DIVINE EMPATHY

DIVINE EMPATHY

A Theology of God

EDWARD FARLEY

SAINT FRANCIS SEMINARY
St. Francis, Wisconsin

FORTRESS PRESS   Minneapolis

DIVINE EMPATHY
A Theology of God

Library of Congress Cataloging-in-Publication Data

Farley, Edward, 1929–
    Divine empathy : a theology of God / Edward Farley.
        p.   cm.
    Includes bibliographical references.
    ISBN 0-8006-2976-0 (alk. paper)
    1. God.   I. Title.
BT102.F29   1996
231—dc20
                                                                    96-33148
                                                                    CIP

The paper used in this publication meets the minimum requirements of American National Standard for Information Sciences—Permanence of Paper for Printed Library Materials, ANSI Z329.48.1984.

Manufactured in the U.S.A.   AF 1-2976

00   99   98   97   96   1   2   3   4   5   6   7   8   9   10

Once more,
almost four decades
after a first dedication,
for Doris

CONTENTS

PART THREE
THEOLOGY OF GOD AND WORLD

PREFACE

I submit this book on the theology of God to public review more in the mood of defeat than victory, of inadequacy than confidence. The reason is simply its subject matter. At every step of the way the words break up on an invisible rocky shoreline. Unlike Eberhard Jüngel I am not confident that *God*, God's concrete actuality, God Godself in the mystery that constitutes it, is thinkable. What we think, what our processes of thinking obtain to, is the situation of God's coming forth as God, the symbolics that attend that coming forth, and certain paradigmatic hints as to how God disposes the world. These are the perennial themes of theologies of God. Yet in spite of the mood of defeat, our theme has a certain inexorability at least for theology. The rocky invisible shore looms ahead of (or within) all of theology's typical motifs: faith, evil, ecclesial community, redemption, hope. Furthermore, attempts to render that shore visible, thematic, or discursive abound in two millennia of Christian texts. This textual tradition, sometimes profound, sometimes unfortunate, continues to shape the way God is understood, bespoken, prayed to, proclaimed, and even worshiped. As a written form of thinking, this textuality is thinkable.[1] Yet if a textuality is all we have, no theology of God is possible. Only if God in some way comes forth (actively, redemptively) can we proceed to assess and reinterpret our textual legacy, and only from that coming forth do we have grounds for appraising the ways we bespeak God and God's activity.

This work is a *theology* and not philosophy of God.[2] That is, it is connected to, even privileges, a specific historical strand of religious

---

1. See chap. 7, n. 5, for a discussion of the "thinkability" and "unthinkability" of God.
2. A rare expression, philosophy of God, is a concept of Bernard Lonergan. He calls chapter 19 of *Insight* a philosophy of God. It means the attempt to know and set forth God strictly on philosophical terms. In Lonergan's project this means the general theme of transcendent knowledge. He distinguishes an objective type of philosophy of God that treats of "God's existence and attributes in purely objective fashion," and another

faith that had its beginnings in the ancient faith of Israel and continues now in the Christian movement. This movement has now become so dispersed and, in the eyes of many, so identified with fundamentalism that one hesitates to use the term *Christian.* "Christian" is probably now a ruined term. Theologies of God that incorporate other historical strands of religious faith are possible, even important, but such a comprehensive way of going about a theology of God is beyond both my competence and available time. To think the theme of God in utter disconnection with all actual historical religious faiths is to move from a theological to some other orientation. It is also to move away from the way God comes forth as God for actual religious faiths.

This essay concludes a series of works that altogether constitute a reinterpretation of some of the belief references or convictions of the Christian movement. As such it is a companion volume to *Good and Evil: Interpreting a Human Condition* (1990).[3] Accordingly, the interpretation of redemption in *Good and Evil* supplies the basis and conceptuality for both my account of the way God redemptively comes forth as God and the way a symbolics of God attends this coming forth. Since I cannot assume that readers of this essay will be familiar with the earlier work, I have offered frustratingly brief summaries of the more detailed analyses of *Good and Evil* that are pertinent to the argument of this work.

To say this work is a theology of God does not mean it is a "systematic theology." Systematic theology originated as an inclusive and pedagogically oriented restatement of the central beliefs of a confessional tradition. The four books of this series are neither specifically confessional (that is, Lutheran, Reformed, and so forth) nor do they restate most of the doctrines or beliefs of the Christian movement. In this respect the project resembles the "philosophical theologies" of Gabriel Marcel, Paul Ricoeur, Martin Buber, or even Sarvepalli Radhakrishnan. At the same time this series is like systematic theology in one respect. It attempts to discover a basic coherence between the way God comes forth as God, the character of redemption, the nature of ecclesia, and theological method. On the other hand, the project resembles philosophical theology not only because of its persistent engagement with philosophical materials and is-

type that sees objectivity as the fruit of authentic subjectivity (*Philosophy of God and Theology* [London: Darton, 1973], 13).

3. The series includes *Ecclesial Man: A Social Phenomenology of Faith and Reality* (Philadelphia: Fortress Press, 1975); *Ecclesial Reflection: An Anatomy of Theological Method* (Philadelphia: Fortress Press, 1982); and *Good and Evil: Interpreting a Human Condition* (Minneapolis: Fortress Press, 1990).

sues but because of its apologetic aspect. The project is an *apologia*, not in the sense of a natural theology, Roman Catholic fundamental theology, or Protestant rationalist apologetics, but as an effort to uncover and display the "reality" dimension of certain themes or convictions of the Christian movement. A negative side of the apologetic aim is the rejection of all interpretations of Christian themes that require or presuppose the retention of prescientific versions of cosmology and nature. A positive side of the apologetic aim is the effort to make sense of faith's "realities" as they take place in the world that we know; a world made up of self-initiating entities, a processing and evolutionary nature, a history comprised of ambiguity and mysterious entanglements.

If the cognitive style of this essay is that of reflective ontology more than rationalistic proofs or "logical" derivations from exegeted authoritative texts, its *tonal* style is more irenic than polemical. For reasons that only savvy psychologists may identify, I continue to be deeply suspicious of theologies whose dominant tonal style is refutation, assault, or discreditation. It is difficult not to suspect in this style idolatrous discipleship, the unqualified allegiance to some single system of concepts or method, the psychology of self-establishment and self-vindication by means of victory over academic enemies, or even a vacuum that has little positive to say. My suspicion is, however, suspended in the case of the efforts of praxis theologies to uncover the way symbols, institutions, and thought systems contribute to the conditions that suppress and marginalize women, the poor, and various minorities. This is not to say that these movements are utterly immune to the dynamics of discipleship and the fixed adoration of almost ritualized concepts and metaphors. My suspicion of polemical theology is not, however, an absolute repudiation. Criticism need not mean superficial academic carping about minor logical unclarities. Whatever its rootage, it can serve to keep conversations open, expose the unclarities, flaws, and gaps in arguments, and voice the limitations of particular approaches.

In spite of my suspicions about polemical theology, I must acknowledge that this essay incorporates polemics or critical theology in at least two ways. First, I try to show (Chapter One) that a number of ways of approaching the question of God are not sufficient simply in themselves. This is not so much an attempt to discredit these approaches as to turn them toward each other and to expose the problems that arise when they would be isolated and self-sufficient.

Second, an implied polemics is at work to the degree that the work departs from or makes little use of some ways of working at theology that were taken for granted throughout the centuries of the Christian movement. Those who interpret the faith convictions of the Christian movement in an unreconstructed way will find three themes missing from this essay. The first is what we might call authority theology. For authority theology, that which initially establishes the truth or reality of a belief is simply its presence in the text of an authority, for instance, a biblical, conciliar, or papal text. Thus if I can show that a biblical text teaches that hell is the final destiny of a portion of the human race, the truth of that claim is settled simply by that showing. Although it is the case that the Christian movement does have "authorities" from which it lives liturgically and homiletically, we misconstrue these authorities when we bestow on their specific texts the status of inevitable and intrinsic truth. I must acknowledge that to depart from authority theology leaves the work of the theologian and the articulation of a theology of God with severe problems. With authority theology intact, we can assemble the "truth" about God from what is said in the texts. We can thus build a symbolics of God by simply restating the metaphors and narratives of the authority. Outside authority theology, the theologian does not work directly *from* the texts but attempts to discover what is at work to prompt the ancient authors to bespeak God as they do. The theologian, in other words, is turned back to the reality itself, that is, to faith, or to the way God arises with redemption, or to the route from redemption to metaphors of God's activity.[4]

The second theme I have made little use of is one that has dominated Roman Catholic and classical Protestant forms of the Christian movement. It is the interpretation of redemption, the event of Jesus, and God Godself in a forensic framework. Coming to the fore in this piety and theology is the human experience of guilt before God, God as an inexorable punisher, and devices by which punishment is mitigated or withdrawn. To those who presuppose this framework (whose construction and privileged status is surely a human work), the double destiny (heaven and hell) of the human being, the eschatology of an ultimate and divine courtroom, and a symbolics of God as sentencer and punisher are all self-evident. When this framework is bracketed or abandoned, other versions of redemption, divine symbolics, and the divine activity arise.

---

4. For an extended analysis of authority theology, and a proposal for a nonauthority theology, see my book *Ecclesial Reflection*.

A third theme that is missing in this account is the interpretation of redemption and God in the framework of ancient cosmology.[5] With this cosmology come notions that the events that brought forth the Christian movement are part of a universal (cosmic) drama that includes the rebellion and fall of Satan, the centrality of this planet in the universe (as the place of the drama), and the end of all things (all billions of galaxies?) by way of Jesus' return to this planet. This cosmology correlates with the symbolics of absolute divine sovereignty, a causal or "ruling" relation of God to whatever happens. Abandoning this cosmology makes possible a reappraisal of the monarchical symbols of God and the monarchical way of relating God to the world. Like so many others, I have taken up the task of a theology of God without appeal to or assumption of authoritative textual demonstration, the forensic framework, and the ancient cosmology.

With the exception of the criticisms implied in these departures, this essay is irenic in tone and in explicit formulation. In fact an irenic and reconciliatory effort marks the very way the problem is formulated and pursued. Accordingly, I have attempted to adjudicate between two fundamentally different ways of going about a theology of God, namely the apparent polarity between the "theism" of the classical Catholic theology of God and the anti-theism of twentieth-century Jewish philosophy and negative and deconstructive theologies. This battle reforms on each of the three fronts of the theology of God: how God is "known," brought to discourse (symbolics), and related to the world. Thus, in each of the three parts of this work, I give an account of this fierce face-off and, incorporating elements from each side, attempt to move to a third position.

Finally, I am aware that essays of this sort are now greeted with a deep suspicion that finds expression in such terms as "essentialism," "false universalism," and "ahistorical generality." The acknowledgment that I am gendered, socially privileged, socialized in a particular time and place, and am a coconspirator in various oppressions may or may not allay this suspicion. Those who think that all discourse that ranges beyond the utter concreteness of politics or autobiography is "essentialistic" will not be content with this acknowledgment. In turn I must voice my

---

5. For a history of "Christian cosmology," see Max Wildiers, *The Theologian and the Universe: Theology and Cosmology from the Middle Ages to the Present,* trans. P. Dunphy (New York: Seabury Press, 1982), chaps. 1–4. For a short but exceedingly clear account of the medieval "model," see the posthumously published lectures of C. S. Lewis, *The Discarded Image: An Introduction to Medieval and Renaissance Literature* (London: Cambridge University Press, 1964), chap. 3.

own suspicion that such a view has turned a legitimate contextualism into a solipsism, a view so private that not even its critique of essentialism could ever be argued in a public way. I submit the arguments of this essay neither as floating above history and contexts nor as expressive of merely local or autobiographical matters. Even if contextuality is inevitable in any and all interpretations of God, God is not simply a name for that particular context. And I submit these arguments not as claims to represent all others but rather to engage others in what is hopefully the interpretive space where people can consider things together and even occasionally come to certain agreements.

As a theology of God, this work takes up questions of the so-called knowledge of God, language about God, and God's activity in the world. Yet, it is the third theme, the divine activity as "divine empathy" that entitles the work. Although this work is not simply about divine empathy, its analyses move ever toward that metaphor. Accordingly, the metaphor of empathy, the understanding of God's activity in the world as an efficacious suffering, is implicit in the first two themes of the redemptive knowledge of God and the ciphers (attributes) of the redemptive God. This is why "divine empathy" entitles the work as a whole.

Prefaces give the author the opportunity to thank those who had some role in the project. In the case of this project those involved are too numerous to remember, much less mention. There are, of course, the many students whose papers and seminar comments turned me toward or away from certain directions. There are those who made possible time off from school responsibilities so the project could be undertaken and completed; thus I thank the Graduate Council of Vanderbilt University, and the Lilly Endowment, Inc. And there are specific individuals who read and criticized portions of the essay: Eugene Teselle, Jack Forstman, and George Kehm. Finally, six chapters of the essay were written at facilities provided by Clare Hall of the University of Cambridge. I am especially grateful to Clare Hall for an appointment as a Visiting Fellow and for providing a delightful environment in which to work.

PART ONE

THE COMING FORTH OF GOD AS GOD

1
APPROACHES TO THE QUESTION OF GOD

> Alack, so sly they are, these scholars old, I can't make out what doctrine I should hold.
>
> *Chaucer,* Troilus and Cressida

THE QUESTION OF WAYS TO THE QUESTION OF GOD

The project here is a theology of God, in itself an outrageous phrase. It seems to promise a successful account of a subject matter or object. Does theology deliver a logos, an understanding of God? We can imagine a logos of nature, of human institutions, of language, because, however much these things frustrate, limit, and surpass logos, they are to some degree available to experience and understanding. And for many, "theology" is no longer a self-evidently clear or even legitimate enterprise. Depending on the interpreter, it is objectifying, religiously provincial, esoteric, Western and Eurocentric in slant, and either a failed foundationalism or a failed fideism. I would hope theology survives these caricatures, but I shall not try yet another time to allay the suspicions. I retain this widely repudiated term, *theology,* for two reasons. First, it says that the project is a struggle with the question of God as a normative or reality question. Accordingly, I am not offering a sociology, cultural anthropology, history, or psychology of belief in God. Second, I choose the term *theology* rather than philosophy of religion or history of religions to locate the project in a specific religious tradition. I have the inclination but not the competence to cast a larger net, to do a comparative theological inquiry. I shall instead privilege a specific tradition, Christianity, in whose history and cultus we find both a developed symbolics and a conceptual elaboration on the question of God. Since the faith of Israel is part of that history, I shall not be departing from what is "Christian" when I make use of contemporary Jewish expounders of that faith. As to the problem of a logos or understanding of God, I can only say that to clarify that is the project itself, the task at hand. "Theology of God" is more a task and a hope than an assumption and a promise.

It seems that a theology of God, a logos of *theos*, would think the unthinkable, the reality of God. This may turn out to mean thinking why the reality of God is unthinkable. But what specifically goes into the conceptual struggle with the question of the reality of God? What sort of questions arise when we would consider God's reality, or God as God and not simply a psychological aberration or a social manipulation? The question is important but it cannot be answered at a universal level above all specific times, places, histories, communities, faith traditions. Any theology of God inevitably takes place in connection with the history and symbolics of an actual religious community. If the God we would think is the God of the Christian community, three questions seem unavoidable.

First, in what way does God come forth as God such as to be "known," "experienced," bespoken, and worshiped? The quotation marks acknowledge that the reader may hesitate before terms like knowledge and experience on the ground that God is just that which we cannot know and experience. This disclaimer accepted, anyone who would think the reality of God faces the question of what justifies any language, any conviction, any posture (even that of worship) concerning God. No term survives the suspicion that arises whenever we concern ourselves with God. We need not construe this first question as a call for a "natural theology," that is, a cognitive and universally convincing demonstration of the reality of God. To be sure, natural theology is one way to answer the question of how God comes forth as God so as to evoke belief-ful conviction. But there are many others; transcendental method, mystical experience, the inherent persuasiveness of authoritative texts. Theology of God's first question then is, What evokes belief-ful convictions of God's reality?[1]

The second question is, How is it that human language is justifiably used to characterize God? I shall call this part of the theology of God a symbolics of God.[2] Whatever the community of faith, God is never a vacuous noncontent, a mathematical symbol, a mere generality. God is bespo-

---

1. The expressions "belief-ful convictions" and "how God comes forth as God" parallel but replace an older discourse that would speak of "revelation," the "knowledge of God," and scriptural texts as the initial step of a theology of God. For example, see Charles Hodge, *Systematic Theology*, Vol. 1 (New York: Charles Scribner's Sons, 1972), chap. 4; and Wolfhart Pannenberg, *Systematic Theology*, trans. G. W. Bromiley (Grand Rapids, Mich.: Wm. B. Eerdmans, 1991), chaps. 1–4.

2. In traditional theologies of God, this is the step that treats of the divine attributes or the divine names. Thus, Hodge, *Systematic Theology*, chap. 5, and Pannenberg, *Systematic Theology*, chap. 6.

ken (related to, proclaimed, meditated, worshiped) in religious faith in and through specific metaphors of God's activity and "character." In these metaphors, God is active and has a determinate character. The theology of God does not itself originate a symbolics of God. It rather takes up the task of assessing, criticizing, and rethinking a symbolics already present in the religious community. This includes the attempt to uncover how a symbolics or contentful language is born from God coming forth as God. It must also struggle with the reality of God not just as a bare facticity but as a rich, symbolic content. And this involves proffering reasons why some contents (symbolics) are important and necessary; for instance, God as love.

Theology of God asks a third question: How does one think God in God's relation to or action upon that which we name as our most inclusive environment?[3] Of the three, this question may most reflect the specific Christian tradition of this project. At the same time, some (Christian) approaches to God virtually abandon this third question as speculative and irrelevant. Since the question directs us to think God's relation to whatever is to be differentiated from God, it seems to require a totalizing speculation. And yet the intent of the question in the specific religious community is not initially speculative. The question arises as soon as the community denies that what it worships is an utterly local entity whose activity is restricted to selected individuals, peoples, or geographical territories. With that negation, the problem of the relation of God and the world comes into the picture. In Hebrew and Christian faiths, this transterritorial conviction about God's activities finds expression in the theme and narrative of creation. The God worshiped in these communities is efficacious for, active toward, anything and everything that is not itself. To think the reality of God is to think, or at least attempt to think, the way in which God is differentiated from, present to, and active in the world.

The theology of God is distributed over these three questions and tasks. However, these questions will not abide mere differentiation. Clearly, they are intermeshed with each other. The symbolics of God, what we mean when we say the word *God*, arises from the way God comes forth as God, for instance, as redemptive. Further, the only materials we have to think God's relation to the world come from the way God is God for

---

3. The question of God's relation to or activity in the world is rarely present as an explicit theme in traditional theologies of God. In place of such a thematization, theologies of God typically expound the trinitarian structure of the divine being (and operation) and such themes as creation and providence. Assumed here is that implicit paradigms of the divine activity are spread over attributes, trinity, creation, providence, and redemption.

us, the attending symbolics, and from our discernments of how the world works. As a theology of God, this project will struggle even if minimally and unsuccessfully with all three of these questions. Thus, as an inclusive project, its version of "the question of God" is this threefold task. The exploration thus moves in a dialectical fashion through these three questions.

To say that the project is a struggle with the "reality" question of God within the framework of a specific historical faith is not to say very much. Ambiguities abound even in that limitation. Because of our historical location, perspectivity, and hidden and overt agendas, there is no single, self-evident *way* to the question of the reality of God. Our locatedness is only partially responsible. The primary reason is that God is not available in such a way as to overwhelmingly determine how God must be approached.

There are those who would disagree. Christology, they say, is the one place where God is self-manifest, and this determines the one and only way of taking up the question of God. Yet, such Christocentrism itself arises from a complex series of theological decisions, valuings, perspectives, and judgments that reflect one way of interpreting how God relates to a specific people and historical tradition. Even in the christocentric framework, a number of approaches to God vie for primacy. Hence, if we adopt the christocentric way, we still face the claims of a variety of approaches. For the question of God is not reducible to a method of deriving language about God from the christological event, texts, or doctrines. It arises in as many ways as the infinite can bear on human reality or the world, or as many ways human beings in their great diversity can be open to the sacred and its symbolization.

The way to the question of God is, in other words, amorphous until something resolves it. This is the case even when God is "traditioned" as a thematic and symbolic part of a people's history. For the symbolic and narrative content found in the textual record of a people's redemptive experience is not as such "the question of God" nor is it as such the way to the question. The question of God is a specific and chosen way of subjecting God (at least as a thematic) to interpretation. This means that something (namely God Godself) has rendered all traditional symbolics and doctrines problematic. This problematic is intrinsic to and constitutive of the traditioned and symbolized God. God being God, all traditioned and symbolic renderings carry with them the unavailability and absence of God, problems of mundanizing divine being, embodiments of oppressive hegemonies, and various logical antinomies. But this intrinsic, internal problematic of God's unavailability is not as such the question of God. The way to the question of God forms when certain internal problematics are privileged, and that which prompts such privileging is always something going on in the interpreter's situation; thus, an epochal shift (the Enlightenment, postmodernity) that discredits the traditioned God, the challenges to centuries-old oppressions, the rise of new modes of thought (process, deconstruction, feminism), or specific events (Hiroshima, the Holocaust). These happenings do not themselves create the intrinsic problematics of God, which are there simply because God is God, but they do give the internal problematics a specific form; for instance, how do we interpret God in the light of the Holocaust, or in the wake of the "death of God," or at "the end of metaphysics"?

Because the question of God is not simply a clear, universal, and self-evident puzzle but something that is constructed in specific situations, it carries with it the problem of the *way* to that question, the determination of that task. This determination thus precedes the question of God itself. In the textual past and present, we find multiple ways to the question of God; mystical, biblical, speculative, demonstrative, practical, and so on. Six of these ways are still with us: tradition retrieval, world puzzlement, historical-cultural analysis, social praxis, fundamental ontology, and redemptive experience. While there are premodern versions of most of these ways to the question of God, historical-cultural analysis and praxis reflect the twentieth-century turn to hermeneutics. Needless to say, there are numerous versions of each of these ways to the question of God. The six ways tend to fall into two general types of approach. Tradition retrieval, world puzzlement, and historical-cultural analysis fall together as *objectivist* approaches. Their path to the question of God passes over the way God is God for human experience. Thus, this path to the question of God offers God as something that arises with human curiosity about the world, or culture, or the authoritative past. Praxis, fundamental ontology, and redemptive experience are *nonobjectivist* approaches. Their path to the question is by way of the engagements, struggles, or situations of human beings.

What this sixfold typology organizes are various *theological* ways of taking up the question of God. Accordingly, it does not pretend to include nontheological approaches: for instance, cultural anthropological analyses of ways different peoples relate to the sacred. Nor does the typology include nontheological versions of the six ways. For instance, Lucretius or Hume attend to God in connection with world puzzlement, Nietzsche by way of history and culture.

Some might want to argue that one of the most widespread ways of approaching the question of God is missing from the typology, the critique of tradition. Criticism in this view is one of the routes to the question of God. This can mean neoclassical criticism of classical metaphysics, deconstructive criticism of metaphysics as such, feminist criticisms of dualisms, hierarchies, and patriarchal metaphors, or biblically prompted criticisms of theology itself. This view invites us to reformulate the theology of God in the light of the specific criticism. In my view, however, criticism exposes paths that cannot be taken but does not itself set us on a path to the question of God. Criticism rather is an important and valid moment of all the approaches. When it does offer a way to the question of God, criticism must attach itself to one of the approaches. These six types reflect more an ideal than a historical analysis. It does not, therefore, organize all the various texts, authors, or religious traditions that might occur to us. We may, indeed, find a certain text, thinker, or even historical period that exemplifies one of the approaches. But it is not untypical to find several of these approaches at work in a single author.[4]

If the typology does not help organize actual texts, what is its use? For this project, the typology is an analytic tool. It helps us to explore what ensues when each way purports to be the *only* way to the question of God. Prompting this exploration is the conviction that the question of God is distorted when it is narrowed to one of these approaches. The typology and exploration of ways to the question of God helps to undercut those kinds of texts that would demand an initial loyalty to one of the ways at the expense of all others. Positively expressed, it helps us discover the interdependence of these ways to the question of God. By negotiating the six ways, we discover that they mutually qualify each other. Exploring these mutual critiques and qualifications is this project's initial way to the question of God. In what follows I shall attempt to show both the importance and the limitation of each type, and I shall argue that all the approaches presuppose in some way the facticity of redemption.

FIVE WAYS TO THE QUESTION OF GOD

Tradition Retrieval

The retrieval of the religious community's authoritative tradition is surely the most widespread theological approach to the question of God. For

---

4. One of the best examples of a theology that self-consciously combines Enlightenment-type criticism, hermeneutics, praxis, and even metaphysics is Peter C. Hodgson, *Winds of the Spirit: A Constructive Christian Theology* (Louisville: Westminster John Knox Press, 1994).

some this is the only genuine theological approach. Theological thinking is thus defined as thinking on the basis of the authoritative past. The aim of the thinking would be to render the retrieved materials into ordered, clarified, and pedagogical form. In the Protestant version, pertinent scriptural resources are assembled and interpreted. The Roman Catholic version ranges over a wider philosophical and textual tradition.

Only the narrowest versions of authority theology restrict theology to the assembling of truths about God from a canon of authoritative texts on God. In most theologies of God, the interpretation of God is part of a larger retrieval, a comprehensive account of "the faith once delivered," the Christian narrative, the revealed doctrines. God is thus approached by way of other theological loci: revelation, Christology, eschatology, sin and redemption. A variety of agendas can prompt this broader retrieval: pedagogics (Philip Melanchthon's *Loci Communes*), apologetics (Anselm's *Proslogion*), or systematics (Karl Barth's *Church Dogmatics*). As the primary way to the question of God, retrieval need not exclude other ways such as liberation or metaphysics.

Moving to assessment, we must acknowledge that historical engagement with the biblical and larger ecclesiastical tradition is an unavoidable moment of any theology of God. Almost all the symbolic contents, imageries, and concepts of God in a current community of faith come from the past. To reduce the theology of God to such a retrieval, however, is to give primary status to what should be secondary. What is retrieved are historically originated symbolics, narratives, and doctrines. What is the status of these traditioned contents? If we presume that what we retrieve is, for some a priori reason, "truth," we have embraced some form of fundamentalism for which past texts are true simply because they are located in an inerrant Scripture or are constructed by an infallible magisterium. Thus, to retrieve *is* to demonstrate. On the other hand, if interpreters abandon the claim that the retrieved texts, symbols, or doctrines are a priori units of truth, they inevitably confront tasks of criticism, interpretation, assessment, and correlation that carry them beyond retrieval. This migration of the question of God from retrieved contents to truth questions should come as no surprise. The actual knowledge and presence of God, even in the ancient, authoritative texts, arises in connection with actual historical deliverances, actual experiences of judgment, liberation, or consolation. The corporate and textualized memory of those deliverances is necessarily secondary to that concrete and actual presence. Nor can we think that textualization and doctrinalization themselves would displace the actual working of God as the way God is known.

Historical-Cultural Analysis

A second way to the question of God is in certain respects the opposite of the first way. It rises from the conviction that radical epochal changes of history have removed the possibility of retrieving the authoritative tradition. Those who take this way range from the radical theologians of the 1960s to certain kinds of deconstructionists. Bridging the whole period is Thomas Altizer, whose lifelong project is to trace the deicidal effect of modernity (or postmodernity) on "God," religion, and Christianity. Accordingly, Altizer is our best guide and example of a historical-cultural approach to God.[5] As the place where all religious beliefs, symbols, and theologies originate, history is the primary passageway to the thinking of God. Since history is a movement and a series of radical displacements and new beginnings, to think God is to discover what God's "fate" in history has been, what history has done to "God." In fact, the question of God itself is not a self-identical question but has a history. A historical time can only ask the question of God that its own character permits. A postmodern age cannot ask the question of God as Plato or Dante did. So, according to this way, one cannot ignore the fate of "God" in the present age and meaningfully pose the question of God. To give an account of that fate calls for both a general tracking of historical beginnings and endings; archaism, the Hebrew prophets, the Christian-Hellenic synthesis, modernity. "God's" fate in modernity begins as early as Aquinas, whose philosophy of existence opened up history to the radically new. The subsequent story is a story of the "death of God," that is, the loss of meaning and positive cultural function of the ontotheological deity as the unity and foundation of an epoch and culture. What has emerged in the wake of this loss is an age that is *a-theos*, incapable of meaningfully worshiping this particular divine entity or grasping its symbolics. This being the fate of "God," it is simply inconceivable to broach the question of God

5. Altizer's thesis is expressed in the preface of his very first book: "A sweeping transformation is taking place in the Church today, and even Catholic theologies are calling upon the Church to enter a post-Constantinian age, a historical era following the collapse of Christendom" (*The Gospel of Christian Atheism* [Philadelphia: Westminster Press, 1964], 10). Virtually everything Altizer has written since this book adds more detail to his portrait of this new era and the collapse of traditional Christendom and the culture it created. This collapse is the background for the apocalyptic genre in which future Christian faiths must be cast. See *The Self-Embodiment of God* (New York: Harper & Row, 1977) and *Genesis and Apocalypse: A Theological Voyage Toward Authentic Christianity* (Louisville: Westminster/John Knox Press, 1990). For a similar view that takes its cue more from Heidegger and Derrida than from Nietzsche, see Carl Raschke, *The Alchemy of the Word: Language at the End of Theology* (Missoula, Mont.: Scholars Press, 1980); and Don Cupitt, *Taking Leave of God* (London: SCM Press, 1980).

as if this cultural event had not occurred. One can only go at the question of God within that event and by means of the interpretation of that event. For Altizer this means that the question of God survives this event of the death of God only as an apocalyptic dialectic of spirit and flesh ever discovering new historical beginnings and endings.

For the postmodern cultural historian, a massive epochal shift (the death of God) inserts itself between all who would "think" God as "God." Hence, a high wall has arisen between the postmodern present and all modalities of thought in which God might be rendered into speech. Thus, the only way to retrieve is to display the now nonfunctioning symbolic tradition. In the sense of a meaningful symbol that functions in the sociology of knowledge of postmodernism, "God" is dead.

At this point I would pose to the cultural historian the same question posed to the retriever of tradition, namely, the question of truth. What is it exactly that is dead; that is, displaced, nonfunctional, without memory? Is it the now demonstrated nonexisting *God* or a culturally constructed modality and symbolics of God? Is the truth proclaimed here the truth of a Godless world or the truth of a historical shift and epoch? If it is the former, then the postmodern cultural approach presupposes or devolves into metaphysical atheism. But surely *metaphysical* atheism is not a possible result, a demonstrated outcome, of a cultural-historical method that has embraced "the end of metaphysics." Cultural analysis as a way to metaphysical atheism is surely an anomaly.[6] If cultural-historical postmodernism is not itself an atheistic way to the question of God, it must then be a *historical* way. Instead of atheism, it is a (nonmetaphysical) deconstruction. But deconstruction can take place either as an extratheological undertaking whose program of textual destabilization is not concerned at all with the question of God or as a moment within the theology of God. If it is the latter, then cultural-historical postmodernism as deconstruction is only a prolegomenon to the question of God and as it takes up the question itself, it devolves into another nondeconstructive set of questions that concern the coming forth of God as God, negative and positive symbolics of God, and paradigms of God's activity.

World Puzzlement

Puzzlement about the world is the third way to the question of God. Insofar as one takes this route, the question of God itself is primarily the

6. This is not to say that the cultural historians (Nietzsche, for instance) who depict this epochal shift cannot be atheists. It only means that if they are, they have other reasons than cultural-historical analyses for the conviction that God (in any and all senses?) can in no

question of how some operation of God, such as final cause, creativity, nisus, or order, accounts for the existence and character of the world. In the history of Western religious thought, world puzzlement and the philosophical way to God are virtually identical. We would be amiss, however, if we implied that world puzzlement is restricted to the Christian, philosophical West. Virtually all religions of the world—early Buddhism and certain forms of Chinese thought may be exceptions—have in their traditions mythologies of world creation. The "world," in the sense of a people's discerned total environment, has posed a puzzle for virtually all peoples. Nor does this puzzle originate simply in the *intellectual* eros, that is, a speculative curiosity about totality. It arises in connection with specific struggles with fertility and birth, the cycles of the seasons, the eerie event of death, and the mysteries of stellar regularity. Human welfare is clearly tied up with the knowledge of how all of this works. The very fact of relatively predictable events, distinguishable spheres, and types of things prompted prephilosophical peoples to mythopoeic theogonies. World puzzlement, then, does not arise simply with the West or with philosophical speculation.

The Hellenic West did, however, inherit from its religious traditions theogonic accounts of creation of and by the gods. Western philosophy is born as a demythologizing of Greek and Middle Eastern creation myths.[7] Its primary questions addressed the puzzle of the world: What is world process (*phusis*)? What is the *ousia* or being of things? Even though the world puzzlement question was symptomatic of a *Götterdämmerung* for ancient mythopoeic thought, those who posed it (Plato, Stoicism) retained elements of metaphor and myth in their account of the puzzle of the world and the theology of God. Both Christianity and Islam appropriated this metaphysical or ontotheological tradition that related God to the puzzle of the world.

The approach to God by way of the puzzle of the world is present in Western philosophy and theology in a variety of formulations: Plato, Plotinus, Aristotle, Benedict de Spinoza, Gottfried Leibniz, A. N. Whitehead—all of these figures respond in some way to the following three issues. First, each figure ponders why there is anything at all and not nothing. Second, each figure offers some detailed account of what the

sense be deemed as real, reasons having to do with internal contradictions, theodicy issues, and the like.

7. For European myths of origin, see F. M. Cornford, *From Religion to Philosophy: A Study in the Origins of Western Speculation* (New York: Harper & Brothers, 1957); and Werner Jaeger, *The Theology of the Early Greek Philosophers*, trans. E. S. Robinson (Oxford: Clarendon Press, 1947).

world itself is; a hierarchy of forms in-forming matter, an aggregate of preharmonized monads, an asymmetrical flow of actual occasions. Thus, to approach the question of God by world puzzlement requires a totalizing act that gathers up the enormous variety and complexity of the world into certain constitutive universal features. Third, each one offers an account of God's relation to or operation in the world such that the world is ordered, moves to novelty, or has a directional character.

World puzzlement approaches to the question of God exploit the non-self-evident and elusive status of the world order or world process. When the approach remains close to its mythopoeic roots—as in Plato, for instance—God and world are so necessarily connected that world analysis is theology and theology is world analysis. Something similar can be said about the amalgam of cosmology and theology in the High Middle Ages. But in postmedieval Western religious thought, a kind of rational theology arose that more or less separated itself from mythopoeic, religious, or fideistic roots.[8] This theologically independent undertaking would then claim to be foundational to all religious faiths that would acclaim God in some universal sense. But this independence is only apparent. Something has already occurred prior to the proof or demonstration of God that provides rational theology with the "meaning" of that which it would demonstrate. The argument of rational theology is that a rational, powerful, and single creator, not an undesignated and contentless X, accounts for the world or world order. Rational theology, in other words, is connected from the start with the symbolics of God already created by religious communities. Rational theology may not be a fideism, but insofar as the God it proves is also the God religious communities worship, it depends on a predemonstrative mediation of the meaning of the divine.

Insofar as rational theology tries to operate above all actual, historical religious faiths, its God is primarily the world-orderer or world-originator of a metaphysics of the world. Even so it presupposes some way in which God becomes thematized to human awareness and knowledge. Most rational theologies assume that awareness of God arises with puzzlement about the world. There is nothing intrinsically problematic about this except for those for whom there is no puzzle of the world. But for Blaise Pascal and his successors (Barth, Gabriel Marcel, and Emmanuel Levinas), God initially comes forth not with the puzzle of the world but in the sphere of *Existenz*, history, faith, traditioning, and the realities of sal-

---

8. It is just this religiously uprooted rational theology that Robert Jenson describes as "theism," the rise and fall of which he treats in chap. 2 of *Beyond Theism: A Grammar of God-Language* (New York: Oxford University Press, 1985).

vation. Even though religious faiths do contain paradigms, metaphors, and even theologies of God's relation to the world, the problem of the puzzle of the world is not their central concern. I can only conclude that while the puzzle of world poses a possible way to the question of God, at least for those who preempt actual religious communities from the approach to God, it cannot be the way to the question of God in a theology of God. That is, it does not explicate the way to the question of God as God is believed, attested, and worshiped by people for whom the metaphysical problem of the world is secondary to problems of *Existenz,* oppression, suffering, and evil.

The Way of Praxis

Theologies of praxis offer a fourth way to the question of God. I shall treat these theologies as a single type rather than interpret the important differences between feminist, womanist, African American, liberation, and other such theologies. As a phenomenon of published writings, theologies of praxis have an academic character and are part of the public world of schools, academic conferences, educated clergy, and even national medias. These are the institutions in which and through which these theologies as "academic" communicate their agendas. Their subject matter and focal concern is any and all subjugated and marginalized peoples; the impoverished underclass, African Americans, women, African American women. The way to the question of God then is determined by a particular version of a way to theology itself. Theology may be in some general sense critical reflection on matters of faith. For praxis theologies the way to that reflection is never formal or general, not even when it is rendered more specific by a connection with "Christian faith," "Catholicism," or "Protestantism." Even the generalized poor is suspect. The way to theology—and thus to the question of God—is a specific, contextual situation of marginalization.

Two things come together in this focus on the experience of a marginalized group: first, faith (in God) typical of the group's experience—thus, its piety, way of reading Scripture, and sense of God or the absence of God—and second, its struggle, what it is up against in a system of oppression. Theology's proper agenda arises with the liminality of a specific group. Its specific tasks include an account of the group's situation and experience, a thoroughgoing critique of the subjugating structures, including religious traditions, and a rereading of the religious tradition so as to bring it to bear both on the oppressive society and on the experience of the group. Methods and instruments of analysis (sociology, rhetoric, exegesis) are co-opted to these ends.

How is this way into theology also a way to the question of God? Theologies of praxis characteristically proceed through three moves. First, they refuse to adopt a distanced and skeptical stance toward the religious experience of their constituency. They acknowledge the authenticity of popular religious piety, as expressed in prayers, preaching, and spirituals. They are unwilling to make philosophical, scientific, or academic criteria the arbiters of that piety. Second, all praxis theologies uncover the way the constituency's experience is a break with, a radical departure from, the tradition imposed on it by the society that has rendered it marginal; for instance, Western, white, colonial, patriarchal, upper class cultures. Thus, praxis theologians offer sharp criticisms of the God of these cultures expressed in such phrases as "the classical view," "the God of the philosophers," and "classical theism." Praxis theology is then a disruptive hermeneutic, a kind of iconocide of the old imageries.

Finally, theologies of praxis move from popular religion and tradition criticism to new iconographies, the construction of alternative imageries of the divine. What prompts this move is the agenda of human transformation. The new imageries function both to expose the disguised subjugating religion of the oppressive society and to mobilize and sustain the experience of women, the base communities, the African American urban poor. The source of the new imageries tends to be some form of tradition; a rediscovered literature of women, or certain symbols and stories from the Bible. Merging to form the question of God are the posited authentic experience of the group, linguistic and social analyses of how subjugation co-opts religious images, and a proposed reimaging. The plausibility (truth?) of this reimaging is rooted in the image's power to actually effect human transformation.

Theologies of praxis are advocative, contextual, and oriented to social transformation. When they move beyond social criticism to constructive proposals, their central agenda is the construction of new iconographies.[9] They would thus reimage sin, salvation, Christ, church, and God for the sake of societal and ecological transformation. The criterion by which

---

9. One of the most important feminist iconographic projects is that of Sallie McFague. See *Models of God: Theology for an Ecological, Nuclear Age* (Philadelphia: Fortress Press, 1987), and *The Body of God: An Ecological Theology* (Minneapolis: Fortress Press, 1993). See also Mary McClintock Fulkerson's *Changing the Subject: Women's Discourses and Feminist Theology* (Minneapolis: Fortress Press, 1994).

these theologies measure their "truth" is the power (of the images) to effect transformation. While there are those in the religious and even secular communities that resist and criticize these theologies, I must concur with their iconographic agenda and their powerful critiques of academic theologies and subjugating structures of society and church.

Praxis theologies contrast themselves to all theologies that do not make social transformation their primary aim. Thus their attempt to support a constituency's struggle by means of a new iconography appears to constitute an independent and exclusive way to the question of God. Is that the case? However successful praxis theology is in advocating the cause of the oppressed and constructing new images, it does pass over certain tasks of the theology of God. For instance, on what grounds does the praxis theologian speak of God at all? Why is it assumed that the proposed narratives and images are accounts of something that is not an image? What justifies attaching one iconography to God rather than another? The classical Catholic theologies of God attempted to show why God was analogically good, knowing, and free. If God is that through which all existents and goods have their being, God must embody in a fulfilled way all the features of which God is the cause. We may not find this argument a persuasive reason for attributing contents to God, but at least it offers a reason. What grounds the imagings (God as person, loving, just) of praxis theology?

I find two ways of justifying ascriptive imagery in the praxis theologies. The first is tradition retrieval, usually carried out as a recovery of formerly marginalized biblical imageries.[10] The second is a kind of pragmatism that justifies the selected imagery by showing its political utility. Both ways have a certain self-evident plausibility. No theologian or believer wants to disconnect the theology of God from the community's memory deposited in its ancient texts. And surely all theologians and believers are of the conviction that the imagery of God is socially and politically transformative. Yet we must ask whether these two ways are in themselves sufficient.

Unless fundamentalist assumptions are at work, the theologian cannot, without argument, simply assume that a selected biblical image sets forth what God is or does. Thus we are passed on to the second way. Praxis theologians do in fact supply an argument. The reason for saying God is just or loving is the efficacy of this imagery in social transformation. Per-

10. An example of the method of underscoring a liberative approach to God by way of biblical appeals is Gustavo Gutiérrez, *God of Life,* trans. M. J. O'Connell (Maryknoll, N.Y.: Orbis Books, 1991).

haps so. But what we have here is a reversed Marxism, and where there is Karl Marx, Ludwig Feuerbach is not far behind. For Marx God-language functions to legitimate social systems. Praxis theology would replace iconographies of oppressive legitimation with a liberating iconography. In both cases we have a use of faith, an apparent projectionist notion of religious language. Can this Feuerbachian turn be held off by alliance with philosophical pragmatism? Pragmatism as a philosophy is not without its ambiguities. Theologians are attracted to pragmatism as an alternative to essence philosophies and as a way beyond both reductionism and idealism. Pragmatism offers a way to retain human values and human transformative agendas while acknowledging the historical, plural, and relative character of human experience. At the same time, pragmatism can be a foil for Feuerbach, a reduction of religious reality to human usages, a divine imagery without God. Yet, African American, feminist, and Latin American liberation theologians do not in most cases embrace this consequence. At the same time these theologies rarely get beyond appeals to biblical imageries and arguments for social usefulness. If neither of these is simply in itself a sufficient basis for ascribing contents to God, it would seem that praxis theology is driven out of its isolation from other theologies to the appropriation of whatever is required to answer the question of how God comes forth as God into human bespeaking.

Fundamental Ontology

The fifth way to the question of God, philosophical anthropology (compare fundamental theology), resembles the theologies of praxis by a deprivileging of metaphysical puzzlements about the world and making human reality the primary field of the question. More specifically, this way follows Immanuel Kant's "Copernican revolution" in philosophy to affirm the transcendental, ontological, imaginative, or hermeneutical entanglements that precede and even construct whatever human beings experience.[11] It argues that the question of God arises first of all with the way human beings are constituted and situated in the world; for instance, their strange and elusive self-consciousness, sense of horizon, or incompleted desire. Thus the question of God arises not "academically," that is, with rational puzzlements and deliberative speculations, but with the human being's very constitution as a self-transcending, self-conscious, de-

---

11. Some examples of this approach are Maurice Blondel, *Action (1983): Essay on a Critique of Life and a Science of Practice*, trans. O. Blanchette (Notre Dame: Notre Dame University Press, 1984); Ray L. Hart, *Unfinished Man and the Imagination* (New York: Herder and Herder, 1968); and Karl Rahner, *Hearers of the Word*, trans. J. Donceel (New York: Continuum, 1994).

siring, and personal *Existenz*. Feuerbach and Freud take this entangle-ment in a projectionist direction while Maurice Blondel, Karl Rahner, and Ray Hart explore it to expose the human openness to what is not simply itself.

The ontoanthropological approach lends itself to at least three quite different formulations. The *transcendental* approach, the one closest to Im-manuel Kant, would explicate the transcendental conditions of the pos-sibility of experiencing or knowing God (compare Rahner and Henry Duméry). The existential turn of this approach (compare Augustine, Blondel, Hart) poses the question of God as arising in connection with the human's being's desiring, imaginative, even anxiously tragic existence. The way of *world experience* takes its start from Martin Heidegger's dis-placement of transcendental consciousness with *Dasein*, that is, concrete human being-in-the-world. Here the question of God arises not with the human being's transcendental or ontological constitution but with its ex-istential world connection (compare Erazim Kohak, John Haught), that is, with the experience of an unfathomed depth of things, the mysteries of nature, or the world as beautiful.[12] This experience should not be con-fused with rational curiosities and puzzlements about the world. This path to the question is less that of cognitive puzzles as an aesthetic en-tanglement of human existentiality and world mystery. The *intersubjective* approach corrects both the transcendental way not by an existential or world experiential turn but by being-with-others. The question of God arises thus with the entanglements of alterity, the mystery of the Thou (Martin Buber), the summons of the violable face (Emmanuel Levinas).

The ontoanthropological path to the question of God has some resem-blances to both praxis theologies and the way of world puzzlement. Like the world puzzlement approach, it begins with a philosophical move rather than the explication of a specific religious tradition and its symbol-ics. Like praxis theologies, it locates the question of God in the sphere of the human, its distinctive agency, world experience, or interhuman rela-tions. It goes without saying that the ontoanthropological approach fails to interest both those who are convinced that reflective, philosophical analyses are cognitively barren and those who see the divine initiative (grace, justification, revelation) as compromised by any correlation with the powers and capacities of human beings. Yet, the ontoanthropological way contributes at least two things to the other approaches. First, its ac-

---

12. John Haught, *What is God? How to Think about the Divine* (New York: Paulist Press, 1986); Erazim Kohak, *The Embers and the Stars: A Philosophical Inquiry into the Moral Sense of Nature* (Chicago: University of Chicago Press, 1994).

count of what makes human beings open to revelation or structurally redeemable undercuts heteronomous and even Manichean interpretations of the human relation to God. If God's revealing or grace has no correspondence whatever to any human need or structure, if it is not dealing with the human being as its own creature, it can only violate the created being of the human being. Second, its account of the role of world engagement, human desire, or imagination in the relation to God undercuts theological provincialism. Provincialist theologies interpret the inevitable concreteness of religious faiths as an absolute and exclusive uniqueness. The religious community becomes then a windowless monad (Gottfried Leibniz). Such Christian provincialism can acknowledge the religious other (the Buddhist, the Jew, the Hindu) as human but not as human under God and in relation to God.

At the same time, as the one and only way to the question of God, ontoanthropology has serious limitations. Beginning with a generalized human being abstracted out of the specific and concrete religious community, ontoanthropology offers a generalized God: a "whence," "being," "horizon," or "infinity." And surely the question of God is not the question of these sorts of things. Here arises a problem we faced in connection with the way of world puzzlement. The God of actual religious practice or faith is worshiped (feared, loved, praised) in connection with actual and specific human problems: sin, oppression, meaningless, moral corruption, life emptiness. Ontoanthropological analysis may help uncover the human dimension of these things and show why redemption confirms rather than violates human being, but that contribution does not itself yield the basis, the symbolics, the world relation of God. Once we abstract away the actual religious community and the concrete dynamics of evil and redemption, we can traverse a path only to a generalized "God" correlated with a generalized human being.

THE WAY OF THE FACTICITY OF REDEMPTION

Each of the five approaches is in its own way persuasive. Few of us would be inclined to deny the importance of tradition retrieval, emancipatory transformation, or the importance of history and culture. Two convictions guide my response to these approaches. First, any comprehensive approach to the question of God would do well to find a way to listen to and embody all of these approaches. This essay will do this only in the most minimal way. The retrieval of tradition will be sporadic and selective. The ontoanthropological approach will appear when I struggle with the relation between the "eternal horizon" of human desire and the "God" of redemptive experience. I shall indirectly address the issue of the cultural death of God in my attempt to adjudicate the apparent chasm between the world puzzlement approach (metaphysics, ontotheology) and antimetaphysics. And, hopefully, a reformulated account of the way God comes forth as God, the symbolics of God, and God's relation to nature will uncover presupposed elements in theologies of praxis. The second thesis is that, at least in a theology of God, the five ways to the problem of God presuppose and devolve into a theology of redemption. To that issue we now turn.

A sixth way to the question of God arises with the privileging of the faith and experience of a specific and actual people. This does not mean a comparative cataloguing of various religions, legitimate as that undertaking is. This route to the question of God is the articulation of the way a specific people symbolize God as redemptively active. For example, if classical Brahmanism is our reference, it would be unthinkable to pose the question of God apart from the facticity of a "redemption" from the rupture of the identity of the true self (Atman) and the bondage of karma. Here the very possibility of posing the question of God is given by the fact of a redemptive change. In Christian faith "God" means that which addresses, is present to, functions toward a cluster of human problems; the network of social evil, the dynamics of individual idolatry, the pangs of finite existence. The "fact" here is not simply the problematic, the bondage, but the experience of some sort of easement, freedom, or empowerment in relation to that problematic. That experience and empowerment can be the annual re-creation of the world in mythopoeic religions, the sense of historical deliverance (Israel), or the sense of acquittal in the face of divine condemnation. In other words, the way God is God, the very meaning of "God" in actual religious communities, is connected to some sort of experienced redemption. I use the word *experience* not to stress something subjective but to contrast what goes on in religious communities with simply theories, hypotheses, or historical descriptions. If Zen Buddhists do actually experience *satori*, if Torah does order and enrich the life of the Jewish community, if certain freedoms (agape, hope) do mark the existence of Christians, if relief from an oppressive power is delivered, if reconciliations do replace alienations, then redemption has a certain facticity about it.

The path to the question of God from the facticity of redemption resembles in certain respects some of the other ways to the question of God.

If redemption is in some sense factical, then all ways to the question of God that bypass that facticity have a secondary or derivative status in the theology of God. Thus, apart from an actual and contemporaneous redemption, theology's retrieval of its authoritative texts and tradition is simply antiquarianism. And if praxis theologies are not reducible to iconographic reimaging, they retain a social and political version of the facticity of redemption. And while theologies that make redemption primary may need the insights of ontoanthropology, the redemption to which they attest is not simply a duplication of general anthropological structures.

In a program of a *theology* of God, none of the five paths to the question of God are independent or autonomous but are derivative of the facticity of redemption. This becomes clear when we confront each approach with the three questions of the theology of God. The iconography of God, ontoanthropology, the retrieval of tradition are not in themselves accounts of how God comes forth as God into the language and experience of the religious community. And if that coming forth (the facticity of redemption) is the primary basis of symbolic language of God and of paradigms that relate God and the world, then these other ways will presuppose some version of that coming forth when they make use of symbols and paradigms. The redemptive coming forth of God as God is then the more primordial, communal, and factical phenomenon. Thus, the theology of God works with ancient texts and traditions, not to bring about redemption, but because redemption is already factical in the remembering community. Cultural historians of "God" may, of course, have no theological orientation. If they are theologically disposed, then the God who comes forth in redemption will not be reducible to the "God" history slays. The philosopher prompted by world puzzlement to speculate on the divine may have no theological orientation. But if the undertaking is a theology of God, then world puzzlement has been taken into an actual community of faith whose God comes forth first of all in redemption. Theologies of praxis clearly root themselves in the symbolics and contexts of actual religious communities. That being the case, the God they attest does not initially arise with reimaging but with the facticity of redemption. They too must attend to that facticity if they would avoid falling back into tradition retrieval or atheological pragmatism as ways of grounding their appeals. Ontoanthropology like world puzzlement may serve a general and nontheological agenda rather than a theology of God. But if the "God" toward which transcendental or interhuman structures correspond has any determinate, symbolic contents, then ontoanthropology has presupposed a historical, factical determination of the meaning of God.

As a theology of God, this inquiry opts for the facticity of redemption as the way to the question of God. That being the case, the question of God becomes the threefold question of how the redemptive coming forth of God carries with it a positive symbolics and a paradigm of world activity. This privileging of redemption does not eliminate or compete with the other ways except insofar as they purport to be independent ways to the question of God. Any contemporary theology of God risks irrelevance and superficiality if it ignores these powerful voices. What theology of God would dare ignore the massive shift of European culture to institutions and cognitive epochs (epistemes) devoid of the sacred? What theology of God can pretend to be theology, thus tied to a specific faith tradition, and ignore the narratives and symbols of the traditioned past? And when the theology of God takes up its third question, a paradigm for understanding God's activity in the world, how can it avoid the centuries-long tradition of speculative thinking prompted by world puzzlement? And can a theology of God settle for the heteronomy that comes with the displacing of the desiring and self-transcending human being with the causal operations of revelation or redemption? Finally, no theology of God is credible if its version of redemption's facticity has nothing to do with a despoiled planet, the genocidal removal of whole cultures, or the continued marginalization and subjugation of women. However meagerly this project carries it out, this synthesis of ways to the question of God within the facticity of redemption seems preferable to methods that opt for a single way.

2
THE CLASSICAL CATHOLIC THEOLOGY OF GOD

> One God, eternal, sole, my creed doth know,
> Mover of Heavens, Being Himself unmoved,
> Loving, desiring, Him, around they go.
> *Dante,* The Divine Comedy

> We must in fact emphatically warn against the common contemporary arrogance with regard to the tradition, and especially against the wholesale rejection of the traditional thought of God. Usually the object of such criticism is nothing more than a dreadful caricature.
> *Eberhard Jüngel,* God as the Mystery of the World

The primary location of a *theology* of God is a specific religious community in its particular time and historical situation. But no contemporary religious community is without a social memory or traditioned past. Accordingly, the Christian community is ever shaped by a legacy of authoritative texts, interpretive traditions, and critical responses to these traditions. In Chapter 1 I offered a brief and inevitably oversimple account of alternative approaches to God in contemporary theological literatures. But these approaches make up only a part of the present situation. Beneath all contemporary approaches to God is a much deeper rift, which for some interpreters is an unbridgeable chasm. One side of the chasm describes the other side in such terms as theism, classical theism, objective theism, and even monotheism. From this perspective, these are all pejorative terms. They represent an approach to God now blown away by the winds of modernity (or postmodernity). The whole cultural world that made "theism" viable and meaningful is gone. In some views "objective theism" is not merely an antiquarianism but an intrinsic mistake, a vehicle too broken to carry a coherent theology of God. From the side of objective theism, such critics appear to be toying with atheism, abandoning the very meaning of God.

SORTINGS

I must confess that this situation of mutual polemic and absolute exclusion appears to be very much of a muddle. Criticisms of "classical theism" attend a variety of approaches: liberation theology, feminism, deconstruction, Heideggerian philosophy, process theology, Jewish dialogical philosophy, radical theology, and Anglo-American analytic philosophy of religion. Sorting out the issues of these polemics calls for some preliminary observations. First, there is no single flaw about "theism" about which all of these critics agree. Second, it is not at all certain that the critics are chasing the same felon. "Theism" seems to wander through these literatures in search of a clear meaning.[1] Third, because critics of theism disagree among themselves about the proper approach to the question of God, they do not altogether comprise a single, coherent, discreditation of theism. My primary concern with this rift is not descriptive, a task that would call for a full explication of the literature. I hope, rather, that a review of these criticisms will help formulate and mediate the apparent incompatibilities between the classical Catholic theology of God and genuine anti-theism. The present chapter offers a minimal account of the classical Catholic theology of God. Because many of the criticisms of "theism" are facile caricatures that confuse the Catholic theology of God with popular (supernaturalistic) theism or with theistic philosophy of religion, I shall begin with some distinctions.[2]

---

1. In some usages *theism* is simply "belief in God" or belief in some eternal reality underlying the world. Charles Gore, *Belief in God* (New York: Charles Scribner's Sons, 1921); Boyce Gibson, *Theism and Empiricism* (London: SCM, 1970). But most authors give the term a more specific meaning. For instance, theism is "the doctrine that the ultimate ground of the universe is a single supreme Being who is perfect or complete in Himself" (W. R. Inge, *God and the Astronomers* [London: Longmans, Green, 1934], 217). Others yet will specify theism to mean a single deity who is independent of the world, eternal, omnipotent, etc. For different meanings of theism, see John B. Cobb, Jr., "The Possibility of Theism Today," in Edward Madden, R. Handy, and M. Farber, eds. *The Idea of God: Philosophical Perspectives* (Springfield, Ill. Charles Thomas, 1968), 100.

2. One widely read work of the recent past that perpetuated the confusion between popular, supernatural theism and the classical theism of the Western theophilosophical tradition was J. A. T. Robinson's *Honest to God* (London: SCM, 1963). In the space of three pages Robinson accuses "traditional Christian theology" of thinking that God is an "entity or being, 'out there,'" (29) and finds that in "the traditional formation of Christianity" God is "the highest Being—out there, above and beyond the world" (30). Gordon Kaufman apparently agrees with Robinson. Speaking of "the traditional western conception of God," he says that God is "conceived as, so to speak, 'outside' or 'other than' the world, as human potters and poets are outside and other than the pots and poems which they create or shape." Kaufman calls this theology "fundamentally dualistic" (*In Face of Mystery: A Constructive Theology* [Cambridge, Mass.: Harvard University Press, 1993], 271).

Popular theism is a mode of believing in and bespeaking God that takes place in the liturgy and piety of Christian communities. Arising from the piety of personal relation with God, it tends to bespeak God as *a* being or individual. Accordingly, popular theism seems to be inherently mythological and literalistic. But the literalism here may be more a mindset of the critic (who takes the language the believer uses literally) than of the believer. The actual relation, responses to, and thought processes of ordinary believers are surely more complex than their linguistic expressions. I have known too many persons who are aware of the failed character of the anthropomorphic and literalistic language they use. Even popular theism is not without its negative theology. Popular theism, then, is itself complex and easily caricatured. But insofar as it does mean a literalistic, mythological way of bespeaking God, it should be confused neither with "theism" nor the classical Catholic theology of God.[3]

Foundationalist theistic philosophy of religion refers to "theism" that has freed itself from the framework of religion to live a philosophical life of its own. Even if it has distant roots in some religious faith, it is primarily a philosophy of God. The work of Gottfried Leibniz, deism, the "proofs" for God wrenched loose from their setting in scholastic theology and postmedieval natural theologies are forms theistic philosophy of religion has taken.[4] The distinguishing feature of this theism is the attempt to establish rational or universal grounds for thinking God exists.

The classical Catholic theology of God names a trajectory of the Christian West whose initial formulation obtained its acme in Augustine and whose more or less definitive expression is found in Thomas Aquinas. In some usages, theism is defined by this trajectory.

Qualified Christian theism is a modification of classical Catholic theology by the introduction of an alternate metaphysical framework, for instance, that of Neoplatonism or process thought. Jacob Boehme, Friedrich Hegel, Alfred North Whitehead, and Charles Hartshorne have proffered such modified theisms.

"Theism" can and does refer to any of these four undertakings. When critics fail to distinguish these various "theisms," the situation is further muddled. It only fosters confusion to try to make a general term, *theism*, apply to all of these views. An even worse caricature is perpetrated when

---

3. For a distinction between "popular supernatural theism" and "classical Christian theism," see David Ray Griffin, "Reply: Must God Be Unlimited: Naturalistic versus Supernaturalistic Theism," in Linda Tessier, ed., *Concepts of the Ultimate* (New York: St. Martin's Press, 1989). The former is the view of ordinary people of faith, the latter of developed theologies of such thinkers as Augustine and Thomas Aquinas (24).

4. This is what Robert Jenson means by "theism." See *Beyond Theism: The Grammar of God-Language* (New York: Oxford University Press, 1985), chap. 2.

the critic assumes that the features of popular theism (literalism, mythology, God as *a* being) somehow apply to all of these "theisms," or assumes that the classical Catholic theology of God is a popular theism. We must eliminate these confusions and caricatures if we are precisely to pose the issues between the classical Catholic theology of God and various kinds of anti-theism.

ORIGINS

Cognitive inquiry, especially when it aims to discredit, tends to force reality into the form of entities. Thus, historical inquiry can foster a kind of epochal literalism that offers up some targeted entity as a sacrificial lamb. For example, we can interpret the classical Catholic theology of God as a discrete, largely coherent system of concepts to be either defended or repudiated. The interpreter constructs such an entity so it can be deconstructed. And many are the constructions of the classical Catholic theology. It is a foundationalism, a natural theology based on *analogia entis*, a philosophical objectivism with little connection with religion or faith, a static or substantialist metaphysics, a dualism, even a mythological theism that thinks of God as *a* being. But these reductive proposals themselves call for deconstruction. Both the historically unreachable "origin" as well as certain aporias (logical contradictions) at the very heart of classical theism prompt us to suspect these interpretations.

One reason the classical Catholic theology of God is not reducible to a single, delimited package of concepts is its prephilosophical origin in the facticity of redemption (the "Christian mystery") and as a Christian way of responding to the Hellenistic world. We surely misconstrue this theology of God if we reduce it to a "metaphysics," an undertaking of the sort we find in Plato's *Timaeus* or Book Lambda of the *Metaphysics* of Aristotle. The primary source of this theology is the Christian movement, a Hebraic type of faith struggling to establish itself in the Hellenistic world. Insofar as this is the case, the various dynamics of redemption—the breaking of the power of idolatry, the worship of one who is the norm of justice—will be at the root of this theology.

A second source of the classical Catholic theology of God is what we might call the "Christian myth," or in more recent language, the "Christian story." This is the story of a once-for-all solution to an apparently unsolvable problem (the Fall and the rule of intractable guilt) by the sacrificial death of the incarnate Son of the creator God, an event followed by the salvific working of the Holy Spirit through the church, such that a

final resolution of history and creation itself is assured. Those who constructed the classical Catholic theology of God were already inscribed by
this story. Their liturgy, preaching, and teaching had this story stamped
on it. The God of this story was the one, internally differentiated (triune),
sovereign, and worshipful creator and ruler of the cosmos.

A third root of this theology of God is the one most emphasized,
namely various appropriated strands of Hellenistic philosophy and culture. More specifically, a qualified Neoplatonism became the framework
for understanding the God of the "Christian story." The initial intent of
this appropriation was not so much to substitute a "Greek" framework
for the Christian story as to use it to differentiate that story from powerful
religious and philosophical movements of those centuries. Thus, so-called
apologists of the second century attacked both the polytheism of Hellenistic popular religion and the several kinds of Gnosticism that threatened to become the interpretive vehicle of the Christian movement.
Second- and third-century Christian teachers opposed all versions of God
as divisible into beings (polytheism), dualisms of a creator God and redeemer God (Marcion), and all notions of God as a metaphysical correlate
of the world, an eternal creative aspect of the world system. Augustine,
the most important patristic source for later Catholicism, inherited these
polemics and brought together the main concepts of the Catholic theology of God: negative theology, creation *ex nihilo*, and God's unity, immutability, divine perfection, and triune self-differentiation. With the exception
of creation *ex nihilo*, all of these concepts had parallels in the middle and
Neoplatonisms of Alexandria, Rome, and Athens. At the same time, the
Christian teachers had strong religious reasons for affirming these concepts. Immutability was, at least originally, an issue of God's trustworthy
character as opposed to the fickleness of the deities of polytheism. Creation *ex nihilo* and God as a unity explicated the religious community's
conviction that the God it knew in salvation was not one of many creative powers.

At the same time, there took place a certain shift of emphasis that
tended to obscure the religious, redemptive, and even polemical roots of
this theology of God. Both internal controversies and external apologetics
pressed the Christian movement and its emerging theology of God toward this shift of emphasis. One result was that "God" as a theme of
conceptual explication began to take on a life of its own apart from its
rootage in the dynamics of redemption. Concepts of God's unity, the internal differentiation of God into hypostases related to each other by procession, *ex nihilo* as an alternative to God as a world correlate, and the nega-

tive theology all lend themselves to a formulation of how God is and is not related to the world. In a subtle way, the God and world relation takes on a certain primacy. And when the God and world problem introduces, dominates, and guides the thinking of God, the classical Catholic theology of God is born. The new emphasis did not eliminate the roots of this theology in redemption and in the Christian story. The combination of these roots in redemption with preoccupation with the God and world relation in the Catholic theology of God brought about its characteristic aporias and laid it open to almost opposite interpretations.

ELEMENTS

The classical Catholic theology of God has seen many explications. They range from comprehensive and technical accounts (for instance, Étienne Gilson) to brief summaries.[5] In some recent treatments, this theology is presented (and thus caricatured) without serious explication. The following summary identifies eight elements: creation *ex nihilo*, negation, self-identity, analogical attributes (names), Trinity, the metaphor of absolute rule, metaphors (analogies) of the personal, and theodicy as problem and task. These themes are tightly intertwined and the absence of any one of them would change this theology of God into something quite different. These concepts are not, however, simply a list of themes. Each of them in its own way explicates God in differentiation and relation to the world. And, with the exception of the Trinity, each of them has a derivative relation to what initially differentiates God and the world, the act or relation of creation.

Trinity

The classical Catholic theology of God was trinitarian. Insofar as this theology is part of a comprehensive soteriological and hierarchical cosmology, the Trinity has an intrinsic place. At the same time, because the Trinity arose primarily in the setting of christological debates and because it

5. See the following chapter-length summaries for brief but helpful accounts of the classical Catholic theology of God: Langdon Gilkey, "God," in Peter Hodgson and Robert King, eds., *Christian Theology: An Introduction to its Traditions and Tasks*, Newly Updated Edition (Minneapolis: Fortress Press, 1994); Étienne Gilson, *God and Philosophy* (New Haven: Yale University Press, 1941), chap. 2; Joseph F. Donceel, *The Searching Mind: An Introduction to a Philosophy of God* (Notre Dame: University of Notre Dame Press, 1979), part 2. For more extended interpretations, see H. P. Owen, *Concepts of Deity* (London: Macmillan, 1971); Richard Swinburne, *The Coherence of Theism* (Oxford: Clarendon Press, 1977); Brian Hebblethwaite, *The Ocean of Truth: A Defense of Objective Theism* (Cambridge: University of Cambridge Press, 1988); and E. L. Mascal, *He Who Is: A Study of Traditional Theism* (London: Longmans, Green, 1943).

was eventually treated in a separate *locus* of doctrine, it seems rather external to the cluster of motifs that comprise classical Catholic theism.

Ex nihilo

Differentiating God from the world is the inclusive task of this theology of God. Religiously symbolized, this distinction is not between a One and a many but between the creator and its creatures. The explicit language of this differentiation is that God creates the world *from nothing*. The "from nothing" says nothing positive about the creative act but does affirm an absolute difference between God and the world. It is important to realize that the content of that difference is unstated. Its only meaning is that God and nothing else is the reason the world exists at all. From this initial differentiation come negation, self-identity, the analogical derivation of attributes, and metaphors of rule and personality.

Negation

In later passages of this essay, I shall argue that faith and redemptive transformation contain elements that destabilize and qualify all discourse about God. Accordingly, a faith-rooted *via negativa* precedes and even grounds the negations advanced by philosophical and theological analysis. But in the Christian movement, the negational element of all bespeaking of God was first articulated and given centrality by the classical Catholic theology of God. However, because that theology was engendered in the first place by an externally directed apologetic that pressed it toward conceptual coherence, its version of the negative way was grounded in that which was its overall concern, the differentiation of God and the world. Thus, if God is the through-which of all that is not God, no discourse (term, name, relation, image) will directly describe God. This presupposes that language arises within and brings to expression the entities and systems of what we call the world. Language is world-oriented and world-saturated. Its referents, formal and material, are things that coexist with human beings in their local and even comprehensive environment. If God is the creative condition of the world and thus of human beings and their systems, none of the referents of language will express the actual being of God. If this is the case, every image, proposition, name, or narration has a built-in negation when God is its subject. Negation, then, tracks every step of the theology of God from accounts of the "knowledge" or "experience" of God through the application of names or attributes to the way of thinking the relation of God and the world.

Self-Identity

Further, if God is the creator, the through-which of the world, the world's being has the status of contingency, an existing-through-another. If that is the case, God's being must be being-through-itself. From this one point unrolls a long train of negative attributes: God as noncontingent (necessary) being, as perfect and complete, unitary, simple, infinite, noncomposite, immutable, impassible, and eternal. The whole "omni" discourse is rooted here in the claim that God as creator cannot itself be contingent and thus must be necessary and self-identical.

Analogical Attributes

God's attributes as analogical to worldly goods are derived from God as self-identical creator. God can be the creative source of all contingents only if God is the realized perfection or Exemplum of whatever exists through God. Thus, worldly goods or perfections are analogous indications of what God must be as their Exemplum. Since God is the Exemplum and the actualization of all goods, it is impossible that God lack any good that creatures possess.[6] Hence, God (analogously) exemplifies the goods that constitute human spirit: knowledge, will, freedom, love, and the like. Accordingly, God is (analogically) personal.

Sovereign Rule

According to the classical Catholic theology of God, God is the absolute origin of all things and as such is an infinite self-identity describable only through analogies indicated by God's relation to the world as creator and which must ever be qualified (negated) for the same reason. Do we have here simply a list of motifs or do the motifs combine into a coherent account? We have already seen the close relation between God as absolute creator and the themes of self-identity, analogy, and negation. But if we stopped at this point, we would have omitted the great metaphor that unites these motifs, the metaphor of sovereign rule. In a rather formal sense, it could be said that absolute creation is the comprehensive metaphor of this theology of God. But why is it important in this theology to affirm absolute (*ex nihilo*) creation? The answer, I think, is that the classical Catholic theology of God arises from one great conviction, even vision, and that is that what we call the world, including human history, is a vast

---

6. "Now since God has been posited as the ultimate Source of all being, he must be at least as perfect as any positive attribute that we find here below in our experience—in fact, infinitely perfect" (W. Norris Clarke, "How the Philosopher Can Give Meaning to Language," in Madden et al., eds., *The Idea of God*, 16).

spectacle of a divine, willful enactment. Many things contribute to this spectacle: the creation and "Fall" of the first human parents, the incarnation, the bringing forth of the church, the eventual cosmic resolution brought about by the Son. Given this unfolding cosmic drama, it is unthinkable that the world not fulfill whatever God wills for it. And if this cosmic drama is a divine enactment, then the world itself must have come about in an act of absolute divine will. Accordingly, there is a metaphor that unifies these various motifs which is not simply one among many metaphors but is a privileged and dominant metaphor, the metaphor of divine absolute rule. If God in the classical Catholic theology is named as "being," it is being that wills, enacts, rules, and brings all things to completion. Roman Catholic "objective theism" envisioned this rule as mediated through celestial, ecclesiastical, and secular hierarchies. The Protestant reformers retained this privileged metaphor of sovereign rule but displaced the cosmic and earthly hierarchies of mediation with a more individual, homiletical, and Bible-central way of conceiving the mediation of grace.

Theodicy

Once the metaphor of sovereign rule obtains a central place in the classical Catholic theology, a severe form of the theodicy problem becomes intrinsic to that theology. It may seem strange to list theodicy as one of the elements of the classical Catholic theology of God. In its broadest sense theodicy is an element in virtually all religious faiths insofar as they relate human suffering and the sacred. But theodicy's narrow meaning as a conundrum reflects a special connection to Judaism, Christianity, and Islam. Here theodicy is the task of responding to the conundrum: "Can the presence of evil in the world be reconciled with the existence of a God who is unlimited both in goodness and power?"[7] This conundrum sets for the classical Catholic theology of God a problem and a task. This is the case not simply because there are in fact numerous responses to the conundrum throughout the history of this theology. The other elements of this theology of God converge to create this severe and inescapable theodical challenge. As the world creator, God is the Exemplum, the eminent instance, of all perfections. When the principle of *actus purus* merges with the metaphors of will, rule, and power, God must be *all* or perfect or unqualified power. At the same time the drama of redemption offers a

---

7. John Hick, *Evil and the God of Love* (London: Macmillan [Fontana Library], 1968), 3. Hick's book is a historical depiction of Christian theology's two major ways of responding to this question.

radical version of the reality of evil, suffering, oppression, and sin. The subsequent antinomy sets the unavoidable task of thinking these things together.

AMBIGUITIES

It is tempting, especially if we think of historical movements as aesthetic totalities, to picture the classical Catholic theology of God as a conceptual gothic cathedral, a finished, unitary, and even beautiful construction. Yet, this very coherence and finished character also makes it into a merely epochal and antiquarian phenomenon. From a different perspective, the classical Catholic theology of God (also like gothic cathedrals) appears to be a mixed conceptual architecture. In other words, major ambiguities, possibly even aporias, attend this theology of God. I shall identify four such ambiguities and then shall restate what may be the general ambiguity of which each is an expression.[8]

The first ambiguity concerns the issue of "foundationalism." We find this ambiguity exemplified in the different interpretations of Anselm's so-called ontological argument. On the one hand, Anselm presents us with a public, objective, rational argument. On the other hand, Anselm's account begins in faith and prayer and a determination of the meaning of God prior to the argument.[9] Is this a foundationalist program? Like all polemical terms, foundationalism itself has its ambiguities. Its narrower meaning roughly coincides with "natural theology" or rationalistic philosophy of religion; that is, the attempt to establish the existence and nature of God without appeal to faith, religion, redemption, and so forth. Thus, some see the classical Catholic theology of God as a foundational, rational

---

8. A huge literature of criticism of the classical Catholic theology of God spans the generations of twentieth-century theology. Boston personalism, English neoclassical theology (Keith Ward), American process thought (Hartshorne and successors), and theological feminism all agree that there is a major aporia at the heart of the classical view. The aporia arises with the combination of the concept of ultimacy (timelessness, changelessness) with concepts of action and relation (love, suffering, responsiveness). The standard way of understanding why the aporia arose in the first place was to trace it to Hellenic and Hebraic roots. See Burton Cooper, *The Idea of God: A Whiteheadian Critique of St. Thomas Aquinas' Idea of God* (The Hague: Nijhoff, 1974), chap. 1. For specific versions of this aporia, see Edgar Sheffield Brightman, *The Problem of God* (New York: Abingdon Press, 1930); Keith Ward, *Rational Theology and the Creativity of God* (New York: St. Martin's Press, 1974), esp. chaps. 3, 6, and 7; Charles Hartshorne, *Omnipotence and Other Theological Mistakes* (Albany: SUNY Press, 1984); David A. Pailin, *God and the Processes of Reality* (London: Routledge, 1989), 27–33; and Grace Jantzen, *God's World and God's Body* (Philadelphia: Westminster Press, 1984), chaps. 2 and 3.

9. See Karl Barth, *Fides Quaerens Intellectum*, trans. I. W. Robertson (Richmond: John Knox Press, 1960); Henri Bouillard, *The Knowledge of God* (New York: Herder and Herder, 1967), part 2; Jasper Hopkins, *A Companion to the Study of St. Anselm* (Minneapolis: University of Minnesota Press, 1972), chap. 2, and Appendix 2.

apologetics built on Anselm's ontological argument or Aquinas's five ways. But would the classical Catholic theology of God disappear if the arguments for God's existence were somehow struck from the record? We recall at this point the roots of the classical Catholic theology of God in the facticity of redemption and its conviction that the world is the creation of God. As a conviction of faith, the notion of God as creator is not dependent on the validity of the five ways. And few would be persuaded by the claim that Thomas Aquinas abandoned and displaced these roots with a rational apologetic.

This much seems clear. The classical Catholic theology of God is not simply a theistic philosophy of religion. Its roots are too bound up with redemption, the Christian myth, and the legacy of church tradition to be utterly dependent on a set of world-to-God arguments. At the same time, this theology of God does have foundationalist elements. However we assess the status of the question, *an deus sit* (whether God exists) in this theology, it is the case that core concepts originate in the way God and the world are differentiated. The difference of God and the world, not Trinity, the Christ, or salvation, establishes divine perfection, unity, analogy, negation, and attributes. And it is the centrality of the God-and-world theme that opens this theology to the criticisms of fideism and anti-theism.[10]

A familiar criticism of this theology of God helps introduce the second ambiguity. Does this theology propose God as *a* being or being? Here we have a deep and pervasive ambiguity in the discourse about God in Western Christianity. An initial inquiry suggests that the ambiguity is brought about by confusing popular theism with the Catholic theology of God. God as *a* being, as *an* entity, is certainly the characteristic language of liturgy and popular piety. This is the discourse of the Christian story

---

10. According to Pseudo-Dionysius, God as primordial cause, the through-which of the world, is the basis of both negative and affirmation theology. See *The Mystical Theology*, chaps. 2, 3, 5. Creation as foundational to everything else is present in the way Claude Tresmontant expounds what he calls the classical "Christian philosophy," or "Christian metaphysics" (*The Origins of Christian Philosophy*, trans. M. Pontifex [New York: Hawthorne Books, 1963], 40). H. P. Owen agrees. Setting forth "classical theism," he argues that the cosmological argument shows why God is self-existent and this basic attribute grounds all the others; see *Concepts of Deity*, 12. Brian Hebblethwaite also maintains the primacy of the God-world differentiation. He argues that God's function as the metaphysical ground of the world (cf. the cosmological argument) is the basis for affirming God as infinite and absolute. And God is personal because only something personal (spirit or mind) can explain the nature and destiny of the world. Thus the "rationally deduced attributes" are based on the creator-creature relation (*The Ocean of Truth*, 7–8). In similar vein Keith Ward says "if our demand for the rational intelligibility of the universe is to be satisfied, God must be a necessary, eternal, and therefore changeless individual" (*Rational Theology*, 3). If God is the explanation of all things (thus is first cause), God must perfectly exemplify all properties (ibid., 56).

minus negations, qualifiers, and metaphorical self-awareness. God is *a* being who first was alone, then created the world some time in the past, and who then made certain crucial interventions that constitute the unfolding drama of redemption. This is also the discourse of personal piety that relates to God (and thus bespeaks God) as an interpersonal entity who condemns, forgives, plans, and punishes. But this discourse of popular religion is not without its own ambiguities. Insofar as it is rooted in redemption, even popular piety will contain unstated but intended negations. The discourse of popular religion sounds mythological but carries with it demythologizing elements. Hence, we are cautioned against a too facile distinction between popular religion's God (*a* being) and theology's God (being or the beyond-being).

Yet the ambiguity of God as *a* being and as being pursues theological discourse as well. Is God *a* being in the classical Catholic theology of God? There are those who interpret it this way.[11] On the other hand, the texts of this theology of God also contain the opposite view. We can see why. The expression, "*a* being," is a literal depiction of an intraworld differentiation. The everyday world is made up of beings (entities) differentiated from each other. To speak of an entity as *a* being is to draw it into focus, calling attention to its temporal, spatial, and contentful differentiation from other entities. This is just what the classical theology says we cannot do with God.[12] The reason is that God is the through-which of the whole order of differentiated entities. To "entitize" God is to mean God

11. Critics like J. A. T. Robinson interpreted traditional Catholic theology this way (*Honest to God*, 30). Another critic of "objective theism," Don Cupitt, also interprets it as a "realism," by which he means that it regards God to be "an actually-existing independent individual being"; see *Taking Leave of God* (London: SCM, 1980), 15. He uses a similar phrase to describe the God of traditional theism, "an objectively existing superperson" (*The Sea of Faith* [London: BBC, 1985], 270). Further, we find the language of God as *a* being, *an* individual, used by philosophers and theologians whose viewpoints are within the theology of God. "In the deliberations that follow, I assume that God (if He exists) is a *being*—a single individual possessing negative as well as positive attributes" (Nelson Pike, *God and Timelessness* [New York: Schocken Books, 1970], 1). Pike goes on to say that God as *a* being is clearly presupposed by Augustine, Boethius, St. Thomas, St. Anselm, and Friedrich Schleiermacher.

12. Joseph Donceel points out that for Aquinas, God is not *a* being but being itself. For to be *a* being would mean *having* an essence and this is what we cannot say of God if God is without limitation. Each created entity is *a* being: God is not. See *The Searching Mind*, chap. 6. Keith Ward concurs. Stressing that Aquinas incorporated the negative theology of Pseudo-Dionysius, he says that for Aquinas, God is not *a* being (which thus would have parts and would fall into a class) but is a universal and pure form. Analogies and their necessarily attendant negations undercut any notion of God as *a* being (*Rational Theology*, 58). Jean-Luc Marion finds Martin Heidegger's presumption that God is *a* being, namely an entity characterized by omnipotence, as far from self-evident. For once "God" is defined as a "being," "his pretension to fix himself as an absolute center becomes a usurpation." Precisely! See *God Without Being*, tr. T. A. Carlson (Chicago: University of Chicago Press, 1991), 50.

as an additional entity along with or "in" the world.[13] Myths of God's creative or redemptive activity may seem to do this, but the classical Catholic theology demythologizes such by its differentiation between God as the ineffable self-identity and the world of beings. The same can be said of the philosophical traditions that inform the classical theology. Plato's "Good" (*to agathon*) and Plotinus's One (*to hen*) are not beings or entities.

In what way is the classical view ambiguous? What would prompt anyone to interpret the God of this tradition as *a* being? Here we recall that which launches this theology of God, the distinction between the absolute creator and creation. The negative proposition of the notion of creation *ex nihilo* preempts the view that God is a metaphysical correlate of the world. The Good of Plato, the world-soul of Stoicism, the One with its processions of Plotinus are such correlates. They represent an eternal, creative, ordering dimension of an everlasting world-process. This creative ordering plus its receptive material (chaos, matter, world body) simply coexist. In the classical theology of God, the world is not coeternal with God and God is not a metaphysical correlate of the world. As creation the world is the result of an absolute act of divine freedom. At this point one could argue that such a claim is simply a negation without positive content and ends any further explication. But some draw a positive implication that presses the doctrine of creation *ex nihilo* toward mythological expressions. If God is not a metaphysical correlate of the world, then God must be metaphysically *independent*. This invites the mythological notion that temporalizes this independence into the distinction of God as first existing alone and then (by creation) existing with a world. The negation of *ex nihilo* is thus transformed into the positive metaphor of independence.[14] And it is just this independence of God that

---

13. For a nonentitative interpretation of Pseudo-Dionysius and the negation theology, see John D. Jones, "Non-Entitative Understanding of Be-ing and Unity: Heidegger and Neoplatonism," *Dionysius* 6 (December 1982): 94–111.

14. Robert Neville has helped clarify the matter by submitting a number of different meanings of independence; thus, self-possession which then comes into relation, in-itselfness, etc. He argues that while in-itselfness is an appropriate term for God, the concept of God as independent arises only with the attempt to know God's relation to the world; see *God the Creator: On the Transcendence and Presence of God* (Chicago: University of Chicago Press, 1968), 96. Robert Sokolowski restates the Thomist view of God's independence in the sense that God is "capable of being without the world," and being without the world involves no diminution of either God's goodness or greatness. He argues, in fact, that this is *the* mark of Christian theism in contrast to the faiths or philosophies of the ancient world that thought of the divine as necessarily entangled with the world. See *God of Faith and Reason: Foundations of Christian Theology* (Notre Dame: University of Notre Dame Press, 1982), 40.

invites interpreters to think that the God of the classical theology is *a* being. For in the world that we know, to be independent is to be *a* being separated from other beings.

Do we have here an aporia, a logical contradiction? To display a true contradiction at this point requires us to exchange the negative function of creation *ex nihilo* for the mythology or literalized sense of God as an independent being. In the classic view, God as the through-which of the whole order of beings cannot be *a* being. Are we to conclude then that God is being? We can find texts that say just that. But neither is that position utterly unambiguous. Do we mean God is the being of beings, that which constitutes beings in their reality? If so God would mean whatever we decide that reality is; eventfulness, temporality, enduring structure, matter. Or do we mean that God is being in the sense of the absolute condition (ground, creativity) without which there are no beings? The classical Catholic theology of God clearly holds to the second alternative. But being in this sense is undesignated. It can be construed as creativity, personality, substance, even an *élan vital*. Insofar as it remains undesignated, there is no contradiction between saying God is being and saying that God acts, reveals, or loves. I conclude that in the classical Catholic theology of God, God as the ineffable through-itself cannot be *a* being, and as world creator, is not simply the *being* of the world.[15] God's relation to being is left ambiguous and unresolved. God is, one might say, objective and referential, but not *an* object nor *a* reference.

The third ambiguity is a tension between a set of attributes derived from God as the necessary and perfect self-existent and the discourse that attributes activity, responsiveness, and personality to God.[16] This tension

15. Contemporary Thomists are quite clear that for Thomas, we do not know *what* God is. And for Thomas to say that God is being (*ens*) is not to identify an essence (*essentia*) of God or a mode of being. Étienne Gilson argues that it is the "religious universe" (Moses and the Scriptures), not Aristotle that is being expressed here. And if "act of being" or "to exist" is what is declared by *ens*, there need be no incompatibility between saying God is being and God is process, dynamic, or action. See Gilson, *The Christian Philosophy of St. Thomas Aquinas* (New York: Random House, 1966), 82–84.

16. This tension or aporia is given succinct expression by Keith Ward: "If our demand for the rational intelligibility of the universe is to be satisfied, God must be a necessary, eternal and therefore changeless individual. But if our demand for human freedom and contingency of the finite world is to be met, and especially if we wish to speak of free creation, either by God or human beings, then it cannot be the case that the universe depends solely upon a necessary being. For the truly contingent cannot arise from the wholly necessary; and if creation, Divine or human, is free and contingent, then creation is incompatible with necessity. If God is the creator or cause of a contingent world, he must be contingent and temporal; but if God is a necessary being, then whatever he causes must be necessary and changelessly caused. On this rock both traditional interpretations of theism founder. The demands of intelligibility require the existence of a necessary, immutable, eternal being. Creation seems to demand a contingent, temporal God, who interacts with creation and is, therefore, not self-sufficient. But how can one have both?" (*Rational Theology*, 3).

has found a variety of expressions: the God of the philosophers and the God of Abraham, Isaac, and Jacob; substance versus process theism; the God of being and the God of revelatory action. Like the other ambiguities, this too can be interpreted as a tension resolvable into the distinction between the popular theistic and the philosophical sides of the classical Catholic theology. Accordingly, we can reduce the tension with a rigorous demythologizing of the popular theistic element. The issue, however, does not disappear so easily. Let us restate the issue. How can we account for God's active relation to the world in the light of attributes that seem to remove God from time, change, and responsiveness? The issue is not a new one. Martin Luther, Blaise Pascal, Jacob Boehme, G. W. F. Hegel, and Friedrich Schelling all challenged the reduction of God to static being. In the twentieth century, process theology has been a persistent critic of classical theism's apparent essentialism, a criticism now taken up in liberation and feminist theologies. In the view of Charles Hartshorne, the classical Catholic theology of God is not a coherent position because it simply combines a static metaphysic with the active and responsive God of religion. On the one side of this aporia, the classical theology seems to conceive God as an absolutely fulfilled or actualized perfection, thus empty of possibilities. Existing above change, God has no past, present, or future. On the other side, this theology attributes to God not only wisdom, knowledge, and love, but also what appears to be genuine action. God possesses all attributes, including personal ones, but in the mode of immutability. The problems arise when one would claim for God not simply simultaneous, essence-type knowledge (or experience) of the world but activities whose responsiveness to contingencies require responsive and (as Hartshorne would say) growing knowledge.

The contradiction between God as timeless and complete and God as active, responsive, and even possible is rooted in a deeper ambiguity that comes with the *via negativa*. Are the negations that arise from God as the through-which of the world metaphysical or nonmetaphysical in character? That is, do they apply to God's being or actuality? To put the question differently yet, are the negations transformable into positive attributes? If we refuse (negate) to apply the category of time or change to God in a direct way, are we at the same time saying that God's being is "timeless" or "changeless"? Pseudo-Dionysius is clear on this point. God is above both change and changelessness.[17] That is to say, no logical or material polarity is directly applicable to God. Thus, it is just as problematic to

---

17. Dionysius the Areopagite, "The Mystical Theology," *The Divine Names and Mystical Theology*, trans. John D. Jones (Milwaukee: Marquette University Press, 1980), chap. 5.

say God is literally changeless as it is to say God literally changes. But an anomaly develops in later applications of the negative way. To claim that God's being or actuality is timeless is possible only if God's being is directly knowable. But this is just what the negative way preempts. Even "revelation" does not enable us to make the cognitive leap from worldly systems into the through-which of those systems. For this reason we qualify (negate) all positive language used of God, thus time and timelessness, change and changelessness. Thus, to regard the negation as itself the basis of a positive claim is to abandon the very thing that calls for negation. Because of this ambiguity, the classical Catholic theology of God has been subjected to very different interpretations. Some interpreters (for instance, Hartshorne) accuse it of maintaining that God is timeless and immutable in a strong metaphysical sense. To the degree that the charge is sustainable, this objective theism is structured by the larger antinomy that combines God as metaphysically absolute and changeless and metaphysically personal and dynamic. Others insist that the negations are not positive attributes and should not be understood as metaphysical descriptions.

The fourth ambiguity often appears in the guise of theodicy problems. I argued previously that the task of theodicy was one of the intrinsic elements of the classical Catholic theology of God. This task is set by what appears to be an aporia. The metaphor of an absolute and sovereign rule, necessarily victorious over all worldly resistance, the affirmation that God wills only the good of things, and the notion that God is the sole and absolute origin of the world system should preempt what this theology of redemption presupposes, a creation gone awry. The Augustinian theodicy of the origin of evil in the freedom of creatures seems to acknowledge that there is something intrinsic about *creatures,* their contingency and nonnecessity of obedience, that makes them able to depart from God's rule. The Irenaean theodicy of necessary conditions and stages (that involve evil) toward the completion of creation likewise qualifies absolute rule by a structural feature of creation. In neither theodicy is *absolute* sovereignty retained. Hence, the standard theodicies do not eliminate but restate this aporia of perfect rule and corrupted creation.

These aporias refer us to a single ambiguity that spawns different interpretations of the classical theology of God. The form in which this theology was originally presented (for instance, Scholastic method) and its rootage in ancient Western philosophies (Plato, Aristotle, Plotinus) prompt some to regard this theology of God as primarily a metaphysics. As a metaphysics it is foundationalist (thus, the "proofs" for God's existence), totalizing in its scope, and focused on God as being. As a metaphysics, its derivation of attributes, including the negative attributes of immutability and timelessness, describe the being of God. On the other hand we have noted ambiguities at all of these points: a nonfoundationalist element, the negative theology that removes discourse from direct description, resistance to ordinary meanings of God either as *a* being or as being. Could it be that the classical theology of God is less a metaphysics than a theology, that is, the explication of a mystery that attends faith? David Burrell reads it this way.[18] Much of the issue turns on whether we regard the negative attributes that come with God as self-identical (eternity, timelessness, immutability, simplicity) as positive descriptions. Is immutability more an agnostic caution against directly applying to God various types of change (demise, fickleness of character, personal development, aging) than a positive description of God's very being as changeless? The same question can be asked of all the negative attributes. If they are more agnostic cautions than positive descriptions, then this theology of God is a very chastened metaphysics of divine being, if, in fact, it is a metaphysic at all. We shall explore this issue in more detail in Chapters Six and Eleven.

18. For Burrell the key to Thomas's way of bespeaking God is something Hartshorne misses, namely, the acknowledgment that we have no knowledge of *what* God is. Accordingly, negative terms like immutability and positive terms like power are not descriptions of God's being or way of being. Thus, Thomas is not making the metaphysical claim that God's being is such that it is literally changeless. To say such a thing would presuppose *knowledge* of God's being. Thus, Thomas's language of simplicity, immutability, and nonrelation to creatures is a set of grammatical prescriptions, not metaphysical descriptions. See *Aquinas: God in Action* (Notre Dame: University of Notre Dame Press, 1979), chap. 6.

3
VARIETIES OF ANTI-THEISM

> Knowledge about God in his true nature, as he is in himself
> and apart from his relation to man, is inevitably objective
> knowledge. Objective knowledge is made possible by a step-
> ping back, in order to discover the contours of what is known,
> of its place in the whole and its relation to other things. The
> Bible does not approve of such objective knowledge of God.
> God is encountered in command and command is an experi-
> ence of the subjectivity of God, of his commanding and ob-
> serving man rather than of man observing him.
>
> *Michael Wyschogrod,* The Body of Faith

> Theism and atheism bear equally upon an idol.
>
> *Jean-Luc Marion,* God Without Being

Anti-theism is now so powerfully articulated and so widely persuasive
that to confess to being a "theist" is almost a breach of theological
etiquette. In spite of the dominance of at least the rhetoric of anti-
theism, the situation is far from clear. We have already noted the ambiguity of the term *theism.* A similar ambiguity tracks antitheism.[1]
As a target of discreditation, theism varies from critic to critic. In
what follows I distinguish five types of anti-theistic criticism: theistic

---

1. Charles Hodge, a nineteenth-century Presbyterian theologian, used the term *anti-
theism* for any and all ways of rejecting theism, which is "the doctrine of an extramun-
dane, personal God, the creator, preserver, and governor of all things" (*Systematic Theology,* Vol. 1 [New York: Charles Scribner, 1872], 241). Since that time, theism has come to
mean philosophy of God, a foundationalist approach to God, an objectivist posture, and
patriarchalist and hierarchalist interpretations of God. Thus, anti-theism is now a term
not just for the rejection of the creator God but for a variety of criticisms of older discourses and frameworks. Accordingly, we have hermeneutic, feminist, Heideggerian,
Whiteheadian, and postmodern anti-theisms. Howard Burkle used the term to describe
such diverse thinkers as Hegel, Sartre, and the Husserlian and Roman Catholic philosopher of religion, Henry Duméry (*The Non-Existence of God: Antitheism from Hegel to
Duméry* [New York: Herder and Herder, 1969]). Burkle is one of the first to accuse anti-
theism of caricaturing theism. (183)

self-criticism, resymbolization, demythologization, deconstruction, and religio-philosophical anti-theism.

INTRATHEISTIC CRITIQUES

Two types of anti-theist criticism remain within the general framework of theism itself. The first type retains the basic approach, agenda, and conceptuality of the classical Catholic theology of God but identifies certain problems to be corrected or tensions to be resolved. An example is Keith Ward, who proposes a way ("dynamic infinity") beyond the dilemma created by the claim that a *necessary* being can relate to *contingency*.[2] The second type, neoclassical or process theism, abandons the metaphysical framework of the classical Catholic theology but retains natural theology, attributes, and the God-and-world problem. Process theology rehabilitates the Platonic tradition (especially the *Timaeus*) by way of Alfred North Whitehead's metaphysics of process. It resolves the ambiguity of classical theology as a metaphysics, and argues that metaphysics, the speculative grasp of the features of any possible world (Charles Hartshorne) or of the world of our cosmic epoch (Whitehead, Robert Neville), is possible as a task and is necessary to any coherent account of God. It charges the classical Catholic theology of God with incoherence for attempting to unite God as a necessary, self-identified, and perfect being in all respects (thus immutable and so on) with God as active, loving, merciful, and seemingly passible. In this rehabilitation, God becomes, at least in one aspect, temporal, finite, and contingent, and themes of creation *ex nihilo*, absolute sovereignty, and God as noncorrelative with the world are abandoned. Strictly speaking, these criticisms are not so much anti-theisms as proposals for a new or qualified form of theism.

RESYMBOLIZING

Two metaphors dominate traditional Catholic and the Protestant ways of understanding God's relation to the world: absolute creation and sovereign rule. As absolute creator, God is self-existent, perfect, and complete,

2. Keith Ward, *Rational Theology and the Creativity of God* (New York: St. Martin's Press, 1974). Ward is critical of Anselm's arguments for immutability and the concept of God as being-itself or pure Form, and argues against Anselm and Thomas that God experiences growth and cooperation with creatures (63, 140). Thomas V. Morris, while critical of the "exotic" and "liberal" character of process theology from the perspective of classical Catholic theism, does qualify the notions of God's a-temporality, simplicity, and immutability (*The Concept of God* [Oxford: Oxford University Press, 1987], chap. 7, #1).

from which are derived other divine perfections. Sovereign rule was a way of understanding God's ongoing and teleological activity in the world. Widespread is the metaphor of kingly rule throughout ancient Western religions. In Judaism, Christianity, and Islam, rule is the primary metaphor that gathers together and interprets metaphors of love and mercy.

Criticisms of the dominance of this metaphor are not unknown in the premodern era, thus, for instance, those of Julian of Norwich. And the first half of the twentieth century contained similar critiques. The Lundensian theology displaced rule with agape.[3] Nicholas Berdyaev, venturing some of the most caustic criticisms of the monarchical metaphor for God in theological literature, replaced metaphors of rule with metaphors of spirit, freedom, and personality.[4] And Charles Hartshorne likewise argued against the monarchical metaphor and sovereignty on both religious and metaphysical grounds. In the second half of the century, we have a continuation of Hartshornian and Whiteheadian critiques by process theologians. And sensing the connection between the monarchical metaphor and patriarchalism, feminist theologies have reformulated the symbolics of God, exchanging metaphors of rule with metaphors of reciprocal relation, thus love, friendship, and parenting.[5] All of these critiques are made on the basis of a resymbolizing of God that either abandons some of the older metaphors altogether or downgrades their status. Resymbolization has in some cases carried over into new metaphorical proposals for the persons of the Trinity.

DEMYTHOLOGIZING

Critical responses to the classical Catholic theology of God by feminist resymbolization and new process metaphysics do not necessarily add up to anti-theism. Process theology retains an essentially metaphysical way of approaching God. I use the term *anti-theism* to express several ways of declaiming against the approach and conceptual structure of "classical theism." Some theologians oppose "theism" by identifying it with the popular theism of a God above or beside the world, God as an entity or

---

3. For instance, Gustaf Aulén, *The Faith of the Christian Church* (Philadelphia: Muhlenberg Press, 1960), chaps. 14, 16; Nels F. S. Ferré, *The Christian Understanding of God* (New York: Harper and Brothers, 1951).

4. Nicolas Berdyaev, *Slavery and Freedom* (New York: Charles Scribner's Sons, 1944), chap. 2.

5. Sallie McFague, *Models of God: Theology for an Ecological Nuclear Age* (Philadelphia: Fortress Press, 1987).

a being. Thus, for these critics, "theism" is a mythical and literalistic way of interpreting God that calls for demythologizing.

Closely related to the charge that theism is an outmoded mythical thinking is the rejection of classical theism as a "dualism." Perhaps there are senses in which that charge holds true. But we should be clear about the various senses in which the classical view is not a dualism. It does not, for instance, propose two ultimate metaphysical principles of reality and nonreality or of good and evil (for instance, Marcion). Doctrines of creation *ex nihilo* and analogy undercut any claim that the world is a metaphysical polarity over against God. "Dualism" may simply mean the view that God is *a* being beside the world, a charge that ignores the negative theology, analogy, God's unknowable self-identity, and God's nonrelation to the world in a positive sense. A mythological construal of creation *ex nihilo* may sound dualistic to some interpreters, but it should be remembered that this doctrine was formulated as an alternative to giving God and the world equal or "dualistic" status. The classical Catholic theology of God originated as an opposition to dualisms of *a* god or gods beside or in the world, two ultimate divinities, or two ultimate realities, God and world. One can only suspect that the charge applies not so much to the classical Catholic theology of God as to world-denying, matter-and-spirit schemes that characterized early Christian asceticism. If "dualism" simply means any and all ways of differentiating God from the world, then the classical theology is dualistic, but then so are *all* religions and theologies that do not simply define God as the world system. These criticisms of "theism" as mythological, literalistic, and dualistic are only pseudo-anti-theisms insofar as they apply only to unreflective and popular forms of discourse rather than to the objective theism of the classical Catholic theology of God.

DECONSTRUCTIVE ANTI-THEISM

I take up now two forms of anti-theism that confront the classical view more directly: radical theology (deconstruction) and religio-philosophical anti-theism. The two unite in their opposition to metaphysics and their conviction that the classical Catholic theology of God is a metaphysics of God. According to the former, the God of classical theism has died; according to the latter, this God never lived.

Using such terms as "theism," "classical theism," and "objective theism," radical theology conducts a funeral for the classical Catholic theology of God. The God of "theism" has not so much been disproved as historically displaced. There is some ambiguity on this point in writers such as J. A. T. Robinson, Don Cupitt, and Gordon Kaufman, who would describe the God of classical theism as "up there," "outside," or "an existing individual."[6] This God is slain both by demythologizing rationality and by the rise of modernity. Since I am persuaded that even popular religion possesses demythologizing elements and that the God of the classical view is not *an* individual or *a* being, I do not agree that demythologizing and the negative theology are inventions of modern (or postmodern) theologies.

On the other hand, Mark C. Taylor's anti-theism is not constructed on the caricature of God as *a* being. For him the issue is not a mythological individual who evokes disbelief but a heteronomous deity that threatens violence against human autonomy.[7] It is difficult to determine whether this is a historical or a philosophical argument. As a historical argument, it describes (from historical evidences) the postmodern type of consciousness that is "its own signification," whose being is the interplay of signs and whose inscription is the play of difference. God thus disappears by way of an epochal shift. Insofar as the God of classical theism is reducible to a violating heteronomy, this historical observation is at the same time an intellectual discreditation not unlike the earlier assaults on metaphors of domination by Nicolas Berdyaev and Charles Hartshorne and more recently by feminist theology. But more is at stake here. For Taylor the postmodern cannot abide *any* alterity: alterity as such is violating. We can only ask at this point whether this identification of alterity and violation has been philosophically established. For Emmanuel Levinas the alterity of the vulnerable face is the primordial redemptive facticity, the fundamental event that launches human beings against violation, totality, and even reality. We must also wonder whether God and the classical Catholic theology of God are so utterly identified that epochal statements about historical shifts apply equally to both. And we wonder what kind of human act is required and what kind of evidences are assembled in order to be certain that God and classical Catholic theism are simply identical.

RELIGIO-PHILOSOPHICAL ANTI-THEISM

In its most formal sense, "theism" can mean any and all ways of believing in and bespeaking God that are distinguishable from polytheism and atheism. In this formal sense most of theism's theological critics are "the-

6. Gordon Kaufman, *In Face of Mystery: A Constructive Theology* (Cambridge: Harvard University Press, 1993), 271.

7. Mark C. Taylor, *Erring: a postmodern a-theology* (Chicago: University of Chicago Press, 1984).

ists." But if "theism" means the approach to God by way of the question of being, the puzzle of the world, the search for a world ground, then we can identify an anti-theism that opposes this approach primarily on religious grounds. Paradoxically, the form this approach takes—and this distinguishes it from Barth-type theologies—is rigorously philosophical. Philosophical reflection is employed to undermine what is sometimes called ontotheology and to clear a discursive space for religious or non-philosophical thinking of God. This anti-theism has Jewish (Franz Rosenzweig, Martin Buber, Levinas), Roman Catholic (Jean-Luc Marion), and Protestant (Robert Scharlemann) representatives.[8] I shall try to synthesize their views into a single case against "theism."

All of the above-mentioned figures share the conviction that rigorous philosophical reflection is a legitimate if not even inevitable modality of "religious" thinking. Further, they all participate in the Kantian disruption of totalizing metaphysics and in the Kierkegaardian turn, if not to the subject, at least to the order of *Existenz*. Primary for them are the interpersonal dealings, distortive idolatries, and the experience of grace of everyday life. In addition, anti-theism directs three refusals to the theology of God in Western thought. First, it refuses to think from the world to God. Put another way, it refuses the question of God *as* the question of being. Second, it refuses to think the *being* of God and thus passes over any philosophical derivation of attributes. Third, it refuses to think the relation between God and the world. This third refusal carries with it a refusal of theodicy as a problem and a task. This repudiation of theodicy stems from the absence in anti-theism of those elements found in the classical view that make the theodicy problem unavoidable. I shall address the first refusal, the issue of the approach to God, in the next chapter, the issue of the derivation of attributes in Chapter Six, and the issue of God and the world in Part 3. In sum, if the "theism" of the classical Catholic theology of God means a thinking that proceeds from the world to God, a derivation of attributes from that proceeding, and a thematizing of the God-world relation, then we can say that these figures represent a genuine anti-theism.

---

8. Franz Rosenzweig, *Understanding the Sick and the Healthy; A View of World, Man, and God* (New York: Noonday Press, 1953); *The Star of Redemption*, trans. W. W. Hallo (Boston: Beacon Press, 1964); Martin Buber, *I and Thou*, trans. R. G. Smith (New York: Charles Scribner's Sons, 1958), part 3; Emmanuel Levinas, *Totality and Infinity*, trans. A. Lingis (Pittsburgh: Duquesne University Press, 1969), and *Otherwise than Being or Beyond Essence* (The Hague: Martinus Nijhoff, 1981); Robert P. Scharlemann, *The Being of God: Theology and the Experience of Truth* (New York: Seabury Press, 1981), and *Inscriptions and Reflections: Essays in Philosophical Theology* (Charlottesville: University Press of Virginia, 1989), part 1; Jean-Luc Marion, *God Without Being*, trans. T. A. Carlson (Chicago: University of Chicago Press, 1991).

All of the anti-theists oppose the identification of God and being. God is not *a* being. God cannot be bespoken by the differentiation of Being and beings (Marion). God is "otherwise than being" (Levinas). What drives this opposition is not the philosophical problem of determining what primary concept "names" God. Anti-theism does not propose an alternate generic concept for God such as process, ground, or the All. Its more fundamental concern is the way the term or problem of being disposes a certain approach to God. The polemic against God as being serves to expose an approach to God that is not ordered by the way God comes forth as God. For anti-theism God does not come forth as God "philosophically"; that is, in connection with the human being's rational puzzlement about the world. In the light of this puzzle and perhaps goaded by religious concerns, Western religious thought from Plato to the present has attempted to think through the world's opaqueness back to what brought it forth and gave it order, direction, or novelty. To name God, being, or to think God as being, is the result of thinking God as in some way the world's ground, foundation, or true reality. What is problematic about thinking God and the world together? What is wrong with the distinction between the ground and the grounded?

The anti-theist figures mentioned above all participate in the modern (or postmodern) opposition to ontotheology, an opposition that has some formidable predecessors. We recall a figure at the end of the Middle Ages whose way of bespeaking God was a break with the movement from grounded world to world ground, namely Martin Luther.[9] Luther simply sets aside as "curiosity" the whole ontotheological tradition and with it all thinking from the world to God. Instead, he would identify how and where God comes forth as God: thus, his declared Word (Scripture), as specifically preached, and the situation of the actual religious life of sin, guilt, despair, humiliation, forgiveness, and worship as all this takes place in the lives of actual individuals. Luther's eyes and ears are turned toward human *Existenz*, the crucified Jesus, and the accusing God who hardens hearts and frustrates pride. There is a negative theology here, but its basis is the ignorance human beings have of the hidden God, the essence of God, and the experience of the paradoxes of the active and declarative God.[10] The mystery of God is especially the mystery of God's inscrutable

9. See, for instance, *The Bondage of the Will*, trans. Packer and Johnston (London: James Clarke, 1957), II, iv–vii; IV, x; V, iv–v.

10. For an excellent account of Luther's negative theology, see Kevin Dodd, *A Transcending Presence: Four Pre-Modern Christian Positions on the Hiddenness of God—Augustine; Pseudo-Dionysius; Aquinas; and Luther* (Ph. D. Dissertation, Vanderbilt University, 1995).

will, not the mystery of grounding Being. Luther can use the traditional language of divine attributes (God as eternal, unchangeable, merciful) but it is clear that these bespeakings are not derived from the difference between the perfect *a se* or *causa sui* and that which is caused. For Luther the attributive language expresses a foolish "knowledge" of God as it is determined by the Scriptures, preaching, and faith.

Luther's is a religiously inspired anti-theism. Twentieth-century anti-theisms have found philosophical ways to express the primacy of religion (faith) in posing the question of the bespeaking of God. While Luther is not part of the religious heritage of all contemporary anti-theists, he nevertheless typifies the refusal to suspend the redemptive coming forth of God as God. What specific reasons do the anti-theists have for refusing to approach God by way of the question of being? For antitheism a philosophical determination of the question of God is just that, a determination. God then is whatever that determination allows God to be. A methodological privileging of philosophy must then set aside God's coming forth as God in revelation, as the eternal Thou, in Jesus, in redemption. For Rosenzweig, ontotheology and the search for foundations is a way human beings would secure themselves against death by their own reflective powers. For Buber ontotheology and thinking from the world to God takes place in the order of the *Es-welt*, the sphere of the primacy of I-It. This objectifies that which does not come forth as a thought or an experiential object. For Levinas to think from the world to God requires an orientation to totality, a concept that embraces both an inclusive cosmic category and the destructive, oppressive, war-oriented outcomes that take place when human beings are determined by objectification. Scharlemann "destrues" (compare Heidegger's *Destruktion*) or deconstructs the history of theism and concludes that in that history, God's otherness, especially God's otherness to the objectified concept of deity, remains unthought. For Marion, any thinking of God that is not evoked by God's own *eikonic* revealing can only have an idol as its object. God as being correlates with an autonomous thinking that can only project its speculative problem of the world onto a screen.

Religio-philosophical anti-theism is, of course, more than a polemic and set of refusals. It would replace thinking from the world (beings) to God (being) with a thinking from the place God comes forth as God. For the anti-theists this place is not a place of God's presence. God remains remote (Buber), a not-being-God (Scharlemann), an invisible depth of an icon (Marion). The place of revealing in the Jewish and Christian types of anti-theism is of course not the same. For the Christians it is the death of God (in Jesus' death) that constitutes a break with religion, attribution, and all cults of divine appearing (Scharlemann), or the place of icons and eucharist (Marion). For the Jewish philosophers, the place of revealing is the sphere of human alterity, thou, and face. Yet there is a remarkable formal similarity between Buber and Marion. For Marion the splendor of the idol fascinates and thus dominates experience and at the same time reduplicates (mirrors) and fulfills the human being's need for splendor. In contrast the *icon* opens itself to the invisible and, like a face (compare Levinas), deepens the visible aspect. This theme of a "deeper" attendant dimension of things is just the way Buber relates the eternal Thou to thous and the way Levinas relates the infinite and the face. In the I-thou relation, we experience a release from being mere entities in the world. Yet no specific thou-entity (each one differentiated from others) effects this release. It is by way of thous and the release to the other that the nonpresent eternal Thou evokes relation to itself. We "know" God not by direct experience but in the transformation that takes place when we experience the reversal (*Umkehre*) and learn to say Thou. Paradoxically this event reconnects us to the world in a way different from objectification. Faith, religion, and relation to God all take place not in flight from but in relation to the world. We can see, now, why this existential, horizontal, (non)-presence of God in the thou or the face eschews theoretical versions of the God-world relation.

ISSUES AND APPRAISALS

I have attempted in these pages to construct what appears at first sight to be an unbridgeable opposition between the classical Catholic theology of God and various forms of anti-theism. This opposition is especially ill-formulated by interpretations that confuse the classical view with popular, supernaturalistic, or mythical theism and the notion that God is *a* being. The apparent opposition between these views is also less sharp when we stress the nonmetaphysical, that is, the nonpositive character of the language of perfection and immutability. Still, the opposition seems unnegotiable to those who interpret the God of the classical view as a violating heteronomy. This charge is easier confirmed at the level of the prevailing metaphors that dominate individual and institutional religion than something literally declaimed by the classical texts themselves.

We must thus pose a question. Is religio-philosophical anti-theism an unambiguous and logical opposite to the classical Catholic theology of God? Anti-theism's stark refusals of certain themes and its privileging of faith to speculation suggest that this is the case. Yet ambiguity shadows even these clear-cut and passionate polemics on two counts. First, as a *religio*-philosophical polemic, anti-theism is an antifoundationalism that insists that God does not come forth as God originally and primarily in the speculative differentiation of God and the world. Let us grant anti-theism this point. What happens when anti-theism moves beyond its polemic to positive language about God, to selections of metaphors, to negative expressions such as God's eternity, or to issues of God's knowledge, freedom, or power? Most anti-theists still use this discourse. We must then ask on what ground? The justification, stated or unstated, seems to be that Scripture has bespoken God in these ways. There is thus a textual event of revealing, the creation of scriptures, and all subsequent bespeakings and thinkings of God imitate that primordial textual bespeaking. Luther certainly assumed this and so does Jean-Luc Marion and the Jewish philosophers.

We find then at the heart of religio-philosophical anti-theism an element of authority theology. "Authority theology" does not mean simply an acknowledgment of a deep correlation between a religious community and the deposit of wisdom in its ancient textual traditions. It is a specific paradigm of the nature and function of these texts, according to which revealing or disclosure is an *a priori* element in discrete, specific, even fragmented passages. Modern religio-philosophical anti-theists are not fundamentalists. They take for granted historical ways of approaching the ancient texts. But insofar as a hidden, textually authoritative *a priori* justifies their actual bespeaking of God, they invite criticism and deconstruction of their authority theology. On the other hand, if they simply repudiate authority theology and yet would bespeak God, appeal to negations, and reinterpret symbols, then they face the issue of the first refusal. In its first refusal, anti-theism rejects foundationalistic approaches to God from the puzzle of the world. But, minus an authority foundation, can it totally preempt the world and say what it even means by God? Opening up here is the larger task of a theology of God that would think God from the way God comes forth as God and on that basis take up the problem of the bespeaking of God and the question of God and the world.

Second, anti-theism repudiates foundationalism and the primacy of the puzzle of the world in the approach to God by rejecting the identification of God and being. But the ambiguity of the term *being* lurks in this opposition. What precisely is the being that anti-theism withholds from God? Let us acknowledge anti-theism's methodological quarrel, its notion that

God as being is a short-cut term for an ontotheological approach and a thinking from the world to God. Does this acknowledgment carry with it a refusal to think from God to the world? What is the relation of the eternal Thou, the crossed-out crucified God (Marion), the God who is "other than deity" (Scharlemann), to being? In this form, the question is far from clear. To say that we are unable to think the *being* of God is not to depart from but to side with the classical view. To deny that God is an ontic referent, *an* existing being, may urge a departure from popular and mythical discourse but not from the classical view. Furthermore, the classical theology would surely agree with anti-theism that God is not the Being (*Sein*) of beings in Martin Heidegger's distinction.

We come nearer to a genuine opposition when we consider that anti-theism appears to reject God as a ground of being (ontotheology), and when we consider that when Aquinas calls God *being* (*ens*), he means just that, that God is the reality through which and from which all else comes. Does this mean, then, that anti-theism's repudiation of the puzzle of the world as the route to God requires it to reject any and all statements that God is the through-which of what is not God? Does the primacy of the facticity of redemption force a rejection of all differentiations of God and the world? Must the symbolism of God the creator (and with it a differentiation between God and world) be dismissed because it contains a remnant of "ontotheology?" I am not sure how anti-theists respond to questions of this sort. The questions do help us pose a single question to anti-theism. Does the primacy of the "religious" over the philosophical placement of the question of God require a *confinement* of the meaning of God or of the divine activity to the sphere of revelation or redemption? Or does the "religious" placement, the sphere of Thou, the face of the other, the crucified Jesus, in some way open up a grace that is unlimited in scope and therefore is as inclusive as the world? At this point a slight crack appears in the polemics of anti-theism. If the reduction of God to redemption is rejected, and some version of a universal relation of God and world is accepted, even as a symbolism, how is the differentiation of God and world made? I would doubt that anti-theists think of God as the offspring of chaotic powers (compare the ancient theogonies) or as simply a competing entity in the world system. With these negations, we find ourselves searching for a discourse, not unlike the classical language of being. God may be loving, merciful, and active. But as world creator God is not simply a loving mundane entity, *a* being who is merciful. Accordingly, the initial refusals of anti-theism may themselves open a way to the tasks of a symbolics of God and a thinking of God's activity in the world.

4

MEANINGS AND EVIDENCES

For in one sense a thing is thought when the word signifying it is thought; in another sense when the very object which the thing is is understood. In the first sense, then, God can be thought not to exist, but not at all in the second sense. No one, indeed, understanding what God is can think that God does not exist, even though he may say these words in his heart either without any [objective] signification or with some peculiar signification.

Anselm, Proslogion

We take up now the first of the three thematics of the theology of God. Yet when we press for a succinct definition of this thematics, we begin to stumble. Our subject is what the other two thematics, the symbolics of God and God's activity in the world, presuppose, namely, an account of how discourse about God arises in the first place. Conventionally expressed, this first thematics is about "the knowledge of God," "the revelation of God," and even "faith and reason." All of these terms address in some way the following question: How is it that something we call God has evoked convictions or postures of belief, trust, or worship? What leads to the conviction that the term *God* names something that could be called actual as over against fictional, psychologically projected, or culturally produced? However much theology is a "way of negation," its subject is not simply a contentless nothing but something (God) that has symbolic content and that is the referent of worshipful acts.

People in specific communities attest to and worship something, however much it is not a "something," however incapable they are of imagining, describing, or conceptualizing it, that is not simply their mirror image. What has given rise to these convictions that this elusive (non)-presence is "real" or "actual?" We are familiar with psychological and sociological explanations that track the convictions and wor-

51

shipful acts of believers to their "causes," explanations that presuppose but do not demonstrate God's nonactuality. The theology of God works from another presupposition. It would articulate (but not demonstrate) as best it can the reasons the community of faith worships and lives before God regarded as something real.

The task of setting forth the way God arises into belief-ful conviction faces the same problem that confronts any and all language that would concern itself with God. Every available term sounds too strong. One hesitates to claim "knowledge" of God or "experience" of God. One hesitates to say that God is simply "present" or that a "revelation" of God has taken place. That which prompts faith to qualify and negate its language about God spills over into the everyday language used to say how God comes into human belief-ful conviction. To say God is present only reminds us that God is ever absent.[1] As the poet Wendell Berry says,

> That we do not know you
> is your perfection
> and our hope. The darkness
> keeps us near you.[2]

To say that we experience or know God only reminds us of the vast difference between what we in fact do experience and know and the way we relate to God.

These difficulties suggest that convictions about God as real do not arise from any direct or immediate divine presence that grounds in an immediate way such terms as knowledge, experience, or presence. Accordingly, I am unable to pursue this first thematic by way of an account of divine presence or of some direct religious experience or knowledge of God. Let us then pose a different question. What *meaning* do we give to the term *God* and how is it we come to think that this meaning or cluster of meanings pertains to something real? In Chapter 1 I argued that God comes forth as God in religious communities in connection with what they experience as redemption. This statement can be interpreted as simply a straightforward historical principle, namely, that redemption of some sort is what unifies the symbols, liturgies, and narratives of religious faiths. The theology of God must take another step. It attempts to understand how the redemption that originates the *meaning* of God prompts at the same time the conviction of the *reality* of God.

---

1. For God as necessarily absent, see Robert Sokolowski, *The God of Faith and Reason: Foundations of Christian Theology* (Notre Dame: University of Notre Dame Press, 1982), 1–2.
2. Wendell Berry, "To the Unseeable Animal," *Collected Poems: 1957–1982* (San Francisco: North Point Press, 1985), 141.

THE REALITY OF GOD AS A PROBLEM FOR FAITH

In contrast to certain philosophies of religion, twentieth-century theologies typically resist the issue or even the expression, "the existence of God." Fideism, biblicism, anti-theism, and existential hermeneutics all have their reasons for refusing to take up the question. They argue that religion, faith, belief, and piety are doxological and doxology takes place in a different order or plays a different "game" than that of objective evidences. At the same time, it does seem to be the case that convictions of reality attend the doxological act. The heart may have its reasons, but at least there are reasons. Believers do not think of themselves worshiping a void, a fiction, or their own subconscious. Thematized or not, evidences lurk in the depths of doxological acts. Negatively expressed, fideism is the term for the refusal to entertain any notion of "rational" or public evidences for God. At the same time fideists do "believe" in God. However radical is their dismissal of philosophy, natural theology, and arguments about God's existence, fideists as worshipers or theologians have their reasons. It may be that faith, not argument, prompts their worship, but how is it that faith has to do with God and not simply an enclosed circle of human experience? How is it that faith is faith in God? Even if the question does not press fideists into the public world of rational argument, it does ask them to explicate the basis for their conviction that God is nonreducible to themselves. Insofar as there is such a basis, we can speak of God's "coming forth" not as something else but as God. Apart from such a coming forth as God, God will not be meant as God but as something else. This then is our question. How does God come forth as God such as to enable God to be meant as God and to evoke the conviction that this meant God is at the same time actual?

From tribal religions to Rudolf Otto, from Isaiah to Martin Buber, from Plato to Alfred North Whitehead, the matter of God gives rise to an extraordinary cognitive situation. The more a thinker tries to render this situation ordinary, the less the thinker has to with God. Neither the would-be believer who would explicate God nor the would-be disbeliever who would establish the vacuity of all God language escapes this situation. We are inclined to resist the distinction between "believers" and "non-believers."[3] Even if there is such a distinction, it is muddied by the fact that the beliefs of both groups have the character of attempts. Believers

---

3. See Robert P. Scharlemann, *Inscriptions and Reflections: Essays in Philosophical Theology* (Charlottesville: University Press of Virginia, 1989), 31. In the light of Scharlemann's comments, I make the distinction only with tongue in cheek, to acknowledge that there are people who use these terms to identity themselves.

and atheists trudge the same path through the same mists before something separates them. The misty path is simply a metaphor for the nonpresentation, nonimmediacy, nongivenness, and nonspecificity of God.

As nonpresentational God is never simply apprehended or experienced. What we human beings do experience and subject to reflection is always discrete, a focused content limited by or to entities and events, or to strata and qualities of events. Such things may serve as theophanies, occasions of worship, or signs of sacred power. They are never the presented God.[4] As nonpresentational God is at the same time nonintentional; that is, unavailable to direct acts of meaning. We human beings move through everyday life by way of multiple kinds of acts directed toward specifically meant contents: friends, physical objects, and abstractions like love or numbers. We never have God before us as this sort of discrete reference. Unable to referentially mean God, we are in a cognitive quandary when we would summon evidences for God, even in the form of reasons for our worship. What sort of evidences does one muster for what one cannot directly mean or have in view?

On the other hand, the failure to mean God as a discrete entity does not mean that God is an utterly vacuous term in the life and worship of believers. God is worshiped by way of a complex symbolics rooted in a millennia-long narrative tradition. God is thus a referentiality but not a discrete reference, a symbolic meaning-cluster but not a specifically discerned meant entity.[5] But what does the believer-interpreter do when she presses behind the symbolics to the question of God? What route is there from the inherited symbolics to convictions about the reality or actuality of God? As we saw in our review of various ways of taking up the question of God, the symbolics of God (imagery, metaphors, narratives, analogies) lend themselves to a variety of projects: historical retrieval and interpretation, praxis criticisms and strategies, doxology and iconography. Important as these projects are, they presuppose but do not themselves answer the question of the reality of God. Something other than simply the existence of symbols evokes, warrants, or founds convictions about the reality of God.

At this point one strand of Western Christian theology has pressed beyond fideist, historical, or praxis appeals to the metaphysical problem

---

4. "In reflection the final judging subject is the reflecting 'I,' and not that about which the judgment is being made. The very structure of this experience excludes, therefore, the possibility that anything could be seen to be God." Robert Scharlemann, *The Being of God: Theology and the Experience of Truth* (New York: Seabury Press, 1981), 95.

5. On the theme of the referential aspect of discourse about God, see David Pailin, *God and the Processes of Reality* (London: Routledge, 1989), chap. 3, #1. In a more general vein,

of the world. Faith's convictions about God's reality may be expressed by historically generated symbolics but they are rooted elsewhere, namely in the way rational, moral, orderly, or aesthetic phenomena indicate a divine source. The symbolics of God is efficacious and communicative precisely because there are signs of God's reality already at work in the human being or in the being of the world. Symbolisms then mediate convictions of divine reality because of universal divine operations in the cosmos or in the human being. The classical "proofs" for God's existence and transcendental analyses are formal expressions of these presymbolic, precultic operations.

Does this combination of historic symbolics and universal analyses adequately set forth the way God comes to be meant as something actual? In this "metaphysical" approach, "God" names a universal function, for instance, cosmic creator or norm for rational order expressed in the symbolics of historical tradition. I note only in passing that these transfideist and universal appeals are an invitation to review the status of the proffered evidences. After such a review, many find them fallacious at worst and nonconclusive at best. To patch universal or totality sorts of evidences onto historical symbolics invites philosophical and logical scrutiny. And one can only wonder whether the convictions that work in communities of faith arise in this way. Some experiential element appears to be at work in the narratives and symbolisms of religious communities that does not depend on universal anthropological or generalized cosmic arguments. Attestations to justice, individual freedoms, and consolation are not simply a sloppy and vague form of natural or rational theology. Recounting a community's narratives and symbolics (historical theology) plus a totalizing rational theology (foundational theology) does not adequately express how the nonpresentational God comes forth as God so as to ground convictions of God's reality.

ATHEISM AND THE PROBLEM OF MEANING GOD

The nonpresentation of God also places would-be atheists in a strange cognitive situation. Because God as nonpresentational cannot be caught in a direct referential act of meaning, belief and disbelief in God can only be ambiguous, self-critical, and dialectical. Insofar as the nonpresentational God frustrates and eludes human knowledge and language, belief

Paul Ricoeur argues (against structuralism) that the move to texts and writing does not remove referentiality. See "Naming God," in *Union Seminary Quarterly Review* 34, no. 4 (Spring, 1979): 215–27.

itself always has an atheist element that refuses to simply "believe in" what is presented, what has come to language. Conversely, genuine atheism retains an element of "belief" that arises insofar as atheism must designate and mean that in which it disbelieves. I use the term *genuine atheism* to describe a disbelief that takes place in connection with a genuine struggle with the question of God.[6] As really concerned with "God," atheism takes a position with respect to the reality of God. This response should not be confused with analyses and theories concerning religion's fate in a specific historical and cultural era or theories that subject "religion" to social, psychological, and cultural causalities. It is common to think of Nietzsche, Marx, Freud, and Emile Durkheim as atheists. And it is probably the case that God had no thematic place in their actual convictional or belief orientations. But social and psychological accounts of the genesis and dynamics of religion do not have "God" as a reference. Even to say that "God" functions as a father figure in human psychodynamics or human culture is not necessarily a statement about the reality or the nonreality of God. If that is so, then such theories are pseudoatheisms and can be embraced by believers and disbelievers. A genuine atheism must have God and not simply the "God" of social functions as the referent of its negative or withholding act.

In similar vein, we should not be too quick to conclude that the criticisms of the God of ontotheology, belief, logocentrism, and foundationalism proffered by antimetaphysical philosophies such as that of Heidegger or deconstruction are genuine atheisms. The target of these criticisms and destabilizations is not God as that with which one struggles in the question of the reality of God. Like some social scientists, the authors of these texts may for personal reasons be genuine atheists but their projects of deconstruction suspend rather than take up the question of God's reality. Deconstruction is surely incompatible with that sort of agenda.

Almost all genuine atheisms or positive disbeliefs in the reality of God are *correlational* atheisms.[7] That is, they correlate with specific forms of

6. Atheism in the sense of a considered, argued, and positive disbelief in God may be primarily a Western phenomenon. Its rise and prominence in the postmedieval West has attracted major historical studies of the phenomenon of atheism. One of the fullest of these is Cornelio Fabro, *God in Exile: Modern Atheism, a study of the internal dynamics of modern atheism from its roots in the Cartesian cogito to the present day*, trans. A. Gibson (Westminster, Md.: Newman Press, 1968). See also James Thrower, *A Short History of Western Atheism* (London: Pemberton Books, 1971); and Michael Buckley, S.J., *At the Origin of Modern Atheism* (New Haven: Yale University Press, 1987).

7. The correlational character of atheism is a frequent theme of the historical studies. The historians reconstruct atheism as a way of responding to theism. This correlation with the

belief and a specific way of articulating the reality of God. This correlation of disbelief with a specific symbolics and conceptuality of God reflects the problem set by the nonpresentational God who eludes acts of meaning. An act of denial, rejection, or the withholding of belief is never merely general or contentless. Like belief it requires a referent. Here the atheist is in the same situation as the believer. God is not a discretely, immediately, or unambiguously given referent. Like the believer the atheist responds not to a directly manifested entity but to a historically (symbolically) mediated or philosophically articulated entity. Responding critically to a process of mediation, the atheist targets interpretations, imageries, and textualities. The atheist may thus find logical or moral reasons for rejecting the reality of the entity of these mediations: the mediated portrayal is internally contradictory (for example, God as an active immutability), morally reprehensible (God as author of hell or the symbolic support of an oppressive class), mythological (God as an entity in or alongside the world), or nonconsequential (God as powerless in the face of evil and suffering).

Several matters here deserve scrutiny. As reactive and dependent, correlational atheism does not itself specify the meaning of God but reviews a historically originated tradition. Is it then responding to, rejecting, disbelieving in God? Here the atheist is in the same puzzling situation as the believer. The problem of meaning God is not simply the historical or philosophical problem of grasping the contents of imageries or the cogency of arguments. That is the hermeneutical problem of interpreting what human beings say, narrate, or argue. Even as the believer refuses to think that God (as nonpresentational) is directly apprehended and successfully meant in the believer's own symbolics, so the atheist has no good reason to identify the criticized mediations of history with God. In other words, the believer and the atheist both confront the negative theol-

way the disbelieved God is represented is what makes atheism such a historically complex phenomenon. Fabro points out that popular, mythical notions of God, philosophical-speculative notions, and revealed-personal notions all evoke different kinds of atheism (*God in Exile*, Appendix). Both Fabro and Buckley offer detailed accounts of how new religious movements, including Christianity itself, are labeled atheistic by the traditional faiths toward which they are differentiated. The Jewish philosopher Benedict Spinoza offered a comprehensive metaphysical system unified by God only to be labeled an atheist by P. Bayle. Jean-Luc Marion takes note of the strange act at the core of correlational atheism that identifies God and the idol, "God." "In what way must one refute something named 'God?' Not, vaguely, but very exactly, for as much as 'the father' in God is thoroughly refuted; likewise 'the judge,' 'the rewarder'; this is to say that refutation implies an identification between the so-called 'God' and the moral uses-names that, de facto, constitute his operative definition" (*God Without Being*, trans. T. A. Carlson [Chicago: University of Chicago Press, 1991], 57).

ogy that demolishes all identities between what is given (interpretations, symbols, arguments) and God.

Because they depend on some meaning designation of God, a correlative atheism of disbelief and the negative theology of belief approach and mix with each other. On the one side, all positive belief has a twofold atheistic character. First, its attempt to symbolically specify God (as one, many, love, feminine, ground, process) displaces other "Gods." Thus, for conventional Greek Olympian religion, Plato is an atheist. For many cults of the first-century Mediterranean basin, Christians were atheists. Second, positive belief as a failed specification (because of the nonpresentational God) critically rejects and qualifies its own symbolics and issues in a neverending dialectic. On the other side, correlative atheism, no more successful than belief in targeting God with an act of meaning, joins with belief in a dialectic of criticism of particular symbolics. At this point, correlative atheism shows a certain instability. Insofar as it fails to successfully mean God directly, it either acknowledges its correlative character, qualifies its own positive conviction that God is not an actuality, and thereby slips into agnosticism, or it is transformed into atheism in a noncorrelative or absolute sense.[8] With this second development, atheism or positive disbelief in God becomes logically odd.[9]

In order to transcend its correlative character and become an absolute atheism, atheism must argue that God in *any and all senses* has no reality. This is a logically odd position for two reasons. First, it refuses the problem of meaning God, hence, denies reality (existence) to what is unspecified. But how can one deny reality in advance of what might arise or be proposed? What possible evidences or bases could such a comprehensive denial have? The denial then has an emotive rather than cognitive or critical character. Second, the denial of the reality of God *whatever* God means is a totality claim in relation to what is and is not. Its positive basis can only be such comprehensive and exhaustive knowledge of what is (world, being, matter, universe, all times and cosmic epochs) that one thus knows what "is not." Noncorrelative or absolute atheism is thus a metaphysics

---

8. James Thrower names the attempt at an absolute disbelief in God "naturalistic atheism." Here atheism's dependence on "theism" or some other specific picture of God is loosened. Absolute or naturalistic atheism (in Thrower's interpretation) ranges over many historical periods and places. It is naturalist in its rejection of any and all claims about the sacred, gods, or God. In its view, the world, human beings, and societies can get along quite well without these fables.

9. Gabriel Marcel depicts the logical oddity of absolute atheism in "Philosophical Atheism," in *Tragic Wisdom and Beyond*, trans. S. Jolin and P. McCormick (Evanston, Ill.: Northwestern University Press, 1973), chap. 11.

in the most speculative and ambitious sense of that word, a cognitively exhaustive specification of what is ultimate. This speculative character of absolute atheism introduces an ironical element into all atheisms that appeal to empirical warrants. Because of its logically odd nonspecification of God and its undemonstrable comprehensive metaphysics, noncorrelational atheism is unstable and easily falls back into a correlational and God-specifying position.[10] Pressed by the failure to grasp a presented and specifically meant God, genuine atheism tends to exist as an unstable dialectic between correlational or relative atheism, agnosticism, and absolute atheism. Pressed by the failure to grasp the presented and specifically meant God, belief is an unstable dialectic of symbolics, foundational-type moves, and negative theology.

THE ANSELMIC PRINCIPLE

It is time to summarize. First, the question of God in a theology of God is the question of the reality of God. How is it that God so comes forth as God as to ground convictions of God's reality? This is the question of evidence. Second, there can be no evidence for or against God without content, without some meaning specification. Neither the believer nor the disbeliever is able to "mean" God in a straightforward and discrete way. Instead of a discrete referent, both belief and disbelief entertain a portrait, a symbolics of divine being. Yet this symbolics is not as such either the meaning nor the conviction-grounding evidence for God. We face here what appears to be a circular requirement. Evidence for God requires that God have meant content and not be simply vacuous. But for God to be meant as God requires that God evidentially come forth as God. The evidence for God and the meaning of God seem to coincide. This is in fact Anselm's intuition expressed formally in the so-called ontological argument. God's essence as *aliquid quo nihil maius cogitari possit* (that than which no greater can be thought) is simply to be.[11] To think or mean God at all is to mean an existent. Insofar as we think God at all (as the *aliquid*

10. Some professed atheists are not simply correlational atheists yet refuse to take the step to absolute atheism. Sensing the cognitive difficulties of positive verification of God's nonexistence and the metaphysical character of a comprehensive positive denial of gods or "God," they refuse to take a position toward either alternative on the basis that the issue itself is unintelligible. See George H. Smith, *Atheism: The Case Against God* (Buffalo: Prometheus Books, 1979). Smith apparently senses the cogency of what I am calling the Anselmic principle, that a case against "God" requires some meaning or designation of the term. Arthur Gibson expounds what I am calling the Anselmic principle when he says that atheism is a faith in the sense of a comprehensive view of the universe and its mysteries (*The Faith of the Atheist* [New York: Harper & Row, 1968]).

11. *St. Anselm's Proslogion,* trans. M. J. Charlesworth (Oxford: Clarendon Press, 1965), 116.

. . .), we must think a reality. The very act of thinking or meaning God is thus evidentiary. With everything else, we can separate our meaning of it and the evidence for its existence. We can imagine its content and also the nonexistence of that content. To think of a nonreal or nonexistent God is not to think God at all.[12]

The standard criticism of this argument accuses Anselm of assuming existence to be a predicate. More specifically, Anselm is charged with fallaciously positing existence in the sphere of thinking (*cogitatio*). Some modern interpreters think Anselm properly answered this criticism when he argued that in God and God alone existence cannot be separated from meaning-content. What intrigues me about Anselm's argument is not his *logical* step from *cogitatio* to existence but his notion that to think God is to think a reality rather than a possibility or an idea. We have here a possible reason why this passage from the *Proslogion* has evoked both pronouncements of a logical failure and defenses of its validity as an argument. There is a reason why the connection of God's existence to the idea of unsurpassability is a valid argument but not a proof for God's existence. If God's existence is in fact connected to the very meaning of God, then it is surely the case that to think God would be at the same time to think a reality. But, does *aliquid quo nihil maius cogitari possit* express an actual thinking or meaning of God? It seems not. The *aliquid quo*, that than which, neither describes nor mediates a referent. As a formal limit to thinking, it is more a disguised form of negative theology. But in this "that than which," this *aliquid*, we do not have a meant or thought entity. This is why the argument, even if valid, delivers no existence and thus does not move the reader from unbelief to belief-ful conviction. Even if it is correct to say that to think God is to think an existent, the argument itself is not a thinking of God. But Anselm's text does illumine the situation of both believers and disbelievers. They can arrive at grounds for positive or negative convictions of God's reality only to the degree that they do think God, that God (and not just an arbitrary definition) is successfully meant. And the more successful they are in pinning down the reference in a meaning act, a *cogitatio*, the less the demand for evidence has to do with God.

---

12. Michael Wyschogrod gives us a terse statement of the Anselmic principle (though not under that name). "The dialectical foundation of the ontological proof is that the essence of God must be admitted even by the atheist to be thinkable, since otherwise he would have no way of identifying what it is whose existence he denies" (*The Body of Faith: God in the People Israel* [New York: Harper & Row, 1983], 151). Compare this also to Boyce Gibson: "How can we set about finding *that* God is without knowing *what* he is, and what is the point of truth to piece together *what* he is without knowing *that* he is" (*Theism and Empiricism* [London: SCM, 1970], 59).

At this point we both acknowledge the Anselmic principle (the connection between evidence and meaning with respect to God) and venture a correction. Anselm's proposal connects the idea of God and God's existence only in a formal, that is, reflective situation. Definition is the "game" of the proposal. But we must ask, does God come forth as God this way? Does this formal definition, this *aliquid quo,* express the God who comes forth in the religious community, in the situation of faith and worship? It seems not. The task set for us then is to explore that situation and see if there is a more concrete way that God comes forth as God, thus evoking a meaning of God that is at the same time an evidence.

5

THE REDEMPTIVE COMING FORTH OF GOD AS GOD

> In the tender compassion of our God the dawn from on
> high shall break upon us,
> To shine on those who dwell in darkness and in the shadow
> of death,
> And to guide our feet into the way of peace.
>
> *Luke 1:77–79,* The Book of Common Prayer

According to the Anselmic principle, the meaning and actuality of God are inseparable. In Anselm's version of that principle, a formal definition of God, the *aliquid quo,* determines the meaning. Yet in the *Existenz* sphere of faith, God does not come forth into conviction or belief by way of this formal definition. How then does the coming forth of God as God evoke belief-ful conviction that God is actual? Neither a historical account of the origin of the communal symbols and doctrines nor a foundational "rational" inquiry describes that coming forth. In religious communities God comes forth as God in connection with what gives them their religious character, the fact and process of redemption.[1] In its broadest sense redemption refers to any and all ways that human beings are transformed in the direction of some good; thus social emancipation, interhuman reconciliation, or personal actualization. Virtually all nontribal religious faiths have as their center some sort of transformation. This present inquiry is not, however, a compar-

---

1. Paul Ricoeur describes a prephilosophical or faith-oriented basis of language about God when he affirms a risk, a believing/understanding, and an already present communal textuality at work in the names of God. See "Naming God," *Union Seminary Quarterly Review* 34, no. 4 (Summer, 1979), 215–20; also in *Figuring the Sacred: Religion, Narrative, and Imagination,* ed. Mark I. Wallace (Minneapolis: Fortress Press, 1995). Others emphasize worship as the primordial act and relation at the root of discourse about God. Thus, according to Boyce Gibson, "All the theologies and philosophies in the world would not make us talk about God unless they issued from the central activity of worship." *Theism and Empiricism* (London: SCM, 1970), 57.

ative theology of God. Its concern is with the redemption attested to in Christian communities, not redemption that takes place in religions of the world. Given the general principle, it would seem that in all of these world faiths, God comes forth as God in connection with the redemption they experience. I shall explore the way God comes forth as God into specific designation by way of the redemptive transformations attested to in Christian communities.[2] And I shall try to show that in the experience of redemption, the *meaning* of God is at the same time the *evidential* basis for convictions of God's reality.

The following analysis privileges the sphere of individual agency over the interhuman and social spheres. This appears to reverse my contention that the interhuman sphere is ontologically prior to the sphere of the individual.[3] I remain convinced that whatever agents experience is by way of interhuman mediation and social participation. At the same time, any account of God's redemptive coming forth as God that bypasses the dynamics, elemental passions, idolatry, and freedom in individual agents will have one of two outcomes. The first turns redemption into an objectivized, external, and social causation. If God does not come forth as God to individuals, God remains simply a content of a society's beliefs and mythology, an item for the sociology of knowledge. The second reduces redemption to metaphysics. If the experience of agents is suppressed, God arises from a rational, objectified, and explanatory argument concerning the cosmos or being. Arguments of this sort do in fact concern the question of the reality of God but not as it relates to individual *Existenz*.[4] And in spite of the element of ultimacy in arguments for God as world ground, these arguments do not constitute a sufficient reason why individuals would relate to God in worship. With the agential sphere restored, we ask how God *so comes forth* as to ground convictions, beliefs, and acts of worship. This question refers us to the facticity of redemption in the sphere of individual agents.[5] I begin with a general thesis. God

2. Much of the material in this chapter is a rather dense digest of more extensive (and I would hope, clearer) analyses to be found in my book *Good and Evil: Interpreting a Human Condition* (Minneapolis: Fortress Press, 1990). Consulting the pertinent passages of that work may be of help in the reading of this chapter.

3. *Good and Evil*, 29, 118, 232–33.

4. For a general, metatheological account of the sphere of individual human agents, see *Good and Evil*, chaps. 3–6.

5. The phrase, "the coming forth of God as God," is my attempt to express the grounds of faithful or theological convictions of God's actuality that is in some sense determined by God Godself. The phrase thus expresses the phenomenologist's concern to open language as far as possible not only to the manifestness of something but also to the mode and place of whatever manifestness is under consideration. Eberhard Jüngel expresses a similar concern through the more traditional and neoorthodox theme of revelation: "Therefore, talk

redemptively comes forth as God insofar as redemption does in fact occur. Something about the transformation of the passions of idolatry into
passions of freedom gives rise to the conviction of the reality of God. This
thesis makes no claim about agents "experiencing" God. Why we must
avoid this language of direct presence eventually should be clear. This
account of agential redemption digests the more detailed analysis of *Good
and Evil*.[6]

The Christian paradigm of individual redemption in the sense of the
actual transformation of agents can be expressed in the two themes of
the hold of idolatry and the new freedoms that arise when that hold is
broken. To help explicate these two themes, I shall offer a metatheological
analysis of the tragic and desiring structure of human agents, a set of
issues more or less at work in the traditional theme of the *imago Dei*.

HUMAN DESIRE AND ETERNAL HORIZON

Primordial righteousness, Fall, original sin, and "flesh" are notions Christian theology has used to describe the "flawed" or distorted condition of
human beings. These notions give expression to our morally skewed history, individual loss of freedom, and dispositions toward cruelty, rapacity,
and coldheartedness. Whence come these deep and enduring distortions
that prompt shame and even despair among human beings?

Biological and cultural anthropology, various religious myths, and psy-
choanalysis have proffered explanations. Granting that human evil eludes
explanation, there is clearly more to it than a self-conscious decision to
do wrong. Human evil displays a characteristic dynamics, and part of
that dynamics are the human being's pain-ridden attempts to cope with
a perilous and tragic world. To call this situation tragic means that suffering, frustration, and nonfulfillments are not occasional or accidental but
are built into organic, historical, and psychological existence. Death may
be the deepest and more dramatic cipher of this situation. Death bespeaks the vulnerability to distortive change that pervades all relations,
accomplishments, attempts, and successes.[7] What gives these tragic elements of human life a special intensity is the structure of desire that con-

about God is responsible when it is its intention to correspond to God. And it *corresponds*
to God in that it *lets him come*. . . . The criterion for the proper usage of the word, 'God,' is
whether human speech allows and achieves this or prevents it. . . . In general God can be
thought as the one who he is only on the basis of revelation which *has taken place*." *God as
the Mystery of the World*, trans. D. L. Guder (Grand Rapids, Mich.: W. B. Eerdmans, 1983), 227.

6. This facticity is described more fully in *Good and Evil*, chaps. 12–17.

7. For an analysis of the tragic dimension of human reality, see *Good and Evil*, 109–11, and
chap. 6.

stitutes human existence. Human beings passionately desire to exist, to retain identity, to be real to others, to have others to whom to relate, to understand what things are. Further, human self-transcendence, its irreducibility to quantity, identity, external causality, and even to descriptive predicates, renders the life of desire complex, rich, and intense.

Desire can of course be trivial, passing, and fulfillable, but the birth to death passions for meaningful existence or for understanding by the personal other are always only partially fulfilled. Accordingly, no specific entity, no actual person, no event or cause, no instance of value, beauty, or reality ever satiates these passions. All elemental passions refer beyond themselves. They take place, we might say, on a horizon that itself is no actual or finite thing. This situation of enduring tragic nonfulfillment, passionate existence, and eternal horizon is part of the dynamics of human evil and redemption.[8] To employ the older symbol, the capacity to desire past the finite toward an infinite and undesignate horizon is the *imago Dei*.

THE DYNAMICS OF AGENTIAL EVIL

According to Jewish and Christian traditions, the "tragic sense of life" (Miguel de Unamuno) is not the basic human problem that calls for redemption. Faith and freedom do not displace the tragic situation. The literatures of these faiths are less worried about the tragic than with the disobedient, hard-hearted turn against God and neighbor manifested in injustice and cruelty. But even these things indicate a deeper dynamic. The life of the human agent becomes structured by idolatry when the insecurities and perils of a tragic world arouse an intolerable anxiety. And these dynamics would never arise if human beings utterly lacked elemental passions or if their world were an unchanging and safe utopia in which all desires were simply fulfilled. Because it is neither passionless nor utopian, human life is structured by deep anxiety. Its very temporality has an anxious quality since what is in store is ever hidden. And the more language renders experience subtle, aesthetic, imaginative, and emotionally intense, the more the human being can sense perils much more subtle and destructive than physical injury or disease, perils in the form of assaults on self-esteem by ridicule and coldheartedness. The fact that human beings are self-transcendent and imaginative intensifies these anxieties and psychic sufferings.

8. For the themes of desire and horizon, see *Good and Evil*, 97–109, 111–14.

Idolatry arises when the human being, unable to abide its vulnerable and imperiled situation, *insists* (in its deepest self) on being secured. The negative side of this insistence is the refusal of the chaos, tragedy, and uncertainty that attend its existential life. This insistence on being secured from inescapable tragedy and vulnerability alters the human being's relation to the resources and "goods" of the world, the important, beautiful, and powerful things on which human life ever depends. For if the human being *must* be secured, what else is there available to do the securing but various goods at hand: the intimate other; the nation, state, or tribe that maintains order and holds enemies at bay; the political cause or party in which one invests hopes for the societal future; the poetic, audible, or visual carriers of beauty; the deliverers of much-needed knowledge (sciences), and the interpreters of the experienced world (poetry, philosophy, religions). In idolatrous mood the human being would exact from these goods something they cannot deliver, a security against the tragic. In idolatrous mood the human being treats the selected goods as if they were themselves the desired eternal horizon rather than what they are—vulnerable, finite, and relative entities much like the human being itself.

With the idolatrous act comes the loss of freedom, not in the sense of the capacity of making choices but in the sense of the power to actualize itself and exist creatively in the world. When the idol takes over the being of the human being, a terrible price is exacted. To pretend that the idol can secure, the human being must deny its relativity and vulnerability and transform it into something absolutely good and powerful. The relation the idol requires of the human being is not the ordinary reciprocity appropriate to finite things but postures of certainty, utter confidence, and absolute loyalty. In these postures human beings and their social systems will do anything and everything in the name of the absolutized finite good. They will identify "enemies" of the idol for the purpose of control and murder, create vast demonic social systems that guarantee the security of the idol itself. From idolatry flows malice, racism, interhuman violence, gender subjugation, and various kinds of abuse.[9]

THE DYNAMICS OF AGENTIAL REDEMPTION

In the religious faiths that spread from ancient Israel, redemption has no single meaning. Its symbolism applies to interhuman, social, and personal spheres. My concern here is with personal and agential redemption.

9. For a fuller analysis of the theme of idolatry, see *Good and Evil*, chap. 6; also 157–64, 171–78, 184–90, 197–206, and chap. 12.

In the situation of organic and historical life, the redemption of the human agent means freedom from the dynamics of idolatry. What could effect such a freedom? Eastern faiths such as Hinduism or Buddhism have their version of the corruptive power of human passions and the dynamics of idolatry. For them the culprit is desire itself. Redemption, accordingly, is a process that releases the human being from desire, and its consequence is the capacity to exist desirelessly amidst life's precarious situations. Tragic existence will continue but its stinger (desire) has been pulled. For the Hebraic and Christian traditions, redemption does not remove desire or passion. In redemptive freedom the human being continues to exist passionately in the world. For these faiths the stinger is not desire itself but the idolatrous alteration of desire.

Phenomenologically speaking, the *experience* of redemption (at least negatively expressed) is the experience of the diminishment of the insistence on being secured by finite goods. Thus, it is the experience of freedom in relation to the hold of absolutized goods over the agent. Symptomatically, it is the experience of freedom from the effects of idolatry on the human being's passionate life; thus, a reduction of the need for certainty, of malicious acts toward enemies, of absolute group loyalties, of various chauvinisms. This diminishment of the insistence on being secured carries with it an alteration of the anxieties that come with passionate existence in a tragic world. This is not to say that these anxieties are eliminated. Specific fears, worries, and anxieties are inescapable attendants of survival-oriented organic life. Yet redemption does affect the deep anxiety that prompts human beings to refuse their tragic finitude and attach themselves to idols. Displacing this anxiety and the insistence on being secured is a certain way of existing in the world and moving into the future, namely, ontological courage. Coming together in this courage is a willingness to accept the relativity and particularity of all finite goods, a consent to finitude as tragic, and a willingness to risk one's actual being in decision and creativity. Insofar as such transformations actually occur, actually give rise to new freedoms, we can speak of the facticity and not just the possibility of redemption. Redemption, accordingly, is not just a theory, a possibility, a utopian projection, or a social ideal, though its symbolic expressions (faith, kingdom of God, reconciliation, righteousness, freedom, and so on) have ideal and eschatological dimensions.[10]

---

10. See *Good and Evil*, chaps. 7–12, for an analysis of the dynamics of individual redemption.

ETERNAL HORIZON AS ACTUAL

What is it that brings about ontological courage and the freedoms that displace the dynamics of idolatry? Hearing and responding to the gospel, believing in something, learning the narrative tradition, or experiencing certain emotions are more symptoms or effects of transformation than that which brings it about. It is not at all evident why any of these human acts as such would reduce the anxiety and the insistence on ontological security or the corruptive idolatrous attachments. We recall again the dynamics of idolatry. In the idolatrous turn, a human passion directed to an undesignated, eternal horizon turns into an anxious insistence that finite goods themselves be that horizon, an insistence that the horizon come forth or collapse itself into the finite good. Does *intellectual* exposure of the illusory and self-deceitful aspects of idolatry and the finite and relative character of the idol break the hold of the idol? Common throughout human history, the critique of idols takes many forms: demythologizing literalistic religion, philosophical analyses, scientific and empirical demystifications, deconstruction, and historical genealogies. These perennial attempts to stage a *Götterdämmerung* are not without a redemptive effect. At the same time, we must acknowledge that all iconoclasms draw those whom they liberate to themselves. An iconoclasm's very power to expose the idol can turn it into a new *eidolon*. So powerful is the human insistence on being secured, it looks for securing from its historical liberators. Thus, we have Marx, science, theology, Freud, postmodernism, historical method, all calling forth iconoclastic discipleships that require the methods of deconstruction, genealogy, and social criticism to be applied to themselves. The iconoclasm of idols sets up an ongoing dialectic of critique and new discipleships: it does not call forth the courage and freedom that displaces the anxious insistence itself.

For redemption to take place, the anxious insistence on being secured must be laid to rest. Mere iconoclasm leaves that dynamics still intact. Something must enable the human being to exist "anxiously" in its inescapable tragic life without being idolatrously secured. Something must alter its lust for securing. This something is a different relation to the eternal horizon. I must acknowledge at this point that the elemental passions under an eternal horizon are passions for a kind of securing. Being grounded in some meaning, having an other who unambiguously acknowledges, understands, and loves one's being, and knowing and experiencing the real all are a kind of securing. We must thus distinguish between the nonspecific securing targeted by the basic passions and the insisted-upon false securing of the idol. But if all the human being has is the empty, undesignated horizon of desire, it turns to the idol. The one thing that can undercut the drive for false securing is not then the ideality of an empty horizon but the actuality of genuine securing. And the one and only thing that can do that is the *desideratum*, the eternal horizon, incarnated into a *bonum adeptum*, an actual fulfillment.[11]

We are faced here with redemption's deepest paradox. Somehow the eternal horizon must so come forth to the *Existenz* oriented to it that the lust to be secured is undermined. To put it another way, the one and only thing that can end the anxious insistence on being secured is an actual being-founded in or by the referent of human desire.[12] The eternal horizon, however, cannot as such found. As a horizon, it is empty and undesignate. If it is the case, however, that the one and only thing that can end the anxious insistence on being secured and the dynamics of idolatry is a being-founded in the one and only thing that can found, then the facticity of redemption attests to the coming forth, the reality, of what outside of redemption is an empty referent. If redemption does take place and if its condition is a founding by the one and only thing that can found, the eternal horizon as actual, then redemption is the basis of the believer's belief-ful conviction of the actuality and not just the possibility of God. In the actuality of redemption as an idolatry-reducing, freedom-giving founding, the nonpresentational God comes forth, not into presentation, but into the determinate designation of that which redemptively founds.

Two questions may help us further explore the necessary connection between being freed from the dynamics of idolatry and being-founded in and by God. First, even if we acknowledge that no finite good can itself be the fulfillment (*adeptum, fruitum*) the human being desires and therefore cannot be what founds, cannot the anxious insistence on being secured be removed simply by a *projected* actuality? Such an option is not without its evidences. In our everyday psychological life, we open ourselves to exaggerated, hyperbolic attachments to things and, under the influences of common sense, psychotherapy, and ethical appeals, we abate these attachments. The dynamics of idolatry seem to come and go as culturally mediated influences lure us toward fanaticism or moderation. Why not simply acknowledge that one of these moderating influ-

---

11. For the distinction between the unfulfilled *desire* for God (*desideratum*) and the fulfillment (*adeptum*) of that desire, see Augustine, *De Doctrina Christiana*, I, 38 (in translation, *Christian Instruction*, trans. J. J. Gavigan [New York: Cima Publishing Co., 1947], 59).

12. See *Good and Evil*, 144–48.

ences is a culturally originated symbol of ultimacy called God, Allah, or Brahman? This projective image could "found" the human being by exposing the destructive character of making finite things into idols. What founds then is simply the narratives or symbolics of communities, not any eternal horizon as actual.

This Feuerbachian and social scientific explanation has its roots in a certain philosophical anthropology. It presupposes that the dynamics of idolatry is a psychological dynamics, that is, a cluster of organically and socially rooted processes that come and go with cultural determinations. Accordingly, one can reduce the dynamics of idolatry by adjusting cultural, symbolic, and other influences. Idolatry then is a "worldview" problem and will undergo diminishment insofar as a worldview of a projected ultimate displaces it. What makes this view plausible is the fact that the dynamics of idolatry are in fact intensified, expressed, and embodied in various psychological and social influences.

At this point we must ask whether the hold of idolatry is a "worldview" problem that disappears under the influence of cultural imageries. If idolatry takes place as a worldview, its location is in the human being's belief-oriented, interpretive life. Since imageries assist human beings to reinterpret things, we can see why they assist the construction of a worldview. Thus, the symbol of a projected ultimate might in fact reduce belief-oriented idolatry. But this version of the dynamics of idolatry suppresses two of its features. First, idolatry is a dynamics of the passionate, not just the interpretive, life. Supplying images to the interpretive life of the human being will not necessarily reach and reform the elemental passions. Second, the passionate life of the human being has to do with the being of the human being, not just the contingencies of everyday psychological life. Worldviews and our constant negotiations with culture come and go. The tragic and passionate way the human being is being-in-the-world does not. Even if the anxious insistence to be secured does not have the ontological status of the elemental passions, it is nevertheless an historically inescapable existential. The anxious insistence that fuels idolatry is neither a psychological need nor a skewed worldview that will recede in the face of certain imageries. The problem itself is not a skewed imagery but a deep ontological rupture that drives the human being toward false securing. A projected ultimate, an offered worldview and symbolics, may evoke "religious experiences" and positive, psychological feeling states. They cannot actually "found," that is, be the ground of meaning of Existenz. Only a coming forth of that to which the eternal horizon ever points and toward which human life is structurally oriented truly founds. A projected symbolic ultimate may expose at an intellectual level the folly of exaggerated and fanatical loyalties. It cannot reach the place where this whole dynamics originates.

The second question is, if being-founded does not in fact secure the human being but leaves it in its tragic situation and in its passionate striving, in what sense *is* there a "founding" at all? Are we talking about a founding that does not really found? If that is indeed the case, the very thing that drives the dynamics of idolatry remains unaffected. The object of idolatry is an actual securing and the human being becomes attached to whatever appears able to accomplish that. But this securing never actually takes place. All would-be securers turn out to be failed securers. What happens then when the human being is "founded"? We have already seen that the human being is delivered from the unfreedoms that rise with the anxious insistence on being secured and from the delusion that the finite securer (the idol) is an absolute securer to a consent to its tragic situation and to freedoms that arise from that consent.

But what is the "founding" that brings this about? There is no utterly specific answer to this "what happens" question. Nothing discrete and actual can be summoned into the order of explanation or even experience that displays "founding." Instead of such a mediation of the concreteness of the divine activity, we can only say that at the level of the human being's *Existenz*, the level of meaning or meaninglessness of being, the human being is engaged with that which is the meaning of things, the "ground" of being (Paul Tillich), the creativity of world process (Nicholas Berdyaev, Charles Hartshorne), the eternal Thou of moral experience (Martin Buber). Once we say this, we must acknowledge that being-founded does not mean that God comes forth into presentation or even that God is "experienced." Rather, the being of the human being takes on meaning by being related to or engaged with the Being of things. Being-founded then is not a mediation of divine being as such. Even in this founding act, God remains nonpresentational, eluding any specific act of meaning that would grasp either its essence or actual existence. God does, however, become designate as that which in this situation of the unfreedom of idolatry transforms the human being toward various freedoms. As that which redemptively founds, God is neither a mere cluster of symbols or images, nor an empty *aliquid quo* (Anselm), Whence (Friedrich Schleiermacher), or horizon.[13] God is the actuality through

13. The reader may recognize a similarity between this analysis of desire, horizon, and founding and Schleiermacher's theology of redemption. Schleiermacher distinguishes between a (formal or prehistorical) transcendental structure that is oriented to God and a

which redemption takes place and in this sense is an actuality, "causality," or presence rather than a theory, idea, or explanation.

SOME CONCLUDING MATTERS

A summary is in order. How is it that God so comes forth as God as to evoke belief-ful conviction in God's reality? I argued first of all that both affirmers and deniers of God's reality face the problem of meaning (conceiving, designating) that which they affirm or deny. All attempts to summon evidences for or against God's reality must at the same time specify what God is, and this implies that evidences for God and the possibility of meaning or conceiving God are intrinsically intertwined. Departing from Anselm's formal definition of God, I proposed that the situation of this coinciding is the transformation from the dynamics of idolatry to the freedoms of redemption. To be sure, this transformation does not bestow on the human being a *capax Dei*, a power to think or mean God. But with the transformation, God comes forth as God in a designated way as the one and only thing that could found the being of the human being so as to break the hold of idolatry. The being (as founded) of the human being is so connected with that which is the meaning of all things that its anxious insistence on being secured is reduced. Accordingly, in redemptive transformation, the belief-ful conviction of God's reality and the meaning of the nonpresented God coincide.

historically determinate self-consciousness shaped by redemption. Literally speaking, the transcendental structure (*Gefühl* [feeling] or immediate self-consciousness) does not have God as its reference but a more generalized or undesignate "Whence" on which the feeling of freedom depends in an absolute way (*The Christian Faith*, trans. H. R. Mackintosh and J. S. Stewart [Edinburgh: T. & T. Clark, 1928], #4 [16]). Accordingly, this transcendental and intentional relation is more a possibility and formal structure of religiousness or piety than piety itself. That being the case, "God" comes into the picture only with history and the actuality of redemption and should not be confused with the undesignated Whence of utter dependence. I have transformed this distinction between the "Whence" of the utter dependence that accompanies the act and structure of freedom to an "eternal horizon" of elemental passions. Schleiermacher locates the formal or general relation to God in a general, reciprocal structure of human-world relation, its feeling of dependence and its feeling of self-initiation (freedom). I have located it in what appears to be not so much a formal structure (immediate self-consciousness) but *Existenz*, that is, human passionate existence in and toward the world. In that respect, this analysis is closer to Augustine and Maurice Blondel than to Schleiermacher. One could say it is a Blondelian twist on Schleiermacher, that twist being the identification of desire as the dynamics of the human being's preredemptive relation to an undesignated eternal. See Blondel, *Action* (1893), trans. O. Blanchette (Notre Dame: University of Notre Dame Press, 1984). For another contemporary approach to God that gives desire a central place, see John Haught, *What is God? How to Think about the Divine* (New York: Paulist Press, 1986). Haught's analysis is historically and anthropologically rich, identifying as it does the *eros* theme, not just in the sphere of truth or reality or in freedom, but in temporality, spatiality, and aesthetics.

In redemptive transformation, does the nonpresentational God come forth into presentation? Does the human incapacity to mean God now become a capacity? These questions confront us with the paradoxical character of all human acts that would entertain (image, think, or envision) God. On the one hand, insofar as redemption (founding) takes place, God is no longer merely an undesignated and empty horizon of desire. God has come forth as that which so founds the being of the human being that its idolatrous passions transmute into freedoms. That which founds has come forth into designation or name, the redemptive one.

On the other hand, this coming forth is clearly not an offering of God's being to the human act of meaning. This is apparent on empirical grounds. Whatever the power and eventfulness of redemptive transformation, human beings do not in fact "experience" God or entertain God as a discretely meant reality. But this nongivenness of God to human meaning is also rooted in the facticity of redemption itself. We recall that what comes forth to found is intrinsically and necessarily the one and only thing that can found, the *desideratum* of human desire. This one and only referent of the existential meaning of the human being cannot be any of the mundane things that disrupt the being of the human being when they are forced to serve as the eternal horizon itself. What the human being is capable of meaning or envisioning is always just such discrete contents and entities: numbers, concepts, events, persons, aggregates, and the like. The failure, the *non capax*, to mean God is not overcome by redemption.

The paradox is that God does comes forth as a designated content (redeemer, founder) but never as *a* being, *a* discrete entity, or specific content. Thus, the belief-ful conviction of God's reality is from the very beginning both a symbolization (God as redemptive founder) and a negative theology. The facticity of redemption, not God and the puzzle of the world problem, is then the original and deepest root of negative theology. From the very beginning, the God who comes forth as God is the one who breaks and surpasses specific meaning designations and direct referential language. Minus this negation, God does not come forth as God but as something else. This initial negation carried in the facticity of redemption will thus attend all discourse of the religious community as it prays, teaches, narrates, symbolizes, and even philosophically conceptualizes divine being.

This argument is neither a "proof for the existence of God" nor a fideism that would repudiate any and all attempts to give reasons for the reality convictions of believers. It resembles fideism in that it makes no attempt to demonstrate the reality or coming forth of God as God outside the specific situations of religious communities and their symbolics, and it does set forth a kind of "logic of faith." It tries to answer the question why participants in religious communities have such convictions. These convictions arise neither from a clandestine rational theology buried deep in faith itself, nor from secondary convictions about the authority of ancient texts, nor from historically retrieved and interpreted symbols and narratives, but from the more primordial facticity of redemption, the actual transformation of idolatrous existence by the one and only reality able to effect that transformation. Such an account will not persuade the nonbeliever, the militant atheist, or the "neutral" intellectual to "believe in God." Arguments of rational theology may or may not do so. Even if these arguments were overwhelmingly persuasive, the ensuing belief would be quite different from the conviction (trust, worship) that comes with the redemptive founding of the meaning of one's being.

I have conducted this exploration in the framework of the Christian community; thus I have set forth the Christian version of "the facticity of redemption" and its version of the paradox of the designated nonpresentational God. I am, however, convinced that this way of connecting the facticity of redemption and convictions of the reality of God is applicable to other religious communities. It does not seem to be the case that beliefful convictions about God in Judaism, Islam, or Hinduism are based on some universal rational theology, authority religion, or the historical mediation of symbols. Something like an actual redemption brings these communities into existence and constitutes their ongoing continuity and deepest reality. In these communities also, convictions about "God" arise in connection with the experience of freedom in relation to suffering, moral corruption, or the hold of desire.

Is this account of the origin of belief-ful convictions about the reality of God in the framework of specific religious communities some kind of exclusion? Can we say, must we say, that the existence, traditions, and mediations of *religious* communities are the *sine qua non* of the move from the dynamics of idolatry to a dynamics of freedom? I am not prompted at this point to argue in universalizing fashion either for "anonymous Christians" (Karl Rahner) distributed over the human community or for some redemptive a priori built into human history as such. On the other hand, I find a positive exclusion of redemptive (non)presences at work in, across, and beyond religious communities impossible to establish. To negate the activity of God coming forth to connect the meaning of the being of the human being and the Meaning of things beyond religious communities is both unverifiable and an a priori restriction on the divine redemptive activity. Christian communities experience God coming forth as God in Jesus as Christ. This does not serve as a basis for some positive claim that God is redemptively inactive in other faiths, nonreligious epochs and cultures, or throughout human history.

PART TWO

A SYMBOLICS OF GOD

6
THE ATTRIBUTE AND ANTI-ATTRIBUTE TRADITIONS

> For these Names express God so far as our intellects know Him. Now since our intellect knows God from creatures, it knows Him as far as creatures represent Him. But it was shown above that God prepossesses in Himself all the perfections of creatures, being Himself absolutely and universally perfect.
> *Thomas Aquinas,* Summa Theologica

> We guess; we clothe Thee, unseen King,
> With attributes, we deem are meet
> Each in his own imagining
> Sets up a shadow in thy seat
> *Gerard Manley Hopkins, "Nondum"*

We move now to the second of the three tasks of a theology of God, the establishment and justification of symbolic bespeakings of God. It goes without saying that the symbolization of God takes place in the religious community prior to theological inquiry or pedagogical formulation. There God is worshiped, prayed to, and interpreted through a multitude of imageries whose roots are the activities and institutions of the religious community. In this discursive imaging activity, human acts, powers, and even feelings are attributed to God. Whence this symbolization? In a theology of God, this is not simply a historical question. It is not answered by tracing the roots of a symbol to the military, agricultural, or governmental institutions of earlier peoples. The concern of the theology of God is with the "truth" and propriety of the symbolic bespeaking of God. Such a concern presumes the belief-ful conviction of the reality of God. Without that conviction, the symbolics of God is simply a question of history or cultural anthropology. Given that conviction, linguistic fidelity to the one who has come forth as God is not a trivial matter. In some approaches, the task of displaying a rationale for a symbolics of God is rendered superfluous by appeals to textual authorities. For instance, we know from Scripture or the church councils that God is holy, triune, just, immutable and the like. Even if one is comfortable with such authority theology, it should be clear that appealing to an authoritative text only pushes the question onto the text. How did the Priestly writer, Jeremiah, or Luke arrive at *their* symbolization of God? If we reject the fundamentalist notion that God simply communicated a symbolics to the community, we face the task of trying to understand the grounds on which the religious communities, believers, or theologians think some symbols properly bespeak the divine reality and others do not.

A distinction is implied in this task of thinking the contents, that is, symbolics, of God. Assumed here is that God does not come forth as God simply as an aggregate of symbols. Granting the negative theology's point that there is no nonsymbolic, positive expression of God, we must nevertheless say that what the religious communities mean by God is not simply a "symbol" or "metaphor." The reality of God is no more that of a symbol than the reality of water or fire are symbols. The religious community relates to, thinks, and worships God through symbols and metaphorical expressions. Insofar as the community and its individuals worship *through* these symbols, the symbols themselves are not the final referent of these acts. The mystery of God is thus not simply the mystery of a symbolic usage, though symbols properly used may help to preserve that mystery.

As referent, God is the "designate" that arises with the facticity of redemption. The facticity of redemption prompts a distinction between God as a designated reference, the initial and primary meaning of God, and the symbolics and concepts that gather around this designate. Thus, the theology of God faces two distinguishable tasks: (1) an account of how God comes forth as a designate, and (2), a genealogy of the symbolics that attach to this coming forth. This distinction can be understood in a variety of ways. For instance, are we distinguishing between a primary definition (or better, specification) of God and the gathered attributions, relations, and acts of God? Examples of primary specifications of God are: "I am that I am," "that than which no greater can be conceived," "that on which all things depend absolutely," "being itself," "the beyond being," and "that which orients history toward redemption." Accordingly, the act of initial designation tends to be the act of discovering God's primary name.

A difficult theological problem for Christian theology is posed by the symbolic legacy of God as triune. Is "Trinity" the Christian designate or specification of God? When we focus on the redemptive or "economic" aspect of the term, we discover that "Father," "Son," and "Spirit" express the redemptive activity of God. Thus, there is no designate or referent, God, of which these terms are simply attributes. The terms rather specify what Christians mean by God. On the other hand, if we focus on the philosophical and speculative background of the term, we quickly confront the Neoplatonic problem of thinking God's relation to the world, the distinction between the undesignatable *beyond being* (the Father, the unoriginate) and the eternal processions through which God is the wisdom (order, logos, creator) and ever-present life of the world. In this sense Trinity is not a religiously originated designate (what God *means* in the Christian community) but a more derivative conceptuality. In classical Catholic and Protestant theologies, the redemptive and the speculative approaches merge to become the authoritative doctrine (or dogma) of the triune God. What is designated here is the primary meaning of God rather than an explication of divine attributes.

In this book, this merged tradition does not have the status of an a priori authority. At the same time, I do argue that the designate, referent, or primary meaning of God is the one who comes forth in the facticity of redemption. For the early Christian community, this coming forth had trinitarian expression as it confessed that the logos or Word of God was enfleshed in Jesus as Christ, and that the divine Spirit continued to mediate that event in the life of the *ecclesia*. In other words, the coming forth of God as God discloses a dimensionality, modality, or living dynamic about God as God. Subsequent theological interpretation of that inner dynamic never specified (except in negative or relational expressions) the unity and differentiation of the "persons." To spell out that differentiation, early theologians had to take up the problem of God and the world and the problem of the inner dynamic of God already given formulation in the Platonic tradition. "Trinity" mixes a primordial symbol of the facticity of redemption with the philosophical speculative tradition.[1] It weds the God who comes forth as God in the facticity of redemption and a more derived and secondary theology of God. To the degree that this is the case, Trinity is a genuine but ambiguous "name" or designate for

1. Cyril Richardson argued that a primary problem with which early Hellenic philosophies struggled was how to understand the relation between that which was ultimate (the One, the source of being) and that which was plural, contingent, and relative. The distinction of the Father as the "unoriginate" and the Son in which the unoriginate expressed and related itself reflects this problem of mediation. But the threefold symbolism of the Trinity did not. Hence, the Spirit is brought in to explain how the Source and the Expression are one being (*The Doctrine of the Trinity* [New York: Abingdon Press, 1958], chaps. 1 and 4).

God. That is, it serves both as a criterion for the theology of God and that which the theology of God critically assesses. This mix may account for the fact that "Trinity," however much it serves as a theological touchstone, has never been the primary name Christians use when they worship, preach, or theologize about the divine. "God" is the preferred term.

Chapter 5 offered an account of the coming forth of God in the facticity of redemption. That account yielded a referent, (what we mean by God) but not a symbolics. How do we get from God as designated in redemption to a symbolics of God; that is, to metaphors and concepts through which God is worshiped, related to, and interpreted? What is the route from the designated referent to its features, acts, or relations? I shall pursue this question in two steps. The first attempts to justify attributive language about God against the charge of idolatry, the task of the present chapter. The second argues that symbols and attributes arise in connection with the way redemption transforms human reality in its three spheres of agency, interrelation, and the social, the task of Chapters 7 through 10.

THE ATTRIBUTE TRADITION

To address and speak of God, religious communities develop a rich, symbolic discourse. They tell stories of divine actions in the past and use adjectival language to say that God is just, loving, eternal, and powerful. Taken literally, this subject-predicate language appears to finitize the sacred by construing God as a specific entity. At the same time there are antiliteralist elements in both religious piety and theological interpretation. We are assured that all such discourse is symbolic, narrational, or analogical, that it presumes the corrections of negative theology, or that it is doxological rather than ascriptive in intent. Perhaps these assurances enable some to participate in the attribute tradition with a good conscience. Yet, even in the face of these assurances, there are interpreters whose shared suspicions of attributive discourse create an anti-attribute tradition. A question may help us understand these suspicions. What is it that drove believers (or theologians) from simply noting what comes forth as God in the facticity of redemption to what seems to be a more remote knowledge carried in ascriptive or attributive discourse? How is it we would ever come to bespeak God as immutable, everywhere present, providentially active, or as creator? Does this sort of discourse presume knowledge we do not have? Does it apply adjectival qualifiers to God's being we cannot justify? Even granting a doxological intent, do not any and all linguistic ascriptions of God transform the relation to God into the I-It of the objectified sphere? Expressed in these questions is the face-off between the attribute tradition of classical Catholic theology and the anti-attribute tradition of Jewish and anti-theistic theologies. Does the symbolics of God in the theology of God survive this face-off?

The term "attribute tradition" refers to the approach to divine attributes characteristic of the classical Roman Catholic theology of God. At the heart of this tradition is the conviction that God has attributes or properties which argument and not just text citation can show (or derive) to be necessary. Deriving the attributes is a theophilosophical and not just exegetical task. These theophilosophical derivations do have a discernible beginning point, a basis that itself may be either argued or posited. This basis is what might be called the facticity of created being dependent on the creator. The derivation of attributes begins by distinguishing between that which exists through itself and that which exists through the through-itself. There are non-Christian versions of this basis from Plato and his successors through medieval Islamic theologians. The doctrine of creation *ex nihilo* marked a Christian departure from both mythical and philosophical cosmogonies of ancient Hellenic thought. Because of this doctrine, Christian theology rejected any view that attributed world origins to a mix of powers or that depicted creation as an eternal struggle between divine power and everlasting chaos. In the Christian view, God was the sole and sufficient reason for the world's existence, telic movement, and specific features (goods, perfections).

Does this beginning point for deriving attributes rest on an extratheological or metaphysical basis? The attribute tradition has no single answer to this question. Some (for instance, Thomas Aquinas) attempt to establish such a basis by way of cosmological and other arguments for God's existence as the single cause of the world's existence. Others work from the received biblical and church tradition of God the creator. However arrived at, the basis of the derivation of divine attributes is the fact of world dependence on God. Implied by this dependence was the notion that since the causality of all things was unambiguously good, the products of that causality must constitute in a derivative and contingent way a realm of goods. Also implied is the notion that if the absolute causality is the real, that which exists through it is derivatively real.

How do the derivations take place? Here we discover an axiom that was more or less self-evident in the world of Graeco-Roman philosophy, the axiom of the necessary superiority of explanatory causes. It may be that behind this axiom is an aesthetic metaphor of the way things come about. The sculpture takes on beautiful form only as something superior to the marble conceives and crafts it. The sculpture's perfections can only come about only through the artist's perfections. This axiom would not be self-evident to either ancient mythopoeic thought (compare Hesiod, for whom the "higher" order comes forth from the "lower" chaos) or to modern evolutionary thought for which "higher" complexities emerge from what is more simple. The axiom reflects Plato's deymthologizing of Hesiod and Olympian religion. According to Plato, only an already existing order of reality ordered under the Good, not primordial chaos, could possibly account for the cosmos. Logos, not chaos, is primordial.

The axiom of the superiority of explanatory causes was the entrance door to the derivation of divine attributes by "the way of eminence."[2] That "through which" the world comes to be cannot be a single, relative, finite entity since all such entities are part of the world of which it is the foundation. Instead of being *a* good or *a* reality, it must be the absolute instance of goodness or reality. Further, given the axiom of the superiority of explanatory causality to what is caused, the world-cause must be the absolute instance of any and all properties that have their existence through it. God then is the perfection, the realization, and the perfect instance of all the relative perfections of created being. And this opens up the route to the divine attributes. The "perfections" or good properties of created being bespeak the properties of God. God then is the perfect instance of existence itself. If one of the goods of the world is a person, God is the archetypal personal being. The world can manifest harmony, beauty, rationality, and life only if these properties are intrinsically combined in God's being.

Terms like attribute or property can mislead us into thinking that attributes are cognitive objects, descriptive adjectives, or mediations of the divine reality. The texts are quite clear on this point. The distinction between the through-itself (*per se*) and the through-another engenders the negative theology aspect of the attribute tradition. Because God is the unique and absolute origin and reason for the existence of all else, nothing in or about the "all else" can be applied directly to God. Thus human beings have neither definitional nor intuitive knowledge of the concrete reality of God. Does this mean that attributes are metaphors? Even if they

2. "Now since God has been posited as the ultimate source of all being, he must be at least as perfect as any positive attribute . . . that we find here below in our experience, in fact, infinitely perfect." (W. Norris Clarke, "How the Philosopher can Give Meaning to Language," in Edward Madden, R. Handy, and M. Farber, eds., *The Idea of God: Philosophical Perspectives* [Springfield, Ill.: Charles Thomas, 1968], 16). See also Eric Mascall, *He Who Is: A Study in Traditional Theism* (New York: Longmans, Green, 1943), 116–17.

have a metaphorical aspect, something is at work in their derivation that distinguishes them from metaphors such as God's hand, voice, or God as male or female.[3] In the attribute tradition, the very meaning of an attribute is something shown to be so. God as living is the perfect instance of the life God has brought about. Accordingly, as human terms, attributes are analogical to what is their eminent instance, the divine reality. On the issue of the attributes as relations, operations, energies (the Orthodox tradition), negations, or immanent properties, the attribute tradition is widely varied. But it does not vary on that which launches the task of derivation and makes possible the approach to God by way of God's relation to the world as its sufficient cause.

THE ANTI-ATTRIBUTE TRADITION

The attribute tradition more or less coincides with the patristic and medieval symbolics of God. According to that tradition, the metaphorical bespeaking of God in liturgy, preaching, and piety can be rigorously grounded by theophilosophical derivation. Attributes, the result of this derivation, are analogously expressed constitutive features of God's being. In present-day theology, mostly outside the Roman Catholic strand, we find widespread criticism of this tradition. Some reject attributes on the ground that they assume "theism," a notion of God as an entity who "exists" alongside or above the world. "Theism" in this view borders on a mythological literalism of divine being. Other critics see attributes linked to an utterly discredited mode of thinking, namely metaphysics and the ontotheological enterprise of the discovery of a world ground. Feminist and liberation theology critics argue that certain metaphors of the attribute tradition, especially omnipotence, immutability, and ontological independence, help maintain hierarchical and patriarchal regimes.

Nevertheless, none of these three criticisms is a direct and precise rejection of the attribute tradition itself. The classical Catholic theology of God from Augustine through Aquinas is not a "mythological" theism. Its negative theology eliminates the mythological God beside or above the world. And while some figures in this tradition offer metaphysical arguments for God's existence, there are also strong mystical and antimetaphysical elements in this theology. And while the charge of oppressive

---

3. Thomas Aquinas distinguishes between names that are simply metaphors (e.g., God as a lion) and names that are used in an exemplary way (e.g., goodness). The distinction is between the metaphorical (*metaphorice*) and proper (*propie*) use of names. The latter are derivable from the divine causality as eminent exemplification. See *Summa Theologica*, I, Quest.13, art.3.

metaphors is surely an accurate one, it does not apply to most of the attributes nor necessarily to this tradition's way of deriving them.

There are older historical movements that anticipate these criticisms. Western religious thought includes an often ignored trajectory of thinking about God that departs from and even opposes the attribute tradition. I shall call this group of texts the anti-attribute tradition. We find versions of it scattered through a variety of religious traditions and theologies of God; classical Reformers (Luther and Calvin), liberal Protestant theology (Friedrich Schleiermacher and the Ritschlian school), contemporary Jewish theology (Franz Rosenzweig, Martin Buber), continental philosophies of religion (Nicholas Berdyaev, Gabriel Marcel, Paul Ricoeur), and other antimetaphysical theologies (Paul Altizer, and theological deconstructionists such as Jean-Luc Marion). One of the first powerful Jewish criticisms of the attribute tradition comes from Maimonides: "you must understand that God has no essential attribute in any form or in any sense whatever."[4] We need not conclude from this statement that Maimonides' God was simply an abstract and contentless vacuum in which all language disappears. Maimonides is quite willing to say that God lives, knows, and loves. He is also willing to direct negations to God and say God is not corporeal. He is not willing to say that God's life, knowledge, and incorporeality are attributes of God's being; that is, specific, positive, adjectival qualifiers. Maimonides anticipated what later became a widespread suspicion of attributes in Reformation, Protestant liberal, and Jewish theologies.[5]

Some common convictions unite these widely divergent oppositions to the attribute tradition. First, they oppose the premise that sets the task of "deriving the attributes." This premise is that the bespeaking of God finds

4. Moses Maimonides, *The Guide for the Perplexed*, trans. M. Friedländer (New York: Dover, 1956), 67.

5. Nineteenth-century liberal Protestant theology did not shun the theological task of articulating divine symbolics but it did change the basis of the derivation. At this point Schleiermacher is a seminal figure. He turns the enterprise from speculation and natural theology back to "religious" concerns, and (like the classical tradition itself) and denies that attributes express knowledge (*Erkenntnis*) of God's nature (*Wesen*). Also like the classical view, he retains the method of causality but alters it from God as world-causality to God as that which transforms the formal anthropological structure of utter dependence into redemptive God-consciousness. This anthropological structure of formal piety reappears in the mode of the sensible self-consciousness in an actual religious community. Thus the experience of redemption through Christ opens up the way to attributive language. We have here a deriving of attributes from the divine causality of redemption. See *The Christian Faith*. trans. H. R. Mackintosh and J. S. Stewart (Edinburgh: T. & T. Clark, 1928), #50–52. For a detailed criticism of the classical approach and a further development of Schleiermacher's method, see J. A. Dorner's work on the immutability of God. Isaac August Dorner, *Divine Immutability*, trans. Robert R. Williams (Minneapolis: Fortress Press, 1995).

its ground in the way the world is related to God. All of these theologies refuse to begin at that point; that is, with the problem of being, the attempted proofs of God's existence, the distinction of the through-itself and the through-the-other. From the start, they are unable to engage in a "derivation of the attributes." Where do they begin and how do they justify the bespeaking of God? The Jewish theologies shall serve as our example. Most of the things that set Jewish theology against the attribute tradition also hold for the other theologies. The following five convictions mark the Jewish approach to the bespeaking of God: the primacy of the community, the existential sphere, the divine Thou, the negative theology, and metaphorical speech.

Unlike many Protestant theologians, twentieth-century Jewish religious thinkers (Rosenzweig, Buber, Emmanuel Levinas, Michael Wyschogrod) are not antiphilosophical. At the same time, they all share a deep suspicion of philosophical attempts to demonstrate God's existence, derive God's attributes, and conceptualize God's relation to the world. They are even suspicious of "God" as a generic symbol or concept. As a generic term, "God" correlates with the universal ontotheological task of discovering a world ground, an enterprise of "totality thinking" (Rosenzweig). But this "God" is not the God of Israel. The God of Israel is always a Something (*Etwas*), and is always bespoken as a Name.[6] The Name that resides amidst the Jewish people is the one with whom they have struggled in the course of their history. Jewish theology begins not with the distinction between God and the world but with its own communal facticity, a facticity of election, suffering, historical drama, disobedience, redemption, dispersion, and holocaust.

Second, the sphere in which God is bespoken is not the rational negotiation of the world but the struggles and mysteries of *Existenz*. God comes forth in the setting of everyday suffering, moral obligation, and social injustice. *Existenz* is not, however, *Dasein*, an individual structure, but an interhuman nexus of thous. For Levinas God comes forth as God only as the invisible infinite that summons the self out of its natural autonomy when it is arrested by the vulnerable face of an other.[7] Because the sphere of God (or Name) is interhuman existence, the only genuine way to be-

6. Franz Rosenzweig, *Understanding the Sick and the Healthy: A View of World, Man, and God* (New York: Noonday Press, 1953), chap. 8; *The Star of Redemption*, trans. W. W. Halo (Boston: Beacon Press, 1964), 5–6, 10–19.

7. Emmanuel Levinas, *Totality and Infinity: An Essay on Exteriority*, trans. A. Lingis (Pittsburgh: Duquesne University Press, 1969, 48–49; *Collected Philosophical Papers*, trans. A. Lingis (The Hague: Nijhoff, 1987), chap. 10; *Otherwise than Being or Beyond Essence*, trans. A. Lingis (The Hague: Nijhoff, 1981), chap. 5.

speak God is the language of address. God is bespoken as human beings pray, trust in, complain to, hymn, grieve before, or praise God. The existential sphere and doxological language are thus interdependent.

Third, the Name with whom the community is existentially and interhumanly involved is an eternal Thou (Buber). Thou is the referent itself, that which is the Name. God's mystery is not the mystery of being or the beyond-being but the mystery of that which can be only a Thou. This leaves the community including its teachers and interpreters with a single problem: how to live before and address the divine Thou. Repentance and worship, not evidence and inference, are the tasks set by the divine Thou.[8]

Fourth, the Name that disposes Israel has no counterpart, correlate, resemblance, or image. It is only itself as Thou. Accordingly, a powerful negative theology attends all bespeaking of God. Contrasted to the Platonic tradition, the negations are not based on the ontological difference between the Cause and the caused, but on the utter uniqueness of the Thou. Negations are born in worship, repentance, and the fear of the idol, not the philosophically based awareness of God's metaphysical transcendence.

Finally, since God (Name) is the mysterious Thou active in the life of the community, human language in all of its complexity and richness is released to bespeak God. At first sight this bespeaking of God rings of literalism and naiveté. The community speaks of the King of heaven, attests to God's emotions, and remembers God's "actions." It does so in metaphors and stories, none of which purport to be descriptions of God's being. The bespeaking of God takes place when the negative theology of the Thou and the conviction of divine activity in the life of the community come together.

Clearly, we have here an alternative to and implicit criticism of the attribute tradition. The activity of God, not the distinction of God and the world, is the starting place. Since the bespeaking of God is either the direct language of address or the metaphorical language of divine actions, it can never lay hold of positive attributes that constitute God's being. God and world, God as the perfect Exemplum of all worldly perfections (the way of eminence), attributes as analogical expressions of God's being are all absent in this existential, interpersonal, and doxological approach. From the Jewish point of view, the attribute tradition is a

8. Martin Buber, "The Question to the Other," in *Between Man and Man* (Boston: Beacon Press, 1955); *The Eclipse of God* (New York: Harper & Row, 1952) chaps. 4 and 8; *I and Thou* (New York: Charles Scribner's Sons, 1958), 75–120.

speculative, objectification of God, a transformation of the eternal Thou into eternal Being, hence an idolatry.

IS DIVINE SYMBOLICS AN IDOLATRY OF GOD?

It would seem from this account that the attribute and anti-attribute traditions are related only by opposition. As a matter of fact, they agree on several important matters. First, the bespeaking of God in attributes or metaphors never mediates God's actual being. Attributes (or metaphors) are not direct descriptions of God. That is, bespeaking God is never an expression of an immediate knowledge of God. Second, that being the case, attributes (or metaphors) do not partition God's being. Third, negations properly attend all bespeaking of God. But at this point, the two traditions part company. The attribute tradition does think it is possible to show in a theophilosophical way why some bespeakings of God do pertain (analogically) to God's being on the ground that God is named by the perfections of which God is the cause. The anti-attribute tradition rejects such a task in favor of a metaphorical bespeaking of divine actions and a relation to the transcendent Name through performative or doxological language.

Moving now to the task of assessment, I find no problems with what the two traditions have in common. No human bespeaking penetrates the divine mystery and directly grasps and communicates features of God. For reasons I shall state further on, I think that a positive symbolics, that is, a theological account of what constitutes the "character" of God, is both possible and important. I do not think, in other words, that the bespeaking of God or divine symbolics should be reduced to citations of authority, pragmatic justifications of attributes on strategic, political grounds, or to existential appeals to the performative function of religious language.

Positively stated, the theological task of attribution is a task of establishing or criticizing the bespeaking of God on the basis of the coming forth of God as God. The attribute tradition has offered one way of taking up this task. It has offered a rigorously argued case for thinking that justice, power, love, or knowledge apply to God's being. It has evoked criticism from the anti-attribute tradition for being only quasitheological. It derives the attributes not from the events that constitute the actual life of the believing community but from the more remote theophilosophical problem of God and the world. To be sure, the distinction of God and the world by way of the symbol, creation, and the doctrine of *ex nihilo* are deeply rooted in the community's religious tradition. Why then does the anti-attribute tradition see this approach as quasitheological? First, the theme of world-founding through divine creativity is a recurrent general religious and philosophical motif. Second, compared to the more concrete and immediate facticity of redemption, it is a secondary and derivative motif. Thus, it charges that the attribute tradition's way of grounding the bespeaking of God avoids the primary way God comes forth as God in the religious community. The way of the attribute tradition—or to use a recent term, the way of ontotheology—is not the way of the facticity of redemption.

The ontotheological way of deriving the attributes is precisely what the anti-attribute tradition rejects. It thus expels from theology the task of deriving, assessing, and interrelating the attributes. Eschewed is the task of grounding the bespeaking of God, of arguing why such things as love or wisdom are not simply deceitful and ephemeral expressions of God. Unlike the attribute tradition, the anti-attribute tradition does begin with the facticity of redemption. At this point, the anti-attribute tradition is an important correction of the attribute tradition. Central to any theological account of the bespeaking of God is the coming forth of God as God, a coming forth connected with the redemptive activity narrated and attested by the religious community. And yet something is left out in this refusal of the theological task of attribution. I shall try to formulate this omission by an examination of the anti-attribute tradition's most radical exponent, Martin Buber.

For Buber God is God only as a Thou. Therefore, God is God only for the primary word I-Thou and for a relation of address. God is God (Thou) for petition, songs of praise, and the like, and God ceases to be God, cannot be God, for the primary word I-It, and for acts that are not direct address such as thinking or interpreting. One can praise God, the merciful one, but one cannot think about God as merciful. Anything else other than God can be subjected to I-It, to being thought about. We can interpret and think about the thous with whom our lives are entangled. God is the one Thou which, to think *about*, is to lose what it is, a Thou. The one appropriate relation to the eternal Thou is faith (*Emunah*) whose primary character is not belief about or belief in but trust. God as Thou evokes faith as trust.

According to Buber, the act of objectifying meaning, meaning of x as y, is utterly excluded from the act that relates to God, the eternal Thou. If that is the case, attribution transforms God into something else and is thus about something other than God. Is this the case? Does a phenomenology of the act or relation of trust confirm that trust contains no elements of objective meaning? Let us examine trust as an interhuman relation and see if the results are in any way applicable for God. In the ordinary sense of the word, trust means a way of relating to persons (thous), not ideas, things, or institutions. As an act or ongoing orientation, trust is directed to an other. Nor is this referent, the thou, simply a cognitive referent. If that were so, intellectual curiosity and rigorous inquiry would be part of the dynamics of trust. Because trust is orientation to a thou, it is never just a quality of the individual's autonomy or isolated self. Trust has been evoked by the other and exists only in interhuman relation. At first sight, trust seems to have the character of a risk, a risking of one's well-being at the hands of another. Yet trust is surely more than simply risk. We "take risks" in hazardous situations and even in personal relations. We risk ourselves when we share our being with another, but that risk is increased when we have doubts about the other's response and reduced when we move toward trust in the other. In trust we do turn our being over to another. This act is not without its reasons but the reasons are not objective evidences by which we predict the other's future behavior so much as a "fellow-feeling" (Max Scheler) for the other's empathy. In trust we relate to the other from our sense that the other is oriented to our own "face," that is, our own vulnerable personhood. Our own vulnerability has engaged the other as to evoke its compassion, responsibility, and empathy. Only then we can subject our being to the other. Only then do we trust.

Is this relation to be interpreted as I-Thou or I-It? For Buber these primary terms describe exclusive relations, hence the one relation exists only as a displacement of the other. Any finite entity can evoke both relations but never simultaneously. At this point we must ask whether those we trust are transformed into the I-It in the situation of absence, when we remember them in modes of joyful anticipation or grief. Is the other simply a non-thou, an "it" in such situations? Even to be able to experience the grief of personal loss carries with it some objective contents (ways of appearance, characteristic idiosyncrasies, enduring traits). And these "it" meaning contents are the contents of an embodied thou with whom, even in absence, we continue to be bound.

On the other side, in situations of presence, "face," and direct relation, are we related to a merely abstract thou, a thou without contents, features, characteristic appearances, and behaviors? No trusted other is such an abstract entity. Thou-ness is never merely formal, empty, or unembodied. For what evokes trust is a concrete entity who has distinctive emotions, habits, and styles, and a certain continuity over time. To refuse or ignore the distinctive, objective contents of a thou is surely to reduce it to an abstraction and thus to violate it. I conclude then that thou and it (meaning contents) are ever enmeshed in the trusted entity. This is the case even if one accepts the distinction between the direct face-to-face relation and the indirect absence relation of recollection or anticipation. This is why the relation of trust need not cease when the trusted one is absent. Furthermore, if thous are always at the same time contents, to relate to a thou is at the same time to direct acts of meaning toward these contents: acts of perception, appreciation, perplexity, acts bound up with recollections of the past and anticipations of the future. Accordingly, interpretation invariably attends "meeting." There are no interpretationless face-to-face relations.

Is God as trusted-Thou an exception to the co-inherence of thou and the embodied contents of "it"? Is God, as Buber claims, pure Thou? Is God violated when contents are claimed and falsified in all relations except direct presence? At this point Rosenzweig seems right when he says God is always an *Etwas*, a something. He does not mean by this that God is a particular finite entity but rather that God is not an empty abstraction.[9] To relate to God even in prayer and praise is to relate to one-deemed-as, as merciful, creative, loving, or holy. To pray to God as loving, creative, or holy is also to interpret. The eternal Thou is, in another words, ever a designated Thou. As undesignate, it is simply vacuous. And no mere vacuousness evokes trust or faith. This gathering of contents into a designated Thou evokes not only trust but interpretation. And with interpretation, critical review of the interpreted contents is both possible and necessary. If these tasks are suppressed, the result can only be a passive relation to skewed, oppressive, or even superstitious ways of meaning God as "something," an uncritical relation to past interpretations that persist in the imageries taken for granted by the religious community. At this point the attribute tradition corrects the anti-attribute tradition by insisting on the possibility of reviewing, assessing, and reestablishing any and all bespeakings of God. To put it differently, the way God comes forth as God in the facticity of redemption evokes a symbolics of God, a metaphorical bespeaking of the content and "character" of God. God's coming forth as God is both the condition and the summons to a theology of attribution, that is to say, a symbolics of God.

---

9. For a similar criticism of Buber's separation of I-it and I-thou, see Michael Wyschogrod, *The Body of Faith: God in the People Israel* (New York: Harper & Row, 1983), 90–91. Wyschogrod argues that Buber's eternal Thou is a universal, general, and abstract "you," not the God of Israel who is a proper name.

Is the theological move from God coming forth as God to a symbolics of God an idolatry? The anti-attribute tradition says yes. To exchange the Thou for I-it ascriptions is to embrace a false God (Buber). To claim that human language can be analogical to divine being idolatrously places God and creatures on a common spectrum (Maimonides). In response to the anti-attribute tradition, I have argued that Thou and it are not exclusive spheres and that the "it" language of contents remains present as an interpretive element even in the situation of address. In response to the attribute tradition, I have argued that it proceeds from the more secondary issue of God and the world rather than the facticity of redemption. Accordingly, I would charge the attribute tradition not with idolatry but with circumlocution. In this I stand opposed to those who would dismiss the whole ontotheological tradition on the grounds that it privileges philosophy at the expense of revelation, "Trinity," or authoritative tradition. Because the dynamics of idolatry are not simply a matter of method, cognitive claims, and interpretation, it is misleading to say they are present in certain approaches to God and absent in others. Idolatry has to do with the way human passions secure themselves by existential attachments to whatever is available to them, including any and all theologies. Accordingly, the dynamics of idolatry can shape even the "correct" trinitarian, revelational, biblical, and doxological approaches (including the present project). The identification of one's own proper method, language, or perspective with what is utterly proper to God, with what God wills or evokes, simply fails to grasp that the theology of God has a kind of failure built into it. Any and all responses to God, be they personal and doxological or reflective and theological, have the pervasive idolatry of the human project mixed into them. In this sense we must acknowledge that the theology of attributes is idolatrous, but in this sense, so is the anti-attribute tradition.

7

A PATH TO A SYMBOLICS OF GOD

Lord! Some assurance please,
that I who kneel before this altar,
molding these few moments the shape of supplication,
am not gaping upon my own face in a mirror
all, all too clearly,
yet catwise clawing behind the glass for
the cat not there.

Vassar Miller, "Embarrassed"

I turn now to the theology of God's second task, a *symbolics* of God.
And I proceed under the correction of the anti-attribute tradition,
which works not from a derivation of attributes from the God-world
relation but from the facticity of redemption. In Chapter 5 I attempted
to show how God comes forth as God in connection with the redemption attested to in actual communities of faith. In these communities,
God as the "one and only" agent of the transition to redemptive freedom is a factical and not speculative reference. Yet the symbol systems
of Christian communities contain far more than this bare facticity of a
redemptive agent or even metaphors of redemption. Cultic, pedagogical, and theological activities bespeak God in symbols, narratives,
metaphors, anthropomorphisms, concepts, and negations. How has
this rich discourse come about? Is it possible that belief-ful convictions
about the divine reality in the community have no relation to the way
the community bespeaks and symbolizes God? It would seem rather
that the redemptive coming forth of God as God, the designated facticity of God, carries with it a complex and various symbolics. In the
sphere of the individual believer, the belief-ful conviction of God's reality fosters specific ways of meaning God precisely because redemption
itself is not a single event but a multidimensional transformation of
human social and individual life. In the third section of this chapter, I

shall try to say what this means. Suffice it now to say that the engendering of a variety of ways of meaning God from the facticity of redemption is the condition and possibility of a theological symbolics of God.

It should be clear then that what a symbolics of God sets forth is a certain dynamics of faith itself. It makes no attempt to give philosophical reasons why God is bespoken as powerful, wise, or creative. That would be to return to the attribute tradition and to ontotheology. The problem before us is to understand how it is that certain ways of meaning and bespeaking God arise with the believer's experience of redemption and belief-ful conviction of the reality of God. What follows here is an attempt to trace the meaning activity (concerning God) that redemption engenders. That believers bespeak God as merciful, loving, or eternal goes without saying. Do they have intrinsic and not just external ("the Bible tells me so") reasons for this bespeaking?

DISCERNMENTS AND THE BESPEAKING OF GOD

The bespeaking of God, with its many symbols, analogies, and even concepts, is rescued from the arbitrariness of subjective projection only if it is rooted in some kind of discernments. Our problem is to uncover where and how these discernments take place. To cite an authoritative text from Ezekiel or the Gospel of John is not to answer the question but to repose it. How does it come about that Ezekiel or John discerned anything about God? And since our question is how discernments arise in connection with the religious community and with ordinary believers, it is not answered by rehearsing the arguments of natural or rational theologies. And because our subject is the bespeaking of God, the divine mystery, we are unable to locate the discernments in some direct perception of the divine being. Authoritative appeal, natural theology, and direct perception are not accounts of how discernments and their attending symbolics arise from the facticity of redemption.[1]

The discernments that ground the bespeaking of God have an indirect or oblique character. Something gives rise to these discernments that is not a direct perception of God but that nevertheless connects them with God. Uncovering this connection is one of the tasks of a symbolics of God. This task is not a repetition of how God comes forth in redemption

---

1. For a fuller treatment of ways in which discernments are a dimension of faith and the community of faith, see my books *Ecclesial Man: A Social Phenomenology of Faith and Reality* (Philadelphia: Fortress Press, 1982), chaps. 8 and 9; and *Ecclesial Reflection: An Anatomy of Theological Method* (Philadelphia: Fortress Press, 1982), chaps. 13 and 14.

as a specified, designated reality. It moves on to ask how this designated redemptive reality is bespoken in symbols, concepts, or attributes. Accordingly, we must move from the general problem of how belief-ful convictions of God's reality arise to specific dimensions of the experience of redemption by individual agents. I shall, therefore, continue to privilege the individual dimension of human reality. I have characterized (in *Good and Evil*) individual redemption as a transformation of specific idolatrous bondages into freedoms. This transformation takes place in a three-step movement. I select as an example of this movement the redemptive transformation of cognitive idolatry into wonder.[2] First, an elemental passion for reality anxiously desires past or through everyday realities (useful, important, mundane, finite things) toward reality as an undesignated horizon. Second, when the human being, driven to secure itself, claims to possess the real, its passion for reality is corrupted into false skepticism (a rejection of the very possibility of knowledge) and cognitive certainty. Third, when being-founded (by God) issues in a security-transcending courage, the corrupted cognitive passion is transformed into a new freedom, the freedom of wonder. The human being, in other words, does not experience redemption in some general sense but rather as specific transformations and empowerments of its passionate life, in this case the release from the hold of cognitive idolatry into the freedom of wonder.

"Being-founded," then, reduces a particular passion's insistence on very particular securings. The undesignated *desideratum* of the passion is the eternal horizon as the Real, the object of the cognitive eros or passion. What happens in this redemptive transformation is that the human being is so founded (by the sacred) that its idolatrous need to make finite cognitive objects themselves the eternal horizon of the Real is weakened. But only the Real itself, that which it passionately desires, could exercise such a founding. Hence, when such a redemption does take place, the desired and undesignated Real is experienced not simply as an undesignate horizon but as the one and only something that could effect the transformation. In other words, it is experienced as actual. This does not mean it is experienced as an immediate representation. Rather, its actuality comes with the event of founding. Thus, the agent of the transformation from cognitive idolatry to wonder is the Real as actual, or, God as the Real.

These elements, the dynamics of passion, eternal horizon, idolatry, and new freedom, appear in all individual redemptive transformations. Accordingly, in each transformation, the eternal horizon of the passion is a

---

2. See *Good and Evil: Interpreting a Human Condition* (Minneapolis: Fortress Press, 1990), chap. 11.

specific *desideratum* which founding appresents as actual (see below). Thus, in the various redemptive freedoms, the human being experiences God as the Real, as the desired Other of its interhuman passions, as the Meaning sought in the passion of subjectivity.

According to the way of eminence in the attribute tradition, God must be the perfect Exemplum of all dependent perfections (goods) that exist through God. In place of this general, and ontotheological principle, I offer the following substitute: *Insofar as God is the founding agent of a redemptive freedom, God must have the character of the actualized* desideratum *of the passion.* We have here, at least in the sphere of human agency, the place and genesis of the symbolic bespeaking of God. The place is the dynamics of agential redemption. The genesis is the discerned connection between the experienced freedom (for instance, wonder) and that which so satisfies the passion (that is, the cognitive eros) that it breaks the hold of idolatry. Because of this connection, the believer discerns the symbolic content of God as the Real, the Life of vitality, the Other who understands.

These are the discernments built into agential redemption. What is discerned is the specific content of the desired horizon as actual. The content is expressed in the bespeaking of God in symbols and metaphors. But only in the rarest of instances would believers submit this whole dynamics to the secondary acts of reflection that uncover and articulate this subterranean connection between founding-transforming redemption and the way they bespeak God. Yet this connection, this fact that experienced freedom depends in some way on God, is a characteristic conviction of believers. To say that conviction is rooted in a discernment means that the believer senses (at some level) that nothing but God could break the hold of the particular idolatry. Because of this discernment, we can say that the bespeaking of God is rooted in "revelation." That is, a manifestation of something contentful and specific to God occurs in connection with redemption. According to this antignostic formulation, revelation depends on redemption; redemption does not depend on revelation. The discernments (revelation) that ground the bespeaking of God arise with the redemptive transformation of idolatrous passions into freedom.

MEANING AND APPRESENTATION

To say that redemptive freedoms have a revelatory aspect is also to say that human beings do entertain God in acts of meaning. It is because God is redeemer and not just an empty horizon of desire that we properly use positive metaphors to say what we mean by God. As a reference of meaning, God is a something, an *Etwas*, bespoken in words and images. Yet have we not said that God eludes human meaning acts? We must inquire then in what way God is and is not subject to meaning.

As we would expect, the term *meaning* is a traffic snarl of equivocations. We use it to express how important something is ("that was very meaningful to me!"). In positivist mood, we hitch meaning to knowledge and verification, and argue that what is unverifiable is meaningless. In a different vein, meaning describes something that attends virtually all of the human being's responses to the world. It shapes any and all ways worldly contents are presented to self-awareness. We can perceive, remember, anticipate, value, or disvalue Lake Superior. But we can perform none of these acts unless we are able to mean Lake Superior as a lake, and, in fact the particular lake that it is. In this sense meaning is an act or relation in which the content of something is entertained as that content. In an ordinary day we mean various fast-moving entities as automobiles, trucks, and bicycles, and certain small living entities as cats and dogs. Further, we are able to mean things (a possible supernova) prior to verification of its existence, and also things that may never have existed (ogres, unicorns).

In addition, an apparently simple act of meaning focused on an apparently simple content is extremely complex. An act of meaning is a focusing act, directed as it is to something differentiated from something else. Furthermore, to mean something is not only to differentiate it as itself, but to place it against the kind of environment appropriate to it, assign it to a type, pull together various aspects of that something into whatever makes it a unity. It is also a positive and not simply a passive act. To mean something is not like taking its picture with a camera but a way of relating to a content by way of one's perspective, preferences, aesthetic and ethical orientation, and future plans. On the other hand, to mean a content is not simply to exercise one's autonomy over the meant. A content makes certain demands on us and evokes from us meaning-acts proper to that content. Hence, only in discourses of jest, hallucination, or poetic simile would we mean a purring cat as a mathematical formula or as a mountain.

Meaning has an aspect that may be pertinent to how human beings discern and bespeak God. To mean something as a content is never to actually apprehend, perceive, or know that something in its totality. In fact, what we do perceive and know is always only a small fraction of the totality we mean. We perceive a physical object on its presented side but not its unpresented sides. We never grasp all sides simultaneously. And when we hold a conversation with another person, most of the actual physical or biological processes, the uncountable billions of cellular and submolecular events that constitute that person are not available to us. Yet we never regard the person before us as lacking those processes or as simply a facade that faces us. We do not, in other words, reduce the living entity to what we immediately grasp. When we mean something as a totality (a cat, a car, a mountain), we simultaneously mean other unpresented aspects, thus various sides, interiority, environmental relations. Nor is this overflow of meaning from what we actually grasp to the total entity an arbitrary act. Without it we could never mean a cat as a cat or a car as a car. Edmund Husserl labeled this filling-out aspect of the meaning-act *appresentation*.[3] Thus, present aspects of things *appresent* other nonpresented aspects. The tree's facade appresents its other side, its interior, its root system. etc.

MEANING AND THE BESPEAKING OF GOD

Let us repeat our question. How is it that human beings assign any content to God given the fact that God is never as such a direct meaning referent? We must remind ourselves again that our exploration has temporarily abstracted the human individual out of the historical legacy and social symbolics which are at work in the very forming of the individual. Yet to reduce the matter to historical and social mediations would be so to capitulate to a social determinism as to suppress the theological question of the ground of the bespeaking of God.

Appresentation

I turn now to the strange act of meaning God that is part of the discernments that come with redemptive freedom. What renders this act of meaning strange is its reference, the one and only thing whose founding could effect redemptive transformation. Acts of believing, praising, or attesting to God may appear to be simple and straightforward. On the contrary, they are convoluted, indirect, and, in a strong sense, inadequate. Even as human beings do not "experience," "perceive," or "know" God in any direct and ordinary way, neither do we "mean" God. All ordinary acts of meaning have to do with our world negations and participations. The features of meaning we described above are features of an act that has a content directly in view. Even the content of a fantasy entity, a uni-

---

3. For an extended discussion of appresentation, see *Ecclesial Man*, 215–31. Edmund Husserl named this subterranean intentional accomplishment in which a presented entity is filled-out with nonpresented contents *appresentation*.

corn, is directly imaged. Most would agree that unicorns are horselike creatures who have a single horn. God is not directly imaged. God does not come into view when redemptive freedom takes place.[4] In place of such a direct presencing, the human being experiences an idolatry-breaking founding that could be effected only by the true fulfiller of the passion behind the idolatry. A content arises here because only that specific fulfiller-founder (God) could found with respect to that specific freedom. In this situation God is not the direct but indirect referent of an act of meaning. For this reason, it would seem that the meaning of God as contentful is something like an appresentation. Is this the case?

At first glance, it would seem that an appresentation is at work in the acts of meaning that ground the bespeaking of God. Something specific, the transition to redemptive freedom, does assign a content to God. And

---

4. Since the thinkability of something depends on the capacity of the thinker to *mean* or conceive that something, I must disagree with Eberhard Jüngel's strong insistence that God is thinkable (*God as the Mystery of the World*, trans. D. L. Guder [Grand Rapids, Mich.: W. B. Eerdmans, 1983], 7–14). Jüngel quite self-consciously opposes his view to Pseudo-Dionysius and the negative theology which, according to him, bespoke God only as the Incomprehensible (234–35, 255–59). Jüngel's alternative to the negative theology is the grasping of God "as a mystery which is communicable in and of itself in language" (260). The basis of this is God's "self-communication taking place as love," which produces an "analogy of faith" that works not in ordinary subject-object signifying but in a speech-event that evokes the language of address rather than description (12). Since God does disclose God's self as "in our midst," God becomes speakable and therefore thinkable. These moves seem to oppose and displace the negative theology. But how would Jüngel respond to the following interrogation by Pseudo-Dionysius? *What* precisely is communicated to thinking in the speech-event when a self-communication of God takes place? Does the self-communication place God's actual and concrete being before human apprehension, perception, or intuition? Presumably not, since it bypasses subject-object relations. But what then does it mean to "think" something that eludes such relations? Does the addressing of God in the speech-event of direct address mediate any direct *meaning* of what God is? Does the self-communication of God make the specificity of God available to a human act of meaning? Is the phrase, God as united with perishability, a direct, literal description? All of these questions can become one question. In the self-communication of God, does God's mystery turn into a manifest presence? On the basis of various texts in Jüngel, I think he would give a negative answer to all of these questions. However much he thinks God has communicated God's self, however much God is not a mere mystery, however much we have a symbolic content that is "speakable" and "thinkable" (thus, love, union with perishability), language, speech-events, analogies of faith, never deliver to us immediate manifestations of God's very reality. Thus, Jüngel too must speak of analogy, not of being, but of faith. It would seem, then, that God's very self and being is not "conceived" by Jüngel, not rendered a discrete target for any act of meaning. I can only conclude that God Godself, even for Jüngel is not thinkable. What *is* thinkable is the place of self-communication (the word) as contents arise in the word-events. What Jüngel does not "think" (because it is not expressly and immediately given to him) is God's concrete being-in-act. My difference with Jüngel turns on a distinction that Jüngel fails to make between God as a specific and concrete referentiality (which is not as such given even in God's self-communication) and the self-communicated or disclosed content of divine being appresented in the situation of redemption. In redemption God, the mysterious Creativity of the world, takes on designated content, but not as a directly graspable referent. In my view we can "conceive" or "think" the former but not the latter.

insofar as this assignment is not an arbitrary act, it is like an appresenta-tion. Something about the transition to redemptive freedom points to and requires this content in whatever (God) brought about the transition. For this reason we may say that the bespeaking of God arises from appresen-tations. Yet, if appresentations are at work here, they are of a very peculiar sort. In ordinary appresentations, the total meaning-act is evoked by something presented: the cat, the car, the other person. The referent ap-presents its hidden side, its nonpresented content. But God or God's sym-bolic content is not a hidden aspect or content of the experienced and presented entity, redemptive freedom. Aspects, contexts, and the like all hold for world situations and entities. Thus, the most we can say is that appresentation is itself an analogy, that the meaning act that leads to a symbolics of God is something like appresentation.

Negation

Why are we pressed to qualify appresentation in this way? To answer this question is to uncover a second element in the symbolic bespeaking of God. Our hesitation to apply appresentation to the meaning of God in an unqualified way is only one instance of a qualification that attends all bespeakings of God. Both worshipers and theologians sense the inade-quacy, the nonimmediacy, the mythological character of their language of praise and concept. Why are qualification and denial intrinsic to the bespeaking of God? In the attributive tradition (ontotheology), negation necessarily attends all positive symbolics of God because one cannot di-rectly apply features, contents, or concepts of created being to that through which it has its being. As world ground, God cannot be identical with that which is grounded. Hence, no feature of the world, no way of thinking the world, no mode of existence in the world can be applied to God in a direct way. But any theology of God that privileges redemption over the God-world relation will not begin (though it may end) with this rationale for negative theology. Nevertheless, the anti-attribute tradition has its own reasons why negation attends all bespeaking of God.[5]

5. Following in the tracks of the Protestant Reformers, Friedrich Schleiermacher also placed the negating element of God language on a different basis than the differentiation between God and the world. Like the Reformers he saw negations arising in connection with religiousness or piety rather than the God-world differentiation. Unlike them he saw negation originating in the transcendental structure of piety, that is, the structure of the immediate self-consciousness (*Gefühl*) as utterly dependent on an undesignated and non-mundane Whence. Accordingly, this nonmundane Whence continued to serve as a correc-tive monitor and norm to all pieties that arose in history to articulate "God." The perennial tendency to mundanize God, that is, to subject God to the sensible self-consciousness, is ever confronted by this nonmundane source of piety itself.

We recall the elements of agential redemptive transformation. Redemptive freedom breaks the power of an idolatrous attachment. Specific idolatrous attachments structure the self when a specific elemental passion (for instance, for reality, meaning, and so forth) insists on being fulfilled. Because the passion's proper object is always transcendent, that is, a horizon toward which penultimate fulfillments point, no mundane entity is able actually to fulfill the passion. This is why the one and only thing that could bring this idolatrous structure to an end is a being-founded by the proper object of the passion. In the facticity of redemption, God is this ultimate *desideratum* become actual. Accordingly, the eternal horizon (*desideratum*) designated as God cannot itself be identical with the failed securers to which idolatry attaches itself. God then cannot be simply the total system of such things (the universe), a micro or macro entity in that system, nor can any relation, feature, genre, or structure of that system. If redemption frees the human being from the hold of idolatry, the through-which of redemption cannot be one of the finite goods (idols) that exercised that hold.

From this general negation at work in redemptive transformation come several types of negations. For instance, the believer realizes that the language which human beings use to negotiate worldly realities, the language of cognition, thinking, reasoning, and the like, cannot express in any direct way the person's *relation* to God. Only with tongue in cheek can the believer speak of the "experience" of God or the "knowledge" of God. The same hesitation holds for meaning and appresentation. Presence and appresence structure the way we are aware of any and all contents in our world. Hence, we qualify even appresentation as a description of the way we discern and mean God.

A second type of negation arises when we realize that different bespeakings of God (names, attributes, ascribed qualities) cannot be accounts of this or that aspect of God. Adjectives and ascriptions do work this way when we bespeak objects or contents of the worldly entities. In the case of a round, blue, plastic ball, each adjective describes a discernible aspect of the ball. Some of these aspects can be altered—for instance, the color—without destroying the ball. If God possessed ascribable features in this way, God would be a discrete, finite entity. Classical Catholic theology expresses this negation in the phrase, the simplicity of God. God must be simple and not composite because God is the condition and source of all compositeness. When simplicity functions not simply as a negation but as some sort of positive ascription, it correlates with a metaphysically timeless deity who lacks internal dynamics, activities, or actual relations. No such construal is possible for negations based on redemptive transformation. God as the one and only founder of redemption cannot be an ordinary finite entity, hence cannot have aspects. But this negation stops short of affirming in a positive way the simplicity of God's being.

This negation does, however, carry with it a positive meaning. If different bespeakings of God (symbols, metaphors, attributes) do not divide God into aspects, they must converge with each other. Thus, the specific bespeakings that arise with the founding of the redemptive freedoms do not describe discrete parts of God nor separate gods. As the Real, as the Other who understands, as the ultimate frame of the meaning of *Existenz*, God is not three Gods nor do these terms name three aspects of God. These bespeakings converge, linguistically, into a name: God the redeemer. In the names of God (Yahweh, Almighty, Holy One, King of heaven) converge a variety of metaphors and contents. And we misunderstand them when we empty them of everything but the metaphor specific to the name.

Finally, as a human act, negation itself is subject to radical negation. Negating, qualifying, distinguishing from are all ways we negotiate the world. They help us to sort out features, contrast entities to each other, and destabilize the language of fixed meanings. A contemporary philosophy (deconstruction) refines and radicalizes this activity. But the negation that is built into the bespeaking of God is not a world negotiation. Hence, it does not simply distinguish God from the world as we would distinguish a rock from a robin. Neither does it deny features of God in the way we say grass is not red. Such negations arise from a direct apprehension of the entity in question and the "is not" is a negative mode of the being of that entity. The direct apprehension founds the negation. Insofar as negative theology is cast in this framework of mundane negations, God will be some sort of worldlike entity beside or above the world. And there are those who mistakenly interpret what they call "theism" in just this way. But in both the attribute tradition and the way of the facticity of redemption, there is a double negation that includes both the negation of world as directly applied to God and the negation of *all world-type negation*.[6]

6. Several contemporary writers have propounded a concept of double negation. Jean-Luc Marion says the following: "Concerning God, let us admit clearly that we can think him only under the figure of the thinkable, but of an unthinkable that exceeds as much what we cannot think as what we can; for that which I think is still the concern of *my* thought, and hence may not to *me* remain unthinkable" (*God Without Being*, trans. T. A. Carlson (Chicago: University of Chicago Press, 1991), 46. In similar vein but connected more to Heidegger's project of *Destruktion* of the history of metaphysics than to Derrida's project of deconstruction is Robert Scharlemann's very nuanced restatement of the negative theology. He too proposes a double negation. For Scharlemann theism makes the single negation based on the fact that God is *not* the world. Thus, "the infinite is not the finite." The result

Can there be an idolatry of God Godself? Since religion itself is *a* if not *the* primary historical promoter and embodiment of idolatry, we are tempted to think so. Religion, including the Christian religion, is especially vulnerable to idolatry precisely because its primary concern is with an ultimate that *really* secures. Religion lives from the conviction that in its cultus, tradition, and teaching, it possesses what *really* secures. And it is only a short step from this conviction to the claim that the things that mediate God and which serve and protect that mediation (sacred texts and verses, holy books, traditions, liturgies, doctrines, institutions) are God's direct and unambiguous command or expression, that in these things we are salvifically founded. In this step, mediation and founding become identical. Religion's idolatry, then, is unique, since it makes an explicit claim that God has rendered the mundane securer absolute. Yet we must say that if God means that which breaks the hold of idolatry, there can be no idolatry of God. The event in which God comes forth as God is a breaking of the dynamics of idolatry. Idolatry then relates to the idol projected as God; thus the class, race, territorial usage, image, or paradigm of God. And surely the most terrifying idolatry of the divine idol is not the naive cultic attempt to bestow visibility and manageability on God but the more subtle usage of the whole sophisticated and complex apparatus of religion for oppressive purposes.

Superlative

The bespeaking of God from redemptive transformation contains a third element that I shall call the superlative. Like appresentation and negation, superlative can be a misleading term. Superlative or great-*est* discourse places God on a comparative spectrum. God is thus bespoken as the greatest being or the greatest power. This language too has evoked the accusation that the God of classical Catholic theology is a quasimundane entity beside the world. Granting that all terms mislead when not attended by radical negation, we shall try to state why there is a superlative element in the bespeaking of God.

Let us begin with the way superlative discourse appears in the attribute tradition. In these texts all the features (attributes) of God occur in the mode of perfection. This follows from the way of eminence, the principle

of the theistic negation is simply to make deity a transtemporal, metaphysical entity. But this God appears not to be God, hence God's being is only thought when "God is not being [this theistic] God." The negation thus places time and activity in God. ("The Being of God When God Is Not Being God," in *Inscriptions and Reflections: Essays in Philosophical Theology* [Charlottesville, VA.: University Press of Virginia, 1989]).

that God is necessarily the perfect instance of whatever exists through God. This classical theology of divine perfection and attributes as perfections can be construed in two quite different ways. The prevailing (metaphysical) interpretation claims that attributes are not just negations but positive perfections of God's being. God's being, God's way of being, the features of God's being are all *pure act*, that is, sheer fulfillment. If this were not so, God would be "imperfect." This view leads to the doctrine of the immutability of God, again not as a mere negation, but as a positive statement that God in no way and in no respects undergoes change. But there is a nonmetaphysical way of construing God's perfection. Here perfection is a negation rather than a positive feature of God's being. Its basis is another principle characteristic of the classical Catholic theology of God, namely the insistence that finite creatures do not have knowledge of God's being itself either in its actual reality or its essence. Thus to say that God is perfect is to say nothing about God's actual being. It simply denies imperfection to God. God does not exist in a birth-to-death cycle nor does God develop over time toward God's own ideal Godness. God thus does not face the task of becoming more eternal, more just, more loving. These negations do not entail any positive notion of immutability. What it means to be God may include activity, responses, and even growth of experience.

I shall not attempt to mediate these opposing interpretations of the classical Catholic theology of God, although I do think that the nonmetaphysical interpretation is more consistent both with the Pseudo-Dionysian roots of that theology as well as with certain of its own premises. Yet we do have from this tradition the legacy of superlative discourse. In spite of the fact that its route to this discourse is by way of the God-and-world problem, the attribute tradition has brought to expression something about any bespeaking of God that goes on in the life of the believer. The discernments that attend redemptive transformation engender not simply "appresentations" and "negations" but "superlatives." Two elements in the transition to redemptive freedom prompt a superlative reading of the symbolic contents of God. The first is a kind of negation. God cannot be imaged as real, just, or empathetic in the mode of particularity or on a spectrum of relative attainments. There is something inappropriate about images of God as partially eternal, partially creative, or partially loving. This language of degree applies to ourselves, not God. For what is at work in redemption cannot itself be a finite, false-promising securer. The one and only thing that can redemptively transform is the true (ultimate) object of human passions. Thus the believer can only refuse the degree language that finitizes God and draws God back into the sphere of idols.

The second element goes beyond negation. God is not simply the *desideratum* of desire but the one who founds with respect to this or that elemental passion. Further, as a nonidol, a noncompetitor among the system of idols, God is the one and only One who can found. Accordingly, God is "appresented" from the very beginning as a kind of ultimate (one and only) sufficiency in positive mode. As founder who transforms cognitive idolatry into the freedom of wonder, God is the "one and only" Real. As the founder who constitutes the very meaning and ground of existential subjectivity, God is the "one and only" Existent. Thus, the facticity of redemption engenders a superlative element in the bespeaking of God. It should not be necessary to say that there is nothing about this superlative language that denies activity, responsiveness, or change in God. On the contrary, redemptive founding would require, it would seem, a dynamic God, a God who is a kind of creativity.

I have been exploring the strange acts of meaning in which the bespeaking of God takes place, acts that arise in connection with the redemptive freedoms. If this is in fact the case, then appresence, negation, and superlative are discernments intrinsic to the life of faith. Accordingly, however naive and unlearned is the person of faith, however "mythological" and literalistic are the ways of understanding and expressing God, appresentational, negational, and superlative discernments are not utterly absent. The reason is simply that these discernments attend the facticity of redemption. Insofar as they do, we are prompted to honor and take seriously popular religion. We need ever to be cautioned against reducing popular religion to idolatry or literalism and locating the "true" bespeaking of God in academic theology. We can interpret the bespeaking of God and its acts of meaning from two quite different perspectives. First, the bespeaking and meaning of God in the life of faith is part of the dynamics and life history of faith. This dynamic is due in part to the social, ontological, and linguistic complexity of the human being. What human beings mean, understand, and bespeak is inevitably entangled with their biopsychological development and their participation in their social world. Because we mean and bespeak God within this entanglement, we do not experience appresentational and negational discernments in a static way. Rather, we realize, suppress, articulate, apply, or expand these elements in our ongoing life struggle.

A second way of interpreting the discernments of the life of faith is more structural. In addition to being dynamic and responsive, the discernments of faith relate to each other in a certain "logic" or pattern. However historical, autobiographical, and dynamic are these bespeakings of God, they do not constitute simply a list or aggregate of attributes. The transformations of redemption not only give rise to a certain symbol (for instance, God as redeemer) but through that symbol open up other strata of symbols. It is in this way that the symbol, God the creator, arises in the community of redemption. The genesis of creation symbolism is not some empirical or speculative discovery of world origins. Something about redemption itself presses the appresentations beyond the name *redeemer* to the name *creator.* This is why the bespeaking of God is not simply a listing of attributes. Rather, it follows a route, a dynamic movement or "logic" that opens up symbols, names, and metaphors of God in their interrelation. There are, in other words, reasons of a sort why the redemptive community has bespoken God in motifs of knowledge, power, all-presence, personality, creativity, and the like. Behind these theological derivations are the primitive discernments, the appresentations and negations, of the life of faith.

INTERHUMAN AND SOCIAL SPHERES OF THE BESPEAKING OF GOD

This account of the genesis of the bespeaking of God and thus of divine symbolics has privileged the meaning activities of human individuals. This privileging of the agent, while provisionally useful, perpetrates an abstraction. Human reality is not just a matter of individuals but includes two other spheres or dimensions: the interhuman (the dialogical and intersubjective reality that forms when human beings are together in relation), and the social (the social reality that forms when human beings create enduring political and other types of institutions). While distinguishable, these spheres have no independent existence from each other. Human beings are individuals only in and from ongoing interhuman relations and within historically formed social structures. That being the case, human individuals never experience the transformation of their idolatrous passions into freedom in isolation from their relational and institutional life. Nor do they cease being agents when they participate in institutions. Human beings experience redemption only through the mediations of the social; thus, through the institutionalized religious community, its remembered tradition, its legacy of language. And the redemptive freedoms are already at work shaping the interhuman relations in which human beings participate. Redemption, thus, is interspherical, and as such, is an entangled transformation of individuals, interhuman relations, and the institution. If this is so, the bespeaking of God does not arise simply from the individual's experience of its own redemptive freedoms but in connection with human interrelation and with culture and politics.[7]

That the bespeaking of God in images and symbols arises in and functions in interhuman relation and in social institutions is a cultural and religious fact. Religious communities symbolize God as a power at work in their history, and draw on the world of social relations for their metaphors. Hence, the symbolics of God is susceptible to historical and sociological analysis. But we must now pose the theological question, How is it that interhuman and social redemptions engender symbols of God? More specifically, do the interhuman and social spheres like the redemptive transformation of individuals "appresent" certain symbolic contents of God? The quotation marks express a certain hesitation before the question. In their most literal senses, appresentation and negation are ways individuals relate to contents, meanings, and objects. An ocean surface appresents to a perceiving individual ocean depths and the ocean bottom. When we say that human relation and sociality appresent matters to *individuals*, we are still in the sphere of individuality. Unlike individuals, social relations and institutions do not discern, mean, or bespeak. Social relations and institutions constitute a special kind of problem for the bespeaking of God. With individual redemption, the one and only One who can found finds designation in the transition to freedom. But claims that God has acted in a certain event of a nation's history or will dispose future history in a certain way do not arise in this way. In relation to individual experience, these claims sound distant and objective.

How then do the spheres of relation or the social contribute to the bespeaking of God? Two ways of answering this question fall outside the theology of God. Authority theology would establish God's activity in the interhuman or in the political sphere by the exposition of texts. Natural theology would uncover something about the interhuman or about social process that requires, indicates, or is explained by the divine working. In contrast to these approaches, we begin with the facticity of redemption. That which calls for redemption is not restricted to individuals and their anxious proneness to idolatry. In the sphere of the interhuman, one-sided violations corrupt human being-together into alienation and guilt. Subju-

---

7. For a fuller analysis of the interhuman and social dimensions of human corruption and redemption, see *Good and Evil*, chaps. 13–16.

gation transforms institutions into structures of oppressive power. This does not mean human being-together and social institutions are evil as such. Like individuals, they are open to redemptive change. Alienation can give way to reconciliation and agapic interrelation, and oppressive social structures can be transformed toward justice. The facticity of redemption, in other words, applies also to these spheres. If there is in fact no reconciliation of alienation and no movement toward justice, there would be no reason to say that these spheres give occasion for the bespeaking of God. But if redemptive change does affect these spheres, they too indicate something about God and God's activity.

We must now be more specific. I have argued that the transformation of individuals is brought about by God, the one and only power able to break the power of idolatry. Something like idolatry is at work in interhuman alienation.[8] The alienation wrought by interpersonal violation has the character of an unhealable wound. The resentment of the violated and the guilt of the violator settle over relation like a shroud. Negotiated settlements, remunerations, and therapies of coping do not remove this shroud. Yet human beings do experience a transcending of the powers that hold them in alienation. Alienated relation is open to a reconciliation that abates resentment and guilt. While never automatic or easy, agapic relation and reconciliation are frequent and "natural" when they take place in the familiar and secure situations of natural intimacy: situations of friendship, family, and erotic love. In these settings agapic relation (the compassionate and obligatory response to the summons of the face) is evoked by the power of natural intimacy. But how would agapic relation and reconciliation ever displace the hard resentments and guilt in relation to the *nonintimate* other? What would prompt agape toward those who make no familial or intimate appeals, agape toward others as such? What can turn any and all alienated relation into a communion that does not simply repeat natural intimacies? What can so "found," lure, or urge a relation structured by alienation toward an utterly open communion? Here we sense something parallel to the "one and only" thing that can break the power of idolatry. "One and only" power moves alienation to a universal, that is, unrestricted, agape, reconciliation, and communion. All human beings transcend their self-interest in acts of caring along preset paths set by biological and social relations. I am not constructing here

---

8. See *Good and Evil*, chap. 13, for an extended discussion of the redemption of the interhuman.

a natural theology argument, an inference of God from the fact of communion and reconciliation. Our problem rather is how the sphere of relation (and not just individuals) generates a bespeaking of God.

How is it that ancient and modern prophets bespeak God in social and political terms? Here too the speaking is from a redemptive facticity, the fact that corrupt regimes are overthrown and justice does become socially embodied.[9] Even as the sphere of relation is rooted in natural settings of intimacy, so the social-political sphere is organized along ethnic, national, and territorial lines. Politics is oriented primarily to the well-being, survival, and power of a territorial unit. Self-interests may prompt politicians and their parties to oppose oppressions and promote justice within the borders of their constituencies. Yet subjugations are at work in all social entities (nations, institutions, cities) and in virtually all types of people who obtain to self-identity of gender, age, race, and class, promote themselves over others. What would ever launch a critique of such subjugation simply as such? What would lure social critique from self-serving, local politics toward a broader concern for the political well-being of strange and foreign others who are not part of one's natural constituencies? What would so relativize a corporation, a nation, or a gender that its concern is not just for itself? What would propel such entities toward a broader and mutual harmony? Redemption in this sense works from a criterion of justice that has no restriction. The concern for well-being opens out to any and all others, including nonhuman others. That which promotes, summons, or founds such a concern coincides with no particular self-interest. Hence, the "one and only" thing that summons in this sense is what the religious community calls God. For this reason, redemption in the sphere of the social and the political bespeaks a symbolics of God not to be found in the individual and the interhuman spheres.

A summary is in order. I have offered an account, a theory if you will, of a route to the bespeaking of God. How do we justify using a particular set of symbols, predicates, or metaphors to express the sacred? The task falls within the theology of God and thus does not suspend but takes for granted the facticity of redemption to which the religious community attests. Insofar as redemption takes place in the spheres of individual agency, relation, and the social, a bespeaking of God will arise in connection with these spheres. In each case, the particular redemption of that sphere engenders a symbolics of the one and only power that could effect that redemption.

9. See *Good and Evil*, chaps. 14–16.

8
CIPHERS AND QUALIFIERS

> The ciphers, futile if seeking Transcendence itself, still guide man's (sic) way, each in its fashion. Our only access to the incomprehensible, the all-encompassing, is by the ever-inadequate, endlessly variable ciphers.
>
> *Karl Jaspers,* Philosophical Faith and Revelation

> It is this great absence
> that is like a presence, that compels
> me to address it without hope
> of a reply. It is a room I enter
>
> from which someone has just
> gone, the vestibule for the arrival
> of one who has not yet come.
> *R. S. Thomas, "The Absence"*

In the previous chapter I attempted to connect the bespeaking of God to different spheres of human redemption. I contended that symbolic expressions of God attend the redemption of individuals, relations, and societies. I turn now to the expressions themselves, the names, symbols, and metaphors human beings use to bespeak God. As a moment in a theology of God, this task is not simply the assemblage of "attributes" into historical typologies or tracing them to social and cultural settings, but an account of why certain bespeakings of God attend the discernments (appresentations, negations, and so forth) of redemption. Another time and approach would call this task "deriving the divine attributes." To say that this is a theological task does not necessarily mean that theology's second-order reflections bring forth the symbolics of God. The first order of language that theological reflection inherits is not that of philosophy or metaphysics but the language of the community of faith. In this sphere of *Existenz* and relation, there is a primary meaning of God that may seem at first sight to be formal and circular. God is that which evokes the distinctive act of worship: the distinctive act of worship is that act which has as its referent God.[1] Some such circularity probably applies to virtually all communities of faith. The theology of God begins here, not with a subject of its own making. Thus, a symbolics of the Worshipful can only be an account of the discernments and negations of a community of redemption. This is the way I shall proceed. I shall try to show how various dimensions of redemption originate particular bespeakings (ciphers) and negations of God. The present chapter will present a general theory of theological symbolics under the rubric of ciphers and qualifiers. Subsequent chapters will analyze the specific ciphers that converge in the name God: redeemer, creator, and the Holy.

The bespeaking of God, needless to say, takes place in and through the grammar of human languages. Nouns, adjectives, and verbs are all employed to praise God, to reflectively consider what we mean by God. We apply to God such apparent adjectives as good, loving, everlasting, and all-knowing. Both Catholic and Protestant theological traditions have labeled these terms *attributes*. And that prompts a question: Do attributes properly bespeak God? We remind ourselves that the "attributes" (features, traits) of anything are never simply objective contents unrelated to our act of grasping and meaning them. Attributes arise only with acts of attribution. We ascribe the attribute, X, to the subject, Q. The fact that we are active in attribution need not imply a subjective idealism. Attribution may be correct or mistaken, have a base in solid evidences or be a self-projection. Nevertheless, attribution is an exceedingly complex act. A superficial analysis of that act discloses the following.[2] To attribute is to distinguish the assigned attribute from the subject, which is thus modified by the attribute. Unless the subject's content is exhausted by the attribute, a situation difficult to envision, the attribute is also distinguished from other attributes that also modify the subject. And to attribute is to

---

1. In David Pailin's view, worshipfulness is one of three criteria for thinking about God (*God and the Process of Reality* [London: Routledge, 1989], chap. 2). Jacques Derrida makes a similar point when he says that a reference to God has already taken place when apophatic (negational) discourse is used. Thus, "In a moment I will try to show how negative theology at least claims not to be assimilable to a technique that is subject to simulation or parody, to mechanical repetition. It would escape from this by means of the *prayer* that precedes apophatic utterances, and by the address to the other, to you, in a moment that is not only the preamble or the methodological threshold of the experience" ("How to Avoid Speaking," in Harold Coward and Toby Foshay, eds., *Deerrida and Negative Theology* [Albany: SUNY, 1992], 5).

2. For an extended and philosophically precise analysis of the act of attribution, see Moses Maimonides, *A Guide for the Perplexed*, trans. M. Friedländer (New York: Dover, 1956), chap. 52.

posit either a formal property (for instance, triangularity) to a formal object or an enduring property (for instance, containing living cells) to an actual object. It is also to posit some relation, even if very ephemeral, between the attribute and the subject: constitutive or definitional (as, for instance, three angles to a triangle), contingent on situations, developmental, and so forth. If this account of the act of attribution is in any way plausible, it is because we can confirm these claims by examples from our experience. We do distinguish "heavy" and "brown" from the dog itself. Inevitably, such examples are taken from the everyday world. Attribution is, in fact, one of the ways we cognitively negotiate the world. As such it presupposes and has to do with specific, distinguishable entities that "possess" or have these traits.

From this we can see why attribution is a problematic activity in a theology of God. An act of attribution is just what we cannot perform toward God. We usually know what we mean when we say a tree has bark and that a bear is furry. Fur is one of many traits of the individuals of this species. But to think of God as "having" traits requires us to differentiate God as an individual entity, and further, as one whose traits are possessed by way of being the type of individual God is. It is, in other words, to reduce God to one of the entities with which we negotiate in the everyday world. This is just what God seems to be in the literalized discourse of popular theism and for those critics who identify "theism" with popular theism. But both genuine, worshipful piety and its theological expressions contain elements of the negative theology that prompt strong qualifications to any entitized God. To bespeak the God who comes forth as God is not to bespeak an entity. We must reject then attribution as a proper act of bespeaking God. In its place is the indirect act of meaning (appresentation) that constantly deconstructs itself (negation) and refuses all attributive partitioning. And if the act of attribution is not a possible or proper act toward God, it seems that God does not "have" attributes.

An alternative strategy is to discover a term unburdened by the problems of attribution. I propose at this point Karl Jaspers's term *cipher*.[3] God

---

3. See Karl Jaspers, *Philosophical Faith and Revelation*, trans. E. B. Ashton (New York: Harper & Row, 1962), Part Four, also, Karl Jaspers, *Philosophy*, Vol. 3, trans. E. B. Ashton (Chicago: University of Chicago Press, 1971), Part One. For Jaspers, ciphers are the language of any transcendence and when they are used for God, they carry negations with them (*Philosophical Faith*, 255–65). Further, ciphers are not simply signs that function in ordinary cognition but are a language that operates in the sphere of human *Existenz*. When we give an account of ciphers, we move outside of *Existenz* to a second, generalized language. He calls ciphers the first or "direct language of transcendence." "Words of power" or "deep symbols" are phrases that may communicate what Jaspers means by ciphers.

comes forth as God in ciphers that arise in the sphere of redemption. I choose this term because it carries with it a secret yet to be disclosed, a mystery yet to be fathomed. Yet we cannot forget that cipher, too, is a human and world-negotiating word. Such words are the only language available to us. Our task, which is at the same time always only an effort, is to so use words that they do not render God into an entity and to avoid the pretension of direct communication. Properly used, ciphers have negations built into them from the start. Accordingly, I shall pursue the question of ciphers in two steps: a look at the character of ciphers and an examination of their built-in qualifiers.

CIPHERS

What do we mean by ciphers? I began to address this question in connection with the account of the way redemption gives rise to a meaning of God. The "one and only" thing able to redeem comes forth as a meaning that, though it never settles into a discrete referent, has the character of metaphor, appresentation, or indirect symbol. The ciphers of God as positive contents are these appresentations. In the attribute tradition, they are analogies, the basis of which is a necessary ontological imitation of the creator by the created. On different grounds (the facticity of redemption), we can say that ciphers necessarily imitate and symbolically express the meaning of God. But because of the way they are qualified, ciphers are not simply metaphors. They are of course metaphorical, but more is going on with ciphers than speaking of God's hands, mouth, needs, and the like. The ciphers of God, like analogies, have a kind of "necessity" about them precisely because they arise with appresentations of redemption.

What is it that ciphers express? It is easier to say what they do not express. Because God ever comes forth as the absent or nonpresented God, no language will express God's concrete actuality. Thus arises the familiar dilemma. If language about God bespeaks neither God's "essence" nor concrete actuality, in what way are we justified in thinking it bespeaks God at all? Could it be that the "real" God is a demonic force clothed in a sham discourse? Could the mystery of God be the mystery of the demonic? Are ciphers simply a screen human beings erect between themselves and an utterly opaque and unknown sacred power? Such a view is not possible if God comes forth as God in connection with redemption. Both Catholic and Protestant traditions agree that because language does not directly deliver God's very reality, "attributes" are accounts of divine relations, operations, or even "energies" (Greek Orthodoxy).

What is it that is manifest in language as God comes forth as God? What nonreferent referentiality is pointed to in our bespeakings? Here I must anticipate the threefold derivation of ciphers in later chapters: God as redeemer, Creativity, and Holiness. The facticity of redemption initially appresents God as the one who redemptively founds. *What* is this that founds? What is God as such? The answer must be some sort of world-pervading creative activity. God as such, the reality of God, is the Creativity on which the world depends.[4] In the sphere of history and humanity this Creativity is experienced as a redemptive activity. This bespeaking neither delivers God's actual reality to our experience or language nor posits a "real" God behind the God who comes forth as God. The one with whom we have to do in redemption—and this remains yet to be established—is the Creativity that disposes the world. Thus, the referent of the ciphers, what they indirectly describe, is the divine Creativity. To say this is to refuse any sharp distinction between God as redeemer and God as creator. It is the world-disposing Creativity who comes forth in redemption. Creativity can mean many things: luring processes in a certain direction, empowering, influencing, founding, calling forth the new. Here, creativity is itself a cipher that expresses what we mean by God in the form of generality. God thus is the Creativity at work in everything whose existence and novelty depends on that Creativity. The ciphers of redemption have as their nonpresentational referent this fundamental and general cipher, and their function is to express the character of that cipher, that is, the character of God's creativity.[5]

QUALIFIERS

No account of the ciphers of God would be adequate that ignored the qualifiers that in a necessary way attend those ciphers.[6] Without these

4. As David Pailin writes, "'If God, then Creator' seems a necessary entailment." Whatever is not "the creative ground of all reality" is not God (*God and the Processes of Reality* [London: Routledge, 1989], 123). For Franz Rosenzweig God the Creator is primary to all other attributes. There must be a self-creation of God, an event in which God's vitality transforms itself to effect a beginning. Thus, "whatever else may properly be designated as divine attribute is, however, included in this attribute" (*The Star of Redemption*, trans. W. W. Hallo [Boston: Beacon Press, 1964], 112). Arthur Peacocke likewise thinks that what God is first of all is a creativity: "But to speak thus is to recognize also that God is *creating* now and continuously in and through the inherent, inbuilt creativity of the natural order, both physical and biological—a creativity that is itself God in the process of creating (*God and the New Biology* [London: Dent, 1986]). See also Gordon Kaufman, *In Face of Mystery: A Constructive Theology* (Cambridge, Mass.: Harvard University Press, 1993), 267.

5. In the chapters that follow, I shall speak of Creativity (capitalized) when it is a term for God Godself, God as Creativity, and I shall use uncapitalized terms to express God as creative, the creativity of God, etc.

6. The concept of qualifier is not new to theology. See I. T. Ramsey, *Religious Language: An Empirical Placing of Theological Phrases* (New York: Macmillan, 1957), chap. 2. Ramsey

qualifiers, the ciphers would not be ciphers of *God* but of some mundane entity. The qualification of cipher language is not limited to technical and academic discourse but is present in the everyday language of individual believers and of liturgical events. God, thus, is not simply "mighty" but *all* mighty, a variant way to express the latinized attribute, omnipotence. Several of the traditional attributes make their qualifiers explicit; thus, (omni)-presence, (omni)-science, (omni)-potence, (in)-finite. And it is not an exaggeration to say that the qualifier is implied, silently present, with all other attributes. A number of traditional terms attend attributes as their silent qualifiers: eternal, infinite, all, divine, ultimate, perfect, ineffable, holy. Even the monarchical imagery of God as king carries with it a silent partner, (heavenly) king. Many of the qualifiers are simply negations. God is *in*-comprehensible, *in*-visible, or *im*-mutable. Others are silent partners of positive metaphors. When believers confess that God is love, they take for granted the qualifier: (infinite) love, (eternal) love. And the anthropomorphic metaphors such as knowledge, freedom, and mercy carry with them the silent qualifiers; (eternal) knowledge, (absolute) freedom, or (divine) mercy. The general function of the qualifiers is clear. They indicate that the positive content expressed in the cipher is to be understood as pertaining to the divine mystery. Thus, for instance, God is loving, powerful, or knowing *in the mode of God.*[7]

The theology of God has not always taken advantage of the presence of qualifying silent partners in its discourse. And when the qualifiers are misused, serious misunderstandings closely follow. A case in point is the concept of positive and negative attributes of God. Ciphers (metaphors) with their stated or silent qualifiers engender the very structure of any and all language about God. Because God is nonpresentational to human

---

argues that qualifiers, intrinsic to any language that is religious, function to prevent taking the models of that language or the naming that goes on it in a straightforward way. David Pailin likewise articulates the linguistic peculiarities of the "omni" terms; see *God and the Processes of Reality,* 27.

7. In my judgment, Eberhard Jüngel's way of interpreting the classical Catholic theology of God is a double caricature: "Although theology is talk about God, the assertion crops up very early in theology that one cannot really say who God is. Talk about God can actually state only what God is not" (*God as the Mystery of the World,* trans. D. L. Guder [Grand Rapids, Mich.: W. B. Eerdmans, 1982], 231). First, what Thomas Aquinas and others in this tradition deny is our knowledge of *what* God is. The reason is that we have no direct perception of God's concrete being. Thus, apart from negative terms such as infinite, we cannot locate God's type of being under any type of reality we already know. Can Jüngel? Second, even the most radical version of the negative theology acknowledges that "talk about God" is more than negations. It is affirmative talk whose negative qualifiers render it analogical. Every ancient Christian theology that I know of is a negative theology in the sense of attaching qualifiers to positive language, not in the sense that there is no positive knowledge of God whatsoever.

experience and language, this structure has no exceptions. Nor can this structure be displaced by a second structure that distributes positive and negative speaking into two kinds of attributes. The outcome of such an attempt is most unfortunate. When construed as attributes, negations become attempts to express some (negative) content of God. This is what happens when the negations themselves are not subject to negations. Without negations they become positive expressions of God's being. We thus apply to God such terms as immutability and eternality in the same way we apply love or knowledge. But at least the analogical or metaphorical character of love or knowledge is clear. Negations too contain metaphors. Change is a metaphor applied negatively to God in the term *immutability*. The negation properly qualifies the metaphor, but when it must serve as an attribute, it suppresses its own negation. It thus appears that God's very being is literally and actually changeless or timeless. What began as a negation subtly becomes a positive claim about God, namely, God cannot change, or God cannot in any way be temporal, or cannot in any way be complex.

Whether or not this view should be attributed to the classical Catholic theology of God is under dispute. However that may be, notions of God's literal timelessness, immutability, or simplicity have been widely held in the theology of God, notions that presuppose the positive applicability of the negations. Yet there are elements in the classical Catholic theology of God that resist these notions. According to that theology of God, human beings do not know God's essence. If that is the case, then the so-called negative attributes do not communicate anything about God's concrete being. This implies the principle that Pseudo-Dionysius explicitly articulated, that *im*mutability is not a positive statement about the status of change in God's being. It simply applies a negation to the direct application of the metaphor, change, to God. In addition, insofar as the classical Catholic theology of God has incorporated the Pseudo-Dionysian negative theology, it will refuse any and all notions of negations as attributes. For Pseudo-Dionysius, negations place God above all the polarities of created being. Thus, both change and changelessness cannot be applied to God. The negation applies to both. If so, to say that God is *im*-mutable cannot mean that God's being is changeless.

Once we are clear that qualifiers, the "omni" language of traditional attributes, are not attributes, we are ready to explore their function toward the ciphers. These functions are operative whether the qualifier is explicitly stated or is a silent partner. The most general function of qualifying discourse is to remove from the cipher its apparent mundanizing of God that reduces God to something other than God. The qualifiers modify the ciphers in three ways: difference (negation), sufficiency, and inclusivity.

Difference

Because the other qualifiers presuppose and in some sense restate it, difference or negation is the initial and primary qualifier of all ciphers of God or Creativity. Although Pseudo-Dionysius gave it its seminal formulation, difference is not the invention of Platonism, mystical theology, or the classical Catholic theology of God. Difference attends in an intrinsic way the redemptive coming forth of God as God. God comes forth as God never into presence or presentation but into absence and nonpresentation. God comes forth only as unpictured, undescribed, and unimagined. This element of difference or negation arises wherever human beings have to do with the sacred, be it in tribal religions, Hellenic and Hellenistic "polytheisms," or the "theistic" faiths of Hebraic, Judaic, Muslim, and Christian peoples. The divine difference (the *mana,* sacred power, the holy) is constitutive of any and all acts that would relate to God.

In a Christian theology of God, the divine difference is specific to the facticity of redemption. The divine difference, the fundamental qualifier of all symbolics of God, produces a unique and paradoxical linguistic situation. As the "one and only" founding empowerment at work in redemption, God is essentially and necessarily different from all else that is unable to so empower. This difference is not itself something known or formulated. Because they contain symbolic content, ciphers such as love or creativity lend themselves to the grammars of language. The divine difference eludes grammar, concept, even metaphor. The term *difference* is of course a metaphor and as such is rooted in the innumerable mundane situations of differentiation in which the acts and even grammar of everyday life take place. Difference as a qualifier of ciphers of God can only present itself as a linguistic and grammatical act and entity. But the differentiation it would articulate is something at work in redemption itself that fractures all linguistic attempts to repeat it. Accordingly, this work of differentiation, rooted in the very creativity and actuality of God, resists reduction to or formulation by the modes of differentiation at work in our world negotiations. For instance, we differentiate logical opposites, withhold or deny certain features to familiar objects, distinguish entities, parts, predicates, and relations from each other. But the difference that is set atremble by Creativity coincides with none of these ways of difference. From the facticity of redemption, we sense the divine difference, but we have no knowledge of it, nor can we formulate it. The divine difference is not given to us thematically but as a question mark placed over every term and metaphor we use of God, a cautionary sense of the nonidentity of God with anything our experience, understanding, and grammar can comprehend. The question mark is thus invisibly present whenever we say God is just, loving, creative, or even when we say God "exists."

Whence comes this sense of difference that qualifies all ciphers of God? How is it that the very facticity of redemption spawns difference? Redemption is distributed across all three human spheres: individuals, the interhuman, the social. In the *individual* sphere the redemptive freedoms are elemental human passions transformed from an idolatrous dynamics to open and courageous ways of living in the world. Since these passions cannot be satisfied by any actual, mundane entity, their formal object is an undesignated horizon, a Whatever, a *desideratum*, a possible but unavailable securing. That which frees these passions from their idolatrous turn is an actual founding by the "one and only" thing that can found, the *desideratum* of the passions themselves. If this is the case, the redeemer God cannot be of the order of entities through which the individual idolatrously secures itself but rather, as founding, must be the horizon or *desideratum* as actual. Here at the heart of individual redemption, the very act of founding, is engendered the divine difference and the impossibility of identifying God with any finite or nonfounding good, any piece of the world-system.

In the sphere of the *interhuman*, redemption takes place in connection with the breaking of the power of human claims on each other in situations of alienation. The "one and only" thing that can break that power is whatever can relativize the absolute character of the claim of resentment and the hold of structural guilt. But the involved parties and would-be mediators can accomplish at best only negotiated arrangements, not reconciliation. Alienation is reconciled only in the face of a summons from that whose concern is the total harmony of all, the summons of an infinite face. Here, too, that which redeems is a radical, unformulatable, and undiscernible difference. In the sphere of the *social*, the divine difference is manifested in the form of a criterion to which all national and institutional self-interests are subject. In the absence of this criterion (justice), social groups simply devolve back onto themselves, settling for conflict, violence, self-promotion, and possible defeat. The "one and only" thing that can draw self-interested groups to a larger harmony is the larger Creativity itself that coincides with none of them. Here the divine difference takes the form of an ideality presiding over the workings of social power.

Sufficiency

In a more general way, I have argued that the "omni" language of the ciphers has the character of a superlative grammar. Whenever we would "mean" God as a referentiality, we engage grammar in superlative mode. This aspect of the meaning of God now reappears as a qualifier of ciphers. A cipher addresses the divine Creativity as a content, for instance, one that has the character of love. But the love that founds is the one and only love that can found. As able to found, it is the original *desideratum*-as-actual of a need and passion for love. Accordingly, expressions of degree, particularity, and ambiguity are inappropriate for ciphers. That which the ciphers manifest is from the start that which is sufficient for redemption. We could also say with the classical Catholic theology that it exists in a mode of maximality or ultimacy as long as we protect such language from a static metaphysics of being.

The classical Catholic theology of God expresses this qualifier through the concept of perfection, a concept retained but revised in neoclassical theism (Charles Hartshorne). In the older theologies, the basis of this qualifier was the way of eminence. God must exemplify in the mode of fulfilled actuality (perfection) all goods that exist through God. I speak of sufficiency rather than perfection in order to sever the basis of this qualifier from the formal through-itself and through-another distinction and to connect the qualifier with the facticity of redemption. One result of letting redemption define sufficiency is that we set aside the contradictions that arise when we hold onto both metaphysical perfection and a discourse of divine action. Thus to speak of sufficiency rather than perfection-completeness is not necessarily to empty God of possibility, temporality, or activity. God's own way of self-actualization, of being temporal, or of acting will be that of God, hence ultimate, sufficient. Sufficiency, in other words, is not a metaphysical or ontological concept. It says nothing at all about God's mode of being. Rather, it qualifies the ciphers by the dimension of ultimate sufficiency.

An example may be pertinent. To apply qualifiers to the cipher *divine knowledge* is to accede to the formal principle that whatever God's knowledge actually is, it is knowledge in the mode of God. To say with Hartshorne that God's knowledge grows over time would not contradict this qualifier, although such a claim would itself call for qualifiers. To apply the qualifier *sufficiency* to the cipher of divine knowledge is to say that

God's knowledge is sufficient to the facticity of redemption and to the activity of Creativity. It does not say anything about God's knowledge growing or not growing, about God foreknowing all things, or about God knowing *totum simul*. Perhaps these notions can be speculatively argued. The qualifier of sufficiency does not depend on such arguments.

Inclusivity

A third qualifier structurally present in all the ciphers can be expressed as a negation. What is negated is all restrictions of the cipher that have to do with scope. Even as sufficiency qualifiers caution against thinking that ciphers apply to God in modes of partiality or degrees so inclusivity qualifiers caution against thinking that ciphers apply only to restricted areas of the world or finite being. If they were so restricted, Creativity would relate to some parts of the world and not others. Divine love would be restricted to some periods of history and not periods, some peoples and not others. As inclusive, ciphers are simply love as such, love without restriction.

The inclusivity of the ciphers has two roots. First, that which is the "one and only" thing that can found the human being in its passionate and anxious life, a *desideratum*-as-actual, cannot be any one of the mundane things to which the human being is drawn to secure itself. It is the Real as such, love as such, and so forth. It should thus be clear that the "as such," or horizonal, ultimate character of the founding Creativity resists regional restriction. Second, if that to which the ciphers refer is the world-disposing Creativity (a point to be argued later), then regional restrictions of the character and work of that Creativity are simply inappropriate.

It is important to keep in mind that inclusivity is a qualifier and negation of a cipher, not a metaphysical claim about God and the world. It is not about "omnipresence" in the sense of an elaborated paradigm of God's activity in the world, the third task of a theology of God. Inclusivity may, however, offer a primarily negative way to interpret the traditional notion of omnipresence. Thus, omnipresence means that God, that is, Creativity, is all present in the nonmetaphysical and negative sense of having no regional restrictions.

I conclude with an observation. Theological symbolics, the derivation and assessment of names, metaphors, and ciphers of God, includes the threefold qualification of difference, sufficiency, and inclusivity. These qualifiers perform a demythologizing work on human imagery and grammar used of God. Furthermore, they originate not in theology itself but in the redemptive facticity from which come the ciphers. They demythologize the "popular theism" of everyday belief in which they originate and all notions of God as *a* being, *an* entity alongside the world.[8] But the function of qualifiers is not limited simply to the symbolics of God. They also perform their demythologizing work in accounts of how God comes forth as God and in paradigmatic reflections on God's activity in the world. They operate, in other words, in all three parts of the theology of God.

---

8. The reason the expression, God as *a* being, calls for a qualifier is that it is a grammar of an everyday world-focusing act. An oak tree is *a* being. God is not. Thus, Robert Neville distinguishes between "real distinctions" (A is really distinct from B) and the distinction being made in the discourse of God as creator distinguished from the created. For Neville the latter will not lend itself to symbolic logic (*God the Creator: On the Transcendence and Presence of God* [Chicago: University of Chicago Press, 1968], 95).

9
CIPHERS OF REDEMPTION

Come not in terrors, as the King of Kings
But kind and good, with healing in thy wings.
H. F. Lyte, "Abide with Me"

I have tried to mark out a pathway from the facticity of redemption to the symbolics of God. To traverse this pathway is neither to speculate nor to appeal to authority. As to the former, I do not begin with an initial philosophical distinction between God and the world nor do I establish the symbolic content of God by citing specific texts. Those who do proceed in these ways may see the path I am traversing as "anthropological," even "subjective." In one sense they would be right. I do attempt to track the symbolics of God back to discernments, convictions, and beliefs of individuals, to human interrelationality, and sociality. The basis of this procedure is that God comes forth as God in connection with redemptive transformations of the spheres of human reality. Accordingly, I shall attempt to discover how these spheres of redemption give rise to "names," ciphers, and metaphors.

Uncovering the divine symbolics that comes with redemptive transformation faces an inevitably muddled and ambiguous situation. The interspherical life of actual human communities is something of a jumble. Empirical and historical accounts of communal life confront an overwhelming variety of names, metaphors, and concepts at work in liturgies, rites, and interpretive activities. Yet within this jumble of things a certain "logic," perhaps even dialectic, organizes the convictional life of individuals and the corporate life of the community. To be sure, if the symbolics of God is about nothing whatever, if it has no referentiality or content, if redemptive transformation has never really taken place, such a "logic" would be difficult to discover. But it is just because redemption does occur, transforming the very structure of agential life and the interhuman and stimulating social emancipation, that the ciphers of Creativity can be distinguished and even, in a provisional way, be ordered. The "ordering" of the ciphers of God may be somewhat artificial, yet it is a useful undertaking because it helps us see why some ciphers have arisen at all and it exposes the abstractions that result when certain ciphers are suppressed. For instance, a suppression takes place when we reduce God to a single symbol such as creator or emancipator.

The following analysis identifies three inclusive names for God: Redeemer (or Spirit), Creativity, and the Holy. Taken together these names say what communities of the Christian movement mean by God. Converging into each other, they add up to a primary designation (though not definition) of God.[1] This convergence is silently present whenever Christians bespeak God in worshipful, didactic, or proclamatory acts. Thus, it would be close to impossible for the Christian believer to think that the God of redemptive transformation has nothing to do with creative activity in the world. This threefold convergence has a certain primordiality for the Christian movement. At the same time, because of the facticity of redemption, the names also come forth in a certain sequence. People in a faith community are not initially concerned with the holy, abstracted into itself, or with the question of what disposes the world. The matter of God arises first from historical and social mediations (exodus, covenant, messianic event) of redemption. Our task now is to uncover this sequence of the divine name, this "logic" of the ciphers.

In communities of faith, the bespeaking of God begins with redemption. In its most inclusive sense, redemption means the transformation of human evil that corrupts the spheres of agency, the interhuman, and the social. In content, redemption means agential freedoms, reconciliation, and emancipation. These three spheres of redemption are rich metaphorical fields for the bespeaking of God.[2] From the transformations that take place in these spheres come ciphers that disclose the character of God or Creativity. When we ask what sort of creativity God is, what its aims are (to speak anthropomorphically), we inevitably turn for our answers to these spheres of redemptive transformation. I have argued elsewhere that in certain respects each sphere has a primacy over the others. Religious faith and redemption surely originate in the interhuman, the sphere

1. To speak of "names" implies a rather imprecise distinction between divine names and what I have called ciphers. As inclusive symbols of divine mystery, the names are of course ciphers. Names also function in the language of address (liturgy and prayer) and also as inclusive metaphors for a cluster of metaphors.

2. For the analysis that distributes human reality over three spheres, see my book *Good and Evil: Interpreting a Human Condition* (Minneapolis: Fortress Press, 1990), 27–31.

where human beings are entangled with each other in mutual, alienating, negotiating, and affectionate activities. Yet nothing would happen at all apart from the mediation of language, customs, and institutional structures in the social world. And surely neither the interhuman nor the social can displace the individual in its irreducible, self-transcending mystery. In order to expose the way the meaning and reality of God comes forth into belief-ful conviction, I set forth the dynamics of idolatry and freedom of individual redemption. I shall continue that privileging of the individual and thus begin with the cipher that arises with the redemption of the human agent.

HUMAN AGENCY: CIPHERS OF FOUNDING

In the sphere of human individuals, redemption has the character of "founding." This is because the dynamics of individual evil (idolatry, fanatical attachments, unfreedom, needs for certainty, malice, and so forth) arise in connection with the existential rootlessness intrinsic to human life. Constituted in the depths of our existence by powerful passions, we human beings cannot abide the intense anxieties that come with our vulnerable, tragically structured, and ambiguous life. Attempting to secure ourselves by means of whatever is at hand, we set up absolutizing relations of certainty and loyalty to what would seem to secure us. In redemption human beings are founded not in the false securer (the idol) but in the one and only thing that can found, that which the elemental passions desired all along. The effect of being-founded is an ontological courage that frees us to exist in and toward the various goods of the world "without idols" and thus transforms our corrupted passionate life. God comes forth then as the founder of being-founded in courage.[3]

Human existence is not reducible to a single fundamental passion, however, for instance, the desire simply to survive. Individual *Existenz* is constituted by at least three basic desires: (1) for *existence*, that is, for the preservation of one's self-transcending, self-determining, and contentful subjectivity; (2) for *others* who will confirm and understand one's *Existenz* and with whom one can enter relation; and (3) for *the real*, that is, the desire to be in and toward what is not merely deceitful or illusory. In the dynamics of idolatry or self-securing, each of these desires turns into an insistence on fulfillment by something that in fact cannot fulfill. Thus we have the passion of *Existenz* corrupted into an oscillation between a brave

---

3. For a more extended discussion of the dynamics of agential evil, see *Good and Evil*, 130–37; for redemptive founding, see ibid., chap. 11.

but false autonomy and a despairing ennui, the passion for the other turned into an unstable wavering between excessive dependence and cynicism, and the passion for the real turned into postures of confident but false skepticism or confident certainty about what we know. Redemption in the sphere of the individual transforms these passions of weakness and fanaticism toward an authentic vitality of subjectivity, agapic freedom toward others, and wonder in the face of the real. This redemptive turn can take place only insofar as the initial anxiety that prompted self-securing is lessened. The one and only thing able to effect a freedom from self-securing is that which itself is the meaning of *Existenz*, the truly genuine Other, and the Real itself. Being-founded, accordingly, does not stop with the bestowing of ontological courage. It transforms the agent at the point of its specific, corrupted passions.

At this point it is important to resist the temptation to overly systematize the analysis by positing a cipher of God that correlates with each redeemed passion. In the concrete existence of individuals, the passions themselves, though distinguishable, are not really separated from each other. Furthermore, this analysis is at best a provisional rather than exhaustive account of human passionate life. It does, however, appear to be the case that a field of ciphers attends the redemption of these passions. The reason we think of God as "real," personal, and as the very meaning of existence is rooted in the experience of founding with respect to these corrupted passions. In the sphere of the individual, God founds the human being as it is rent by terrifying anxieties and desperately self-securing postures. To exist in the world nonidolatrously is to exist in and from this founding empowerment. Being-founded in such an ultimate founder evokes ciphers of God as ground of meaning, utterly real, the ultimate other. Expressing these ciphers in the texts and traditions of the religious community is a rich cluster of metaphors; God as just and merciful ruler, shepherd of lost sheep, father, betrayed spouse, and, more recently, as friend and mother. These metaphors of popular religion all point to a single cipher, the cipher of redemptive founding. This cipher discloses Creativity from the perspective of individuals trapped in their anxiety and evil and who experience a founding that frees.

In using the term *founding* I am not unaware of the vigorous challenges to the language of founding (foundation) and the language of "reality" by certain forms of postmodernism. I must say, first, that founding and being-founded has little to do with "foundationalism."[4] Because it works

---

4. For an excellent summary of the concept of foundationalism, see Francis Schüssler Fiorenza, *Foundational Theology: Jesus and the Church* (New York: Crossroad, 1984), 285–92. Fiorenza distinguishes rationalist and empiricist, hard and soft, foundationalism. In philos-

from the facticity of redemption, the concept of "founding" constitutes a criticism of foundationalism. An older challenge to the notion of existential founding comes from radical, secular existentialism (Sartre, Camus). Sartre offers a phenomenological ontology of the human being (the "for-itself") according to which being unfounded is not only the actual and empirical human situation but its unavoidable destiny. The for-itself (*pour-soi*) is ontologically incapable of being founded because its very being as freedom is constituted by nihilation. To found human being is to destroy it. Accordingly, Sartre concluded that the human being's closedness to founding was at the same time a closedness to the possibility of God.[5] Here we face the usual difficulties of simply identifying onto-anthropological analyses and the possibility or impossibility of God. A huge gap yawns between the phenomenological ontology of human being and analyses that proceed from the facticity of redemption. Because of this gap the theology of God can even accept Sartre's claim that human self-transcendence, lacking an intrinsic founding meaning, exists in the form of anxious nihilation. And yet redemption happens. The passionate (and nihilating) life of individuals turns into freedoms, not in Sartre's empty and dizzying sense of absolute existential choice but of passions of wonder and agapic concern. The nihilism of Sartrean existentialism and the facticity of redemption are not sufficiently similar to be logical exclusions.

A second challenge to the notion of founding comes from all philosophies and theologies that reject *being* as the primary name of God. Although I have not used the term *being* in these analyses, it does hover near by. To say that God answers to the human being's passion for the real, the genuine other, or founding meaning sounds very close to the metaphysical language of *ens realissimum*. Does the notion of founding return us to ontotheology? Here we must recall the place or moment in the theology of God of these present considerations, ciphers that arise in the sphere of individual redemptive transformation. The problem before

ophy the Cartesian attempt to locate and expose the ultimate bases of rationality is the prime example of foundationalism. For Richard Rorty ancient Platonism is foundationalism's real root. In that view the foundations of knowledge are "truths which are certain because of their causes rather than because of the arguments given for them." Nonfoundationalist philosophy goes back not to some (founding) relation to objects known but to arguments (*Philosophy and the Mirror of Nature* [Princeton: Princeton University Press, 1977], 157, 32–35). According to Fiorenza, foundationalism appears in the history of theology in both rationalist (natural theology) and transcendental undertakings. In general, a critique of foundationalism exposes "the cultural, social, and hermeneutic dimensions" of all foundations. (Fiorenza, 289)

5. For a close analysis and critique of Sartre's argument, see Robert R. Williams, "The Problem of God in Sartre's *Being and Nothingness*," in William McBride and Calvin O. Schrag, eds., *Phenomenology in a Pluralistic Context* (Albany: SUNY Press, 1983).

us is not God and the world, not one and many, not Being and beings, and not being-through-itself and being-through-another. It is what is appresented when human *Existenz* experiences redemptive freedoms. If *being* means the one and only thing able to found *Existenz*, then that which redemption appresents is being. But this founding is not simply a relation to or cognitive claim about some impersonal substratum of the universe. On the contrary, the one and only "being" that could found *Existenz* evokes metaphors of care, concern, and intimate relation. The real in the sense of founding is already in some sense a personalized cipher.

THE INTERHUMAN: THE CIPHER OF RECONCILING LOVE

In the the sphere of the individual, redemption means founding, and God comes forth as the one and only founder (reality) of *Existenz*.[6] But human reality is not simply individuality but a dimensional complex that includes the sociopolitical and the interhuman, spheres that also undergo redemptive transformations. If redemption were limited to the sphere of the individual, it would not really transform the distorted self-preoccupations that arise with anxiety and evil. Individual redemption does involve a breaking of the hold of idolatry. When passions for the other and for the real are transformed into agapic freedom and wonder, the individual is released from the narrow circle of self-preoccupation to enjoy, relate to, and interact with others and with the world. But insofar as the interhuman and the sociopolitical are absent, the emphasis is inevitably on the *individual's* fulfillments, enjoyments, and freedoms. The individual sphere (subjectivity, *Existenz*, self-transcendence, passions) alone will not pull the individual into relation.

At this point, then, I correct the abstraction I have perpetrated by taking up the interhuman. The facticity of redemption applies not only to individuals but to relation, a sphere of human reality irreducible to the experiences of individuals. In this sphere of relation occur the distinctive corruptions of alienation: violation, resentment, and guilt. Violation restructures human interrelation into relations of resentment and objective guilt. Presiding over all relation from the very beginning is the irreducible alterity of thous and the violable face of the other (Emmanuel Levinas) that seizes and interrupts the individual's natural egocentrism and summons it to acknowledge the vulnerable other. Resentment and guilt accompany relation because of alterity and the face. The summons of the

---

6. For the human being as *Existenz*, see Karl Jaspers, *Philosophy,* Vol. 1, trans. E. B. Ashton (Chicago: University of Chicago Press, 1969), 54–60.

face confronts the violator with an unsolvable problem, an alienation no compensation can remove. This unsolvable problem is what renders guilt into a structural, relational, and not just a "feeling," phenomenon. Interhuman violation brings about what appears to be a permanent structure, an unredeemable state of affairs. Negotiations, strategies, and penalties in the objective order do not reach it. In the situation of violation and the alienation that follows thereon, the element of face is reduced to an accusing vulnerability.[7]

And yet redemption does in fact take place in the sphere of relation. Even as there is a facticity about individual transformations toward freedom, there is likewise a facticity about interhuman reconciliation. Reconciliations are not simply successful negotiations of compensation, a phenomenon that takes place more in the order of the sociopolitical than the interhuman, but are genuine removals of resentment and guilt as structural elements of relation. But these removals cannot occur as long as the face remains simply the violated and accusing face. Somehow face itself must be released from the accusatory posture into which alienation has transformed it. According to texts and traditions of the community of faith, the one and only thing that can break the power of alienation is repentance and forgiveness. Whence come such things? They are possible only if there is a releasement of face from mere accusation. Resentment can diminish only as the violated does not reduce the violating other to its crime. In other words, the violating other must come forth to the violated as itself a vulnerable face. And that which uncovers the vulnerable face of the violator and thus reduces resentment is the violator's own repentance, genuine sorrow, regret, and sympathy for the violated. But what would ever arouse such repentance? Somehow, the violator must be confronted not simply with the *accusing* face but with a face that, sensing the vulnerable face of the violator, can forgive. This dynamics of interhuman reconciliation that disempowers accusation, resentment, and guilt is very much a dynamics of mutuality. Empirically or psychologically speaking, it could be initiated from either side. But the reality of the reconciliation itself is a mutual sensing of a face behind the accusing face.

Looked at his way, the reconciliations of the interhuman are ordinary human acts. People violate each other, quarrel, and make up. Something similar could be said about the redemptive transformations of individ-

7. For a fuller discussion of the corruption of the sphere of relation, see *Good and Evil,* chap. 13.

uals. But the religious community has given expression to another dimension of reconciliation, the depiction of which we find especially in twentieth-century Jewish philosophers. Something draws relation toward this mutual dynamics of repentance and forgiveness. In the face that is irreducible to mere accusation, that is ever at work prior to violation, the community has sensed an infinite summons.[8] Or, to express this in a negative way, the summons of a face is not totally subject to the "rationality" of compensating wrongs. That which calls the alienated into mutual reconciliation without calculative transactions is simply love as such. For this reason, the religious community has sensed in the mysteries of human reconciliation a cipher of God, namely Creativity as reconciling love.

THE SOCIOPOLITICAL CIPHER OF JUSTICE

As human beings organize their lives by way of enduring patterns of activity, expectations, and order, they bring about the sociopolitical sphere. With the social come stratifications of function and power and a variety of institutions, some small and ephemeral, some large and centuries old. Thus we have tribes, societies, hierarchies, armies, monarchies, trade guilds, corporations, and bureaucracies. And with the social comes a distinctive way human beings perpetrate and undergo evil, namely subjugation. Violation and alienation are features of the interhuman. Subjugating structures that oppress, enslave, disenfranchise, and remove basic rights are the work of the social sphere. So subtle can be that work that mythologies, role definitions, and the social unconscious can disguise the oppressive structure and make it appear normal.

The facticity of redemption likewise reaches the social. To those who think that social ills are simply matters of social determinates, any claim about their redeemability sounds fantastic and utopian. It is important at this point not to confuse social ills with the inevitable instabilities and tragic aspects of the social. Nor should we confuse social redemption simply with the inevitable vulnerability of all social powers. Oppressive institutions can be weakened and even eliminated by their own internal instability, by external events, and by competitors. "The captains and the kings depart," as Rudyard Kipling says. Such upheavals break the hold of an oppressive regime only to be followed by new regimes and their victims. The *redemption* of the social replaces oppressive structures with social orders that empower the victims, restore their rights, and redress

---

8. Emmanuel Levinas, *Collected Philosophical Papers*, trans. A. Lingis (Dordrecht: Nijhoff, 1987), 169.

their misfortunes. Social redemption involves much more than the elimination of an old order. It subjects the oppressive order to critique, exposes the subtle masking of oppression as a normalcy, and reverses the humiliating social roles, status, and location of the disenfranchised. Actions such as these require resymbolization and a new discourse. And because such things do happen in the social order, we can speak of a social facticity of redemption.

Why is it that religious communities of the past and present, especially liberation types of theologies, speak of these transformations as a work of God? One can of course interpret social redemption as simply a human work, even the outcome of a social determinism. Why think of the sphere of the social as open to a divine redemptive activity? Criticisms of oppressive structures and proposals for large social harmonies that recognize the rights of all take place under a rather strange criterion. Temporally speaking, this criterion pertains to future possible developments and thus concides with nothing in the present. Spatially speaking, it cannot be reduced to the interest of any particular group, not even the inclusive social unit (for instance, the nation) in which the oppression takes place. The criticism of the regime that perpetrated the holocaust has no territorial, national, or institutional entity as its model or criterion. The criterion that would prompt a leadership to envisage a future sociality that would be a harmony of various constituencies coincides with no actual social system. Such a criterion has the character of ideality, even eschatology. As such it relativizes the self-interested claims of all social entities and locates them in a broader harmony. So far this criterion sounds like the pragmatic criterion of the greatest good for the greatest number. Yet, something in the criterion undercuts this quantification. At work in this eschatological criterion that presses toward emancipation are the vulnerable faces of human participants. It is just this element of face amidst the social that evokes resistance to dehumanization and presses us to consider basic rights. And when redemption takes place under this criterion which I shall now call justice, it is not the work of any one historical, delimited, self-interested social entity. All such entities are measured by that which is concerned for all together. Nor is it possible to delimit that to which the criterion applies. "All together" comes finally to mean any and all entities in the world system. Resembling the horizon of individual passions, the criterion of justice is a horizon of social good. And when redemption takes place under this (eschatological) criterion of justice, religious communities see the hand of God. Accordingly, they attribute to the Creativity they worship the character (cipher) of justice.

GOD AS SPIRIT

To divide the facticity of redemption into three spheres of human reality is, by the nature of the case, misleading. Redemption never occurs in any one sphere without influencing and being influenced by the other spheres. Individuals freed for nonidolatrous and compassionate life in the world and enduring and reconciled human relations are powerful redemptive forces in the sphere of the social. Parallel to this point, our triple division of the ciphers of Creativity is likewise misleading. To say that Creativity is what *founds* human individuals, releases the accusing face of relation into reconciling love, and is the inclusive criterion of justice is not to think three things. Founding, love, and justice converge into a way of envisaging God in a name and that name is Spirit.[9]

In the long sweep of history and its overwhelming linguistic variety, spirit has meant many things. In a dualist metaphysics or supernaturalist religion, it expresses a form of reality that transcends, even animates, the "physical" entities of the everyday world. In more recent times and especially in post-Enlightenment European philosophy, spirit (*Geist, esprit*) has described human reality itself in its irreducibility to external causality or quantification. Capturing the complexity of human reality, spirit is that in which individual agency, interhuman reality, and sociality merge. On that basis spirit comes to be a dimension of history, or, if taken widely enough (compare Hegel), a way of understanding nature and even being. Needless to say, a postcritical or revisionist theology of God would prefer the anthropological to the supernaturalist meaning of spirit. But does the anthropological meaning of spirit open the theology of God to anthropomorphism? The *desideratum* (horizon) of individual desire is not simply vacuous. That which founds human *Existenz* in its desire to be itself, to be with and from the other, and to experience the real, that which summons the contracted face into reconciliation and contracted societies into justice and harmony, cannot be utterly unlike human reality itself. The character of Creativity at work in these ways is something like an agency, a loving other.

At this point it is difficult to avoid a theme about which popular religion (in a certain sense) is quite comfortable and theological reflection uneasy. Does the name *Spirit* contain a claim that God is a "person" or personal? If we answered positively, we could take the position that the three ciphers of redemption so converge as to appresent God as personal.

9. See Peter C. Hodgson, *Winds of the Spirit: A Constructive Christian Theology* (Louisville: Westminster John Knox, 1994), 284–87.

If we add the qualifier to this, (divinely) personal, we have God as unenvisionably personal in the mode of utter sufficiency and inclusivity. Several reasons prompt me to resist this version of God as Spirit. First, it synthesizes the various metaphors of redemption not into a cipher but into a referent, God as person. But the referentiality of the ciphers is Creativity. To make it a "person" is to mythologize it. Second, person and the personal arise in the sphere of agency.[10] Even if they are always interpersonal, persons are individual agents. But the metaphors of redemption do not converge into one of the spheres: they rather express how interspherical redemption applies to Creativity. Third, person and personal are entities. To use person as a cipher is to confirm anti-theist suspicions that "God" means a specific entity. And entity or person language about God opens the door to discourse of a divine psychology; God as thinking, anticipating, remembering, feeling emotions, choosing between options, and so on. Perhaps there is a place for such language in a liturgics and even poetics of God. But if this language is to retain its theological character, there must be an initial clarity that there is no entity whose psychology it describes. Nor does the act of worship require God as a personal entity. God is the worshipful precisely because God is not an entity alongside others whose psychology we can envision or linguistically express. We are content then to say that the ciphers of redemption (founding, love, justice) appresents the character of the Creativity we worship.

I conclude then the exploration of the cipher of redemption. If the approach had been ontotheological, that is, proceeding from God as the through-which of the world, I could have called this cipher by the more abstract and general term, the goodness of God. I have replaced that general term with the metaphors that converge into the name *redeemer.*

---

10. For a sharp criticism of God as person, see Robert Neville, *God the Creator: On the Transcendence and Presence of God* (Chicago: University of Chicago Press, 1968), 191–93. Compare Neville's criticism to Tillich's rejection of the phrase, God *as a* person (*Systematic Theology,* Vol. 1 [Chicago: University of Chicago Press, 1967], 244–45).

10
CIPHERS OF CREATIVITY AND HOLINESS

> Sweet, sweet, sweet, O Pan!
> Piercing sweet by the river!
> Blinding sweet, O great god Pan!
> The sun on the hill forgot to die,
> And the lilies revived, and the dragon fly
> Came back to dream on the river.
> *Elizabeth Barrett Browning,*
> *"A Musical Instrument"*

> And one called to another and said: "Holy, Holy, Holy, is the
> Lord of hosts; and the whole earth is full of his glory." And the
> foundations of the thresholds shook at the voice of him who
> called, and the house was filled with smoke.
> *Isaiah 6:3–4,* RSV

The task before us is a "genealogy" of the symbols of God as they arise
in a community of redemption. Having explored ciphers that arise
with redemption itself, I move now to ciphers connected with God as
Creativity and as Holy.

CREATIVITY

I have proposed that the referent of the ciphers of God is the Creativity
that disposes the world. Ciphers of redemption give content to that
referent. But creativity is itself a metaphor and content. As a "name"
of God it is thus both a referent, that which God is, and a cipher. Our
present task is to explore why this is the case, why creativity arises as
a motif in the community of faith at all. Does not the introduction of
the motif of creativity contradict our thesis that God redemptively
comes forth as God, collapsing the theology of God back into ontotheology and problems of God and the world? I can only respond at
this point that if ontotheology means any and all ways of thinking God

as world-disposer, then the theology of God does have an ontotheological element. On the other hand, if ontotheology means any and all proposals about "God" that arise from the problem of being or the puzzle of the world, then the cipher of creativity falls outside of ontotheology.

Creativity as Referent

Stories, metaphors, and even doctrines of God as Creativity (creator, maker, world-origin, providential orderer) abound in virtually all religious faiths. Ancient goddess and tribal religions, henotheisms (such as ancient Babylonian religion), polytheisms (such as Olympian religion), and the so-called theistic faiths all think of God as in some sense the power(s) at work in the fecundity, order, and novelty of nature.[1] These faiths could not conceive a divinity or sacred power totally disconnected with how and why the world is what it is. Whence comes this virtually universal motif of creativity? The question intensifies when we recall that religious faiths are centered in the practical concerns of everyday life, not speculation. Yet most world faiths contain a "cosmic" element. For instance, in tribal religions, everyday life depends on the fecundity of nature that calls for a neverending ritual renewal of the powers of creativity. In the West Hesiod systematized the mythical origin of these powers that order the world and bequeathed to Hellenic philosophy the speculative problematic of world origins. Thus, Platonic, Stoic, and Neoplatonic philosophers struggled in speculative manner with the "puzzle of the world" in relation to the sacred. Although the theistic faiths of the West constitute a break from the ancient shamanistic and fecundity religions, they too think of God not just as a redeemer but as world creator. Whence this orientation to the totalistic problem of world order and world origin? The question is a theological one. What is it about these faiths as faiths that engenders the theme of a universal creativity?

I begin with a thesis. Redemption itself bespeaks the divine creativity. The thesis has both negative and positive grounds. I previously argued that redemption gave rise not only to ciphers but to qualifiers of the ciphers. One element in the qualifiers is a negation of all restrictions of the

---

1. Many recent studies and anthologies indicate how widespread is the motif of creation in ancient and modern religious faiths: E. Ehrhardt, *The Beginning: A Study in the Greek Philosophical Approach to the Concept of Creation from Anaximander to St. John* (Manchester: Manchester University Press, 1968); Marta Weigle, *Creation and Procreation: Feminist Reflections on Mythologies of Cosmology and Parturition* (Philadelphia: University of Pennsylvania Press, 1989); Mircea Eliade, *The Myth of the Eternal Return*, trans. W. R. Trask (New York: Pantheon Books, 1954); Charles Long, *Alpha: The Myths of the Creation* (New York: Braziller, 1963); Barbara C. Sproul, *Primal Myths: Creating the World* (San Francisco: Harper & Row, 1979).

scope of the cipher. As the "one and only" thing that can found *Existenz* and free from idolatrous attachments, God cannot be one of or even a cluster of the finite entities that constitute the world. It is just the idolatrous dependence on such entities that distorts the self and its relations and removes its freedoms. The "not" of this negation makes it unthinkable that God as founder can be restricted to a region, physical area, ethnic group, nation, or genus of being. Given this negation, whatever God is or does can have no restriction in scope. The cipher of redemption applies then to something that in principle does what it does wherever and whenever anything exists. It is, in other words, coextensive with what we call the world.

Redemption, however, launches the theme of creativity not just from a negation. One of the redemptive transformations that individual agents experience concerns the cognitive life. Idolatry structures the cognitive (reality-oriented) self into the paradoxical mix of skepticism and certainty that redemption can transform into open-ended postures of wonder. At work in these idolatrous dynamics is a passion for the real which, when transformed into wonder, combines a mix of openness to and participation in whatever manifests itself as real. The initial *desideratum* of this passion is simply the real as the horizon of all sorts of specific cognitive curiosities and puzzlements. But when cognitive idolatry is transformed by being-founded, that which founds is not simply the empty horizon of the real but the horizon of the real as actual. One senses in a vague way that the Reality that evokes wonder is in some way that which founds and connects all events, objects, and relation of the world. In the redemption of the interhuman, the cipher of reconciling love brooks no stipulated limitation. It is simply love. And insofar as it is actual, it is unimaginable that it would distribute itself piecemeal through the universe. Similarly, the cipher of justice cannot be regionalized, as if it applied to one galaxy and not another. In other words, the ciphers of redemption are universal in scope. And insofar as redemption actually takes place, they refer not simply to an empty horizon but to something actual. If that "something" is *utterly* unrestricted in scope, it is an activity that founds, reconciles, and emancipates whenever and wherever there is anything at all. Because the aim of this nonrestricted operation is both to assist entities to move toward the future by way of wonder and new responses and perpetually to reconcile entities with each other, redemption has the character of creativity. Thus begins a dialectic of novelty in which stable social conditions assist the creative work of individuals and individuals contribute to new social structures. And when all restrictions of scope are removed, this creativity is at the same time the creativity at work in the world. Thus, when the community of faith experiences redemption in this sense, it bespeaks God as a universal creative activity in the totality of things.

Creativity as Cipher

What ciphers refer to is a universal, world-disposing Creativity, not a being, entity, or piece of the world itself. Manifest in ciphers of redemption, this Creativity is not a vague force empty of content. But creativity, itself a metaphor, contains ciphers that call for interpretation. What symbolic content do we find in this cipher? Here I recall the distinction between two tasks of the theology of God, the derivation and interpretation of a symbolics of God and the construction of a paradigm for understanding God's activity in the world. One way to uncover the content of the cipher of creativity is to move directly to the second task, a move that would land us in the conceptual thickets grown by Duns Scotus Erigena, Gottfried Leibniz, Alfred North Whitehead, and others. Postponing this move, I shall keep this exploration within the confines of a symbolics of God. What symbolic contents or ciphers do we find in (divine) creativity? I shall continue to let redemption guide the inquiry.

When we ask for the content of the cipher of Creativity, we find ourselves caught between the direct language of popular religion and the conceptual world of metaphysics. Continuing to give primacy to redemption, we push metaphysics into the background. But does the eschewal of metaphysics at this stage turn us over to the mythical discourse of popular religion? A word about popular religion is in order here. Insofar as the face of popular religion, at least as a discourse, is the face of mythology and literalism, the theology of God cannot avoid a demythologizing and deliteralizing relation to popular religion. But popular religion is inevitably more complex and subtle than its discursive facade.[2] Even if it eschews a conceptual and interrogative discourse, it is as faith rooted in the events and processes of redemption. Even if popular religion *bespeaks* God anthropomorphically, that bespeaking contains piety-rooted qualifiers and negations. Fundamentalism is another matter. Fundamentalism appears to be popular religion unchastened by the qualifiers that origi-

---

2. The authenticity and centrality of popular religion has been an important theme in Latin American liberation theology. See, for instance, Juan Luis Segundo, *Liberation Theology*, trans. J. Drury (Maryknoll, N.Y.: Orbis Books, 1979), chap. 7. The emphasis of the liberation theologies is the religious insightfulness that comes with marginalization, an insightfulness that senses the legitimating character of the theologies and ecclesiastic institutions of the religious majority and that enables marginalized religious people to read the old texts in new ways.

nate in redemption. The following analysis is concerned more with the literalistic facade of the discourse of popular religion than its deeper complexity.

The only way we human beings can conceive creativity in a positive way is by way of the creativity we perform, observe, and are. Accordingly, our direct accounts of creativity employ a discourse of intervention in which creativity means keeping things from happening, aesthetic composition, invention, manufacturing, urgings, and lurings. All of these terms originate in the way we finitely exist in our environments. Thus, drawing on these various senses of creativity in the everyday world, we express the divine creativity as the work of an entity (God) who faces possibilities, makes a decision to create, and does what is necessary (speak a word) to bring the new thing about. Thus, in its literalistic sense, creation *ex nihilo* means an event that happened far in the past. It should not be necessary to say that this whole discourse is less a cipher of creativity as a literalized metaphor or set of metaphors. The *doctrine* of creation in the classical Catholic theology is not simply this literalized myth. However, its central concept, *creatio ex nihilo*, can be interpreted either by way of the myth or as a negative qualifier. If we construe creation "from nothing" as a positive statement, we find ourselves back in the myth. That is, we try to think the "from nothing" as depicting a creationless state of divine being, interrupted (a long time ago) by a decision to create. As a qualifier, creation from nothing expressed the Christian movement's rejection of the prevailing Hellenistic notion that divine creativity was an everlasting relation to an everlasting world. I shall take up this issue in a later chapter. Setting aside mythical and literalistic accounts of creativity, I find three ciphers at work in the symbol or metaphor of (divine) creativity: empowering, eternality, and aim. These contents converge to form the meaning of symbol itself.

Empowering

In the classical Catholic theology of God, empowering finds expression in the monarchical metaphors of sovereignty and rule and in the concept of omnipotence. Since an attribute in that theology is a metaphor in the mode of completion or perfection, the power of God means *all* power.[3]

3. John McTaggart's criticisms of the doctrine of God's omnipotence assume that omnipotence means all-determination without exception, a determination that would apply to the laws of logic as well as the actual universe (*Some Dogmas of Religion* [London: E. Arnold, 1930], chaps. 6 and 7). For a similar criticism, see David Ray Griffin, *God, Power, and Evil: A Process Theodicy* (Philadelphia: Westminster Press, 1976), chap. 17.

Insofar as power means willful determination, it is *all* determination. When redemption is the source and route to the ciphers, no such notion arises. In redemption we grasp the divine founding, reconciling love, and summons to justice; we do not experience all-determination. On the other hand, redemption does attest to an empowerment that takes place in all three spheres of human reality. Individuals are empowered in their struggle amidst tragic finitude toward empassioned freedoms. In the interhuman, the reconciliation of alienation and violence empowers relation and opens it to ever-new possibilities. Emancipation empowers not only disenfranchised and subjugated peoples but the total society as it would reduce disharmony, corporate misery, and conflict. If creativity is redemption writ large on the face of the universe, it is a form of empowerment.

Eternity

The second cipher of creativity has to do with time. Like power, time has found expression in the biblical and theological literature of the Christian community. In popular religion caricatured as literalized anthropomorphism, God is temporal in the same way as any actual entity, namely as a process in which future possibilities become actualized. Trees, cells, galaxies, and human beings are all temporal in this sense. Eternity then means an everlasting persistence. The classical theology of attributes would have it reversed. Positing perfection or utter completion of possibility as a positive feature of God's being and not just a qualifier, it denies that God has possible states and thus denies temporal actualization in God. That being the case, God's eternity means timelessness. The classical theology could have taken this in a different direction. Since God is the eminent instance of all that exists through God (existence, life, knowledge, goodness, and so forth), why not conclude that God rather than being timeless is eminently temporal? Further, a consistent application of Pseudo-Dionysian negative theology would place God beyond both time and timelessness. Some texts in fact lend themselves to a nonmetaphysical interpretation of God's eternity. Instead of being interpreted as a timelessness, eternity would be simply a qualifier, not a positive description of God's relation to time. Eternity is simply the divine (sufficient, inclusive, nonidentical) time. This is just the view that the approach from the facticity of redemption requires. The Creativity that is the referent of redemption not only spans the universe (that is, whatever exists) in scope but also in time. It is unimaginable that so many billion years ago, this Creativity began. As the referent of redemption, God's Creativity cannot then be temporally restricted. Yet as a redemptive Creativity God must be temporal in whatever way the task of redemption requires. And this rules out timelessness as a positive attribute that renders a divine activity impossible.

Because of the negations that attend redemption, we cannot interpret the divine temporality by way of human time-consciousness. In self-aware anthropomorphic and liturgical language, we may speak about God remembering, forgetting, anticipating, waiting, and the like. But because finitizing negations must be themselves subjected to negation, neither do we attribute to God "timelessness."

Aim

Is it conceivable that creativity disposes the world in an utterly random way? Can it be an activity indifferent to outcome? We confront here the issue that arose in Hellenic philosophy and that entered the early Christian movement under the term *providence.* When its governing (*gubernatio*) aspect combines with traditional eschatology, world process marches toward a final and assured outcome. I shall take up this issue in connection with the third task of the theology of God, a paradigm of divine activity. I find neither the concept of a final cosmic denouement or completion nor that of an gradual and necessary cosmic progress to be required by the ciphers of redemption. On the other hand, these ciphers do call for a stronger notion of creativity than simply a random process. Redemption itself as founding, love, and justice indicates a creativity that opposes idolatry, alienation, and subjugation. In other words, these ciphers do assign aim or direction to creativity. And if creativity is utterly inclusive (as the qualifiers would have it), then no aspect of created being or world is without aim. However, the negations and qualifiers prevent us from anthropomorphic versions of this cipher that posit a discrete entity that wills things and then causes them to happen.

I have argued that creativity is both a cipher and the name (Creativity) for the referentiality of the ciphers. How does such a view compare with the Thomist identification of God and being and the mystical tradition's claim that God transcends being? These two views may not be in direct opposition. In Anselm's formulation, God as the *per se* or self-existent is necessarily a superlative existence or being (the real) in its fullest sense. This must be the case if that which does not exist through itself (the world, creatures, finitude) exists through God. Insisting on a negative qualifier for every positive term, the mystical tradition does not so much oppose as qualify this view. Does the notion of Creativity as referent and subject of the ciphers depart from the view that God is being? The emphasis of Thomist theology is on the distinction between the actualized perfection of God (being) and the contingent goods of creatures. Critics of this tradition from Charles Hartshorne to Jean-Luc Marion have argued that this distinction results in a "static," inactive, timeless, and unchangeable God. Whether the criticisms hold depends on whether the term *being* is a positive content and applies directly to God's actual being or whether it is primarily a term of negation. If the identification of God and being relates God to the world in structural rather than dynamic terms (for instance, an eternal content of immanent ideas in God in which creatures participate), then the notion of God as Creativity departs from the classical view. God as Creativity is more the child of Plato's *Timaeus* than Plato's *Republic*. However, if we think of being not as substance, structure, or actualized perfection but as process, event, or activity, in other words, as creativity, then it may be the case that God and "being" are identical. But the mystical tradition must have the last word. There can be no direct identification of the nonpresentational God and creativity. As a cipher creativity refers but does not directly describe. As a name, Creativity is the nonreferent referentiality who avoids direct description.

THE HOLY

We come now to the cipher that shatters all ciphers, in which the ciphers gather and disappear. Without this (anti)-cipher, that which comes forth in redemption and obtains symbolic expression would not be God. Since we continue to use language, continue to symbolize, we must acknowledge the cipher character of the Holy. As a cipher it draws from metaphorical fields that express otherness; thus, the divine distance, height, unfathomable depth, ineffability, and even danger. As with all ciphers these metaphors are born in human experience but their function is to undermine the cipher itself. The religious faiths and philosophies of the West express this cipher in such terms as the Holy, the One, the Ungenerated (*agenetos*), transcendence, mystery, and the beyond-being (*hyperousios*). A similar discourse is at work in Eastern faiths. In these terms we confess the failure that attends the bespeaking of God as redemptive and creative. Thus, the negative function of this cipher is to display the poverty of all ciphers. And in the term *the Holy*, the nonpresentational God has found a name. Why is this (anti)-cipher part of a symbolics of God?

The metaphors of otherness that would bring this name to expression can mislead us into thinking that what we have here is a repetition of the negative theology. And we must acknowledge at this point that in the name *the Holy One* we have the apex, so to speak, of the negative theology. As intrinsic to redemption, negations and qualifiers attend the way God comes forth as God. Hence, they chasten and qualify the ciphers of redemption as they point toward and give content to Creativity. And once we understand that it is the very Creativity of the world with which we have to do in redemption, a new phase of negation arises. The theme of a world-disposing Creativity demythologizes the ciphers of redemption because it preempts their tendency to reduce God to the locales and carriers of redemption: the tribe, the people, the nation, or the individual. But Creativity is a cipher that carries with it its own mythologizing tendency to reduce God to *a* being or *an* entity. Negations and qualifiers must attend any account of creativity even as they attend all ciphers. Yet Creativity too calls for demythologizing. We who think of God *as* creativity need a cautionary word concerning the *as.* Does "creativity" capture, express, exhaust God's being? At this point the (anti)-cipher of holiness issues the cautionary word. In this sense, holiness expresses once again the negative theology.

Yet the Holy One is more than negation.[4] It would not be inaccurate to say that holiness expresses the divine otherness. But otherness can be construed as simply differentiation or opposition. If that were the case, our sense of the holiness of God would increase as we differentiated God from all metaphors, ciphers, and contents, including creativity itself. Taken all the way, holiness as utter opposition would no longer name the God who comes forth as God.[5] The human being, we might say, responds to holiness, to God as the Holy One, in postures of amazement, astonishment, and awesomeness. The reason for these responses is not simply the abstract sense of divine otherness, a sense that could arise with struggling with the puzzle of the world. Rather, the sense of holiness increases as we consider how God comes forth as God in redemption. That which awes is not an unfathomable abyss—a cosmic black hole would qualify

---

4. Franz Rosenzweig formulated the complexity of negation as follows: If we acknowledge that God is not reducible to the (redemptive?) symbolism of historical redemption but is first of all the creative vitality of things that far exceeds what is manifest in the symbolism, we have God both as an unthinkable ground and as an unthinkable surplus. In other words, God's reality precedes, succeeds, and far exceeds the symbolics of creation and redemption. This exceeding, this surplus, is what I am trying to express in the cipher, holiness. See *The Star of Redemption*, trans. W. W. Hallo (Boston: Beacon Press, 1964).

5. It is just this possibility of an extreme and undialectical negative theology that Eberhard Jüngel opposes so vigorously. For Jüngel the Pseudo-Dionysian tradition simply identifies God with the contentless dark, hence turns away from the God who is united with perishability (*God as the Mystery of the World*, trans. D. L. Guder [Grand Rapids, Mich.: Wm. B. Eerdmans, 1983], 15).

as that—but an unfathomable, reconciling love, a voice that summons seemingly invincible historical powers to justice, a creativity that knows no bounds. God's otherness is, in other words, God's unswerving aim to (creatively) redeem. The religious community knows no other holiness than this, the awesomeness, the incomparable character of that which creatively disposes the world. This is why the holiness of God is not a mere negation. On the contrary, it is the very Godness of the God who redemptively creates. Before a mere otherness, an abyss, a darkness, we contemplate and perhaps even tremble: before holiness we worship.

The (anti)-cipher of holiness should be differentiated from two similar notions that arise with the mystical tradition of early Christian Platonism. According to the Neoplatonic tradition, God disposes the world through a hierarchy of descending operations. The world obtains order, regularity, beauty, and life through an immanent divine reason (*nous*) and an immanent enlivening movement (*psuche*). Although divine, reason and soul do not exhaust God's being. Both proceed from that which they presuppose, the unfathomable One (*to hen*) that is beyond being. It is not difficult to uncover a formal resemblance between holiness and the unoriginate One of the metaphysics of emanation. In fact, the Eastern church's formulation of the Trinity embodies the motif of descent, distinguishing as it does the unoriginate (compare the One), the logos (compare *nous,* reason), and the Spirit (compare *psuche*). But the (anti)-cipher of holiness is not simply the One of an emanational metaphysical scheme. It is not a cipher that arises with the problem of the God-world relation but rather as the (anti)-cipher of God coming forth as God in an awesome redemptive creativity.

The second notion of the mystical tradition reverses and existentializes the emanational scheme. Its problem is not the relation of God and the world but the salvific ascent to God. That which resembles what I am calling the Holy is the divine dark. Here we have the God beyond God, the God we arrive at only by leaving or transcending the symbolics of God. The rapture of this union is evoked only by leaving redemptive creativity behind. I would not disparage the lives and teachings of the great mystics. I do want to insist that although the (anti)-cipher of holiness does negate, it leaves nothing behind. If "rapture" comes with redemption, it is a rapture before the divine Thou, the redemptive face of God, the Creativity of the world.

A final question: Is holiness a synonym for transcendence? Is this (anti)-cipher a way to formulate the transcendence of God? In spite of the popularity and widespread usage of the terms transcendence and immanence (and the fact that long ago I wrote a book on the subject), I do not find these terms very useful in the theology of God. They invite us to the rather vague task of deciding whether we should emphasize "transcendence" or "immanence," and to easy polemics against one emphasis or the other, all without very precise struggle with the essential ambiguity of these terms. One gets the impression one should be "for" immanence rather than transcendence, or the reverse, or one should subject them to a balancing act. There is a reason why these terms lend themselves to such vague agendas. Used outside of any framework of divine symbolics or a God and world paradigm, these terms are vague to the point of being interchangeable. What do we mean by God's immanence? Is it God's *relation* to the world? Even if that is the case, we must remember that *God's* relationality is something quite unique, other, and incomparable. For what can relate to, create, be present in the world as such but God? As immanent in this way, God is awesome, other, different. As Hartshorne says, to be maximally *related* to the world is to be "surrelative" and this is a transcendence.[6] What would we mean by transcendence? Surely, we would not turn the term over to the spatial literalism of a caricatured popular religion. It thus must mean the divine otherness, uniqueness, awesomeness, but to explicate that is to take up the divine symbolics, the distinctive divine activity in the world, and therefore immanence. Transcendence and immanence seem to be terms more suitable for a liturgical rather than a conceptual discourse, that is, terms for the expression of a sense of God's nearness and a sense of God's "Godness."

UNITY, TRINITY, AND THE SYMBOLICS OF GOD

Our task has been to understand how God's coming forth as God in redemption gives rise to a bespeaking of God, to a theological symbolics. The analysis led to a threefold naming of God as Redeemer, Creativity, and the Holy One. Do we have here a back-way route into a reformulated doctrine of the Trinity? Since I see this triune symbolics as neither a restatement of the classical doctrine nor in discontinuity with it, some clarification is in order.

To take up the question of "the doctrine of the Trinity" is to be launched into the midst of a wide range of attitudes toward and theological accounts of the history and nature of Christian doctrine. A more Catholic posture distinguishes elemental dogmas (mysteries) given to the church

---

6. Charles Hartshorne, *The Divine Relativity: A Social Conception of God* (New Haven: Yale University Press, 1948). Hartshorne is arguing that God's very relativity and relationality is "surrelative" and therefore a kind of transcendence.

to guard and interpret and the particular doctrinal formulations that vary from age to age and thinker to thinker. A more Protestant approach assumes that the great truths of the Christian faith are contained in some form in the Scriptures. One thing seems clear. The more a doctrine (dogma) expresses the universal consensus of a church body (Orthodox, Catholic, Lutheran, and so forth), the more its formulation has a general character and is comprised of negations; thus, for instance, the great ecumenical creeds of the first four centuries. By the same token, the more a doctrinal formulation obtains conceptual preciseness, the more it is the work of an individual author; for instance, Thomas Aquinas or Jonathan Edwards. This principle presses on us the following question: Where is *the* doctrine of the trinity to be found—in the primarily negative (antiheretical) formulaic and liturgical expressions of creeds and confessions, or in the highly variable but specific interpretations of individuals such as Origen, Augustine, Aquinas, John Calvin, or Karl Barth?

According to the ecumenical creeds, God is eternally structured by three hypostases (*personae*) whose distinguishability does not eliminate God's unity. If these are the minimal contents and distinctions of the doctrine, I find no author in the New Testament who thinks of God in that way, even those who think that God was incarnate in Jesus or that the sanctifying Spirit of Pentecost was divine. The early church did inherit a triform baptismal formula from the New Testament but not a concept of a triune hypostatic structure of God. If *individual* formulations of the triune structure of God serve as our benchmark, there are no grounds for speaking of *the* doctrine of the Trinity. Consider the following.

In the first two centuries after the death of Jesus, the Christian movement was occupied with issues raised by the Arians, the outcome being that the Word was consubstantial with the Father. Little attention was given to the relation of the Spirit to God. Even in the fourth century, says R. P. C. Hanson, "The surprising thing is not that more attention was not paid to the Spirit, but that the theologians continued to include the Spirit in the framework of their theology.[7] For one theologian, Marcellus, the Holy Spirit "simply was God in his temporary function as Logos before the incarnation."[8] For certain Egyptian Christians, the Spirit did not name anything fully divine. Responding to these views, Athanasius launched a defense of the Holy Spirit as divine and the Cappadocians completed the project. The stage is thus set to use the triform baptismal liturgy as a

---

7. R. P. C. Hanson, *The Search for the Christian Doctrine of God: The Arian Controversy 318–381* (Edinburgh: T. & T. Clark, 1988), 739.
8. Ibid.

formula for the internal differentiation of the very being of God. In the course of this project, individual theologians (in some cases branches of Christendom) could not agree on (1) what the terms (hypostasis, persona) for distinguishing the persons mean; (2) what precisely distinguishes the persons; (3) the character of the inner relation between the hypostases; and (4) the distinguishing content of the Spirit as one of the persons.

As to the first issue, there was no consensus among theologians about what a hypostasis (the Eastern term, initially resisted by Western theologians) or a *persona* is. This initial nonconsensus plus the burden of what came to be an essentially individual, psychological term (person) pulled both Catholic and Protestant popular religion in the direction of tritheistic understandings. That is, each person is viewed as a center of initiating activity toward other members of the Trinity or toward the world, and as a cultic object each person evokes distinct relations of prayer and piety. Close to this development in popular religion is the fairly widespread theological view that the persons of the Trinity constitute some sort of internal intersubjectivity, a communion of love. When the older meanings of hypostasis and person are transformed into the modern notion of person as a discrete, self-initiating entity, we think of God as a gathering of mutually loving individuals, a view hard to distinguish from the tritheism of popular religion.[9]

As to the second issue, the terms are initially used to express different salvific operations of God. But once these "persons" were thought of as consubstantial with each other, all the attributes and even acts that constitute God had to be applied to all three. This created a new problem of distinguishing the persons, which was solved by affirming the formal relations of unbegotten, begotten, and bestowed. Residing in this formalistic way of distinguishing the persons is the question of what the content or function of each person is other than simply the mode of derivation. For instance, is the Son distinct as the agent of creation? Is the Father distinct as the active source of creation? Such questions pressed patristic theology in the direction of the psychological analogies of Augustine. The formalism of distinguishing the persons by their relations was overcome by positing, analogically, something like a structure of divine consciousness. In spite of this development, there has never been a consensus among individual theologians concerning what specific psychological el-

9. This appears to be the view of Thomas V. Morris, who describes the Trinity as made up of "three divine individuals or persons," thus distinctive individuals whose wills are necessarily in harmony ("God and the World: A Look at Process Theology," in *The Concept of God* [Oxford: Oxford University Press, 1987], chap. 7).

ements (wisdom, love, will, and so forth) are to be identified with each person.

As to how the hypostases are related, there is general agreement that they are identical in that all of the divine attributes apply to all three. A Neoplatonic Christianity sees these "persons" related by way of an eternal derivation. Another view sees them as coinherings of whatever complexities are required if God is personally active or self-revealing. As to the fourth issue, there is little consensus among individual theologians as to what precisely distinguishes the Spirit. At the formal level Eastern and Western churches debate whether the Spirit derives not only from the Father but also from the Son. Beyond this formal level, the Spirit's actual meaning changes from text to text; as that which unifies the Father and Son; as the relation of love between the other persons (Peter Lombard), as will (Aquinas), as that which sanctifies, as that which illumines the Word (Clement) or assists our understanding (Tertullian).[10]

Can we then speak of *the* doctrine of the Trinity? Trinitarian formulas have a central place in the liturgies of Catholic and Protestant Christianity. And the creeds and confessions of various branches of Christendom contain general (formal) and primarily negative trinitarian phrases. At the level of authoritative tradition, the Trinity is primarily a negative criterion, a caution against believing the persons are less than divine and against rank polytheism. At the level of the conceptual interpretations of specific thinkers throughout the history of theology, we have a variety of proposals about what the Trinity means. Instead of a something conceptually specified, Trinity is a kind of blank tablet, an invitation for each new generation of interpreters to say what it means. For example, Karl Barth proffered a rather ingenious proposal that grounds the threefold structure of divine being in the threefold structure of revelation, a view whose very originality suggests that once again the blank tablet has been covered with a new writing. If the Trinity *means* this (or any other specific proposal), then *the* doctrine arises only as the proposal is made. Like the

---

10. A fifth unresolved issue seems to have arisen in the twentieth century, namely, the question of the content of the *symbolism* of each person in the triad. Feminist theology would replace the language of Father and Son. When we look at the history of confession-making in the Presbyterian churches in the last thirty years, we find that "God" has replaced the Father as the first person of the Trinity. ("The Confession of 1967," "A Declaration of Faith," "A Brief Statement of Faith," in *The Constitution of the United Presbyterian Church in the U.S.A.: The Book of Confessions.*) While it is the case that certain theologians of the past have used the term *God* to mean the Father, a convention also present in the apostolic benediction, this confusion in a confessional statement eliminates a genuine trinitarianism. Since God is the one whose being is triadically structured, such a formulation seems to have no first person at all.

Wandering Jew the dogma of the Trinity eternally searches for a conceptual homeland.

This migration of the meanings of the hypostases, the role of the Spirit, and so forth, from one proposal to the next, this millennia-long attempt to translate a symbolics into conceptual specification is not a historical accident. The doctrine of the Trinity arises from and thus attempts to combine two quite different orders. In the one, we try to understand the symbolics of divine redemptive activity, for instance, as taking place through Jesus or in the immediacy of Pentecostal inspiration. In the other we try to solve the problem of how God can be so internally structured as to relate to, create, and redeem the world. Instead of *the* Trinity we have a history of proposals that paste together a redemptive symbolics of God and a more speculative genetics of divine being and activity.

Is the triune symbolics of God as redeemer, creativity, and holiness a reinterpretation of *the* doctrine of the Trinity, another attempt to fill the blank tablet? I must acknowledge a certain resemblance between the three ciphers or names of God and at least some versions of the doctrine of the Trinity. Holiness could resemble the ineffable, unoriginate of Neoplatonic Christianity. Creativity rings of the ancient *logos* theology, and concrete redemptive founding could be said to be the work of the Spirit. It is thus tempting to exploit the migratory character of the doctrine of the Trinity and claim that this triune symbolism resolves the general and formal language of the creeds into a specific interpretation. To make that work, I would have to construe the three ciphers as "hypostases" or "persons" and I would have no idea what it would mean to say that. I begin then by acknowledging that this analysis does not coincide with the triune hypostatic structure of the God of the creeds. In the sense of being a referent, the analysis has only one "hypostasis," God as Creativity. Redemption gathers ciphers that describe the character of that hypostasis and holiness attests its Godness. Nor are these ciphers related by way of a structure of generation (begetting) whereby two of the ciphers are eternally spawned by the primordial hypostasis. Nor do the three ciphers organize psychological analogies for the divine internal complexity, which is a necessary condition of divine activity.

On the other hand this triune account of divine names is in continuity with at least some elements in the classical trinitarian doctrine. First, the emergence of ciphers from the facticity of redemption parallels the way the "persons" arise in the "economy" of salvation. Second, one of the issues posed by the classical symbol is whether or not God is to be internally differentiated, whether there is an immanent complexity to God.

Internal differentiation is implied in the dramatic, active, and empathic metaphors for God in Hebrew religion. Showing the influence of the Platonic tradition, late patristic and medieval Christian theology (although retaining the trinitarian Symbol) had doubts about any internal complexity in God. However philosophically satisfying this notion of divine simplicity was, it was a poor vehicle for expressing the active and reactive God of redemption. Plotinus and other Platonists responded to the problem with an emanational version of divine differentiation that was highly influential on the Christian movement. Because of the "Hebraic" strain of the Christian movement and the fact that its God was from the beginning the God of redemption, it had strong reasons for some version of the divine internal differentiation. Neoplatonic emanation, eternal processions in God, offered one of these versions; thus, God as unbegotten, begotten, and bestowed. The psychological analogies of Augustine was another.

Insofar as the trinitarian Symbol means a notion of internal differentiation in God, my analysis is in continuity with that Symbol. Accordingly, God is a world-disposing Creativity whose creative activities have a redemptive character. As such God is a self-active, self-differentiated, empowering love. What I have not done is what trinitarian proposals try to do, namely, show that God's internally differentiated structure coincides with the threefold liturgical formula of Father, Son, and Spirit, a task that calls for great inventiveness and not a little bit of speculation.

A final question: Do we have in this symbolics of God a "monotheism" versus a "polytheism"? My initial response is that these terms as well as the distinction itself arise from a perspective external to religious faith. The observer notes that some "religions" worship many deities and other religions worship one deity. When the distinction is fostered by a religious faith, it tends to serve a polemical and empirical orientation; that is, an aim to displace the God or Gods of another religion with its own God or Gods. In the religions themselves the situation is more fluid and unstable. Religions that experience and symbolize the sacred as a multiplicity of powers tend to see each power as dangerous, awesome, and worshipful because it is connected with Power itself and is a manifested or regional form of sacred power. Religions that attest to the sacred as a single power tend to develop multiple symbolisms of the presence and operation of that power; thus, "persons" of a trinity, multiple names, or a hierarchy of mediators. The reason for this fluidity and ambiguity is that the sacred resists typological distribution into either a one or a many. God (sacred power, Creativity) names neither an entity (*a* being) nor a plurality of entities. Insofar as religions of a plurality of powers and religions of the single name sense this, the resulting demythologizing places sacred power beyond numbers. For instance, we must literalize and mythologize Olympian religion to make it a "polytheism" and we must literalize and mythologize Hebraic religion to make it into a "monotheism." The resulting argument is thus between two mythological literalisms, the divine as one (entity) and the divine as many (entities).

The problem here is the metaphorical character of both number and of the concept of unity when applied to the nonpresentational God. Unity (oneness, singleness) is part of a formal system of meanings that assists human beings to interpret and function in the everyday world. Thus we use the concept of unity to sort out entities from each other (for example, apples and oranges), to identify *an* entity in spacetime, to grasp how multiple aspects of an entity are mobilized toward an actualization or aim, and to grasp certain inclusivities (*genera*, cooperations, aggregates) by which entities are compared or contextualized. None of these unities applies directly to God. God is not one, does not have singularity, in any of these senses. Popular religion that lacks a self-demythologizing element may be "monotheistic" or "polytheistic" insofar as it suppresses the metaphorical character of number and thinks of the sacred as *an* entity, or *a* person with mental processes. I conclude then that the ciphers of divine symbolics refer neither to a single nor a multiple entity but express Creativity that is neither one nor many.

PART THREE

THEOLOGY OF GOD AND WORLD

11
METAPHYSICS AND ITS CRITICS

"My mother is like old George the Third," said the Vicar, "She objects to metaphysics."

George Eliot, Middlemarch

But here, if anywhere, this question cannot be avoided, since religion loses its nerve when it ceases to believe that it expresses in some way truth about our relation to a reality beyond ourselves which ultimately concerns us. It is more possible for other forms of thought and expression, such as art and science, to go on doing their specific work without raising metaphysical questions. Religion, when its implications are thought out, must raise them in an acute way.

Dorothy M. Emmett, The Nature of Metaphysical Thinking

Facing us now is the third task of the theology of God, thinking the relation between the world and God or, to express it differently, constructing a paradigm of the divine activity. The great texts of the past that attempt this sort of thing work from a proposed root metaphor: final causality (Aristotle), inclusive organism (Charles Hartshorne), procession (Plotinus), sovereign rule (John Calvin), preestablished harmony (Gottfried Leibniz). These constructions vary in the extent to which they subject the root metaphor to conceptual elaboration. Such elaboration is minimal in Calvin and extensive in Plotinus, Leibniz, and Hartshorne. With conceptual elaboration, the metaphor takes on the character of a paradigm; that is, it brings a wide variety of concepts into coherent relation. These concepts include but go beyond the ciphers of the bespeaking of God. Because the task is a thinking of the world and God together, the concepts must also include history, nature (life), and cosmos. Accordingly, thinking the relation of the world and God is always more than metaphor construction. For insofar as the metaphor is appropriate, defensible, or illuminating, it must interpret not just the divine activity but the "the way the world is." To establish, clarify, and express the coherence of the metaphor, for instance, that of sovereign rule or organic inclusion, is inevitably a conceptual task. Thinking the relation of God and the world tends to involve paradigm as well as metaphor construction.

The paradigm constructions of Western thought from Plato to Alfred North Whitehead constitute a metaphysical tradition (ontotheology) whose very possibility is brought into question by David Hume, Immanuel Kant, Martin Heidegger, Anglo-American empiricism and pragmatism, and deconstruction. According to Kant, such an endeavor is at best an "empirical synthesis," and the "synthesis of all possible things in general" must always remain an ideal rather than an accomplishment of reason.[1] When reason attempts to think such matters as the origin, composition, or direction of the cosmos at the level of "absolute completeness" or the absolutely unconditioned, it only arrives at antinomies. In the wake of Kant has come a theological or religophilosophical literature (Søren Kierkegaard, Paul Ricoeur, Martin Buber, and other Jewish thinkers) that more or less abandons the task of thinking the relation of God and the world. We have, in other words, not simply an issue between variant philosophies—for instance, deconstructionists and process thought—but between theology (insofar as it takes up this task) and antimetaphysical philosophy. We must acknowledge, then, that this third task of the theology of God is to many contemporary theologians neither legitimate nor important.

In earlier chapters, I broached this issue in a general way by articulating the face-off between the classical Catholic theology of God and varieties of anti-theism. I must now assess this confrontation and explore the possibility of mediating what appears to be an unnegotiable rift. On the one side are those who are persuaded that some form of metaphysics (Platonic, Thomist, Whiteheadian) is both possible and necessary for the theology of God. On the other side are those who have announced "the end of metaphysics" and for whom to attach metaphysics to theology is like throwing an anchor to a drowning person. I have attempted to get beyond the impasse of ontotheology and anti-theism by means of an account of how God redemptively comes forth as God (Chapter 5) and by a theological symbolics determined by that coming forth (Part Two). I move now to a third attempt to get beyond the impasse, focusing now on anti-

---

1. Immanuel Kant, *Critique of Pure Reason*, trans. N. K. Smith (London: Macmillan and Co., 1961), 385.

theism's refusal to think the relation of God and the world. I shall explore this stand-off in three steps; a review of the matter from the side of classical Catholic theology and contemporary process philosophy, a case for the task of thinking the relation between God and the world, and a review of issues between antimetaphysics and metaphysics.

METAPHYSICS IN CLASSICAL AND NEOCLASSICAL THEOLOGIES OF GOD

The classical Catholic theology of God and process theology are usually thought of as opponents. In its Whiteheadian form, process thought substitutes process, temporality, eventfulness, and novelty for the conceptual apparatus of ancient philosophy. At the very center of the Hartshornian form of process thought is a severe criticism of the classical theistic tradition. Yet from the perspective of religiophilosophical anti-theism, classical and neoclassical (process) theisms are up to the same thing, the formulation of a coherent conceptuality of God in the framework of an objective, metaphysical account of what it means for anything to exist.

Closely examined, the classical Catholic view is not a pristine, clear, and unambiguous conceptual accomplishment easy to dismiss out of hand. Reducing this theology of God to the provinciality of a discredited historical epoch is one way of effecting this dismissal. If this past epoch is discredited, and if the classical Catholic view is simply epochal, it hardly needs philosophical criticism. Historical observation will do. Whatever validity this theology of God may have had is an epochal validity; that is, a contribution to the needs and problems of the Middle Ages. In spite of the criticisms of the Catholic theology of God by process thought that exploit its ambiguities in the direction of a hardened or "metaphysical" notion of divine immutability, the classical theology poses issues that stubbornly refuse to go away. We have in these texts a legacy of God as a problem of thinking and conceptuality. The bespeaking of God does not float automatically out of biblical texts or religious experience, but passes through the task of thinking. Even if the so-called "proofs" for God's existence are not persuasive as objective demonstrations, they do offer a way to differentiate God from that which has its being through God. And with this differentiation came the negative theology and its cautions against anthropomorphisms and mythologies of God of popular theism. Further, the differentiation of God from the world displays the most general ontological feature of the world, namely, the world's non-self-dependence, its need for a positive operation of God in order to exist. This tradition has also taught us that the world's non-self-dependence and God's positive operation are connected in some way with the task of explicating a symbolics of God. To summarize, the theology of God may imperil itself if it ignores the legacy of these classical texts. Process theology would address this task by way of a departure from classical Thomism, but it has not eschewed the legacy of these issues. At the same time, for process thought, the central task is the explication of God's relation to the world not the derivation of God's attributes.

The symbolics of God and a God-and-world paradigm are legacies from the classical Catholic theology of God. For that theology the importance and possibility of these tasks was self-evident. Taking place in a period in which metaphysics is repudiated by most other philosophies, process thought has had to argue the case for metaphysics and has had to address those historical circumstances that have converged to render discourse about God meaningless.[2] The process theologians are less concerned about rational demonstrations of God's existence—although some such as Hartshorne have addressed this issue—than with rendering the concept of God credible, that is to say, coherent. They have little sympathy with approaches that sneak God through the back door of nihilism or build faith and its symbols on the despair and emptiness of modern life. They do take such things seriously, but they focus on one strand of the modern situation, the apparent incoherence of any and all notions of God to postmoderns.[3]

To render the concept of God coherent, process thought appropriates a metaphysical scheme (Whitehead) that both relates God to the world of modern sciences and arrives at an internally consistent concept of God. In so doing it tends to minimize the first and second tasks of the theology of God, an account of the way God redemptively comes forth as God and the symbolics internal to that coming forth. Process thought tends to begin and end with the problem of a coherent concept of God's activity in the world. As a necessary instrument in specifying this activity, meta-

---

2. David Pailin argues this point. See *God and the Processes of Reality* (London: Routledge, 1989), chaps. 1 and 2.

3. Process thought as an *apologia* underwent a shift of emphasis from its first generation (A. N. Whitehead, Charles Hartshorne) to recent decades. The primary concern of Hartshorne was to correct the metaphysical incoherence of classical Christian theism. Although all process thinkers concur in this criticism of classical Christian theism and oppose in its place an alternate metaphysics, its present representatives are more centrally concerned with movements of culture for whom God language is meaningless or marginal. See John Cobb, *A Christian Natural Theology* (Philadelphia: Westminster Press, 1965), 13–14; Pailin, *God*, chap. 1; Marjorie Suchocki, *God, Christ, and Church: A Practical Guide to Process Theology* (New York: Crossroad, 1982); David R. Griffin, ed., *God and Religion in the Postmodern World: Essays in Postmodern Theology* (Albany: SUNY, 1989).

physics is present at the very beginning. In this respect process thought resembles the classical Catholic theology of God. In the process view, no coherent articulation of God's operation in the world is possible without metaphysics. The reason is that the object of metaphysics, the necessary features of any possible world and the most general features of this world, is the condition of thinking itself. If God means that apart from which nothing else can be, to bespeak God as a coherent concept must involve an account of what that "everything else" is and the way that "what" depends on God. The process theologians are quick to acknowledge that philosophy of religion is not a substitute for worship, for relation to God in faith. Their point is that if we prefer coherent bespeaking of God to contradictory, vague, and muddled discourse, then a metaphysical explication is unavoidable.

METAPHYSICS AND THE THEOLOGY OF GOD

The classical Catholic theology of God and process theology are prominent examples of approaches to God that require the explication of general features of "what there is" or metaphysics. Under the term *anti-theism* I reviewed thinkers for whom the employment of metaphysics in theology is a serious mistake. Given its Hebraic roots and its dependence on the facticity of redemption, how did the Christian movement's liaison with metaphysics ever take place? We can construe this as either a historical or theological question. As a historical question, it invites studies of the strategic responses, co-options, and polemics of the early Christian movement to Platonic, Stoic, and other philosophies of its time. As a theological question, it invites us to explore what there is about the Christian version of the redemptive coming forth of God as God that presses its thinking toward metaphysics. I do not venture to interpret this "pressing toward" as an inevitable development as if metaphysics were an *a priori* element in faith or theology. Yet those who have appropriated metaphysics for the task of theology have reasons for doing so that go beyond an appeal to past tradition or matters of taste. Four of these reasons come to mind.

First, the theology of God is never sheer, imaginative proposal. It arises with a historically and culturally formed religious community and therefore works from legacies of world interpretation, liturgical symbols, social corruptions, and various "grammars" of language. Any specific theology of God will inevitably reflect all of these things. At the same time, the theology of God is ever a critical response, an assessment and an imaginative construction that transcends the entangled web fostered by the past. Such transcendence is called for not only because of the corrupted and fallible past, but because theology interprets its ever-changing situations under an inexhaustible mystery. Theology inherits from the past both a symbolics of God and ways of drawing symbols together into an interpretation of God's relation to the world; for instance, as a sovereign rule or as an external intervention. Present in the ordinary language of piety, biblical stories, hymnody, and preaching are overt and covert ways of thinking how God relates to the world. If the theology of God ignores this legacy and situation, it repudiates a certain service it could render to the religious community, the subjecting of prevailing metaphors, paradigms, and modes of understanding to critical review. If it does take up this critical task, it will find itself faced with questions concerning "how the world works," or how this sort of world could be an environment of divine activity.

Second, with the facticity of redemption comes a designation of the meaning of God that launches thinking toward further specification. Earlier on I argued that in redemptive founding that which was only an empty horizon of desire took on specific content as corrupted human passions were released into freedom. This move to content (specification) is what makes the symbolics of God possible. I also argued that the reference of this symbolics, the *what*, was a world-disposing Creativity, related to human agents as a founding creativity, to the interhuman as a reconciling creativity, and to the social as an emancipating creativity. I further argued that to found, reconcile, and serve as a criterion of justice, Creativity could have no regional or temporal limitation. God as Creativity cannot be reduced to what is creatively at work in a specific nation, individual, or epoch. This means that as Creativity, God's operation extends to whatever exists. Whatever the "world" is specifically, it is the environment and outcome of that Creativity. And this is what summons the theology of God to a second specification, which goes beyond the thinking of specific symbolic contents to a thinking of God (Creativity) and the world. Even as the facticity of redemption prevents theology from thinking of God as a contentless vacuity but presses theology to explicate and assess the metaphors and ciphers that arise with redemption, so it prompts theology to explicate or think God's relation to the world.

We have reviewed two reasons why theology is pressed toward metaphysics. The third reason is the irrepressible wonder that attends human freedom. Here we ask, How is it that thinking God and the world calls for metaphysics? In *Good and Evil* I offered some illustrations of what happens in the transition from the hold of idolatry to redemptive free-doms. In one of those transitions, the human desire for the real (the "cog-nitive eros") is transformed from self-securing modes of certainty and scepticism to wonder.[4] This wonder is the cognitive eros freed from nar-rowed, reality-denying "knowledge" and opened onto the endless mys-tery and beauty of the world. Wonder is what gives agential redemption a world-participating rather than a world-denying orientation. In wonder we are oriented to whatever form, sense, or dimensionality the real takes. The real thus is never a given totality. To claim cognitive access to and comprehension of the absolute conditions of the world is not wonder's way. This is because that which opens wonder to the real is the "mystery of the world," whose concrete operations are never available to our cogni-tive processes. In wonder we are open to totality, not as a given or a manifestation, but as a horizon. But it is just this wonder, limited as it is, that prompts us to bespeak the world not as an autonomous aggregate of things but as that of which God is the mystery. Shaped by wonder the theology of God is pressed beyond the symbolics of God to the world's very constitution and to a thinking of God in relation to that.

A fourth reason presses theology toward the problem of God's relation to the world. I maintained earlier that theodicy in its narrow and techni-cal sense was an intrinsic element in the classical Catholic theology of God. The narrow problem of theodicy arises when we try to affirm to-gether the reality of evil, God's perfect goodness, and all-determining power. Does this mean that some forms of the theology of God avoid the theodicy problem? This seems to be the case if theodicy is reduced to the conundrum created by the above three elements. Yet a kind of theodicy task arises simply with the coming forth of God in redemption. As the one who founds, God paradoxically reduces the desperate and idolatrous insistence on securing foundations. Redemptive existence is then a way the human being exists toward suffering and toward its own tragic condi-tion. Yet since the one who founds cannot be any specific, regional power (idol), its operation is without limit. It is the Creativity at work in the mystery of the world. No rationalistic theodicy problem is promulgated by these notions. Yet, in the order of *Existenz*, there does arise the existen-tial question of the status of suffering in a world disposed by Creativity. This is not the "why me" question born from a perplexed resentment that assumes that God as all-powerful could have prevented the catastrophe.

4. *Good and Evil: Interpreting a Human Condition* (Minneapolis: Fortress Press, 1990), chap. 11.

It is a "why" question that would discover the relation of suffering to Creativity. In this broader sense, a kind of theodicy task does arise with the facticity of redemption, and once arisen it presses the theology of God to a thinking of how God is active in world.

CHARGES AND REJOINDERS

I have reviewed some reasons why the theology of God includes questions of God and the world and with that whatever metaphysical inquiries that would respond to those questions. Yet we must acknowledge the opposition to metaphysics that has been part of the Christian movement since the time of the Reformation.[5] Fueling this opposition have been *sola Scriptura*, post-Kantian polemics against totality-oriented, objectivist metaphysics, varieties of empiricism, and liberation and feminist theologies that see antimetaphysics as a way to expose the patriarchalism and hierarchicalism of classical modes of thought. I cannot do justice to the extent, subtlety, and depth of these criticisms. Yet I cannot simply pursue this third task of the theology of God as if these criticisms were irrelevant. I would assume neither that business is as usual with "metaphysics" nor that a theological battle of Waterloo has occurred leaving anti-theism utterly victorious.[6] On at least three issues, anti-theism and metaphysics do not appear to be in direct conflict.

Before taking up these issues, I shall try to set aside what seem to be two pseudoissues. The first is the charge that theologians who appropriate metaphysics—for instance, process thinkers—displace faith, religion, or revelation with "natural theology." I have criticized approaches that so privilege the God-and-world problem as to pass over the first two tasks of the theology of God. But this privileging is not necessarily a denial of redemption or revelation. The issue thus is not between "metaphysics" and "theology" but between two cognitive styles of pursuing theology. The second pseudoissue has to do with concepts and conceptualizations. As far as I know, no metaphysically oriented theology of God utterly repudiates metaphors or pretends to conceptualize the being and reality of God, nor does any anti-theism and fideism that I know avoid

---

5. For an older and polemical description of various types of "antimetaphysics," see R. J. Collingwood, *An Essay on Metaphysics* (Oxford: Clarendon Press, 1940), Part 2.

6. For an older account (1945) of the malaise of metaphysics, see Dorothy Emmett, *The Nature of Metaphysical Thinking*, chap. 1. For Emmett, metaphysics is a kind of analogical thinking that takes concepts that presumably function in ordinary experience to throw light on reality and compares these concepts to various enterprises that make claims about reality, the sciences, for instance (2, 3).

concepts and conceptualization. I turn now to three issues that seem to create an unbridgeable chasm between anti-theism and metaphysically oriented theology: objectification, totality (including autonomy), and substantialism.

Objectification

A basic conviction of antimetaphysical theology is that relation to God and the discourse proper to that relation take place not in the order of objectification but in orders of *Existenz*, the personal, praxis, or relation.[7] Accordingly, it would seem that metaphysical theologians "objectify" God and nonmetaphysical theologians do not. Because of the ambiguity of object, objective, and objectification, however, this opposition is far from clear. Objectification can be a code word for foundationalism, the attempt to think God in the order of general "rational" evidences. But Thomists and process theologians may or may not think such an endeavor is possible or very important. The process aim at conceptual coherence may not be constructed on a foundationalist claim.

Objectification may also refer to an empiricism in which reality means the discrete, quantifiable, testable, and measurable units of the sciences. But process philosophy arose in the first place as a criticism of that empiricism (compare Whitehead's fallacy of misplaced concreteness); nor could we ever say that the classical Catholic theology objectifies God in this sense. Objectification can also mean what happens when God is simply subjected to third-person discourse, an act that transfers God from the sphere of Thou (face, address, Between) to the sphere of It. What is intrinsically relational is turned into a content. We must acknowledge that discourse does bring about such a transition. Accordingly, theology constantly struggles with the deicide that ever imperils any and all bespeaking of God. Theology counters this potential betrayal by means of the negative theology, poetics, indirect communication, reflexive philosophical styles, and of late deconstruction. However heroically they are carried out, these ploys do not prevent the transition from taking place. At best they express the tragic loss or destruction of God as God in the bespeaking of God. With the exception of the languages of logic and mathematics, this destruction is only the most severe instance of a tragic loss that comes with all language that would bespeak *Existenz* in its concreteness or in fact anything that is actual. Insofar as God is not an utter

7. For a brief and sympathetic account of the criticisms of theological objectivism, see Claude Geffré, "Non-Metaphysical Theology," in Johannes B. Metz, ed., *New Questions on God* (New York: Herder and Herder, 1972).

vacuity, in other words, is bespoken at all, God will have some discursive content. If objectification attends any and all bespeaking of God, it seems to be as much a part of antimetaphysical as of metaphysical theologies of God.

Do the criticisms of objectification undermine the ideal of coherence stressed in process theology? Coherence has the character of a categorial ideal, a kind of paradigm of reason, that presides over a theology of God. One of these paradigms is an extreme and confident rationalism whose systematizing lust would violate the mystery, density, and novelty of the real. Yet coherence need not be something merely imposed on the world. Except for certain kinds of human babbling, the merely incoherent has no existence in actuality. To exist at all requires a certain degree of successful inheritance from and continuity with the past, a synthesis of enough inherited traits to enable the entity to function, however momentarily, in its environment. This is why "world," inevitably a constructed and perspectival notion, is not simply a mirroring of subjectivity. One could not even establish the fact and "truth" of perspectives and constructions without presupposing certain syntheses and interrelations of what is actual. Furthermore, it would be peculiar to acknowledge this minimal and inevitable element of coherence in what is actual and then propose that the Creativity that disposes and redeems the world is somehow incoherent. Such a view would undermine all discourse of God as love, justice, or creativity. Further, the thematizing and analytic thinking inevitable in a theology of God does not take place *as* a Thou relation, *Existenz*, or face, but in the third-person relations of the it-world. However much they are determined to avoid the idolatries of objectification, the writings of antitheists, as writings, are objectifying activities. As writings, they are not face, *Existenz*, or relation. They objectify by thematization, differentiation of theme, linear development of thought, appeal to evidences, and the selection of one word usage over another. To expose that which disrupts the objective, they must enter and dwell in the objectifying sphere.

The issue of objectification is closely related to the now universally despised "God of the gaps." The case against the "God of the gaps" seems foolproof. The "God of the gaps" is a code word for a device that would insert God into some sphere of inquiry to "explain" a yet unsolved puzzle. In its crudest form this device is directed to not-yet solved puzzles of the sciences; for instance, the origin of life. It can also be a code word for foundationalism; that is, any attempt to argue in a metatheological way for God as world-ground. On the other hand, we should avoid letting our fear of this device preempt all discourse about God as Creativity or

God's relation to the world. I have argued that such discourse originates in the way God redemptively comes forth as God, not in scientific or ontotheological puzzles about the world. When this origin is suppressed, the resulting either-or seems to be a "God of the gaps" speculation or an utter repudiation of any and all relation of God and the world. Without a rootage in the way God comes forth as God, all God-and-world discourse seems to be a gap-filling maneuver.

So we confront the issue. *Is* all God-and-world discourse an exploitation of scientific unknowns, of yet-to-be-solved empirical problems? To say yes is to christen science as the omnicompetent arbiter of reality before whom the very mystery of the world itself will eventually fall. So arises then a new foundationalism that would replace God with the alternative "ultimate" explanations of astrophysics. In face of such a possibility, we cannot avoid asking whether the mystery of the world is itself a "gap." If the oxymoron of an "empirical metaphysics" prompts an affirmative answer, the implication is that the very existence of the world is a problem solvable by experimental and mathematical strategies. Stated this way the issue is between science itself as a metaphysics and nonscientific or philosophical metaphysics. The theology of God does not begin with either alternative but with the facticity of redemption. The God of redemption, Creativity, is not the God of gaps but of the mystery of the world. There is thus an incompatibility between the theology of God and any discourse that empties the world of that mystery.

Totality

Antimetaphysical theology's second charge against theologies of God that retain metaphysical elements finds expression in the code word, totality.[8] The issue goes back to Kant's distinction between concepts that synthesize (generalize) what appears empirically and concepts of "unconditioned totality" that express the "conditions of all possible things in general." In Kant's view the latter concepts are either *ideals* of reason, though not the products of its work, or expressions of transcendental subjectivity. Totality thus ever eludes reason's attempt to objectively grasp

---

8. Kant does appear to be the originator of the concept of totality as it now functions in twentieth-century Jewish and other philosophies. Pure reason begins with particularity but eventually demands "absolute totality." But what pure reason actually attains is a set of antinomies (*Critique of Pure Reason*, trans. N. K. Smith [London: Macmillan and Co., 1961], 385). Stephen Toulmin identifies two stances toward totality, one that extrapolates specific entities or features to totality, the other a skepticism about totality or a belief that religion, not science, delivers it. He would find a middle way between the two (*Return to Cosmology* [Berkeley: University of California Press, 1982]).

it. Franz Rosenzweig gave this theme an existential twist. He pressed a different question: Why must human beings pretend to have access to, know, and conceptualize a totality they do not in fact possess? His answer is that the human pretension to possess totality is a way of struggling with the fear of death. Totality pretensions show a false consciousness, a diseased reason (*apoplexia philosophia*) rooted in the human incapability of existing amidst a death-structured finitude. To cognitively penetrate the world totality (*die Allheit der Welt*) is to place all, explain all, and inter-relate all, including death itself. But what human beings are actually given is not unconditioned totality but manifestations that display them-selves against a background that shades off into the unknown. In other words, we are given cognitive location and perspective, not penetration of the all.[9]

Emmanuel Levinas continues this theme but gives the existential ele-ment a social, historical twist. He agrees that pretensions to totality con-tain a self-securing element. Thus he correlates pretension to totality with human autonomy. But human autonomy is not simply a matter of indi-vidual *Existenz*. When the human being remains simply in the circle of its biological, psychological, and social dynamics, unchallenged and un-disrupted by what Levinas calls the face of the other, it perpetrates not simply protections against death but death itself in the form of war. Pre-tension to totality is not then an innocent cognitive curiosity but an alter-native to the one thing (the face) that can summon the human being out of its socially oppressive, war-making autonomy.[10] Jean-Luc Marion con-tinues this quarrel with totality under the rubric of being.

Do these powerful polemics against philosophies of totality (metaphys-ics) undermine any and all metaphysical elements in the theology of God? More specifically, is it self-evident that the use of Plato or Whitehead in the theology of God is an exercise in idolatry, autonomy, and social oppression? The matter is surely more complicated than this face-off of two apparently exclusive views. Few would question the claim that patriarchal, hierarchical, and ethnocentric elements in the classical Catholic theology of God legitimated centuries of sexist, anti-Judaic, and class oppressions. I only note at this point that no religious faith, however

9. See Franz Rosenzweig, *The Star of Redemption*, trans. W. W. Hallo (Boston: Beacon Press, 1964), 5–6; and *Understanding the Sick and the Healthy: A View of World, God, and Man*, trans. N. W. Glätzer (New York: Noonday, 1953). This English title is misleading, obscuring the phrase in the German title, that speaks of "sick and healthy reason."

10. See Emmanual Levinas, *Totality and Infinity: An Essay on Exteriority*, trans. A. Lingis (Pittsburgh: Duquesne University Press, 1961), 21–40. For a connecting of Levinas's critique of totality with feminist concerns, see Wendy L. Farley, *Eros for the Other: Retaining Truth in a Pluralistic World* (University Park.: Pennsylvania State University Press, 1996).

metaphysical or antimetaphysical, that has obtained institutionalization and interpretive traditions has ever avoided being a vehicle of oppressions. Furthermore, there are powerful elements in the classical theology and in process theology, even in their metaphysics, that explicate antioppression criteria. These empirical and historical ambiguities call for a closer examination.

First, speculative efforts (for instance, Plato, G. W. F. Hegel, Whitehead) to think the determinate in relation to more general concepts may well end up in antinomies, promote postures of autonomy, displace spheres of face, Thou, faith, and *Existenz*. At the same time, these general criteria may also serve to summon human societies beyond their provincial aims, their self-absolutizations that end up in the bloodbaths of war. Human societies are pushed toward conflict, war, and oppression not only by totality thinking but by self-absolutizing provincialism.

Second, is the pretension of a cognitive mastery of or penetration of world totality the specific possession of "metaphysics"? The grand metaphysical schemes of Western history may have a more nuanced sense of the mystery of the world than cognitive movements that would repudiate totality and metaphysics under what seems to be unrevisable and even unformulated notions of reality and knowledge: thus, behaviorist psychology, social Darwinism, or certain kinds of Marxism.

Third, let us grant to Buber the irreducibility of the primary word, I-Thou, in the sphere of the human and the sphere of faith, and let us grant to Levinas that only the face can summon the human being out of the enclosure of autonomy. Do these primacies eliminate the sphere of I-it, the issues of human-world relation, and phenomenological, linguistic, and scientific efforts to understand and bespeak such things? Even if face is not a product of the human structure of intentionality, does it thereby displace that structure? These questions are of course rhetorical. The writings of Buber and Levinas are filled with just such ontological analyses. Why is it, then, that the affirmation of the primacy of *Existenz*, the interhuman, and the face *displace* wider, generic analyses of nature, history, or world? To pursue such analyses as if they were adequate to the bespeaking of the human being, its redemption, or God, would falsely displace what is primary. But it is not clear why world-generic analyses simply forbid or exclude existential and interhuman primacies.

Substantialism

Along with objectivity and totality, substance and substantialism have become code words of antimetaphysics. And like objectivity and totality, substantialism summarizes a serious critical reaction to metaphysics.

Having said this we find ourselves forced to make some distinctions. Forgetting some of its meanings in Hellenic philosophy, some see substance as some sort of "stuff," a notion now replaced by modern science. But in the history of philosophy a substance (*ousia*) can be any specific thing that has properties, a term for what specific things share, a term for primary genres or types of things, and a formal term for being. Since ordinary and even scientific language has equivalent terms for all of these older meanings of substance, it would be an exaggeration to say that now we have gotten beyond "substance."

At the same time, we must acknowledge that substance is also a code word for an aspect of ancient Western philosophy that modern philosophies strongly oppose. In this opposition, substantialism means a view of "being" as a static, hierarchical structure. This is not to say that Plato or Aristotle saw the world as without change. Plato's demythologizing of the ancient theogony resulted in a quasimythological picture of a perpetual *becoming* in which chaos is at least partially and perpetually ordered.[11] Twentieth-century interpretations of Plato (Henri Bergson, Nicholas Berdyaev, Whitehead, Hartshorne) accuse him of being "substantialist" partly because he identifies being or the real with order, with the unchanging constitutive ideas that are the referents of genuine knowledge, and partly because the world is simply this endless struggle of order and chaos, or the perpetual in-forming of matter. Omitted in this "Platonism" is genuine novelty in which even structures themselves undergo transformation. Put this way, substantialism not only names a criticism of metaphysics by antimetaphysics but is an issue between *types* of metaphysics.

Deconstructive antimetaphysics is not just a restatement of Kant, the fate of pure reason under unconditioned totality, nor is its concern the distortions that arise when thinking is severed from *Existenz*. Nor is it satisfied by metaphysical corrections, as, for instance, those of process thought. For deconstruction all metaphysics including philosophy itself is "substantialist." Here the term is given another twist yet. Substantialism is any attempt to think a content in a straightforward way, to trace language back to what simply presents itself. Substance here means any and all intended and linguistically expressed presence. Yet all presentings take place in the form of masks and suppressions. For all linguistically expressed presences, simply because they are expressed, suppress the oppositions they carry with them, the multidimensional historical layers of meaning, and the "play of difference" that destabilizes fixed mean-

---

11. This more dynamic way of thinking of world is the theme of Plato's *Timaeus*.

ing.[12] Philosophical deconstruction is a willing ally of historical, social, and feminist deconstruction because the suppressed historical layers of meaning disguise how power structures have disposed language. Thus, for deconstruction, a process metaphysics is substantialist insofar as it fixes the world into a conceptual scheme, even the conceptual scheme of novelty.

As opposed by process thought, substantialism is any view that privileges structure over novelty. As opposed by deconstruction, substantialism is the suppression of the hidden oppositions and instabilities of meaning and presence. In the first case, we do not have an abolishment but a correction of metaphysics. Does deconstruction effect such an abolishment?[13] The antinomy that arises with all would-be abolishers of metaphysics prompts us to say no. To establish in a positive way that any and all accounts of world totality are impossible can only take place in the form of a totality argument. Something about knowledge as such, world as such, the human situation as such, conspires to bring forth this impossibility. Deconstruction thus has the same relation to metaphysics that it has to other linguistic ventures. It exposes, destabilizes, and opens up language. Doing this toward the law does not eliminate law. Nor are the arts, sciences, or theology eliminated by historical or linguistic deconstruction. To be a cultural assassin, even an ontocide, deconstruction would have to turn into its own opposite either in the form of an empirical critique of empirical undertakings, or a metaphysical (totalizing) interpretation of what language, world, and human beings "really" are.

Objectification, totality, and substantialism have all drawn the fire of antimetaphysical criticism. At the same time all of the antimetaphysical critics draw on and therefore do not abandon ideals of coherence, appeals to manifest evidences, and differentiation of meanings. Have they then eliminated metaphysics? I shall take up this question in the following chapter.

---

12. See Jacques Derrida, "Différance," in *Margins of Philosophy*, trans. A. Bass (Chicago: University of Chicago Press, 1982), 1–27.
13. Jacques Derrida rejects the possibility of an absolute break with or elimination of metaphysics. Even to use signs at all is to retain a metaphysical element (*Positions* [Chicago: University of Chicago Press, 1981]), 17, 36

12
ON THE WAY TO A PARADIGM

> Never known as anything
> but an absence, I dare not name him
> as God. Yet the adjustments
> are made. There is an unseen
> power, whose sphere is the cell
> and the electron. We never catch
> him at work.
>
> R. S. Thomas, "Adjustments"

As the critical explication of the way God redemptively comes forth as God, the theology of God is not "metaphysics." Because the way God comes forth as God contains ciphers that have to do with God's relation to the world, however, the theology of God contains a metaphysical element, the world interpretation required by any attempt to interpret the divine activity. Our task now is to explicate what goes into a thinking of God's relation to the world. In this explication I shall review the contributions of anti-theism, the several faces of metaphysics, and the nature of the task itself.

THE CONTRIBUTIONS OF ANTI-THEISM

At various points of the argument, I have attempted to mediate metaphysical and antimetaphysical approaches to God. Before the jury of anti-theism, I have argued the case for metaphysics. It is now time to consider anti-theism's case. Are we in any way in debt to anti-theism? Is anti-theism an important resource for the theology of God? Two anti-theist themes stand out as important cautions to theologies of God that use speculative philosophy. From Martin Luther through Emmanuel Levinas and Jean-Luc Marion resounds a powerful negation. God does not come forth as the God who founds, frees, or redeems in connection with the puzzle of the world or with conceptual schemes that would render that puzzle explicit and coherent. Metaphysical schemes that translate totality into categorical form originate independently from the theology of God, and show from the start a primarily philosophical concern. Characteristic of these schemes is some attempt to show philosophically that a world such as ours requires a divine activity and that this activity is what indicates the character of the divine. And while the theology of God may well appropriate elements of these schemes for its purposes, it cannot simply ground its convictions about God's reality or its symbolics of God directly in such schemes. This is simply to repeat the primordial character of God's redemptive coming forth as God in the theology of God.

The second theme of anti-theism confronts speculative philosophy in a more aggressive way. Anti-theism questions the very possibility of metaphysics in the sense of a truly cognitively grounded explication of "what is" and its ground. I am not suggesting that metaphysics must be defined this way. Many speculative philosophers make no such claims. Paradoxically, the confident claim to have cracked the secret of the world is often found in antimetaphysical thinkers.[1] Antimetaphysics is itself a phenomenon of philosophy. Immanuel Kant, pragmatism, analytic, and deconstructive philosophies have all had their go at metaphysics. But theological anti-theism works from a different angle. Its suspicion about the possibility of cracking the secret of the world flows directly from its theological posture. The world's secret will not be solved precisely because its mystery is the mystery of God. Given the reality of God, metaphysical (rational) explication of the secret of the world is preempted. This is not to say that God displaces metaphysics as the "true" explanation of the world. That would only be metaphysics once again. The point, rather, is that if God is the world's creativity, the world takes on a depth or mystery that will not be dispersed with the advancement of scientific knowledge, with persuasive and coherent categorical analyses, or even with the theology of God itself.[2]

THE MANY FACES OF METAPHYSICS

Concepts that express inclusive and complex undertakings and that persist over long periods of time tend to gather multiple meanings. That is to say, they become more and more ambiguous. It is this ambiguity that

1. For instance, P. W. Atkins, *The Creation* (Oxford: W. H. Freeman, 1981), Preface and 126–27.

2. "God is the ultimate limitation and His existence is the ultimate irrationality. For no reason can be given for just that limitation which it stands in His nature to impose. . . . No reason can be given for the nature of God because that nature is the ground of rationality" (David Pailin, *God and the Processes of Reality* [London: Routledge, 1989], 130).

prompts the interpreter to use quotation marks whenever the concept is recalled. We are not, therefore, surprised to find that ambiguity trails any proposal to eliminate or make use of "metaphysics" in the theology of God. In its strongest sense, metaphysics means any attempt to discover, demonstrate, or dissolve the mystery that attends the very existence of "what there is." Metaphysics in this sense need not be limited to philosophy. Scientists engage in it insofar as they claim that the specific paradigm of knowledge and reality they are using is inclusive and exhaustive. Religious thinkers become "metaphysical" when they think God or gods are exhaustively explanatory.

Second, metaphysics can mean the attempt to discern features necessary to any and all possible worlds and existents.[3] Third, metaphysics can refer to the speculative—one could say imaginative and coherent—attempt to explicate the most general features of existents in our present "cosmic epoch" (A. N. Whitehead). In this sense, metaphysics has more the character of a descriptive ontology of what constitutes the universe of which we are a part.[4]

Siding with anti-theism, I have argued that the theology of God is incompatible with metaphysics in the first sense. If God is the Creativity of the world, then the world will always have an unpenetrable mystery about it. The theology of God does seem to imply at least one statement about the world that has an *a priori* character and that seems to qualify as metaphysics in the second sense. If the world and God are not simply

---

3. According to Charles Hartshorne, metaphysics is the search for necessary and categorical truths. Such truths are such that "no experience can contradict them" and "any experience must illustrate them" (*The Logic of Perfection and Other Essays in Neoclassical Metaphysics* [LaSalle, Ill.: Open Court, 1962], 285). For Hartshorne's notion of empty or formal metaphysics of any possible world, see his essay in the above-cited volume, "Some Empty Though Important Truths."

4. David Pailin does not distinguish *a priori* and cosmic or epochal metaphysics. In my judgment Hartshorne attempts the former, Whitehead the latter. Whitehead, accordingly, would see the features of actual entities not as *a priori* traits of any possible existence but as pertaining to our present cosmic epoch. On the other hand, Pailin interprets Whitehead as "referring to whatever could possibly be as well as to what has been and is the case" (*God*, 42). An example of metaphysics in the cosmological sense is Robert Neville's *Recovery of the Measure: Interpretation and Nature* (Albany: SUNY Press, 1989). David Ray Griffin discusses this difference under the terms of Hartshorne as a rationalist who makes coherence the central ideal and Whitehead as an empiricist who sees metaphysics as a descriptive science. He then argues that this difference is not absolute. Granting these qualifications, it seems to me that Hartshorne does see metaphysics primarily in terms of necessary truths applicable to any possible world, and Whitehead sees metaphysics, or at least the speculative philosophy in which he is engaged, as a description of the general features of the present cosmic epoch. See Griffin, "Hartshorne's Differences from Whitehead," in Lewis S. Ford, ed., *Two Process Philosophers: Hartshorne's Encounter with Whitehead* (Tallahassee: American Academy of Religion, 1973), 45–48.

identical, if they are differentiated at all, and if that differentiation means that the world is in some way dependent on God, that dependence is the world's most general *a priori* feature. In the classical Catholic theology of God, this feature is called contingency. While this feature is fostered by the differentiation of God and the world, it does not express God's actual relation to or operation in the world. That undertaking involves metaphysics in the third sense, that is, the attempt to discern at levels of generality "what there is" in the world that we know.

Why would the theology of God ever take up metaphysics in the third sense? Why would it not simply try to discover how God relates to the world as described in astrophysics, quantum physics, biochemistry, and molecular biology? We must remind ourselves at this point that we have no access to the way God is related to any specific world operation. We cannot discover (if in fact there is something to be discovered) how God functions in the complex world of the cell, the replications of DNA, the engulfing of whole solar systems by a black hole, or the play of subatomic particles. To plot any specific and actual function would mean the uncovering of a divine "causality" at work in the specific worlds of cells, quarks, and galaxies. We must decide at this point what we mean by the "world" of the God and world relation. It would seem that the world is not reducible simply to what the various sciences, oriented as they are to causal and structural explanation, deliver to us, but also something available in broader discernments. Showing itself in these discernments are such features as eventfulness, autonomy, tragic structure, competition, and cooperation. These traits of the way the world works better pose that to which we would relate the divine creativity than subatomic particle events or cell metabolisms. In such concepts as these, yielded by descriptive metaphysics, we struggle with what it means to say that God is the Creativity of the world.

I am attempting to make the case of an appropriation of a generally descriptive metaphysics that makes no claim to "explain" world totality. Behind this attempt is an assumption concerning the way the "realities" of faith are related to the environments in which they take place. This relation is not so much a correlation as a mutual participation in which the realities of faith influence and are influenced by their environments. This was the method of the theological anthropology of *Good and Evil*. Rather than correlate sin or redemptive freedoms with human biology or intersubjectivity, I attempted to explore how such freedoms became biologically embodied and how they themselves had a transformative effect on biologically based aggression. Divine activity in the world sets a similar task. Given the world to be what it is (tragic, eventful, processive, and the like), how is it that the world is open to or dependent on the divine creative activity?

ON THINKING GOD'S RELATION TO THE WORLD

Up until now, I have simply been clearing some brush, proposing ways of adjudicating metaphysics and antimetaphysics. I concluded that while totality metaphysics was incompatible with the theology of God, metaphysics as descriptive ontology of the world was not. But it would be facile to assume that adjudicating metaphysics and antimetaphysics is itself a thinking of God's relation to the world. We do not think that relation simply by uncovering general features of world process. At this point we must ask whether the relation of God and the world can be thought at all, and if so, what that thinking would involve.

Such a question prompts us first to cast a suspicious eye on the phrase "God's relation to the world." Does this expression contain an intrinsic distortion? Actually, a certain skepticism properly attends the thinking of any relation; for instance, a pencil lying on a table. The thinkability of the pencil-table relation rests on a third something, the thinker, who is outside that relation (though not outside relation *to* it) and whose external vantage point over the terms of the relation permits an objectifying analysis and discursive description. But that is not our situation with respect to God and the world. We are not related to God and the world as something *in* our environment like pencil-table. We are neither external to it, nor do we comprehend the terms.

We can respond to this rather paralyzing suspicion in several ways. The easiest way, especially for postmodern anti-theists and followers of authority theology, is to abandon the project of thinking God's relation to the world. Since this relation is sufficiently clear in the ancient texts or in the concrete faith experiences of the religious community, thinking it is both impossible and superfluous. A second response moves beyond the examination of texts and explicates God's relation to the world simply by uncovering the contents of the ciphers of God. This approach assumes that the God and world relation is specified in such ciphers as creation or redemption or in the persons of the Trinity. Thus, to think God's relation to the world is to explicate God's love, justice, mercy, or incarnational presence. We have here a credible beginning. But once this explication begins, it quickly presses us beyond cipher explication. If we assume that each cipher expresses or implies a distinct way God is active in the world, the explication of the ciphers leaves us with an aggregate, a list of expressions that does not itself express God's relation to the world. Further, the ciphers are not really separate but are mutually interrelated. To explicate a cipher as a world relation poses a second task of describing the world's receptivity, of saying what opens the world to love, the Spirit, and so forth. Cipher explication then turns quickly into a larger task that involves some account of world process itself and the way in which all ciphers conspire together in world relation.

A third response turns us in the direction of natural theology. We try to locate something about the way the world works that eludes ordinary explanation and then show how this working uniquely depends on God. The classical Catholic theology provides an instance of this response. Drawing on Aristotle's concept of a first mover and the hierarchical cosmology of the Platonic tradition, it portrays God as moving the world through angelic, celestial, and terrestrial orders. When this classical Christian cosmology finally gave way to the nonhierarchical sun-centered mathematical-mechanistic world picture of sixteenth- and seventeenth-century sciences, the way was paved for another version of this third type of response.

In the Middle Ages, cosmos meant an inclusive system whose beginning, descending order of influences, and final outcome are ordered by the divine causality. After the Middle Ages, cosmos means a totality of interrelated processes and entities, whose beginning, ending, and operation are understood through mathematical and efficient causal analyses. If these analyses are sufficient and exhaustive, the need for an explaining divine causality is removed. Thus is born a new problem: If all specific world processes are understandable without God, how can the relation between God and the world be conceived and explicated? Yet from Issac Newton through John Polkinghorne, there have been scientists who resist scientifically originated deicide, the removal of any and all divine activities in the world. Using their extensive scientific knowledge, they would discover something about the way the world works that leaves room for, even requires, the divine influence. Such proposals smack of deism, not in the narrow sense of proposing a divine maker of the world machine, but in the broader sense of locating a divine operation somewhere in the cosmological apparatus. Even if these efforts offer us a God of the gaps, they express a negative religious conviction, the refusal to grant to the cosmologies of natural science the status of ultimate explanations.

At the same time, these proposals are troubling in several respects. The first is what appears to be a dilemma, with problems on both sides. On the one hand, one type of proposal claims to discover the actual way God is active in biological, quantum, or astrophysical environments. But surely such an activity is not actually discoverable. A successful description at this level would have to meet the condition of grasping any function or relation, namely the capacity to comprehend in an external way the terms involved. But if we abandon this effort, the other alternative is a *deus ex machina* where God is attached to a conceptual system as the explanatory entity for some designated feature of that system. But the stability of a *deus ex machina* device is subject to the character of that which evokes the explanation. Either the to-be-explained is an *ordinary* sort of problem within the system (cosmos, quantum world, and so forth), in which case it is the type of thing subject to future possible empirical explanations that would replace the *deus ex machina*, or it is some *extraordinary* problem that *in principle* cannot be replaced. The theology of God quite properly hesitates to insert the divine operation into the gaps of potentially empirical explanations.[5] But when we move to the second option, something in the world system unexplainable *in principle*, we are talking about the intrinsic mystery of things, not a specific feature of a scientifically described system. Accordingly, with the second option we move outside of the realm of explanation.

Inserting God into the unexplained aspects of scientific explanatory schemes is also troubling insofar as it suppresses other considerations and criteria needed by a paradigm of divine activity. Only two things are involved when we relate God to the world by way of gaps in scientific explanations: some general meaning of God and the puzzle of a world operation. What is not considered is the way God redemptively comes forth as God, most of the symbolic content of God, the historical dimension of divine activity, and a general ontology of world process; in short, the elements and criteria needed in a paradigm of divine activity.

To summarize, God and the world are not terms to which human beings have an external relation, comprehensible in the same way as intra-world relations. Thus, there is no direct account of the divine activity. Yet, because the way God comes forth as God is a world relation and because the ciphers themselves express God-world relations, these initial steps of a theology of God contain materials for a paradigmatic thinking of God and the world. The mere explication of ciphers stops short of this think-

---

5. See Robert Neville, *God the Creator: On the Transcendence and Presence of God* (Chicago: University of Chicago Press, 1968), chap. 5. God as indeterminate being-itself cannot function as an explanation. Thus, the only explanations possible at the level of cosmology take place by reducing the subject matter of the cosmos to certain first principles, the sort of thing we find in Paul Weiss or Alfred North Whitehead.

ing, and the relation of God to specific cosmological elements ends in an aporia. The way beyond these options lies in the development of a paradigm in which converge elements appropriate to the thinking of God and the world.

ELEMENTS OF A PARADIGM

In this present chapter I propose a path to the thinking of God and the world. Even as we do not capture God's actual being in the ciphers that attend redemption, neither do we expect to envision and articulate God's concrete activity in the world. In the symbolics of God this failure of direct cognition is expressed in the term *cipher.* In thinking God and the world, it is expressed in the term *paradigm.* Paradigm is what we have when, in some measure of coherence, we would conceptually explicate the meaning of God as the Creativity that disposes the world. And even though we may sense some mutual interrelation between the ciphers, that interrelation as such is not a paradigm for God's relation to the world. A paradigm arises when we assemble materials and criteria pertinent to the understanding of the divine activity.

Because God comes forth in redemption as that which founds, reconciles, and summons to justice, the paradigm we seek expresses not simply a structure, an *a priori* aspect of something, or an abstract goal of things, but an activity. The one and only thing that can redeem is the Creativity of the world itself. Accordingly, that which the paradigm attempts to express is not how a structure (God) and a totality (world) are related but what it means to say that Creativity is active in world process. If that which the paradigm would express is an activity of some sort, we have some indication from the start what sort of elements would constitute the paradigm. Political activity, for instance, is not simply a structure, an idea, even a fixed entity but a situation involving aims, strategic planning, and action, and a certain kind of environment to which aims and actions are adapted. If we would understand a politician's activity, we try to uncover her aims or agendas: self-serving reelection goals, constituency orientation, or ideal criteria. We need some sense of the strategy or means by which the politician "gets things done," has an effect on things. And we need some grasp of the character of the environment (congress, political party, power coteries) that may be both receptive and resistant to those aims and strategic actions. Since the divine activity is not that of *an* entity *in* a world, it is not as such imaginable. Nevertheless, if it is an activity at all, it would have certain formal features of activity. Thus, to understand Creativity as an activity would include the aim or content, the means through which it takes place, and some notion of the environment in which or toward which it addresses itself. That which indicates the aim of the divine activity is the way God redemptively comes forth as God, bespoken in the ciphers and qualifiers. Apart from an account of redemption and a symbolics of God, a paradigm of divine activity would be vacuous.

As to the second aspect of Creativity, where do we look for the "divine strategy," the divine way of making a difference in things? Where is there any instance of divine activity? Here we become aware of the abstract character of the account of redemption at work in these pages. To be sure, to discern redemption at work in agential, interhuman, and sociopolitical spheres corrects the abstraction that reduces it to any one of them. But the focus was entirely on a general description of what the redemption of these spheres means. What we have not asked is how emancipation, founding, and reconciling take place. Even if we agree that individual redemption begins with a being-founded, what mediates that founding? How is the redemption available? One thing is clear. The redemptive coming forth of God as God does not take place by way of a divine-human immediacy that bypasses language, institutions, and history. Being-founded is not a supernatural intervention in a human psyche. It occurs only in connection with something that alters language, calls forth new communities, and resymbolizes tradition. The historical (linguistic, symbolic, cultic) mediation of redemption is not unique to the Christian movement but is the way redemption happens in any and all faiths. In Hindu, Buddhist, and Islamic faiths, ritualizations, written scriptures, stories of sages and saints, and specific institutions all mediate redemption. When the Christian movement describes its own historical mediation, that which brought forth a language, community, and tradition, it engages in Christology and ecclesiology. Accordingly, the facticity of redemption is not limited to the effects of redemption on agents, the interhuman, or society but includes the epoch-making event(s) from which came the *ecclesia*, and with that a new ritual, symbolics, collection of writings, and subsequent history of reinterpretation. At least in the Christian movement, it is in this event of the crucified messianic teacher that we find the historical mediation of the divine activity. What prevents this turn from being utterly arbitrary is that founding, reconciling, and emancipation are connected with this event. The event of the suffering messianic teacher is not, of course, a photograph of the divine activity. We have no direct access to that. It is, however, an expression of a change in history, which change is the "objective" condition of the ongoing effects of redemption.

The third element of a paradigm of divine activity is an account of the environment(s) in which that activity takes place. The very distinction between an activity at work in an environment and the environment itself implies both a receptiveness to that activity (else the activity would not exist) and an opposition to that activity (otherwise it has no function, fulfills no need). Since actual things are never in utter harmony with each other in their environment, all environments (actual things in their non-harmonious relation) will offer resistance to whatever is active in them. This appears to be a general principle of any environmental activity. And there are strong reasons for applying this principle to the divine activity. To relate God to whatever we call redemption, either of individuals or of societies, is to posit both a resistant (since redemption is needed) and receptive (since redemption takes place) environment. World, creation, and finitude have served as terms for the environment of God's creative activity. In their theological sense, these terms are not simply interchangeable with cosmos, universe, or nature. The formal meaning of "creation" is the "whatever is" of which God is the creativity. The task of an ontology of world in a theology of God is to specify in what way world is open to and resistant to the divine creativity. And once we take this step, we have before us not world in the formal sense of that which depends on God but world as a determinant set of overlapping systems or levels of activity.

The three systems we are accustomed to differentiate are cosmos, nature, and history. And while human perspective inevitably shapes the apprehension of each system, these systems are not simply perspectival terms. *Cosmos* names the inclusive, astrophysically, and quantum and mathematically apprehended epochal system of spacetime that began with the Big Bang. *Nature* names the planetary ecosystem, the biosphere of living things as they are bound up with the nonliving conditions on which they depend. Nature is distinguishable from cosmos not only as part to a whole but to the degree that the dynamics and structures of living things—for instance, cells and their nucleic acids—are not reducible to the entities or structures of astro- or quantum physics. Nature (environments of life) may in fact be distributed throughout the cosmos. But the only nature we know is our own planetary biosphere. *History* names the system of interpersonal, social, and other interactions that arose when human life took on the dimension of language. There may be something like history on other planets in the universe. The only history we know is limited to our own planet.

Are we to conclude then that thinking God's relation to the world can only be a threefold thinking of God's relation to cosmos, nature, and history? While I do not want to dismiss the possibility of exploring distinctive ways God may be related to these inclusive systems, three considerations caution me against such a conclusion. First, the undertaking will surely be frustrated if it attempts to relate God to the specific operations described by cosmologists, biologists, and historians. It is difficult to imagine what it would mean to discover divine activity in spacetime, quarks, supernova, cell replication, or the behavior of international markets. Second, even if these endeavors had some success, they would not constitute a thinking of the divine activity in relation to the world, the total environment of these systems. Third, one can so exaggerate the differences between these systems as to undermine the way in which they depend on each other and the sense in which they constitute the world.

What, then, is the use of distinguishing these systems or world environments? First, the very existence of history, the realm of human institutions, symbols, corporate memories, and power struggles, constitutes something not reducible to the other two environments. And as the environment of agential, interhuman, and social redemption, history has a certain primacy in relation to cosmos and nature. Without God's activity in that sphere, little could be said of God's relation to the other two. In history we initially meet both the resistance and receptiveness to divine activity. Second, the operations of each of the environments provide materials for a general ontology of the world. We learn of the world's complexity, competition, eventfulness, and tragic structure only as we experience history, nature, and cosmos. Attending to the way these environments work, we become aware of general features of the world to which we would relate the divine creativity.

To construct a paradigm of the divine activity, we must bring into interrelation to each other the symbolics of God, the objective (historical) mediation of redemption (the event of the suffering messianic teacher), and ontology of the world. Is the construction of such a paradigm the construction of a metaphor? Are paradigm and metaphor identical? Since any understanding of the way God and the world are related is inevitably metaphorical, the constructed paradigm will have a metaphorical character.[6] At the same time, paradigm construction goes beyond the proposal

6. Stephen C. Pepper distinguishes what he calls world hypotheses and root metaphors. World hypotheses are comprehensive conceptual ways of understanding the world; thus, for instance, Lucretius's *The Nature of Things* or Darwin's *The Origin of Species*. For Pepper a root metaphor is what grounds and unifies the elements of a world hypothesis. According to the theory, all comprehensive ways of understanding the world have adopted a comprehensive metaphor; for instance, the metaphor of structure, machine, organism, or accidental happenings (*World Hypotheses: A Study in Evidence* [Berkeley: University of California Press, 1961], chaps. 1, 4, 5).

of a metaphor. The liturgy, doctrine, and piety of the religious community can take place under the aegis of a dominating metaphor without much attempt at critical paradigm construction. Thus, sovereign rule has been Christendom's dominating metaphor for expressing God's relation to the world. But this metaphor can function in the life of the community without being critically established; that is, without any attempt to root it in the way God redemptively comes forth as God or relate it to an ontology of world. On the other hand, influence (lure) is the dominant metaphor of process theology, but it functions as a kind of shorthand term for a detailed conceptual way of understanding world process and God's relation to it. I conclude that an inclusive metaphor is useful for giving a paradigm a unitary expression but to propose a metaphor is not necessarily to construct a paradigm. The distinction is between unconceptualized inclusive metaphors and metaphors that express an extensive, coherence-oriented conceptualization. Focus on conceptualization alone may fail to subject metaphors to analysis and criticism. Focus on metaphors alone will fail to relate divine creativity to the structure and processes of the world.

METAPHYSICS AND HERMENEUTICS: A METHODOLOGICAL QUERY

A paradigm of divine action calls for three resources: divine symbolics, historical instanciation, and an ontology of the world. Because the first two resources concern redemption and the third has to do with the world, this paradigm construction appears to be a method of correlation. In that method an independent ontology of the world becomes a framework in which symbolic contents are conceptually reexpressed. As I understand it, something of the sort takes place in process theology. The Whiteheadian conceptual scheme serves as a framework that makes possible a coherent restatement of Christian symbolic contents. Anti-theism and other theologies (Barth, hermeneutics) object to methods of correlation on the grounds that the philosophically derived conceptual scheme ends up dominating and diluting the facticity of redemption. More specifically, to grant utter autonomy to metaphysics at the point of world interpretation implies that nothing about the world is disclosed by redemption. Two things combine to bring about this problem. Because it is impossible to relate God directly to actual world occurrences as described in the sciences, the theology of God is pressed toward metaphysics or general ontology of the world. Because redemption gives rise to ways of interpreting the world, the theology of God cannot regard metaphysics as the sole source of knowledge of the world.

One reason why anti-theism has trouble with objective metaphysics is its commitment to a hermeneutic turn of thinking. This hermeneutic element is as much present in Luther and Blaise Pascal as in Karl Barth, Heidegger, Hans Georg Gadamer, and Ricoeur. The main principle of this turn is that existential, social, and linguistic participations give all thinking the character of interpretation. Thinking's claim to objectivity undergoes assaults from two sides: from idealism that sees the human being enclosed in subjectivity, and from empiricism that sees even human thinking as a causal outcome. According to the hermeneutic turn, the ontology of the world can never be a direct, objective apprehension that transcends participation and perspective. That being the case, an ontology of the world is not something simply discovered by an objective discipline (metaphysics) and handed on to another discipline (theology). The world itself is experienced perspectively and through participations that reflect aesthetic orientation, religious faith, and historical epistemes (Michel Foucault). Redemption, thus, is not simply an individual salvific relation to God but a form of world interpretation. The facticity of redemption engenders perspectives on and insights into the world. I shall postpone for now a detailed account of how redemption gives rise to perspectives on the world. But I must anticipate this account in order to show how metaphysics and hermeneutics come together.

According to "the principle of positivity," the determinate realities of faith have a transforming effect on the situation of faith. This is why the general ideas and categories that express that situation do not remain unchanged in theological interpretation. To assume that they remain unaffected is the tendency of what I have called a "generic hermeneutics."[7] In *Good and Evil* the application of this principle yielded the way in which generic or ontological features of human individuality and sociality are distorted by human evil and are carried to new levels of freedom by redemption. In other words, all the things that constitute the human being socially and psychologically (the three spheres of agency, the interhuman, and the social) are open to both distortion and redemption. Because of these distortions and freedoms, the theology of human reality neither repeats nor simply correlates with the data of the sciences or philosophy.

When a theology of God applies the principle of positivity to the relation of God and the world, it faces a situation that resembles theological anthropology. Here too we find a more generic reality (world) to which a

---

7. See my book *Ecclesial Man: A Social Phenomenology of Faith and Reality* (Philadelphia: Fortress Press, 1975), 58–59.

more determinate symbolism (the ciphers of God) is related. To discern this more general reality, we conduct an ontology of the world ranging across the spheres of cosmos, nature, and history, an ontology that yields such notions as time, complexity, stratification, determinacy, order, entity, and differentiation. Yet world interpretation is not exhausted by this scientifically informed and philosophically based ontology. The redemption of human individuals results in specific ways of being in the world. One of these ways arises when agential freedom transforms cognitive orientations of idolatrous certainty or skepticism into wonder. In addition, agape is an orientation of empathetic participation and delight in any and every worldly other. In these postures human beings are oriented not just to the data, objectivity, structure, or events of the world but to the vulnerability, tragic structure, and legitimate alterity of worldly things. In the older traditions, world is depicted as fallen, "groaning in travail," or marked for a dramatic and fulfilling ending.

I shall not attempt to rehabilitate these quasicosmic, if not mythological, notions. On the other hand, empathetic wonder does sense a kind of tragic fallenness about cosmos, nature, and history. The world's generic features of chaotic randomness, provincial self-interest, incompatibility, and competitiveness constitute a resistance to God's active creativity. At the same time, empathetic wonder also discerns about the world a certain receptivity to creativity that prevents fallenness (resistance) from being the final word. In a theological perspective, the world is not just tragically fallen but open to new possibilities of cooperation that transcend the natural structure of self-interest necessary to natural and historical entities. Thus, arising with the facticity of redemption are world orientations that set for the theology of God a *hermeneutic* for world interpretation, a hermeneutic structured by the three motifs of createdness, "fallenness," and redeemability. This is why the theology of God does not simply relate God to a "world" delivered to it by metaphysics or an ontology of the world. Instead, under the principle of positivity, it tracks the way its own hermeneutic of the world transforms or reinterprets the more generic ontology of the world. We can call this task a hermeneutic ontology or a theophilosophical ontology of the world. To carry out this task, we bring together scientific accounts of cosmos and nature, ontologies of the various spheres of the world, and postures on the world born in the dynamics of redemptive freedom.

As a final step along this path toward a paradigm of the divine activity, I would listen again to the cautionary voice of negative theology. Negative theology accompanies the theology of God every step of the way; from the undesignated horizons of human elemental passions to the qualifiers of the ciphers of God. But we do not leave these qualifiers behind when we take up the task of thinking the relation of God and world. Even as ciphers fail to describe God's being, so do paradigms fail to describe in a direct way God's world relation and activity. If they did perform that feat, they would have become explanations in competition with the more or less direct explanations of the sciences. A paradigm for God's creative activity does not exploit the leftover puzzles of the sciences or metaphysics but arises as the ciphers, Christology, and a theophilosophical account of the world are brought together. Such a paradigm will attempt to specify what it means to say that God is a creative activity and if this awesome Creativity of the world is that which evokes worship, a paradigm of the divine activity will also set forth God as the worshipful.

13

THREE-DIMENSIONAL WORLD: COSMOS AND NATURE

> For nature, heartless, witless nature,
>   Will neither care nor know
>   What stranger's feet may find the meadow
>   And trespass there and go,
> Nor ask amid the dews of morning
>   If they are mine or no.
> > A. E. Housman, "Last Poems, XL"

> . . . . but truly now we drift
> a slow lost way upon a minor arm
> of one faint nebula while millions more
> beyond the utmost void all shine and spin.
> Still from black holes that suck creation in,
> to antimatter that eludes our grasp,
> hiding perhaps some mirror shape we fear,
> Still, still, from all of this who brings form in,
> Analyses, discards it, age to age?
> > Loren Eiseley, "His Own True Shadow"

Our task now is to begin to assemble the pertinent sources for a paradigm of God's relation to the world. One of those sources is world or *the* world and its way of working. *The* world is what the astrophysicists and biologists deliver to us. It is world interpreted as cosmos, thus a single, objective totality studied by the sciences. Those who study *the* world agree that we never experience this objective totality as such. *The* world is not like the particular occupants or objects we experience in *the* world. We do not experience *the* world as an entity over against us: rather, experience itself is worldly. We are of (the) world, structured by worldliness, as we experience whatever we experience. To express this human-world mutual participation, I use the term *world* without the article. World without the article is a term like being, time, space, history, or nature. Because our historicity is a condition of our study of history, we do not speak of *the* history. Nor do we speak of *the* time, *the* space, or *the* nature. World without the definitive article means the network of happenings in which we participate that all objective studies presuppose. Like cosmos, world connotes a totality but, unlike cosmos, this totality is openended and dimensional rather than bounded and objective.[1]

From the perspective of individual agents, world means the inclusive environment in which they find themselves and in which they pursue their aims. They may understand this environment to be very small, or, with the help of objectifying instruments, very large, even to the point of infinity. More reflective postures will sense that this inclusive environment has a dimensional character. If we privilege physical existence, we will limit this dimensionality to three dimensions of space plus time, an analysis that has more to do with *the* world (cosmos) than with world. But world as our participated environment and, in a sense, a mark of our own existence, is dimensional in a different sense. We experience it by way of participation in three spheres that are distinguished by the kinds of entities, behaviors, and even structures we find in them. I shall call these spheres or dimensions, cosmos, nature, and history.[2]

Cosmos names what we sometimes call *the* world, the spacetime aggregate of clustered galaxies and their sun systems that provides both the location and the "stuff" (molecules, atoms, and subatomic particles) of both nature and history. *Nature*, the sphere of life, names something that

---

1. For "world" (cf. also "life world") in this sense, see Maurice Natanson, *Edmund Husserl: Philosopher of Infinite Tasks* (Evanston, Ill.: Northwestern University Press, 1973), chap. 7; Martin Heidegger, *Being and Time*, trans. J. MacQuarrie and J. S. Robinson (London: SCM, 1962), Part One, III; Quentin Smith, *The Felt Meanings of the World: A Metaphysics of Feeling* (West Lafayette, Ind.: Purdue University Press, 1986); and Conrad Bonafazi, *A Theology of Things: A Study of Man in his Physical Environment* (Philadelphia: Lippincott, 1967).

2. Three of the five parts of Paul Tillich's system are spheres that reflect human participation; being, life, and history. Missing here is what I am calling cosmos. Accordingly, Tillich could correlate religious symbols to life (nature) and to history, but not *the* world or cosmos. But when Tillich thinks of history in relation to the human individual, he sees it as one of four "dimensions," the other three being the inorganic, the organic, and the psychological. And each "dimension" embodies four categories of being: space, time, causality, and substance. Tillich, accordingly, is treating cosmos under the rubric of being. However, Tillich never inquires into cosmos on its own terms in the same way as life or history. Further, in his treatment of being he combines a general ontology of what is (cf. ontology of world) with a specific phenomenology of cosmos. The result is that history and life make little or no contribution to the way Tillich conceives of being. Or, to put it differently, Tillich's philosophy of being recapitulates distinctions found in ancient and especially Platonic philosophy, thus, dynamics and form, freedom and destiny, individuality and participation. Thus the sciences and even various philosophies of world have little influence on the way Tillich philosophizes about world or being. See *Systematic Theology*, Vols. 1 and 3 (Chicago: University of Chicago Press, 1963, 1967).

at present we know only in connection with our local planetary biosphere. It is the closely interconnected system of living things that arose on our planet with macromolecules. Life presupposes cosmos. *History* names the sphere of activities that take place in connection with the human populations of our planet, activities made possible by the traditioning power of language and institutions. History presupposes both cosmos and nature. Complexity increases from cosmos to nature to history. Because of leaps in this complexity, these dimensions resist reduction to each other or to a single reality. Whatever continuities there are at the level of world itself, they are ways these distinguishable spheres are connected rather than a single identity to which they are reduced. Since history presupposes nature and both presuppose cosmos, there is a certain directionality in the way the dimensions are connected. Events in the cosmos influence nature and history. The life-forms of the biosphere influence history but have minimum cosmic influence. Human being is the one life-form now able to influence and even eliminate the whole planetary biosphere. Because of this, nature and history are spheres of reciprocal influence.

Our cognitive access to world is only by way of our participation in the three spheres, their continuities, and mutual influences. Accordingly, any general account of world concerns not just these distinguished spheres of world but world continuities and features of world participation. I shall offer here an outrageously simplified account of the three spheres as a prelude to a philosophy and ontology of world. Working from these spheres, a philosophy of world may discern certain continuities that constitute world as such. To say that there are such continuities and general features need not commit us to a static view of world. General features of world may be such things as process, change, evolution, temporal differentiation, and novelty. A *theology* of world would consult the way redemption opens human reality onto the mystery of world.

COSMOS

The attempt to grasp the origin, development, make-up, and structure of the universe (cosmology, cosmogeny) is not simply a modern undertaking. For Euro-Mediterranean peoples, it originates in Babylonian and Egyptian mythopoeics and develops by way of Hellenic and Hellenistic philosophies into the medieval Catholic cosmology. Given poetic expression in Dante and conceptual expression in Bonaventure and Thomas Aquinas, "Christian cosmology" united early Hellenic speculation, especially Plato's *Timaeus*, with elements of Semitic cosmology taken from the Bible. The displacement of this "Christian cosmology" in the Renaissance is a familiar story that begins with Nicolas Cusanos in the fourteenth century, develops through Copernicus, Tycho Brahe, and Johannes Kepler, and is given observational confirmation by Galileo. Isaac Newton and the seventeenth century more or less completed this phase of the displacement and marked the beginning of modern cosmology.[3] By the time of Newton, overwhelming evidence had given rise to a new if minimum consensus about the cosmos. Neither the earth nor the earth's sun is the center of the universe. The earth is one among several planets orbiting the sun and, like other planets, is subject to the laws of moving bodies. The Newtonian constituents of the cosmos were bodies whose mass and motion lent themselves to mathematically formulated laws. Such was the first revolution in cosmology.

In the early decades of the twentieth century, physics, and with it cosmology, underwent a second revolution. In its narrowest sense, this revolution was prompted by Albert Einstein's work on special (1905) and general (1915) relativity. Broadly interpreted, this revolution took place as new technologies were brought to bear on stellar and nuclear exploration. A new picture of the size, age, and constituents of the universe emerged from geology and chemistry as well as astronomy and physics. If there is a third revolution in physics (Paul Davies), it came about when physicists realized that the primary road to the "problem of the cosmos," (its origin, development, and structure), is not just the macromathematical study of the heavens by means of ever more subtle instruments but the study of subatomic particles.[4] From this merger of particle physics and astrophysics has come a proliferation of subsciences: quantum optics, X-ray and gamma ray astronomy, quantum electrodynamics, and so forth. The third revolution in physics, and with it cosmology, may be, as some argue, an extension of Einstein's work. But it is a vast extension that includes black

3. For the shift from a Christian to Renaissance cosmologies, see Max Wildiers, *The Theologian and the Universe: Theology and Cosmology from the Middle Ages to the Present*, trans. P. Dunphy (New York: Seabury Press, 1982), chaps. 5 and 6; E. A. Burtt, *The Metaphysical Foundations of Modern Physical Science* (Garden City, N.Y.: Doubleday and Co., 1924); Alexandre Koyré, *From the Closed World to the Infinite Universe* (Baltimore: Johns Hopkins Press, 1957); and A. N. Whitehead, *Adventures in Ideas* (Cambridge, Eng.: Cambridge University Press, 1935), Part 2.

4. On the broad front of this third revolution are black holes, subatomic particles, chaos theory, self-organizing chemical reactions, and, of course, the ever-present search for a grand unified theory. See Paul Davies, ed. *The New Physics* (Cambridge: Cambridge University Press, 1989).

holes, quark theory, chaos theory, and gauge theory (the theory of invariance or symmetry in an electric field). Contemporary cosmological science appears to be distributed over three main areas of investigation: the spacetime structures of the universe (relativity theory and astrophysics), the constituents of the universe (particle physics), and the origin of the universe (Big Bang, inflationary physics), which draws on the first two areas. Together, these three areas of investigation now give us the meaning of "cosmos."

The Structure and Development of the Cosmos

When cosmology and physics were given a new mathematical foundation by Kepler and others, they became esoteric sciences. The nonmathematician can of course grasp certain gross facts such as descriptions of the surface of the planet Venus or the claim that a galaxy is disk-shaped. But the lay person cannot enter into contemporary macro- or microcosmology at the point of its primary evidence. Higher mathematics bars the door both to relativity theory and particle physics. Being a lay person, I can only present contemporary cosmology in broad and gross terms, minus its mathematical evidence, which means for the cosmologists themselves, minus its very meaning.

One way contemporary cosmology can be summarized is in the phrase, "things are not what they seem." All premodern cosmologies have one thing in common. Dependent on human powers of observation unaided by technology, they have a common sense orientation. Once the instruments of modern technology were employed, almost everything the ancient and medieval world thought about the cosmos turned out to be either wrong or drastically limited. First, calculating the population of heavenly bodies as well as their distances involves unimaginable numbers. A single galaxy may have a hundred billion suns, many of which have a good chance of having planetary systems, and there are a hundred billion galaxies. Second, the size of the universe involves unimaginable distances, expressible only by the speed of light. Earth is forty thousand light years from the center of its galaxy, and its galaxy is part of a cluster of galaxies that would take twenty million light years to cross. Third, the age of the cosmos is not calculated in millions but billions of years, from twelve to twenty billion earth years back to the Big Bang. Fourth, the entities that constitute the cosmos are immensely hot (to the point of nuclear reactions) condensations of cosmic gas (giant molecular clouds) we call suns, plus in many cases, various cooled fragments they have thrown off (planets, moons, asteroids, meteors). These sun systems are arranged into galaxies that themselves have spiral or elliptical organization and that tend to fall into clusters.

Fifth, the innumerable galaxies and suns do not exist as an ageless, timeless structure. Like the planet earth and human history, there is a cosmic story. The cosmos changes over time in a directional way in at least two senses. First, it changes by galactic expansion. Whether this expansion will go on to infinity or, because of gravitational pull in relation to the speed of expansion, collapse back on itself is not yet resolved. Second, it changes by way of entropy, the gradual decay of heat and energy into disorder. Within these overall directions are innumerable events of coming into and passing out of existence. Suns form, do their nuclear cookery, and explode, sometimes collapsing from their own gravitation into a black hole. Galaxies and their multiple suns are born and pass out of existence, sometimes engulfed by black holes. At this present time, multiple worlds have already come and gone. Other forms of change characterize the cosmos. Planets rotate on their own axes and rotate about their suns. Suns have orbits in their galaxies and galaxies themselves rotate.

Finally, according to relativity theory, space and time are neither separate from each other nor are they absolute concepts according to some universal standard that can identify where or when something exists in relation to everything else. There is no single simultaneous time of occurrence for the cosmos as a whole. The entities of the cosmos have no simple location in space and time. The fact that light is drawn to objects indicates a distortion of space, something massive bodies also can effect. Here, spacetime determined by and relation to bodies is curved and expands as bodies expand.

Constituents of the Cosmos

The question of the make-up of the cosmos was taken up initially in Euro-Mediterranean culture by the philosophers of Ionia. Speculation merged with common sense set the approach. The ordinary "stuffs" of the everyday world (water, fire) were proposed as the world's primary substances. Somewhat in the line of ancient Pythagoreanism and Platonism, Renaissance sciences used mathematics to track the behavior of moving bodies. For René Descartes, Newton, and others, the universe was comprised of physical bodies understandable in terms of mass, weight, and extension.[5]

5. See Ivor Leclerc, *The Nature of Physical Existence* (New York: Humanities Press, 1972), chaps. 15–18.

Although the bodies in question were such macrobodies as planets or stones, some thought that these bodies were comprised of irreducibly small bodies or atoms. According to Renaissance and Enlightenment sciences, the universe is made up of matter, that is, bodies that exist in space and are subject to the laws of motion.

All this changed with quantum physics. While microbodies subject to the laws of motion were not eliminated from the cosmos, they lost their status as the ultimate constituents of the universe. What comprises "bodies"? The chemistry of basic elements marked one step toward the answer. Molecular theory and the eventual observational confirmation of that theory was a second step. The discovery of atoms as composite systems led to the subatomic particle physics of today. But sketching the make-up and behavior of subatomic particles has not come to an end. Quark theory with its hadrons (heavy, strongly interacting particles like neutrons) and leptons (light, weak interacting particles like electrons) may be coming close to the ultimate building blocks of the universe. But with these concepts so elusive to the nonscientist, we have little more than a typography of the very small. For particle physics the universe is comprised not just of entities (atoms and their constituents) but forces. And there seems to be a good bit of consensus that there are four fundamental forces at work in the particles: gravity, electromagnetism, and weak and strong nuclear forces. The very frontier of particle physics is the understanding of the attractions, repulsions, and symmetry (gauge theory) of these forces.[6]

One of the spin-offs of particle physics and the concept of matter is a reformulation of what the ancients called chaos. Like atoms chaos is a motif of ancient Western cosmogonical myths (the *Enuma Elish*, Hesiod's *Theogony*) and partly demythologized philosophical cosmologies (for instance, Plato's *Timaeus*). Nor is the motif limited to particle physics in contemporary sciences.[7] Chaos is formulated both as an incalculable complexity of turbulent systems (the molecular activity in the wake of a boat) and as an element in algorhythm complexity theory. In quantum physics it was initially articulated as the uncertainty principle (Werner Heisenberg), the concept that all modes of observing the particle world have an

---

6. See Rudolf Peierls, "Particles and Forces," and Abdus Salam, "Unification of the Forces," in J. H. Mulvey, ed., *The Nature of Matter* (Oxford: Clarendon Press, 1981).

7. See James Gleick, *Chaos: Making a New Science* (New York: Viking Press, 1987); Joseph Ford, "What is chaos that we should be mindful of it?" in Paul Davies, ed., *The New Physics*; and John Polkinghorne, *Science and Creation: The Search for Understanding* (Boston: New Science Library, 1989), chap. 2.

effect on what is studied.[8] The only particle world we observe is what we have already modified. Furthermore, there seems to be spontaneous activity in the particle world, even a spontaneous activity toward organization that resists explanation. The use of computers has greatly enhanced this sense of a chaos element. The more detailed the computer program becomes in taking account of factors that would enable prediction, the more it simply copies the situation and thus recedes as a predictive instrument.

"Origins"

I shall postpone to a later section the ambiguities that attend the concept of origin. I note that even some physicists (Stephen Hawking) are nervous about the term.[9] Obviously, any science of the cosmos is incomplete insofar as it lacks an account of how the cosmos came to be a cosmos. In recent decades this project has had stunning success, effecting a virtual consensus among astro and quantum physicists. They agree that the universe, the spacetime continuum, originated some twelve to twenty billion years ago when a very hot, dense, unstable, and relatively small set of conditions suddenly expanded in such a way as to produce conditions, cooling for instance, in which atoms could form from preatomic particle collisions.[10] Three discoveries marked the route to this consensus about what is metaphorically called the Big Bang. First, Hubble, using a new and very powerful telescope, discovered a Doppler effect (a light shift to the red), that indicated that distant suns were receding. We have then, an expanding rather than steady state universe.[11] Second, radio astronomy discovered a residue of the Big Bang in the background radiation distrib-

---

8. Werner Heisenberg, *The Physicist's Concept of Nature,* trans. A. J. Pomerans (New York: Harcourt and Brace, 1958), chap. 2; and J. Paul Davies, *Other Worlds: A Portrait of Nature in Rebellion* (New York: Simon and Schuster, 1980), chap. 3.

9. Stephen Hawking has tried to formulate the conditions in which a universe comes about without having to appeal to boundaries, edges, or times of origins. Thus he speculates that four-dimensional space curves around to form a closed surface in four dimensions, which as "finite and unbounded" requires no boundary conditions. And if that is so, it makes no sense to ask what occurs "before" the Big Bang. See "The Edge of Spacetime," in Davies, ed., *The New Physics,* 68–69.

10. At the time of this writing, data made possible by the Hubble telescope has engendered some new estimates concerning the age of the universe and thus a new ground of discussion about the Big Bang. But for classic Big Bang theory see P. W. Atkins, *The Creation* (San Francisco: W. H. Freeman, 1981); Stephen Hawking, *A Brief History of Time: From the Big Bang to Black Holes* (New York: Bantam Books, 1988); James Trefil, *The Moment of Creation: Big Bang Physics From Before the First Millisecond to the Present Universe* (New York: Charles Scribner's Sons, 1983); Paul Davies, *The Edge of Infinity: Where the Universe Came From and Where it Will End* (New York: Simon and Schuster, 1981); and Steven Weinberg, *The First Three Minutes: A Modern View of the Origin of the Universe* (New York: Basic Books, 1977).

11. See Alan Guth and Paul Steinhardt, "The Inflationary Universe," in Paul Davies, *The New Physics.*

uted uniformly throughout space. Third, quantum physicists were able to reproduce in the laboratory the subatomic conditions of the first minutes and even seconds of the Big Bang, that is, conditions necessary for the overcoming of and canceling out of particles and antiparticles so that atoms could form and endure and not be immediately disintegrated.

It is at this point that the Big Bang becomes ambiguous as an explanation of the "origin" of the universe. One of the problems that has troubled Stephen Hawking are certain nonexplained elements in the Big Bang.[12] Even when the standard theory works back to milliseconds from the Big Bang, it must simply posit an initial unexplained condition, a singularity that precedes space and time (since spacetime begins with the Big Bang) and thus evades the laws of physics. Reacting to this and other such problems, physicists have supplemented the standard theory with an inflationary theory. Without attempting to assess the theory's explanatory power, I can only say that the language that seeks to overcome the penultimate explanation of the standard theory with an exhaustive explanation has a peculiar, almost metaphysical, ring. The universe originates as a "quantum fluctuation" from "absolutely nothing." Even though the universe "started out in a fairly smooth and uniform state," it has no boundary conditions, but is "self-contained."[13] The universe begins in a "nothing," an "extreme simplicity" prior to spacetime, a "structureless spacetime," a geometrically amorphous "dust," or "structureless dust points."[14] I realize that lay persons such as myself are supposed to be properly respectful if not intimidated by the mathematical complexities of this literature, thus should accede to whatever is propounded. But I must say that Hesiod's account of the origin of the world from chaos in terms of the struggle of titans and their children makes as much sense to me as the pretense that "nothingness," "dust points," and "quantum fluctuations" are exhaustively explanatory.

I have no desire to spin theological garments out of failed explanations. But the explanations do seem to have the character of stipulations or constructions prompted by a certain scientistic pretense, namely that a science, in this case, the science of cosmology, must be able to totally explain that with which it deals.[15] But a vicious circle attends this pretense. The

12. Stephen Hawking, *Brief History*, 133, 173.

13. Ibid., 136, 173.

14. Atkins, *The Creation*, chap. 5: ". . . spacetime emerged by chance out of its own dust" (103).

15. As we would expect, conversations between cosmologists and theologians, almost unheard of in the recent past, are beginning to take place. In some cases, challenges have been thrown out by theologians. See Langdon Gilkey, "Whatever Happened to Immanuel Kant?" in *Nature, Reality, and the Sacred: The Nexus of Science and Religion*, Theology and the Sciences (Mineapolis: Fortress Press, 1993), and, Wolfhart Pannenberg, *Toward a Theology of*

claim to total explanation is not based on actual, successful explanation but on a claimed *a priori* feature of science, in this case physics, as capable of explaining its subject matter by way of its discovered laws. If cosmos is a term for the All and if cosmos is the subject of cosmology, cosmos must be explainable without remainder. To repeat, the basis of this principle is not an actual, empirical discovery, an accomplished explanation, but a self-definition of a science (total explanation) brought into connection with a subject matter (cosmos). Why would cosmologists be drawn into such a vicious circle? Something intrinsic about the cosmos itself rather than any specific failed explanation is at work here. Consider the alternatives. The cosmos is either (1) a single system that actually began "a long time ago," whose beginning engendered spacetime and the laws of physics; (2) a single system everlasting in time; or (3) one of a multiplicity of systems that everlastingly succeed each other, the Big Bang thus being the "origin" of the present cosmic system. In none of these three situations is cosmology as a macroastronomical, mathematical, or quantum endeavor able to meet the conditions of explanation. It cannot obtain to the situation of transition into cosmos without positing *something* (dust particles, extreme heat density, quantum vacuum), and no laws of physics will account for an everlasting system, everlasting multiple systems, or the transition in which those laws arose.

Such then is the cosmos delivered to us by quantum and astrophysics. It is clearly not simply a very large machine made up of small, indivisible

Nature: Essays on Science and Faith, trans. Ted Peters (Louisville: Westminster John Knox, 1993), chap. 1. In addition is the debate over creation and the Big Bang between William Lane Craig and Quentin Smith. See their *Theism, Atheism, and Big Bang Cosmology* (Oxford: Clarendon Press, 1993). Craig argues for the necessity of a creator, even given the Big Bang. Smith offers an "atheistic cosmological argument" that appeals to wave-functional analysis (cf. Hawking). Combining both theological and cosmological viewpoints, a physicist (Polkinghorne) dismisses the physicist's (Hawking) debate over a singular condition as having no theological significance. For Polkinghorne, divine creation is always taking place, hence it cannot be assigned to some function at the boundaries or edges of spacetime. Thus even if physicists are right when they say that the universe emerged out of a "pre-existing quantum vacuum," this is not the *nihil* of the religious claim that God creates from nothing. John Polkinghorne, *The Faith of a Physicist: Reflections of a Bottom-Up Thinker* (Minneapolis: Fortress Press, 1994, 1996), 74. At stake here is whether or not there can be an "end of physics" in the sense of an arrival at complete explanation without remainder. See Stephen Hawking, *Is the End in Sight for Theoretical Physics?* (Cambridge: Cambridge University Press, 1980). Hawking argues (against seventeenth-century theologians) that the initial conditions of the universe is as suitable for scientific study as local conditions. To study such conditions may not necessarily be an example of scientific hubris that David Lindley opposes. If it pretends to be an exhaustive theory of everything, then it claims more than it can deliver. "This theory of everything, this myth, will indeed spell the end of physics. It will be the end not because physics has at last been able to explain everything in the universe but because physics has reached the end of all the things it has the power to explain" (*The End of Physics: The Myth of a Unified Theory* [New York: HarperCollins, 1993], 255).

bodies that obey laws of motion. At the macro level a portion of its entities display a regularity.[16] But the only regularity of the cosmos as a totality appears to be its move toward energy loss and disorder.[17] The cosmos also has a kind of randomness about it, a chaotic element that operates in the behavior of subatomic particles, in complex, turbulent systems, and in the ever-present tendency both to disorder and the generation of novelty and new order. Further, cosmos includes multiple levels of things from the particle world to vast suns, with behavior changes at all levels. There are specific directional activities as galaxies and suns are born and die, but there appears to be no total teleological fulfillment in the future of the cosmos. The cosmos as the single system originating in the Big Bang does appear to be limited in time but the ultimate circumstances of that beginning appear impenetrable. Cosmos thus has a cognitively impenetrable aspect, a face turned away from us. In other words, cosmos does have an edge, a boundary, a kind of underside. These metaphors describe the very facticity of the cosmos as evoking a kind of astonishment. This is why cosmos is not a sheer given, a discrete object comprehensible to whatever science or speculation would subject it to explanation. At this point cosmos or the universe resembles what I have called world.

NATURE

The second sphere or dimension that constitutes world is nature, that system of interdependent living things to which our planet has given rise.[18] Earth is the name and metaphor for our planet as the host of life.[19]

16. For a comprehensive picture of the symmetries, structures, and regularities of the universe at both macro and micro levels, see Frank Wilazek and Betsy Divine, *Longing for the Harmonies: Themes and Variations of Modern Physics* (New York: W. W. Norton and Co., 1988). See also Guy Murchie, *The Music of the Spheres: The Material Universe—From Atom to Quasar Simply Explained*, Vol. 2 (New York: Dover, 1961), chap. 9.

17. There are dissenters to the "big crunch" scenario of the end of the universe. Hawking speculates that quantum theory gives a third alternative to the old dilemma of a beginning at some point in time or an everlastingly existing universe. In quantum theory spacetime would have no boundary and thus no singularities at the beginning or end, thus is simply "self-contained," neither created nor destroyed (*Brief History*, 135–36). Freeman Dyson writes, "The laws of physics do not predict any final quiescence but show us things continuing to happen, physical processes continuing to operate as far into the future as we can imagine" (*Infinite in All Directions* [New York: Harper & Row, 1988], 115).

18. On the ambiguity and variety of concepts of nature, see Gordon Kaufman, "Theology and the Concept of Nature," in *The Theological Imagination: Constructing the Concept of God* (Philadelphia: Westminster Press, 1981). See also Langdon Gilkey, *Nature, Reality*, chap. 6.

19. In this threefold analysis of world (cosmos, nature, and history), I am using nature and life more or less synonymously. Nature, in other words, is world in the sense of a sphere of living things. On nature *as* life, see Gilkey, *Nature, Reality*, chap. 7.

Given the number of galaxies, suns, and probable sun systems (in the thousands of billions), life is statistically probable throughout the universe. But the only system of living things we know is that of our own planet. While chemical, atomic, and other continuities pervade the universe, life represents something of a break from nonliving or inorganic entities. This break is established when entities emerge that reproduce their kind through cell replication and speciation takes place through cell mutation. Speciation has occurred when reproduction is limited to individuals of a specific group. Life then is a distinctive phenomenon and sphere, not reducible to the macroentities of the cosmos (suns, planets) or to cosmologically distributed chemical and atomic particles.[20]

Because nature is the sphere we occupy and is what we ourselves are, and because we respond to living things in aesthetic, cognitive, and practical ways, it evokes from us multiple interpretations. When we describe life as participants, we attend to the ways our entanglements in the ecosystems of life structure our everyday experience. This is the life (nature) of the seasons, of light and dark, hunger, food gathering, and predation. This is the "nature" of tribal religions and their mythologies and rites and also of the common sense, practical orientations of all peoples.[21] And this is the "nature" that ever presents to human beings the perils and obstacles as well as the resources for their struggles for survival and well-being. And these struggles with nature have fostered attempts to understand the workings of the sphere of life. In recent centuries these attempts have taken the form of vigorous, controlled, experimental, and technologically managed investigations; in other words, the sciences. But the human struggle with nature has also prompted other kinds of understandings of the sphere of life. The mystery that comes with the sphere of life, the rigorously focused work of the sciences, and the destruction human

20. Technical definitions of life abound in the biological sciences. Jacques Monod proposes that something is living if it has three properties: teleonomic behavior (acting toward ends), autonomous morphogenesis (self-reproduction), and reproductive invariance (the reproduction of *kind* over generations) (*Chance and Necessity: An Essay on the Natural Philosophy of Biology*, trans. A. Wainhouse [New York: Alfred A. Knopf, 1971], chap. 1). For distinguishing features of both inorganic and organic spheres, see Arthur Peacocke, *Science and the Christian Experiment* (London: Oxford University Press, 1971). Compared to this precise definition, Paul Tillich's use of the term *life* is both general and confusing. See his *Systematic Theology*, Vol. 3 (Chicago: University of Chicago Press, 1963), Part IV: I. According to Tillich, the ontological concept of life is the "actualization of the potential" (12). Such a definition fails to distinguish life from cosmos and from the inorganic, since actualizations of various kinds take place in the particle world, crystals, and other levels of actuality. Yet Tillich's proposed features of living things (self-integration, self-creativity, self-transcendence) seem to pertain to organic entities but not the inorganic (30–88). The confusion here is between life defined simply as actualization and life as marked out by transinorganic features.

21. Gilkey, *Nature, Reality*, 81.

societies are able to wreak on the sphere of life have evoked poetic, reflective, moral, integrative, and speculative interpretations. In what follows, I shall put such interpretations temporarily aside to focus on how biological sciences portray the sphere of life. I postpone the broader issues until the next chapter.

So astonishing, so world-changing have been the scientific discoveries of the last one hundred or so years that we sometimes speak of them as a series of "revolutions." These revolutions have given us a physical universe whose sizes, distances, times, and contents now escape the pictorial imagination. Even those who conduct the experiments and grasp the mathematics have no way of actually thinking or conceiving numbers in billions, distances of light years, or time intervals of nanoseconds. The more precisely we understand with the aid of the new scientific instruments the less we can actually picture or imagine. Powerful telescopes, radioscopes, computers, and cyclotrons have given us the expanding universe. A similar technology has revolutionized the sciences of life.[22] All of the old geological timetables, the old paleontology, genetics, and chemistries of living things, are now replaced or vastly extended. New paleontologies and biochemistry have changed our notions of the history of life and the world of the cell as much as quantum and astrophysics have altered our notions of the cosmos. Accordingly, the sphere of life is much older, more varied, more complex, and more interrelated than earlier generations ever suspected.

Research on three different levels has given us this new picture of the sphere of life: macrobehavioral (natural history), evolutionary, and the microstructural. Perhaps a better way to express this threefold division of labor is to say that the old "natural history" of life forms has splintered into behavioral-structural-environmental, evolutionary, and microbiological undertakings. Thus any one life form, a species of beetle for instance, can be studied in all three ways.

Natural history has been part of Western thought since Aristotle and Pliny. Until Gregor Mendel and genetics, Charles Darwin and evolution, and Louis Pasteur and the world of microbes, biology was more or less a gathering of descriptive information about the classification, distribution, behavior, and physiology of various forms of life. Descriptive natural history has not so much been replaced as expanded into a galaxy of specialties that include ethology (the science of animal behavior) and ecology

22. For a popular historical account of the revolution in biology, see Horace Freeland Judson, *The Eighth Day of Creation: Makers of the Revolution in Biology* (New York: Simon & Schuster, 1979).

(the science of life systems). Ethology has studied animal behavior in its enormous complexity, breaking down older mechanistic notions of animals as units of "instinct," and sciences such as primatology and the study of cetaceans have uncovered continuities between human and other life forms. Ecology has given contemporary societies a sense of the interdependence of all life forms in the biosphere of our planet.

No account of "the way nature works" is now possible without attending to the overwhelming evidence for the evolution of species. We should not let the ambiguities of the term *evolution* obscure or dismiss this evidence. Evolution can mean an essentially philosophical pretension to an exhaustive explanation of whatever human beings are or do, a kind of worldview. It can also name one of several "theories" concerning the dynamics of species development.[23] But such things should not be confused with the fact of species development, the evidence for which not only lies in a detailed fossil record whose sequence is fixed relatively precisely with the help of advances in the dating of ancient strata but also in direct observation of speciation, for instance, the genetic manipulation of fruit flies. The contents of this basic fact are the following. There is continuity between all earth life forms at the level of macromolecules and the nucleic acids of proteins, and beyond that, there is continuity between all life forms and the basic chemistry and atomic structure of the cosmos. These chemicals of life were "cooked" in ancient suns. Second, all groups of life forms (species) develop from other life forms, hence, life in our biosphere is not only a matter of individual birth and reproduction but a sequence of species that is irreversible.

Most controversies about evolution are concerned with the dynamics of evolutionary process, especially the Darwinian notion of natural selection.[24] In spite of qualifications and refinements, especially proposed by sociobiology, natural selection ("Darwinism") continues to be the prevailing view among biologists. Consider the following: First, a species reproduces itself by the replication of genes, and the gene pool of a species contains an enormous number of variations, most of which pertain to

---

23. The major issues that evolutionary biologists debate are the locus of evolution (groups, species, individuals, genes), the degree to which the environment plays a role in genetic variation (Neo-Larmarkianism), the gradual and slow versus episodic and rapid (Stephen Jay Gould) nature of evolution, and whether selection targets and is the explanation for all the features of organisms. See Arthur Peacocke, *God and the New Biology* (London: Dent, 1986), chap. 3.

24. See Michael Ruse, *Taking Darwin Seriously: A Naturalistic Approach to Philosophy* (New York: Blackwell, 1986), chap. 1. See also Arthur Peacocke, *Science and the Christian Experiment*, chap. 3. For evolutionary process in microbiology, see Jacques Monod, *Chance and Necessity*, chap. 7.

individual features (size, color of fur, and soon) compatible with the general requirements of survival. Within this gene pool cellular variations (mutations) are constantly taking place. Some of these variations are incompatible with the survival of individuals and fade out. Others are neither adaptive nor counteradaptive. Second, individuals of the species carry these variations (for instance, larger or smaller wings) and respond to the challenges of their environment accordingly. Because they carry mutated features, some individuals will possess possibilities of response (for instance, a certain kind of beak), which in the ordinary environment of the species has little or no advantage, but in a new environment may be survival oriented. Third, no environment of a species and its individuals is static. Weather patterns, predatory groups, and available food all change over time. Hence, those individuals that carry a particular mutated feature will adapt to the change and others (or at least their offspring) lacking the feature will be eliminated. What was once an irrelevant mutated feature takes on a positive survival function due to the challenge of a new environment. For instance, the darker color fur disguises the animal from a new type of predator that has moved onto the scene. Finally, gene replication continues to pass the trait on to new generations, and those individuals that lack the trait fail to survive. On the basis of this "Darwinian" account, we need not conclude that every trait of a species or its individuals is present because of a successful adaptation. Many traits are neutral to adaptation and are present simply because of mutation. Some traits such as the huge antlers of the Irish Elk are counteradaptive and will either disappear as traits or will assist in the elimination of the species.

It is clear that the concept of evolution is not simply the common sense observation that living things develop. Evolution is the very condition of life as we know it. If DNA were utterly invariable, perfectly replicating every trait, nothing would have developed out of the primeval algal matter. Further, even if an existing species was created all at once by a divine magician, but utterly without cell mutations, it would not have a variable enough gene pool for its individuals to be able to adapt to changing conditions. Such a species, doomed to exactly repeat itself and unable to adapt, would succumb to the first environmental change. Hence, the randomness of cell mutation is a *sine qua non* for the origin and continuation of any and all species. Evolution then is the necessary condition of organic life in a changing environment.

The world of the cell is the third horizon of present-day biological sciences. Like particle physics, microbiology originated and progressed with the aid of new technologies. When the world of the cell and its nucleotides were uncovered, it provided evolutionary biology with the specific mechanisms of gene replication and showed how that replication could be varied. From microbiology came an astonishing world (the cell) more complex than the particle world. The discovery of the cell is basic to virtually all the sciences of life. Since the cell (or cell in combination) and its proteins and nucleic acids are what maintain the delicate metabolic conditions of life, cell and genetic biology is the key to understanding the conditions of life itself. Looked at one way, we have in the chemical processes of the cell a kind of "molecular engineering" (Jacques Monod) or a mechanism of chemical activity. The molecule thus stores memory, processes and passes on information, and assists different compounds to interact. And the sequences of these activities is found in all living things. By means of this "engineering," a life form reproduces its own type, traits are passed to the next generation, food is metabolized, energy is stored. In this perspective a living organism seems to be a kind of machine, comprised of cellular cybernetics. But if this were the whole story, life would not emerge at all. For the molecular world of the cell is also a quantum world, a world of particle play. Thus the cell is not a machine but a complex environment of various kinds of accidental or random events, beginning with the incalculable operations of atomic particles and continuing into cell mutation. Like the organisms of which they are a part, cells can respond, adapt, and entertain novel contents. If this were not so, a living thing would be utterly changeless, unadaptive, and would never come to be in the first place.

STRUCTURAL FEATURES OF THE SPHERE OF LIFE

In actuality the contributions of the sciences of life are too vast and too complex to be communicable in short summaries. At the same time, we can identify certain themes in the sciences of life that supplement and enrich world simply as cosmos. On the basis of the life sciences, we can identify seven general features of the sphere of life: levels, teleonomic behavior (responsiveness), parasitism, cooperation, environmental interdependence, direction, and suffering.

Levels

The sphere of life is not simply a multiplicity of living individuals or kinds but is distributed over levels.[25] If the metaphor of levels means rule

25. The metaphor of levels is fairly commonplace in philosophies of nature. See Arthur Peacocke, *Science and the Christian Experiment*, chaps. 2 and 3; Harold Schilling, *The New Consciousness in Science and Religion* (London: SCM, 1973), chaps. 1 and 3; Michael Polanyi,

from the top, it is surely an inadequate metaphor. No top stratum controls the sphere of life through a hierarchy of servant powers. To avoid this notion, Paul Tillich proposed a "democracy" of dimensions.[26] Yet his dimensions (inorganic, organic, spirit) are interrelated not by democratic input but by a one-way dependence of the organic on the inorganic, and so forth. In other words, they turn out to be levels. Nature or the life sphere is comprised of levels of entity types. Thus, no one would say that while organisms exist, species and cells do not. The range of the life sphere includes the micro world of cells, membranes that connect cells together into organs, composite entities (roots, leaves, organs) that make up an organism, the species and families of the organism, and the kind of environment necessary to the survival of all these things. Each level has its own complexity and distinctive make-up and requires distinctive methods and concepts to understand it.

Responsiveness

Everything that is actual changes over time. Living things not only change but respond. They are not simply objects utterly passive to external forces, blank tablets on which external causalities write certain contents. Even cells display teleonomic activity. And when cells gather into a more complex organism, that organism constantly responds both to its own internal events (injury, malfunction, disease) and to the environment that impacts it. This capacity to respond is not a contingent feature of living things but a necessary condition of their survival. Because all living entities require specific environmental conditions, their lives become precarious when those conditions begin to change. If a living thing is unable to respond to minute or massive changes, it quickly succumbs. "Responsiveness" is only a minimal and abstract way of expressing this trait. In their constant search for sustenance and for situations in which propagation can take place, living things not only respond but initiate. Response need not be self-aware or deliberate. When cells mobilize chemical resources to resist a bacterium, a kind of response is taking place. For microbiologists, quantum or particle events and cell mutations introduce a chance element into what lives. But the unpredictability is intrinsic to a life form insofar as it is responsive to its environment. The strongest way to express this trait of living things is to say that they exist creatively. Insofar as living things seek and find solutions to problems fostered by

Personal Knowledge: Towards a Post-Critical Philosophy (New York: Harper & Row, 1964), chaps. 12 and 13.
    26. Paul Tillich, *Systematic Theology,* Vol. 3: 12–15.

their environment, they originate situations that never before existed. In other words they are units of genuine novelty.

Parasitism

Environmental events can detrimentally affect life forms and their species. These imperilments include but are not limited to predation and intraspecies competition. Half of all marine species were eliminated when vast areas of the continental shelf on which those species depended disappeared when continental drift formed a new single continent (*pangea*). At the same time, life forms can live only at the expense of other life-forms. Here we have life-forms not just competing for space or food but dependent on other life-forms for nourishment. All species exist in a food chain of some sorts, even the very large and apparently invulnerable animals such as lions, bears, and whales. As large and successful predators they may be at the top of their food chain, yet they too are objects of insect and microbe predation. Because of competition for space and the special vulnerability of the young of species to predatory and environmental hazards, there is an enormous profligacy of numbers in the reproduction of plants, fishes, insects, and bacteria. Such profligacy is an adaptive response to the fact that most of the young of these life-forms do not survive into adulthood. Parasitism or the predation of life forms on other life-forms comes with life itself. For most species what provides energy to living cells are not the chemicals of inorganic substances. At the same time, parasitism is a necessary condition of ongoing life. Its elimination would be the death of the biosphere. And since the drastic reduction of a species by some herbivores or carnivores (croppers) frees space for other species, parasitism promotes diversity of life-forms.

Cooperation

To portray life in the dramatic language of "red in tooth and claw" yields a skewed picture. To focus solely on parasitic behavior, the food chain, the demise of species, and profligacy of reproduction may prompt us to overlook an equally important feature of the behavior of living things. Even in the particle world negative repulsion between particles had to be overcome for atoms to come into existence. Forces of attraction and binding together are necessary for the existence of atoms and thus the universe itself. Could the sphere of life ever emerge at all and be successfully maintained if its sole feature were the principle of parasitism? Even parasitism depends on the existence of species and thus on successful reproduction and survival. And the survival of species and of individuals in species does not depend simply on the efforts of survival-oriented solitary individuals but also on cooperation. Living organisms are not a windowless monad (Gottfried Leibniz) whose harmony is "preestablished" but are rather intrinsically interdependent. Thus, mutual attractions prompt cells to form into larger units, individuals of species to develop survival-oriented social behavior, and even species to develop cooperative behaviors with other species. And once life becomes propagated through gender differentiation, cooperation takes the form of propagative acts and enduring gender units of protection and nurture. Without organizational structures that promote survival, mutual attraction, and cooperative behavior, the human life form would surely be a failed biological experiment on this planet.[27]

Systemics

One of the great discoveries of modern biology is now part of everyday awareness and even politics, the interdependence of life forms in their specific environment and the whole biosphere as a delicate balance of conditions for life. Some species come to be dependent on each other. Some local environments, for instance, a small pond, maintain a seasonally phased balance between the micro world of bacteria and the macro world of fish, insects, birds, and mammals. But beyond these locales of interdependent life forms is a systemic interdependence as broad as the planet itself. Life on a planet came about in the first place from the pres-

---

27. In Darwinism the primary thing that pushes evolution along is each entity's survival orientation, hence competition and predation. But in the nineteenth century, one of the Darwinians added to the dynamics of evolution the motif of cooperation or "mutual aid" among animals. In the 1980s a Russian zoologist, Karl Kessler, delivered a lecture entitled "On the Law of Mutual Aid." This lecture helped stimulate a set of articles by Peter Kropotkin written in the 1890s and collected under the title, *Mutual Aid: A Factor of Evolution* (New York: New York University Press, 1972); see chaps. 1 and 2 for a study of mutual aid among animals. The main point was that evolution proceeds not simply by competition and survival of the fittest but by mutual interdependence and aid. From the early 1970s to the present, this theme has received new attention. See William Trager, *Symbiosis* (New York: Van Nostrand Reinhold, 1970), 2. Symbiosis works across the whole range of organisms from protozoa (cf. microsymbiosis) to vertebrate animals. This older motif of symbiosis has evoked new interest under the term *mutualism,* "a mutually beneficial relation between (or perhaps more) species" (Joel Cohen, "Concluding Remarks," in Hiroye Kawanabe, J. Cohen, and K. Iwasaki, eds., *Mutualism and Community Organization* [Oxford: Oxford University Press, 1993]). In the view of the contributors to this volume, mutualism arose as a corrective emphasis in biology in the early 1970s. Its main insight is that "positive relations have an important position in the discussion of the organization of natural communities" (2). Some argue for a distinction between mutualism and symbiosis. Mutualism can include *brief* positive interactions such as pollination. Mutualistic symbiosis has some degree of permanent interdependence (D. C. Smith and A. E. Douglas, *The Biology of Symbiosis* [London: Edward Arnold, 1987], 1). For an excellent introduction to the topic, see Jan Sapp, *Evolution by Association: A History of Symbiosis* (New York: Oxford University Press, 1994).

ence of very specific conditions having to do with light, moisture, temperature, and even gravity. The total loss of the ozone layer, the loss of the oceans as life-supporting environments, the elimination of all green plants would drastically affect the planet's capacity to support life. Ecological balance, the interdependence of species with each other and on environmental conditions, is both a local and a planetary principle.

Direction

To biologists teleology is a pejorative term for the view that life on the planet is following a preset direction to a preset end, and-or, a way of explaining particular biological phenomena by assigning some preset and guiding intent. For instance, God (or something) gave fins to fishes so they can better function in water. Biologists aggressively reject teleology in both senses, partly for lack of evidence for such, and partly because other explanations (natural selection, cellular chemistry) are deemed to be adequate. This repudiation of teleology is not necessarily a denial that life is directional. We would expect to find direction in the sphere of life simply because directionality is a universal feature of everything that is actual from the cosmos itself to atomic particles. In the sphere of life directionality takes a distinctive twist. To say this is not necessarily to claim some overall direction of the life sphere, an issue I shall postpone for the present. Direction in the sphere of life shows itself in the life span of individual organisms, in trends at work in species, and in specific regions and epochs of time. Teleonomic or self-maintaining and responsive behavior in the struggle for life and well-being of individuals is directional, as is their maturation from infancy to adulthood.[28] At the species level, evolution itself is directional as mutated traits enable successful adaptations to a changing environment. Speciation itself is directional, arising as it does on the basis of an enormously varied gene pool whose ongoing mutations prevent the exact replications or cloning of individuals. Further, direction is present in the "histories" of specific environments, for instance, the spread of Douglas fir trees in the Northwest of North America, or the rise and subsequent erosion of mountain ranges. To conclude, in nature direction is displayed in individual growth, teleonomic behavior, regional and epochal trends, and evolutionary speciation.

Is the sphere of life marked by any *universal* directions? Does the sphere of life give any sign of direction as betterment or progressive movement

---

28. Monod, *Chance and Necessity,* chaps. 1, 2, and 3.

toward some value? Biologists unite at this point in a negative consensus. There is no built-in, inevitable movement in the biosphere that began with the primeval algal soup and proceeded from there to a certain end.[29] The one possible candidate for such a trend is the rather formal notion of movement from simplicity to complexity. It is the case that the biosphere is more varied and complex now than it was in earlier times. And yet there have also been movements in the direction of simplification. Due to mass species elimination, there are fewer species now than at certain times in the past. And it is quite possible that some future planetary event could again eliminate most species, leaving a much simplified biosphere. This qualification has less to do with the biosphere and its life forms, however, as with the vulnerability of that sphere to environmental conditions. The reduction of marine species by continental drift is a kind of external accident rather than something arising within the sphere of life itself. Even when we acknowledge the vulnerability of life forms to environmental conditions, it seems to be the case that the biosphere displays a general directional trend. Because of mutations, teleonomic struggle, and adaptation, individuals of species attempt to solve the problems they confront in their environments and species tend to fill what space they can. The result is that "nature" selects or promotes entities with ever more increased sensitivity and capacity in monitoring their situation. Because of environmental factors and accidents of mutation, most lines of direction are evolutionary dead ends, that is, the species fails to survive. Yet the trend is ever in the direction of increased sensitivity. Biologically speaking, one can only say that the emergence of mammals, primates, and human beings is an "accident." At the same time, there is something about selection and adaptation that presses in the direction of complexly responsive entities.

Suffering

Contemporary cosmology presents us with a stellar world of unimaginable events of destruction (supernovas, black holes engulfing whole sun systems) and a micro world of untrackable randomness. At work in the apparent regularities of the stars and in seemingly stable and solid "matter" are elements of chaos. When life emerges, chaos (randomness, disorder) takes new and intense forms. The old theodicies could explain hu-

---

29. This view is challenged in a recent article that lists evidences for the probability of life emerging if certain chemical conditions are in place. According to the author of the article, James Trefil, "The business of the universe is creating life." ("However it began on Earth, life may have been inevitable," in *Smithsonian* 25, No. 11 [February, 1995]: 40).

man suffering as an effect of the Fall but they still had to struggle with the pervasive phenomenon of animal suffering. And the notion of a pre-Fall painless Edenic existence only intensified this problem. To speak of a "tragic" dimension of the sphere of life may be unnecessarily dramatic. Yet if the tragic means the structural interconnection between conditions of creativity and sensibility and vulnerability to suffering, something like a tragic structure is intrinsic to all forms of life.[30]

Teleonomic and responsive forms of life exist at some level as modes of feeling, able to sense how their environment impinges on them. To speak of a cell's "suffering" may not be simply an anthropomorphic exaggeration. If suffering means the capacity of an organism to sense in a qualitative way distorted alterations of its own embodiment, then something like suffering appears to attend all living organisms. This suffering increases in intensity with neural complexity. Living entities are subject to suffering in at least three ways. First, all life forms are subjected to assaults on their embodiment, the distinctive imperilments of injury, disease, and death. Mountains and planets may come to an end but do not undergo these sorts of imperilments. Furthermore, because life forms mobilize their resources to resist them, we can say that they experience these imperilments. Second, because living entities are teleonomic, pursuing nourishment and situations of reproduction in a struggle to survive their imperilments, a gap between their pursuit or set of needs and what would answer to these needs structures their very being. There is nothing accidental about this gap. It is present by virtue of the fact that the entities are alive and are teleonomic. In human beings, this structural break between desire (eros) and end occurs in intense, self-aware, and symbolized ways. Third, living things are both the victims and actors in the food chain of predation. In this parasitic situation, predators reduce the population of the species on which they feed and are themselves reduced. Parasitism is the primary though not only imperilment of most living things. Suffering, then, is intrinsic to the sphere of life. Apart from suffering, life could neither come about nor be maintained.

In the twentieth century, physics and microbiology have made astonishing strides toward understanding "how the world works." So much is this the case that some scientists are confident that a total and exhaustive account of "all things" has been in principle accomplished. In connection

---

30. One of the general features of evolution listed by Arthur Peacocke is the sacrifice of life based on the principle that new forms of life can arise only by displacing or modifying what already exists. Thus, competition and struggle are intrinsic to evolutionary process (*Science and the Christian Experiment*, chap. 3).

with the cosmos, I argued that since scientific explanations can only take place in terms of the laws that are immanent in the world system, it can never explain the sheer facticity of this system. Cosmos thus presents to science a boundary, a depth of mystery. And this mystery only intensifies with the emergence of life. There are those who identify that mystery with the failure of biology to explain or reproduce the conditions of life. Because there are chemical and atomic continuities throughout the universe we should not be surprised if science discovers and even reproduces the transition from nonlife to life. I hesitate to make too much of this gap in present scientific knowledge. I prefer to say that nature, like cosmos, presents a boundary to its inquirers. The play of particles is one kind of boundary to explanation. The phenomenon of self-initiating, responsive entities confronts explanation with another kind of boundary. These entities resist explanation not because of chance or statistically unpredictable events but simply because they *act*. Insofar as an internally born action is not the passive receptivity to an external cause, it cannot be causally explained. And this is the mystery, the elusiveness of life's facticity, the sheer unexplainable fact of self-initiated action.[31]

31. Thus, Paul Weiss argues that the constituents of reality, "primary actualities" or "beings," all have an impenetrable "inside" as well as a manifestness (*Nature and Man* [New York: Henry Holt & Co., 1947], 39–41). The "ontological creative act and its source" is, for Robert Neville, what is responsible for the "that it is-ness of the world," one could say, its sheer facticity, that eludes explanation in terms of itself (*Recovery of the Measure: Interpretation and Nature* [Albany: SUNY Press, 1989], 115).

14
THREE-DIMENSIONAL WORLD: HISTORY

> The modern idea of history is a dynamic principle for attaining
> a comprehensive view of everything human. . . . The more this
> idea of history has been emancipated from extraneous meta-
> physical prejudgments and gained recognition as a way of
> thinking independent of the formulation of concepts that takes
> place in the natural sciences, the more it has demonstrated that
> it is the matrix out of which all worldviews take shape.
>
> *Ernst Troeltsch,* The Absoluteness of Christianity and the
> History of Religions

> We contend that what is *primarily* historical is Dasein. . . .
> World-historical entities do not first get their historical charac-
> ter, let us say, by reason of an historiological objectification;
> they get it rather as those entities which they are in themselves
> when they are encountered within-the-world.
>
> *Martin Heidegger,* Being and Time

Human beings participate in world not simply as cosmos and nature
but as history. And while world as history involves "subjectivity," it is
not merely subjective. As a term for that whole complex of human
groups, institutions, cultures, and symbolic systems, history does not
simply repeat what we find in the cosmos or the biosphere. Even the
attempt to eliminate history from world must make use of language,
evidences, symbolic forms, and even power considerations that arise
in history. The task before us is a general one. I shall not try to cata-
logue the way history is interpreted in various religious traditions or
track competing philosophical plottings of the "meaning" or "meaninglessness" of history. Granting that my interpretation will have been
influenced by these traditions, my explicit aim is more general than a
"theology" of history.

Insofar as cosmos and nature are somewhat delimited fields of inquiry that lend themselves to scientific specialties, they seldom evoke

philosophical questions as to their meaning. But history as a sphere of human activity retains complexities and ambiguities that evoke disagreements even about what it is and how it should be studied. Accordingly, a general account of history cannot avoid some preliminary clarifications. An initial ambiguity is easy to resolve. History can mean an academic discipline, located either in the social sciences or the humanities. The subject of this discipline is the recoverable past, and the methodological problem (historiography) this discipline faces is how to best go about that recovery.[1]

History can also be an inclusive term for the sphere of the human as opposed to "nature," a flowing complex of human individual and corporate activities. We have here a distinction, common in various texts, between history as the subject of a scholarly endeavor and history as concrete, human temporality. In the first sense, history arises by way of a selective retrieval and imaginative construction. History thus is something we recover only by abstraction. I mean by that, a rigorous and evidence-oriented reconstruction of the past requires a focused, selective act that by its nature must obtain a distance from the flow of historical process. It should not be necessary to say that when we speak of a "theology" of history, or of God's relation to history, we are not talking about this abstracted, focused academic enterprise. What sense would it make to say that God is related to the *reconstruction* of travel practices of the Italian aristocracy of eighteenth-century Milan?

On the other side of the distinction is what some interpreters have called concrete or inner history.[2] Here arises a fascination with the phenomenon itself, the very facticity and mystery of the way human corporate reality perdures through time. It is history in this sense that prompts us to think about the "meaning of history," the general dynamics of historical movement, and such issues as history's uniqueness, direction, conflict, patterns, and indeterminacy. Those who explicate history in this sense perpetrate an abstraction, not of focus and selection, but of generality. We should be careful not to permit the distinction to harden into sepa-

---

1. For an excellent overview of history as an interpretive activity, see Marc Bloch, *The Historian's Craft*, trans. P. Putnam (New York: Knopf, 1953).

2. On "inner history," "our history," or history as lived, see H. Richard Niebuhr, *The Meaning of Revelation* (New York: Macmillan, 1946), 56–90; and Nicolas Berdyaev, *The Meaning of History* (London: Geoffrey Bles, 1936), chap. 3. For Berdyaev there is only one history, the realm and movement in which human freedom operates and in which the enrichment of human experience takes place. Objectified history for Berdyaev is pseudohistory (*The Beginning and the End* [New York: Harper & Bros., 1952], 200–22). Karl Jaspers has a similar view; see *Philosophical Faith and Revelation*, trans. E. B. Ashton (New York: Harper & Bros., 1967), 196.

ration, as if there were two histories. There is, in the end, only history, whose multidimensionality invokes a variety of relations to it and ways of speaking of it. When we actually participate in what H. Richard Niebuhr calls "our history," we are close to concrete history. We are only a slight step away from participation when, aware of oppressive history, we give voice to that oppression under agendas of liberation. We distance ourselves further when, like Tillich, we do a phenomenology of historical process. We are farther yet when we would recover a selected strand of the historical past in as much detail as possible. According to the following account, three features come together in the historical as a distinctive dimension of world: bearers, historical passage, and ambiguity.

BEARERS

The old adage about time also applies to history. We know what it is until we attempt to define it. Yet a formal definition comes easily. History is past, temporally sequenced, human corporate life. The matter becomes more opaque when we try to understand what is distinctive about history's temporality. What is it in this temporality that is temporal? What, in other words, is our subject?[3] When historians retrieve the historical, what do they retrieve? These questions have no single answer. In one sense, the answer must be inclusive. If history is about the whole human complex, and if that complex is connected with nature and cosmos, "all of that" is what history would retrieve. Yet precisely because history is the sphere of the human, certain things are inevitably privileged. For instance, we would not be talking about history at all if we made no room for human agents. History as human corporate temporality is what it is only because it is a web of individual, purposive activities. History thus includes the mystery, complexity, and multidimensionality of human passions as they are rooted in organic drives, self-transcending subjectivity, and the tragic conflictual character of these things. Human agents as we know them exist as a distinctive temporality that orients them to past and future by way of language and symbols and that gives their life a tone of anxiety, rooted in a generalized awareness of their imperilment. In con-

---

3. Several historians and philosophers of history have come to the same conclusion as to the bearers or carriers of historical passage. Ernst Troeltsch proposes life unities in which individuals, classes, peoples, and communities all come together. See Peter Hodgson, *God in History: Shapes of Freedom* (Nashville: Abingdon Press, 1989), 174–79. For Paul Tillich, the group is history's primary bearer (*Systematic Theology,* Vol. 3 [Chicago: University of Chicago Press, 1963], 308). Individuals then are indirect bearers. In similar vein, Maurice Mandelbaum says that the object of history is a "societal order," and this sets the primary task for the historian, the study of the character of societies (*The Anatomy of Historical Knowledge* [Baltimore: Johns Hopkins University Press, 1977]).

nection with these things come exaggerated valuations of whatever eases the perils of life and a dynamics of evil that issues in malice and murder. These agential dynamics bestow significance, depth, and aim on groups, institutions, trends, and traditions of human corporate life.

Yet it is clear that human individuals are not simply separated entities that exist simply in themselves alongside each other. Prior to individuality in the sense of "consciousness" and "self" are various ways of human being-together. Concretely this being-together means both the intimate and anonymous relations that constitute families, tribes, workplaces, and peoples. Philosophically expressed, it is the intersubjectivity that engenders and structures the human self and a set of relations (the interhuman, the Thou, the "face") that deobjectifies human being-together and summons human individuals into mutual responsibility.[4] Human being-together is also a bearer of history and the "stuff" and subject of history. This is why historical passage is not simply a flow of individual biographies. And like human agency, being-together is a kind openness toward the future. Intimate relations, too, have a past, a direction, a "history," a horizon of future possibilities.

Yet to stop our analysis of the "stuff" of history with individuals and their being-together would promote a serious distortion. Human beings ever struggle to maintain their existence, well-being, meaning, power, and security. In this struggle human being-together takes on enduring patterns, organization, and roles. The most ancient form of institutionalization and always its deepest stratum is tradition. Human beings move from the past to the future not simply as conscious individuals but by means of deep structures of value carried in symbols, narratives, customs, and laws. Some have argued that tradition is so central to human history that its loss (as in the postmodern world) would threaten human historicity itself. But institutionalization is more than tradition. Institutions are any and all ways human reality so organizes itself that structures of cooperation, mutual effort, and habitual procedures can be taken for granted. Arts and armies, corporations and bureaucracies are all institutions. Depending on their time and setting, they may or may not be severed from tradition.

4. Both Reinhold Niebuhr and Paul Ricoeur think that human intersubjectivity is the primary locus of history. For Reinhold Niebuhr, historical realities are carried in "dramatic patterns" that originate in active and ongoing dialogues that take place in families and in local and national communities (*The Self and the Dramas of History* [New York: Charles Scribner's Sons, 1955], 193). Ricoeur argues that historical causality needs "relay stations" and these are "first order entities" or "social entities" in which individuals are together in a narrative. For Ricoeur the bearers of history are not simply groups but "entities of participatory belonging" (*Time and Narrative*, Vol. 1, trans. K. McLaughin and D. Pellauer [Chicago: University of Chicago Press, 1984]).

Personal agency, being-together, tradition, and institutions are the "stuff" of history's actual passage. History is borne in these things. At this point the historian senses that the analysis has omitted something important. What historians actually record are not these elements of historical passage. The "stuff" of historical writings is something else; trends, events, corporate entities (for example, nations), regions, individual lives, conflicts, and time periods. If we were content to simply separate concrete history from recorded history, we could ignore this unfortunate dualism. But the "stuff" of recorded history is not simply invented but discerned. Human agents, forms of being-together, and institutions do undergo beginnings and endings, form themselves into regional entities, and perpetuate bounded events. History passes not just in individuals and their traditions but in ethnic groupings, nations, and peoples. To focus exclusively on these entities of recorded history is to miss history's primordial bearers, the very stuff of its passage. To focus exclusively on the bearers is to miss history's epochal and local concreteness.

HISTORICAL PASSAGE

Whatever else history is, it is a movement. Of course the past as such has no movement, but that which is past once moved. Hence, to remember or retrieve the past is to address a movement over time. But to say this is to say very little. Whatever is actual in cosmos or nature also moves. Because of its distinctive "stuff," historical passage is not simply an instance of the movement of cosmos or nature. It is rather the peculiar way in which corporate human reality is temporal.[5] Three themes arise when we would understand this distinctive corporate temporality or historical passage: conservation and novelty, conflict and responsibility, and patterns and directions.

Conservation and Novelty

Like macroeconomic trends, historical passage resists prediction and even exact description. Yet it is not simply an anarchy of unrelated happenings. We who are part of historical passage do have expectations

5. See Tillich, *Systematic Theology* 3:326–39. Tillich gives us an extraordinarily insightful account of the temporal aspect of history or history as passage. As an ontology of historical passage, his analysis is much more formal than Peter Hodgson's, who combines a Hegelian approach, deconstruction, and liberation and praxis theologies to stress the "de-configurative" element in historical passage. See Peter Hodgson, *God in History*, chaps. 3 and 4. See also Langdon Gilkey's analysis of historical passage in *Reaping the Whirlwind: A Christian Interpretation of History* (New York: Seabury Press, 1976), 37–46.

about the near future, which is to say, historical movement displays some continuity, a limited sense of pattern. We may be unable to predict whether or not a certain nation will declare war, but we can discern patterns in its history that remove the surprise from the declaration. Postmodernism is an age of difference. Difference, change, novelty, nonidentity, and instability are what fascinate us. Logos, structure, pattern, and continuity are fascinations of an older time. Between the two, continuity may be the more difficult theme to discern and articulate. Given the complex and rapid alterations that take place at every level of world, we sometimes wonder if there are any continuities. Yet tradition, institutions, and individuals require continuity to exist at all. Even a seemingly momentary event embodies a minimum continuity over time. In nature (life), continuity is obtained initially by replications of genetically based characteristics, behaviors, and responses. In history what endures is the group: the tribe, sect, or committee. Assisting this enduring are deposits of language, symbols, ritualistic patterns, organization, and role distribution that serve the group's aims. Thus, history's enduring takes place as a conservation of the past.

At the same time, historical passage is a movement into novelty. At this point history's movement resembles the assymetrical and irreversible passage (evolution) of nature. And, like nature, history moves in part by way of individual entities. The fact that the group is history's primary unit of passage does not exclude the contribution of participating individuals. Any group has a dynamic life because of the never-ceasing activities of self-transcending, passionate individuals, connected with each other in the dynamics of being-together. This is not to say that historical passage is simply an aggregate of individual activity. Human beings together in their groups exercise creative responses to their situation. If we do not overly literalize this point, we can say that historical units have "a mind of their own." Nations, committees, clubs, and families all respond to what imperils their existence and well-being. At work in these responses are assessments, deliberations, and discernments that find their way into corporate action. Historical movement into the new occurs as human beings are together in the mode of cooperation. This cooperation is not simply the phenomenon of modern democracies. Cooperation goes on in tribal, tyrannical, and bureaucratic groups. Nor should we interpret the historical passage toward the new as something necessarily "good." The novelty that comes about may be a new and frightful form of human being-together that oppresses its own members and works genocide on its neighbors.

Conflict and Responsibility

A second duality of historical passage has to do with power and its molli-fication. Conflict is a mark of historical passage. Struggle, competition, and opposition are recurrent features of the history we know. The strug-gle ranges from clan and tribal warfare to the massive economic and mili-tary conflicts of the twentieth century. A reductionist approach will argue that such conflicts only repeat the biologically based tendencies of all life forms. But such a view sounds like a mere stipulation when we consider the distinctive microelements of historical passage, the self-transcending individuals in their being-together, and the complex way they participate in the social units of history. Historical struggle takes the form of a con-flict of powers. All the bearers of history embody power by the very fact that in them human individuals have pooled their resources to achieve certain aims. Thus, history moves through time as corporate *powers* com-pete with each other, sometimes to the point of tense coexistence, some-times to the point of mutual devastation.

At the same time, historical passage as struggle has another side. To ignore this other side is to invite reduction of human history to cynicism and the "naked ape" anthropology. Human being-together in forms of intimacy (family, small tribes, friends, towns) is never mere conflict. Something is at work in these relations that transcends oppositions and evokes mutual respect, affection, and responsibility. In these forms of being-together human beings are attuned to human vulnerability. While this attunement originates in the intimacies of families, it can become a more broadly oriented posture. Accordingly, human being-together takes on a moral dimension that engenders opposition to murder and violation and ideals of justice and compassion. These interdicts and idealities origi-nate in familial and intimate relations but they can spread into other bear-ers of history. Thus historical passage takes on a dimension of ideality that is in tension with competition and power. The idealities of responsi-bility and justice, expressed in the rites, symbols, and narratives of tradi-tion, confront and limit human conflict. Historical passage takes place in the tension between competitive power and elements that would reduce and tame such power.

Patterns and Directions

A third duality of historical passage confronts us with an endlessly ar-gued theme of philosophy or theology of history, the "meaning of his-tory." Does history have a teleological character? Are certain recurrent patterns intrinsic to history? Is there a directional movement about historical passage that makes history a single story? With a few exceptions, most contemporary interpreters of history oppose religious (God is leading history to some preappointed end) and secular (history ever progresses toward the better) universal teleology.[6] The basis of this opposition is that there are no *a priori* reasons, religious or secular, for such a teleology and there is overwhelming empirical evidence against the notion of a single, unidirectional development. If such a teleology is judged to be the necessary condition of history having a "meaning," then this negative consensus has surely abandoned the concept of a universal "meaning" of history. There is a similiar widespread suspicion, again prompted by empirical evidence, about all attempts (for instance, Arnold Toynbee) to show that historical passage has certain inevitable and recurrent patterns; for instance, a cyclical pattern or a dialectical spiral. For history as a totality, teleology, progress, and patterns seem not to apply.

Yet, the opposition to universal teleology may miss something about historical passage. If we think of historical passage not as "history" but as histories, something like patterns, direction, and the like are not utterly absent. Like nature, history is an accumulation of events. This accumulation takes place not so much over the totality of time or space of what we call history but in strands of tradition, geographically located peoples, and epochal periods of time. Any one bearer of history—a corporation, nation, tribe, or institution—may have a "history," a beginning, development, denouement, and end. Some of these entities and their epochs develop over vast periods of time, thus, Celtic, Chinese, or Roman civilizations. Some of these very inclusive histories may well have discernible patterns; for instance, patterns that arise in transitions from agricultural to industrial and village to urban life. I conclude then that historical passage is directional and open to patterns at the point of specific locales, traditions, and periods.

AMBIGUITY

From Reinhold Niebuhr and Paul Tillich to the present, interpreters have noted the ambiguity of history.[7] Here we move beyond the initial struggle

6. For two very extensive and detailed theological analyses of these issues of the meaning of history that argue for the possibility of direction and the new (cf. eschatology) but who criticize the idea of overall, inevitable progress, see Gilkey, *Reaping the Whirlwind*, chaps. 5 and 10, and Hodgson, *God in History*, chap. 4.

7. See Tillich, *Systematic Theology* 3:339–48; Gilkey's discussion of the issue of ambiguity in *Reaping the Whirlwind*, 122–30; Ruth Page, *Ambiguity and the Presence of God* (London: SCM, 1985), chap. 2. For Page, ambiguity is not so much a positive "force" as the malleability of

with the ambiguity of the term *history* to the ambiguity of history itself. What does it mean to say this? Something is cognitively ambiguous to the degree that it resists our attempt to apprehend it in coherent conceptual accuracy, prediction, or structural pattern. It is existentially ambiguous if it frustrates our attempts to make it a trusted haven, a source of security. History is ambiguous in both senses. The indeterminacy, complexity, and multidimensionality of concrete history make it cognitively ambiguous: its nonteleology and tragic character make it existentially ambiguous.

From the human perspective, the sphere of nature is constituted by microworlds of particles and cells in which work elements of chaos. Accordingly, we would expect such entities to give to history a certain indeterminacy. But because of the self-transcendence of its individuals and the enormous complexity of the bearers (being-together, institutions), history is indeterminate in a distinctive way. The resulting indeterminacy is not simply a temporary cognitive failure that future generations of data-gathering techniques will defeat. It is rooted in historical passage itself as a movement into novelty, a gathering of individual responses, and the accumulation of ever-new syntheses of events. On the other hand, a deterministic approach to history *is* a phenomenon of method or cognitive effort. Thus, it is successful to the degree that it can abstract concrete history into patterns or isolate its elements of continuity and repetition for predictive purposes.

History is also ambiguous when it is approached as a foundation of human existential meaning. The idolatrous impulse would have it otherwise. In idolatrous mood, human beings would attach themselves to an unambiguously good and trustworthy historical bearer; for instance, a nation or a religion. But history frustrates such hopes not only because of its indeterminacy but because of its nonteleological and tragic character. I have discussed the widespread opposition to universal teleology. What does it mean to call history "tragic"? In nature the tragic emerges because life and novelty come about only through inter- and intraspecies competition. History is no exception. It too includes competition between human groups and both micro and macro forms of life.

But history is also tragic in a distinctive sense. Sigmund Freud described how civilization itself inevitably effects repression that tames and structures the ecstatic self. Repression is unavoidable when individuals are subjected to the complex requirements of being-together and institu-

---

anything that is actual to being reshaped. Ambiguity thus is a negative ontological feature of any and all worldly realities, apart from which they could not even exist.

tionality.[8] A further repression and conflictual structure comes about as human passionate life and intimate relations are taken up into the more anonymous groups and institutions of a civilization. The perennial complaint about governmental and bureaucratic over-management signals the tragic conflict fostered by the very existence of bearers of history. This tragic conflict between the needs of concrete individuals in their specific situations and the demands of organized society shows up in the struggle between history's ideal element and its units of power. For a human group to endure over time requires a struggle with and against the natural and human environment, a struggle that taps resources for the uses of power. And organized power carries with it corruption and dehumanizing control. Human cultures have found ways to limit power by subjecting it to such idealities as justice, mercy, and responsibility. But the conflict goes on, and it is a tragic conflict because a society by definition is a gathering of power.

History's deepest tragic aspect may be the fact that history itself is imperiled. In its most formal and superficial sense, history is human corporate temporality perpetuated through language and institutions. In a deeper sense, concrete history is deep tradition that drives human groups to realize a self-perceived destiny. In this second sense, it is clear that history is not *a priori* to human life. History as tradition is surely imperiled in the "brave new world" of postmodern societies. For it is tradition that formulates and conserves human being-together and the idealities that arise therewith. Without tradition, "history" becomes a merely external passage, and the tragic conflict between ideality and power is supplanted by a victory of power. History then is replaced by nonhistorical bureaucracies that construe the past as a chronology of preserved information. History, like cosmos and nature, has an underside of mystery. This underside is not simply the impenetrable facticity of the strange and elusive character of life but rather the mystery of self-transcending individuals in their being-together over time. This mystery has many faces: tradition, the interhuman, evil, and ideality. With the help of discourse and interpretation, we illuminate but never cognitively manage these things.

8. Sigmund Freud, *The Future of an Illusion*, trans. W. D. Robson-Scott (Garden City, N.Y.: Doubleday & Co., n.d.), 3–20.

15
MANIFESTED WORLD

> There is no abiding city, no, not one.
> The tower of stone and steel are fairy stories.
> God will not play our games nor join our fun,
> Does not give tit for tat, parade His glories.
> And chance is chance, not providence dressed neat,
> Credentials hidden in its wooden leg.
> When the earth opens underneath our feet,
> It is a waste of brain and breath to beg.
> No angel intervenes but shouts that matter
> Has been forever mostly full of holes.
> *Vassar Miller, "The Wisdom of Insecurity"*

The third task of a theology of God is to think, insofar as it can be thought, the way God is active in the world. Since we have no direct access to this activity, we can only think it by constructing a paradigm. Since world is where the divine activity takes place, any such paradigm must portray what the world is and how it works. A first step in this portrayal was taken in the brief and oversimplified retrieval of world in natural and humanistic sciences, world as cosmos, nature, and history. I must now ask whether that portrayal is exhaustive, whether world *is* simply cosmos, nature, and history. Is world an aggregate term for the totality of ever-expanding information delivered to us by scientists and historians? Positivism and reductionism take that position.[1] I recall at this point the oft-repeated observation that positivism and reductionism are metascientific, "philosophical" ways of construing knowl-

---

1. An older criticism of reductionism is advanced by Michael Polanyi, *Personal Knowledge: Towards a Post-Critical Philosophy* (New York: Harper & Row, 1964), 382. For a more recent criticism, see Arthur Peacocke, *God and the New Biology* (London: J. M. Dent and Sons, 1986), chaps. 1 and 3. Both Polanyi and Peacocke present an analysis of world by way of levels, each of which is irreducible to that on which it depends or from which it emerged.

edge and reality, not scientific observations, experimental conclusions, or even inferences therefrom.

There are strong reasons against reducing the constituents and workings of world to the world-picture advanced in cosmological and life sciences. No specific objectifying or quantifying experiment captures the strange phenomenon of knowledge itself, the perspectival activities of objectifying, perceiving, sorting, meaning, evaluating, selecting what is important, and the like. Furthermore, the primary world we human beings know and experience is the common sense world of everyday life, and the sciences both refine and correct but also presuppose and build on the way we are entangled with and participate in the common sense world.[2] World-for-us precedes and is assumed by all the enterprises that would abstract pieces of the world for precise study. In addition, to recall a point from the last chapter, scientific and historical explanations are necessarily intraworld undertakings. An "ultimate" or "total" explanation appeals to intraworld laws and concepts (since they are what is to be explained) and thus requires a standpoint outside the world to account for the very facticity of the world. Such an explanation would also require assurance that every type of reality lends itself to objectifying, structural, or causal explanation. It is clear that no specific science or human cognitive enterprise can meet these conditions on its own terms, that is, by using its own methods, types of evidences, and categories. To argue that the sciences have limitations and boundaries is not necessarily to adopt a subjective idealism that invites us to construe the world as we please. Nor does it propose gaps in the scientific world picture to be filled by religion or philosophy. The point is that science itself is one way of relating to and knowing world and that the complexity and very facticity of world overreach all specific, focused projects of research.

Accordingly, to understand the world and its workings we must attend not only to what the sciences are uncovering but to other ways human

2. For Edmund Husserl that which lies behind such acts of reduction is a metascientific posture or attitude (*Einstellung*) which he calls the "naturalistic posture" (not to be identified with the "natural posture," which is our concrete participation in everyday life. See "The Attitude of Natural Science and the Attitude of Humanistic Science," in Appendix III of *The Crisis of European Sciences and Transcendental Phenomenology,* trans. David Carr (Evanston, Ill.: Northwestern University Press, 1970). For the same point, see Appendix VII, "The Lifeworld and the World of Science." This notion of the concrete, experienced world is irreducible to the scientifically studied world and the prescientific importance of common sense and world participation is argued by Robert Neville. Thus, world, not interpretation, not the cognitive accomplishments of the sciences, is the "measure" of our claims. *Recovery of the Measure: Interpretation and Nature* (Albany: SUNY Press, 1989), Division III. Primary for Neville is common sense, world participation, and value.

beings are aware of and participate in the world. There are terms for these "other ways" and as soon as we use them, we invite negative knee-jerk philosophical reactions. World, the experienced world, the common sense world, the world in its mystery is the concern of speculative philosophy, primary cosmology, ontology, metaphysics, and phenomenology. In the eyes of many, these centuries-long efforts present a story of cognitive confusion and moral distortion. They are unverifiable (the positivist point), essentialist (the existential and pragmatic point), meaning-fixing (the deconstructionist point), and hierarchical (the liberation and feminist point). Because we take these "points" seriously, we cannot use these terms as if they had no history, as if they stood for self-evidently important and automatically successful disciplines. Yet to dismiss them out of hand is to invite the sciences to become all-controlling cognitive empires. If world means "scientific world," and if science means valueless, perspectiveless, objective data collection, then the world with which we are entangled, the world of light and dark, being and nonbeing, ambiguity and boundary, value and beauty, is a false world, a world of discredited myths, fantasies, romances, and cognitive mistakes. The only world of God's activity, if there is such an activity, would be the world of the specific scientific experiment and its resultant information. In other words, the elimination of metascientific attempts to understand the world leaves us with a world we do not recognize, a world in which God's activity is superfluous. This is why the theology of God is driven in the direction of something like a metaphysics or ontology of world.

At this point of the analysis, I shall not attempt to rehabilitate "metaphysics" as a discipline or simply appropriate texts from some existing metaphysic. In a more direct fashion, I shall take cues from world itself. The result is a threefold problematic: the problem of world as it appears in our own primordial entanglement with it (world-for-us), world as a set of manifested, intrinsic features (the being of the world), and world as comprised of basic constituents related to each other in some comprehensive root metaphor (metaphysics of world).[3] These three problematics are, respectively, experiential ontology of world, descriptive ontology of world, and speculative philosophy of world. The first two problematics lend themselves to intuitive types of verification. The third problematic requires the more speculative method of general coherence.[4]

3. An example of a more direct and inclusive metaphysical program is that of Robert Neville. In his view metaphysics addresses three questions. What is it to be a thing (the question of identity)? What is the connection of all things such that they can be said to be? And what are the basic categories of reality? *Recovery of the Measure*, 95.

4. I must acknowledge that these three problematics do not organize the *literature* of metaphysics nor are all three necessarily found in all thinkers of world. Erazim Kohak and

WORLD-FOR-US

A certain kind of objectivism, scientific or metaphysical, approaches world as an external content unaffected by our relation to it or by what we must do in order to understand it. Challenges to this objectivism have been advanced not only in philosophy (Immanuel Kant, Edmund Husserl, A. N. Whitehead, Thomas Kuhn) but also in science (for instance, Werner Heisenberg's principle of indeterminacy). All of these critiques of objectivism portray the human-world entanglement that necessarily precedes and, in a sense, grounds all specific, technical knowledge. Formal, technical, and explanatory ways of knowing are derivative ways of relating to the world. Primary world relation is by "presentational immediacy" and aesthetic feeling (Whitehead), practical orientation (John Dewey), or life-world participation (Husserl). This primordial experience in which the world is manifest is our initial access to the actual world that the sciences would study. Because they see science or scholarship as necessarily proceeding through focused and isolating inquiry, the critics of objectivism work to correct the abstractions that technical, focused study perpetuates by a return to the concreteness of world.[5] The resulting categories (process, events, beings, times, modes of being) may themselves seem abstract, but the aim of these concepts is to portray nature or reality as it is in fact experienced. We do not experience quarks and nanoseconds of time. We do experience events (a thunderstorm), entities (a person), and relations (a friendship). To identify world itself with the results of focused inquiry is what Whitehead calls the "fallacy of misplaced concreteness." Ecologically oriented critics of objectivism challenge the policies that flow from an objectivist view of world as something not only to be objectively known but to be managed and controlled.

Antiobjectivism is not, however, a single voice. It includes an *idealist* type (Kant) that would display the nonobjective (transcendental) struc-

Conrad Bonifazi focus primarily on experiential ontology of world. Although his approach is not so poetic and existential, F. J. E. Woodbridge includes in his descriptive ontology of nature the way the world is for us in everyday life. Bertrand Russell and Wilfred Sellars are concerned primarily with descriptive ontology of world. Paul Tillich's ontology of world has both experiential and descriptive aspects. The problem of the basis constituents of reality (*res verae*) related to a root metaphor is present in Gottfried Leibniz, Whitehead, Hartshorne, and Ivor Leclerc. Paul Weiss offers a descriptive ontology of world which is at the same time a proposal about ultimate or irreducible reality constituents.

5. Edmund Husserl expresses this point by contrasting the immediacies of the life-world to the secondary, derived, or abstracting cognitive studies that presuppose such. In a very different philosophical tradition, A. N. Whitehead expresses the point by contrasting focused, "abstract" cognition (cf. scientific knowledge) to the vivid awareness and feeling prehensions of actual entities. This distinction creates a space for the task of philosophy, namely a restoring of thinking to the concrete (*Science and the Modern World* [New York: Macmillan, 1925], chap. 10; and *Process and Reality* [New York: Macmillan, 1929], chap. 1).

ture that shapes and constructs whatever is manifest to it. A *common sense* type would press beyond nature as a mathematical structure to underlying practical relations to the world of light and dark (F. J. E. Woodbridge), means and ends, events (Dorothy Emmett) and processes (Whitehead), or to the life-world and its lived space and time (Husserl, Alfred Schutz).[6] A *process* type sees something like human experience (feeling, prehending) as a pervasive characteristic of anything that is actual. Here we have a speculative universalization of concrete experience. A more *experiential-existential* type (Erazim Kohak) would uncover the concrete ways in which we actually experience (and not just have knowledge of) nature.[7] Kohak highlights this experience by contrasting it to the loss of the concrete world in urban styles of life. Thus, nature in her dark and perilous beauty, her unfathomable mystery, even her living things that evoke respect and care, is only dimly remembered by those whose very being has become a *technê*, a deployment of managing skills. Langdon Gilkey makes a similar point in his claim that archaic religions have something to say to postmoderns about nature.

To conclude, the world that is our world, is never merely a world-in-itself but is a world-for-us.[8] The only world we know is through our participative and experiential entanglement. It is by way of this participation, not the distancing acts of observation and analysis, that we have primordial access to world. And it is by this participation that we would correct the root metaphors that identify world with what is discovered by abstracted, focused, and causal-oriented modes of inquiry.

THE BEING OF THE WORLD

Setting forth our world entanglement and world-for-us is only one of several problematics of a philosophy of world. We do discern certain features of the workings of the world in connection with our everyday activities. Philosophers disagree about the status of these discernments. An earlier type of process metaphysics (Charles Hartshorne) would discover the features of any and all possible worlds. A latter generation (Robert Neville) is content with a "primary cosmology" oriented to the features

6. F. J. E. Woodbridge, *An Essay on Nature* (New York: Columbia University Press, 1940), chap. 2; Dorothy Emmett, *The Passage of Nature* (Philadelphia: Temple University Press, 1992), chap. 1.

7. Erazim Kohak, *The Embers and the Stars: A Philosophical Inquiry into the Moral Sense of Nature* (Chicago: University of Chicago Press, 1984).

8. See Harold Schilling, *The New Consciousness in Science and Religion* (London: SCM, 1973), chap. 1; Conrad Bonifazi, *Theology of Things: A Study of Man in His Physical Environment* (Philadelphia: Lippincott, 1967), chaps. 8 and 9.

of this particular cosmic epoch.[9] How are these features discerned? One possibility is that they are implicit in and even constitute the scientific world picture. If this is the case, the philosopher is a kind of generalizer who weaves scientific discoveries into a garment of totality. And the scientific world picture has figured into the descriptive ontologies of Bertrand Russell, Whitehead, Wilfred Sellars, Woodbridge, Paul Weiss, Neville, and many others. Yet something else appears to be going on in these analyses than simply inductions from or synthesis of scientific discoveries. What makes this something else possible is that we do in fact participate in world and that participation yields modes of world manifestation available to reflective analysis. Human beings do not need laboratory experiments to know that the world contains events, processes, and entities and to grasp the features and relations of these things. Descriptive ontology of the world takes place not by speculation but rather by direct inspection and lends itself to intuitive verification. To be sure, philosophical (ontological) accounts of world vary widely.[10] Yet many, if not most, of the general features keep turning up in these accounts, and the descriptions of these features tend to be grounded in sharable or publicly communicable intuitions.

I shall not attempt here yet another descriptive ontology of world. My concern is to give an account of what we mean by world and its workings that includes but goes beyond the scientific world picture, and that poses the issues necessary to a paradigm of God's activity in the world. Accordingly, I shall incorporate both the generalities of the scientific world picture and materials from descriptive ontologies of world into three major themes: chaos, order, and direction. Versions of all three themes recur in the three main sources to be consulted in an account of world: common sense orientation, scientific inquiry, and philosophies of world.

Chaos

Common sense experience, the sciences, and philosophies of world all have voiced the theme of chaos.[11] The work of chaos in everyday life may

9. Neville, *Recovery*, 115–19.

10. Paul Tillich proposes four categories of finite being: space, time, causality, and substance. Paul Weiss Identifies three modes of finite or worldly being: actualities, idealities, and creative fields (God is a fourth mode of being). (*Modes of Being* [Carbondale: Southern Illinois University Press, 1958]). In self-avowed dependence on Plato, Robert Neville sees ontology as dealing with things, their connections, and basic categories, which at one level are time, enduring, space, motion, and causality. Whiteheadian philosophers work with actual entities of experience and eternal objects. For Langdon Gilkey, five common sense categories express world constituents: power, life, order, redemptive unity, and disruption (nonbeing) (*Nature, Reality, and the Sacred* [Minneapolis: Fortress Press, 1993], chap. 6).

11. For an experiential account of chaos, see Kohak's description of "the gifts of the night," thus, pain, *skepsis*, "the spell of the demon," and nothingness. On nature's destruc-

be the reason it is a prominent theme in archaic religions and early Western philosophies. In these religions world is a scene of mysterious, fearful, and fecund powers whose renewal and mollification requires constant ritual activity. Ever hovering at the edge of order are the chthonic, Gaian, Dionysian powers of earth and other regions. In everyday life chaos means what surprises us, what overturns the protective orders we construct, what erupts from an apparently predictable nature or society.

When we add scientific and philosophical sources to common sense experience, four themes expressive of chaos emerge. The first is the way any entity that can respond to its environment, initiate action, and bring about the new alters the world. Indeterminacy is a rather weak way to express this element of chaos. In the panpsychic schemes of Whitehead and Hartshorne, the actual entities that constitute the very reality of things are responsive and self-initiating. Even those who remain unconvinced by panpsychism will acknowledge that even the strange occupants of the particle world respond to attraction and repulsion and the cells of the world of life are complex worlds of chemical and electrical events through which they relate to their environments. In the sphere of nature (life), entities respond, initiate actions, even develop something like strategies. Insofar as a response requires a reading of the situation, a taking into account of things to avoid, attach to, take in, or conform to, it is a kind of creativity. Responsive acts are never merely passive mirrorings of an external causality nor are they exact replications of some earlier state of affairs.

A second aspect of the chaos element of the world arises when we consider the effects of a multiplicity of responses; that is, the situation they produce when they affect each other and their environment. An untrackable and everchanging complexity arises when self-initiating entities relate to, influence, and respond to each other. This complexity is not simply the complexity of a structure whose details are beyond our power to innumerate but a network of ongoing occurrences, each related to the others and to the past, and changing with breathtaking rapidity with which cognition never catches up. This dynamic complexity introduces an unquantifiable and surprising dimension into all ordered systems.

What is the connection between chaos and the complex situations that self-initiating entities bring about? Self-initiation resists explanation by

tiveness (as well as creativity) see Schilling, *New Consciousness*, chapter 8; cf. John Haught, *Nature and Purpose* (Lanham, Md.: University Press of America, 1980), chap. 6 on perishing and the fragile universe. In biology chaos is interpreted as chance and "accidental perturbations." See Jacques Monod, *Chance and Necessity: An Essay in Philosophical Biology,* trans. A. Wainhouse (New York: A. A. Knopf, 1971), chap. 6. For a full account of chaos in physical science, see James Gleick, *Chaos: Making a New Science* (New York: Viking, 1987).

efficient and external cause. As utterly determined, the entity would be simply an aggregate of manipulable parts, passive to all external influences. If it is not so manipulable, its responses will affect, prompt changes in, and evoke responses from whatever is in its environment. Because responsiveness is never an activity of mere conformity or replication, it introduces an unaccountable, surprising, indeterminate aspect into the systems of which it is a part. However much entities and processes seem to repeat each other, however strong a trend seems to be, there are always factors at work in the cosmos, nature, or history that can disrupt, reverse, even destroy those things. Accordingly, chaos attends the self-initiations of worldly entities and systems. This is why all actual things are subject to reinterpretation. Nothing living or actual is interpretable as if it existed all at once, utterly complete, or exhausted in content. All things are on the way.

Third, a tragic element is intrinsic to the world as we know it. Worldly things are subject to demise, nonfillment, and (at the level of experience) suffering. No ordered system is immune from forces that undermine or work against that system. The world does not single out some aspect of itself, human beings for instance, to immunize against these things. Nothing that is actual has a privileged immunity from demise, failure, or suffering. To use the term *tragedy* for this element is not necessarily an anthropomorphic projection but arises with the observation that in order simply to be and to act, anything that is actual requires a split between its actual state and the ideal environment it needs for its preservation and fulfillment.

A closer look at this split reveals a tragically necessary maladjustment at work in all ordered systems. Insofar as a worldly entity is real, that is, has its own content such that it is other to what is not itself and is able to affect others, it is not a mere projection, mirroring, or replication of anything else. Hence, what it needs to survive, to actualize itself, to have well-being, to effectively respond, can never coincide with the needs of any other entity. Accordingly, the environment of a multiplicity of entities can never be a system of resources perfectly and exhaustively oriented to the well-being of any one entity or all the entities together. Only in magic land do we find such environments. The very flexibility entities need to operate in an environment requires that their environment not be magically adapted to them. A maladjustment between the environment and the needs of each of its members is necessary to the reality and responsiveness of each member. Maladjustment means that entities experience both a lack of absolute confirmation and a certain resistance to their needs on the part of any and all environments in which they exist.

World as order (compare logos) evokes and makes possible explanation. If chaos also means that about world that defies explanation, then chaos attends the very fact that the world exists. Chaos thus will frustrate anyone who would explain the very phenomenon of world, who would employ causal or speculative explanation to discover the world's secret. As chaotic the world keeps its secret. It presents itself to our inquiries in the form of a limit that has several dimensions. One limit arises with any and all self-determining entities who thus have what Paul Weiss calls an "inside," an interior perspective, content, or experiencing unreachable by inquiry. Another limit arises with the infinite combinations of events and relations in the micro and macro world, only a fraction of which will ever be subject to inquiry. A third limit is the very facticity of the world that eludes causal explanation because such explanations can only pertain to intraworld processes.

Indeterminacy, elusive complexity, the tragic, the deep secret of the world's facticity all signal a chaos that is not simply an interdependent aspect of order. Expressed in such terms as *me-on, das Nichtige,* and *Ungrund,* ultimate chaos is an uncreated obstacle that yields to ordering or creativity (compare logos) but is not thereby eliminated.

Order

According to both common sense experience and to various sciences, world is in some sense ordered. Order too is an ancient motif in Western mythologies and philosophies. The very existence of order and ordering processes was the primary fascination and philosophical problem of Hellenism. In Hesiod's *Theogony,* chaos (the titans) is subjected to order by the birth and eventual victory of the gods and goddesses. Demythologizing this theogony, Plato and other philosophers reinterpreted the ordering powers as the *ousiae* of things, forms that organize and structure chaotic matter. With Renaissance and modern scientific mathematics and technologies, the Hellenic fascination with order becomes a fascination with calculable laws of nature, predictable regularity, and causal systems.

Insofar as the machine is the root metaphor of world working, chaos means the chance or randomness and order means predictability.[12] When we take into consideration both common sense and philosophical analyses of world, we find that order and chaos are not reducible to the meta-

---

12. According to Stephen Pepper, the machine (mechanism) is one of the basic root metaphors for understanding order. But order can also be interpreted in organic and structural metaphors (*World Hypotheses: A Study in Evidence* [Berkeley: University of California Press, 1961], chaps. 8, 9, 11.

scientific issue of causality and chance or to determinism and indetermin-
ism. "Chance" and "predictability" are not so much world features as
degree terms for statistical analyses. They arise with one kind of attempt
to know things. Low degrees of predictability (chance) arise both in the
particle world and in the macro world of complex interacting systems;
for instance, the economics of industrial states. But world in its actuality
is not captured by this spectrum of degrees of predictability.

At the level of intuitive world discernments, we find three different
senses of order, none of which reduce to statistical predictability. First,
there is continuity in the features, structures, and behaviors of entities as
they persist over time. Nucleotides pass on very precise genetic information to succeeding generations of cells. Individual organisms retain the
features of their species and even their own individual genetic inheritance as they develop. Human communities survive generations of time
through enduring customs, traditions, symbolic structures and institutions. A kind of order comes about when multiple aspects merge into a
composite entity. Molecules, cells, and human beings do not simply disperse into billions of unrelated parts in every nanosecond of time. They
exist as complex systems in which the multiple entities that constitute
them cohere into a unity.[13] Without coherence, there would be no entities,
not even atoms, and no enduring continuities. Third, we discover order
in the fact that both the coherence and continuities of entities require
delicate and precise environmental conditions. And an intrinsic aspect of
those conditions is the way entities are systemically interdependent.[14]
This interdependence ranges from galaxies to life forms in the biosphere
to the molecular environment of an organism to social groups. Order,
then, is not simply a statistical phenomenon related to predictability but
the necessary presence of continuity, coherence, and systemic interdependence in whatever is actual.

Directions

Common sense, the sciences, and philosophies agree that the world we
know is in passage, or better, is itself a passage or process. Process or
time may be the most general thing we can say about world. World as a

13. "Gregariousness" is Harold Schilling's term for the attraction between things in the
particle world (*New Consciousness*, chap. 1).

14. Two texts, one older and the other more recent, interpret the interdependence of
things by way of the metaphor of a symphony. (Schilling, *New Consciousness*, chap. 4; and
Guy Murchie, *The Music of the Spheres: The Material Universe from Atom to Quasar Simply Explained*, Vol. 3 [New York: Dover, 1967], chap. 7).

whole contains processes and is in process.[15] To speak of process does not mean simply that states of affairs or entities succeed each other in time. Rather, the units of process gather up what has happened previously, past contents so to speak, and undergo or perpetuate changes in these contents. A state of any actual thing in the world or the world as a whole is never identical to its predecessor state. Changes are occurring over time from the particle world to the ways human beings experience things.

Can we speak of process or passage as having some sort of direction? At first sight, this seems to be what is at issue between a scientific and "religious" way of interpreting the world. For scientists, teleology is the insect pest in the garden of science, something to be quickly eradicated wherever it is discovered. For it is just teleological explanation that prevents thinking about a happening scientifically. Scientific explanations appeal to conditions and (efficient) causalities, not to deliberate, immanent, guiding purposes. And we must acknowledge that the sciences have successfully displaced the kind of teleological thinking that sees God giving creatures this or that feature in view of some future need or function. And this same nonteleology applies to the cosmos as a whole. There is no actual evidence that the universe with its myriads of galaxies is following a preset path to some salvific fulfillment.

At the same time, scientific antiteleology does not utterly eliminate direction from world process.[16] On the contrary, direction is a pervasive feature of the world as passage. First of all, if process is not a mere succession of contents, each isolated from all others, then process itself is directional. A molecule constituted by atoms reflects a movement toward synthesis. The same is true when further syntheses produce crystals, cells, and organisms. If each moment of time receives, builds on, and alters past contents into new contents, these new contents set a direction or trajectory over time.

---

15. Dorothy Emmett, reflecting the strong influence of Whitehead on her early work, proposes process as *the* comprehensive category of nature. The now vast literature of process philosophy is an ever-extended exposition of world as process. See Emmett, *The Passage of Nature*, chap. 1, and A. N. Whitehead, *Modes of Thought* (New York: Macmillan, 1938), chap. 5.

16. For discussions of the issue of purpose and direction in nature, see John Haught, *Nature and Purpose*, chap. 5; Gilkey, *Reaping the Whirlwind: A Christian Interpretation of History* (New York: Seabury Press, 1976), chap. 11; Gordon Kaufman, *In Face of Mystery: A Constructive Theology* (Cambridge, Mass.: Harvard University Press, 1993), chap. 19; David Pailin, *God and the Processes of Reality: Foundations of a Credible Theism* (London: Routledge, 1989), chap. 8; Emmett, *The Passage of Nature*, chap. 8; Woodbridge, *Essay on Nature*, chap. 3; Richard Overman, *Evolution and the Christian Doctrine of Creation: A Whiteheadian Interpretation* (Philadelphia: Westminster Press, 1967), chap. 4; Arthur Peacocke, *Science and the Christian Experiment* (London: Oxford University Press, 1971), chaps. 2 and 3.

Second, most cosmologists affirm that the universe as a whole is directional, not toward fulfillment in the sense of maturation or perfection, but toward a steady state of energy. Suns, planets, and life forms are all centers of energy gradually being dispersed. But the very fact of entropy suggests a sense in which the cosmos is directional. Originated in the Big Bang so many billions of years ago, the cosmos has a kind of "history"; thus, early pregalactic states, stages in which galaxies form, stages that include conditions of life on planets. Such a direction in itself neither requires nor eliminates theological ways of interpreting world.

Third, in the biosphere of earth, we find distinctive kinds of directions. All living entities are directional both in the sense of proceeding from birth and infancy toward maturation and in the sense that they pursue certain ends connected with survival, reproduction, and well-being. Furthermore, the evolution of life forms is directional, not in the sense of a single aim but rather as a passage toward complexity and increased organic sensitivity. Catastrophic geological events and interspecies competition can eliminate species and reduce the number of species on a planet. But because they are then set to respond to new and complex environments, the surviving species develop new and complex capacities of adaptation. Insofar as this is the case, a development toward complexity also may aim toward what Whitehead calls intensity. For as capacities of adaptation increase in complexity, they also increase in the intensity and quality of world participation; that is, qualities of enjoyment and suffering. Finally, direction also takes place in world as a kind of cooperation between mutually assisting species, between individual life-forms, and even in the attractions of the subatomic world.

In sum, neither science nor ontology of the world disclose to us a world totality that proceeds toward a predesigned perfection. On the other hand, world contains directional processes that include the development of the conditions of life, the dispersal of energy, the teleonomic behavior of living entities displayed in their struggle for what is valuable or important to them.

WORLD CONSTITUENTS AND ROOT METAPHORS

Concepts of chaos, order, and direction lead naturally to the third problematic of a philosophy of world. The first problematic prompts analyses of modes of world experience; the second, analyses of the being of the world. Both endeavors make direct intuitive claims. But something about world still looms beyond these analyses. The cognitive eros that world awakens in us remains unsatisfied by ontological descriptions of what is intuitively given. It drives us on to the two intertwined questions: What is it that ultimately constitutes what we call world; and what root metaphor most adequately captures the workings and interrelations of world? The first question is the philosophical issue of the *res verae*, the units to which all apparent powers, entities, or activities reduce.[17] The second question asks for a comprehensive paradigm, unavoidably cast as a metaphor, for world working as a totality. Both questions have roots in the mythologies of archaic religions, and both questions are present at the birth of Western thought as Ionian thinkers reflected on what basic substances constituted reality. The symbols and stories of both archaic and postmodern industrial societies specify what is and what is not to be regarded as real. And modern societies typically look to the sciences to learn what constitutes the real (the atom, forces of energy, spacetime) and how to think of the world totality (for instance, a mechanism).

Two general comments may help introduce the philosophy of world totality. First, proposals about what constitutes the real (*res verae*) and how to think the world totality tend to correlate with each other. If the basic constituents of world are physical atoms whose behavior is governed by the laws of Newtonian physics, the root metaphor for world totality will tend to be mechanistic. If the root metaphor of world totality is organic, a different kind of *res vera* is implied. Second, to work at both of these problems calls for speculative thinking for the simple reason that we have no direct, external, nonperspectival access to that totality. Thus, we can only imaginatively construct that totality out of our limited experience of world.[18] To claim that astrophysics gives us immediate access to world totality assumes that world totality is synonymous with the observed universe. On the other hand, some might argue that we do have cognitive access to the basic units of world. That depends, of course, on what units are proposed. Events, self-initiating things, processes, and facts (Bertrand Russell) are all available to intuitive discernment. But what we do not intuitively grasp is evidence for the claim itself, namely that one of these things is the *basic* unit of the real. How then are proposals about world constituents and root metaphors grounded? Here specu-

17. For what may be the best philosophical account of the history of the issue, see Ivor Leclerc, *The Nature of Physical Existence* (New York: Humanities Press, 1972). Leclerc traces the concept of physical existence from Aristotle through the Middles Ages to Descartes, Leibniz, and Whitehead. The work is both a constructive philosophy of physical existence as well as a profound historical study.

18. "Imaginative construction" is a recurring term in the later works of Gordon Kaufman. A. N. Whitehead may be the source of the phrase (*Process and Reality: An Essay on Cosmology* [New York: Macmillan, 1929], 7).

lative philosophy must take the nonintuitive path of comparative coherence. A proposal about basic constituents and a root metaphor is "better" than another proposal if it avoids the incoherence of dualism and if its concepts can account for various activities and entities we do intuit in the world.[19] Such has been the method of speculative philosophy from Plato and Plotinus to Whitehead and Weiss.

Most modern philosophical proposals about root metaphors and basic constituents are responses to the kind of metaphysics that appeared with Renaissance and post-Renaissance sciences. For this metaphysics world means cosmos and its observable contents, and reality means micro (atoms) and macro entities whose behavior follow mathematically formulatable laws. That persons, consciousness, life, value, religions, and morality are explainable by these laws was either stated or implied. This situation gave rise to what is now called the Cartesian response, the attempt to "save the appearances" by affirming two basically unreducible types of reality: the *cogito* serving as the locus of the spirit, value and morality, and *extensions* describing the material world. And while it is customary to pretend that we have discredited and overcome such dualism, the vilification of René Descartes being a required philosophical ritual in virtually all academic fields, the insistence on a nonreductionist metaphysics tends to make Cartesians of us all.

To divide nature (world, reality) into what we concretely experience (perceptual qualities) and what we subject to research is to bifurcate nature.[20] To overcome that bifurcation has been speculative philosophy's modern project. Some schemes would accomplish this by uncovering emergent, unreducible levels. Some would discern in these levels a life force that accounts for the emergence itself. The most ambitious and detailed attempt to supplant the bifurcation of nature is surely the project of Whitehead, carried on largely but not exclusively by philosophical theologians. This project sees the *res verae* not as ultimate physical entities but as actual occasions that receive past content and preserve it for future entities in what looks like a structure of experience. Some process thinkers exchange this panpsychist element for levels of analysis.[21] Other philosophers are influenced by Whitehead but would replace bifurcated nature with processes, events, facts, or a combination of such.

19. See Pepper's excellent analysis of the tests to judge adequate and inadequate world hypotheses in *World Hypotheses,* 115–37. Thus, the adequacy of a hypothesis depends "upon its *precision* in dealing with individual facts and its *scope* of factual corroboration" (118).

20. Alfred North Whitehead, *The Concept of Nature* (Ann Arbor: University of Michigan Press, 1957), chap. 2.

21. Pailin, *God,* 55–56; Neville, *Recovery,* 191.

How are these proposals of basic units of reality and a comprehensive root metaphor related to the theology of God? Liberation, feminist, neo-orthodox, biblical, and deconstructive theologies tend to spurn the project of a metaphysics of world. Not only is it not demanded by their own project; it smacks of ancient epistemologically and morally discredited systems and ways of thinking. Only historical, social, political, and linguistic workings of world are theologically pertinent. But this bypassing of all philosophies of world may carry with it a new "bifurcation of nature." The old dualism separated the objective world and transcendental consciousness. The new binary opposition sets world (the realm of objective sciences) over against the political sphere. Religion and theology continue to occupy the sphere of practical reason over against scientific (objective, analytic, ontic) reason.

This exclusion of philosophy of world exacts a hefty fee from the theology of God. First, to refuse absolutely the problem of the basic constituents of world is to abandon the field to a variety of postmodern reductionisms that suppress the personal, the aesthetic, and the moral by academic specialization, the technological preoccupations of postmodern sciences, societal consumerism, and romanticisms of warfare of a cultureless society. Second, if theology opposes these developments by articulating new comprehensive root metaphors about the world that incorporate moral resistance and aesthetic and personal experience, it must recognize that such metaphors require and imply some version of the constituents of the world. A metaphysic of world is sometimes dismissed by theologians as a "foundationalism," a return to natural theology. But the attempt to interpret the activity of God in a conceptual scheme that expresses how the world works is not so much a founding as a specifying act. Its question is what we mean when we say that God who redemptively comes forth as God, the unthinkable Creativity of things, is active in the world.

ENTITIES, RELATIONS, EVENTS, AND ENVIRONMENTS

A comprehensive and constructive philosophy of world is beyond the scope of this essay and the powers of the author. Yet the scientific world picture and the ontology of the world together suggest some concepts useful for a provisional philosophy of world. Reality in its most inclusive sense is clearly a process or group of processes. Also, in the most inclusive sense, world is a setting, location, or a group of locations. Processes are not simply "nowhere." World, in other words, is temporal and spatial and both together imply that it is an environment of whatever constitutes it. What does constitute it? What is it that is a process or is in process?

Entities

Both common sense experience and the sciences suggest the same answer. The world is made up of *entities*. Entities are what we experience when we negotiate the world and participate in the flow of process. Are there *basic* entities that constitute all things and to which all composite entities can be reduced? A philosophical tradition from Epicurean atomism to Whitehead has answered in the affirmative. It is important, however, not to turn this question into a quasiphysics, an instrument-aided search for the ultimate materials (chemicals, elements) and units (molecules, atoms, and particles) of the cosmos. The aim of such microexplorations is to explain by way of constituents. In reductionist mode, this explanation ends up reducing the composite to its parts. But the entities that constitute the three-dimensional world (cosmos, life, history) should not be confused with explanatory microunits. What constitutes the real are various kinds of composites: atoms, suns, crystals, flowers, human beings. Accordingly, it is misleading to apply a size classification to them and assign them to micro or macro worlds.[22]

What are these entities that make up the world? The most general thing we can say about them is that they are collections of energy, ways of being so organized as to have a distinctive affect on whatever is in their reach. In its minimalist sense, an entity is something that has a capacity to make a difference in world. Entities, thus, are foci of activity. We need not take this statement in a panpsychist way, that is, a claim that all entities display the character of living things. If life requires certain conditions for its emergence, it cannot be a trait of all entities. Yet it would be equally misleading to think of entities as merely passive to their environment. As collections of energy, all entities are able to influence what is around them. Thus, they can repel, attract, or change the motion of other entities. For reasons that physicists and biologists best understand, entities even in the particle world seem attracted to each other. So much is this the case that the world we know is comprised of innumerable types of composite entities whose complexity is the outcome of attraction and synthesis.

22. I am drawing on Leclerc's account of Aristotle's criticism of the concept of ultimate, individual, and actual units (atoms). For Aristotle, any body that has extension is divisible. Thus, no continuum is dividable into indivisibles (*The Nature of Physical Existence*, chap. 14).

Relations

Because of their extensiveness, location, and duration, entities are constituted by *relations* that pertain both internally to their own aspects and
externally to whatever is in their environment. To speak of relations is
not to say very much. The relations between entities (focis of energy and
activity) have the character of mutual actual influencings. But the very
existence of composite entities attests to something else at work in these
relations. Atoms exist only because there is a sufficient overcoming of the
repulsion of their particles to create a nucleus. The same kind of attraction
or coming together into an enduring composite is necessary for the existence of cells, and multicelled organisms can exist only as cells are able
to combine into larger organic systems. What prompts this movement
toward synthesis, this attraction between units? In the world of particles,
we can do little more than describe or note the attraction. At more inclusive levels, levels of more complex behavior, attraction seems to have
an aesthetic element. An intrinsic attractiveness (beauty?) appears to be
at work in drawing entities together. Insofar as the entities are self-
determining, this aesthetic element qualifies and limits their struggle to
survive, their natural self-preoccupation.[23]

At the same time, this phenomenon of attraction and synthesis so necessary to the being of entities has a negative side. For as entities come
about, increase in complexity, and develop into "higher" forms, they must
struggle to meet the conditions of survival, and in this struggle on their
own behalf, entities and their groups develop postures and strategies of
self-defense, competition, and predation. Suffering, therefore, is intrinsic
to the being and situation of entities. The interactions that constitute the
environment of entities thus have the paradoxical character of aesthetic
attraction and massive suffering.

23. Themes of mutual attraction, cooperation, symbiosis, and mutuality recur often in
ontologies of being, biology, and the physical sciences. See James Gleick, *Chaos*, for the
concept of "strange attractors." Schilling notes a gregariousness at work at the level of ele-
mentary particles (*New Consciousness*, chap. 1). Robert Neville sets forth several senses of
harmony as a feature of things that have achieved unity, one of which is a harmony of the
components of an entity. Also, to be an entity at all is to have some place and movement in
some larger harmony (*Recovery*, 157–58). Paul Weiss argues a similar point when he describes entities as not only centers of resistance and interiority but as making constant
adjustments to possibilities and of other actualities. In this sense, entities have a kind of
eros for other entities (*Modes of Being*, 32–55). Guy Murchie writes, "A being is something
like an idea or a song or an organized system. Where was the telephone in A.D. 1890? Where
were you and I? None of us had yet been born. All the elements of our future composition
were in the world but not organized into integral system. . . . thus an organizing of life is
basically much the same as an organism of systematic ideas—an abstraction, a new combination, a larger reality" (*Music of the Spheres*, 2: 595).

Events

A third basic unit of the world of both common sense and the sciences is the *event*.[24] The everyday life of human beings is a succession of overlapping events; overlapping because events have no objectively specified spatial or temporal scope. There are events of individual set-tos in the larger event of a battle that occurs in the still larger event of a war. The event of a thunderstorm may precede but persist in and influence the battle. Events are the result of the composite, relational, processive, and active character of entities. Events come about when all these things converge to produce a new and distinguishable state of affairs; a supernova, earthquake, birth, or historic revolution. Looked at simply as a state of affairs, they are event-facts. Looked at as units of time, they are event-processes.

Environments

A fourth basic element, though not unit, of world is the system of relations or environment in which entities and events are located.[25] As specific locales, environments, like events, overlap; for instance, a biological system of relations in a rural region overlaps the social environment of the farmers. Any and all actual things exist in a system of relations, and because entities are actions or influencings, this system is never simply an ideal structure but a place of dynamic interactions.

Do active and processive entities, relations, events and environments with their aesthetic (attractive) and suffering interactions suggest a root metaphor? Two root metaphors do not appear capable of combining these things: the root metaphor of the machine and the root metaphor of the organism. Mutual attraction and competitive entities that perpetuate events and develop over time do not have the features and behaviors of a machine. Neither do the interactions of the cosmos (galactic events) and history (economic trends, warfare, migrations) display the sort of interrelations that constitute an organism. Any adequate root metaphor for world totality would bring together the fact of directions, the dimension of the tragic, and the constituents of world (entities, events, and so on). Contextualism (Steven Pepper) seems better able to bring these various features into coherent interrelation.[26] Contextualism would interpret

24. For an analysis of events, see Emmett, *Passage,* chap. 2; and Pepper, *World Hypotheses.* 232–42.
25. A. N. Whitehead, *Adventures in Ideas* (Cambridge, Eng.: Cambridge University Press, 1935), chap. 13.
26. Pepper, *World Hypotheses,* chap. 10.

world totality as something like a contemporaneous historical event. It does seem to be the case that the various elements of world are together in a moving context. But something is omitted when event is expanded to an inclusive concept. An event organizes subevents and entities into a movement over time, but it excludes elements of attraction and synthesis by which entities, groups, and systems come about in the first place. More adequate yet is the metaphor of world as an ecosystem. The cosmos itself is an interrelated system of galaxies in spacetime. And wherever there are entities, there are tendencies toward merger and cooperation as well as competition and repulsion. And this is just what we find in all ecosystems: entities, events, a systemic environment, balances of cooperative effort, and competition. This is not to claim that in some literal sense world is an ecosystem. It is to use the metaphor of ecosystem to unify what appear to be the main ingredients and features of world.

16
WORLD AS CREATION

> . . . We know, have known
>   for many centuries,
> our language is not appropriate to gods, beast voices
> retain the mystery, elder things hidden in rough coats.
>   *Loren Eiseley, "I Heard It Breathing*
>   *in the Lizard Dark."*

> Then he stopped and looked and saw
> That the earth was hot and barren,
> So God stepped over to the edge of the world
> And he spat out the seven seas—
> He batted his eyes, and the lightnings flashed—
> He clapped his hands, and the thunders rolled—
> And the waters above the earth came down,
> The cooling waters came down.
>   *James Weldon Johnson, "The Creation"*

The task before us is to assemble sources pertinent to the construction of a paradigm of God's active relation to the world. One part of this paradigm has to do with the world and its workings. Accordingly, I have given brief accounts of *the* world of the natural sciences and of "world" in philosophical reflection. For some, what sciences and philosophies offer exhausts the matter. If this is in fact the case, the few cognitive crumbs left to theology (or faith) concern a preworld subjectivity or a transworld divine realm but not world itself. Such a view erases world from faith's system of symbols. But faith itself cannot be quite content with this erasure. There is a lot of "world" in the symbols and doctrinal traditions of the Christian movement. One of the ways early Christian theology distinguished Christian faith from Hellenistic faiths and philosophies had to do with world as creation. World has been a theme throughout the Jewish and Christian textual tradition and was part of Christian theology from its beginning.[1] The role of religious symbolics in the Western exploitation of nature, postmodern alienations from nature, and the planetary ecological crisis have goaded some modern theologians toward a theology of nature. The theology of God cannot then assume that only sciences and philosophies have something to say about world. If this is so, one of the elements in the paradigm of God's activity in the world is faith's own world orientation and the consequent theology of world.

THEOLOGY OF WORLD

Making a plea for the importance of a theology of world is one thing; responding to that plea is another. There are strong historical reasons why many nineteenth- and twentieth-century theologians more or less limit theology to history, politics, or the human subject. Throughout most of the history of Christendom, the church regarded the Scriptures as a source of factual and unrevisable information about the world. When scriptural facts were merged with certain common sense notions and the cosmologies of Ptolemy and Aristotle, scholastic Catholicism, and, to a certain degree, Protestantism, promoted a Christian cosmology that contained elements of astronomy, geology, biology, and cosmic chronology. According to the Catholic cosmology, the cosmos is a hierarchy of spheres that organizes the heavens in relation to a single earth. In the heavens order and beauty reign. Angels have cosmological assignments. The total cosmos exists for the sake of the drama now taking place on earth. Accordingly, the incarnation of the logos in human history is at the same time an event in and for the cosmos as a whole. Earth and the cosmos are part of a divinely originated teleological plan that will have a preordained outcome. The creation of the earth is an event a few thousand years in the past. That creation proceeded step-by-step to bring about animal and human life on the planet, all of which are fixed, nonevolving types of being. Causality tends to be teleological, proceeding from what is superior to what is inferior.[2] The temporal and spatial structure of cosmos are thus both geocentric and anthropocentric. Claimed by this cos-

---

1. Some helpful studies of creation in both the Hebrew Bible and the history of Christian theology are: Bernard Anderson, *Creation versus Chaos: The Reinterpretation of Mythical Symbolism in the Bible* (Philadelphia: Fortress Press, 1987); Ernan McMullin, "Natural Science and Belief in a Creator: Historical Notes," in Robert J. Russell, ed., *Physics, Philosophy, and Theology: A Common Quest for Understanding* (Vatican City: Vatican Observatory, 1988); Langdon Gilkey, *Maker of Heaven and Earth: A Study of the Christian Doctrine of Creation* (Garden City, N.Y.: Doubleday and Co., 1959).
2. Keith Ward, *Rational Theology and the Creativity of God* (Oxford: Blackwell, 1982), chap. 3.

mology are certain unnegotiable truths necessary to Christianity itself: absolute beginning and end, a fixed place of earth and the heavenly spheres, fixed species, and fixed places of destiny (heaven, hell, purgatory). When an official Christian cosmology is intact, theology of world means the one, unchanging, divinely authoritative factual truth about what we call the universe.

It is not an exaggeration to say that virtually every feature of this rather beautiful and coherent world picture has been eliminated by modern physical and biological sciences. Gone are the earth as the *raison d'etre* of the cosmos, the changeless tiers of heavens, the fixed spheres, the hierarchy of causes, the geological time span, the fixed species, and the teleological destiny of the cosmos (or even the solar system). One implication of the disappearance of the Christian cosmology was that factual and empirical knowledge of the world cannot be taken directly from sacred writings or church traditions. Whatever a theology of world is in the time after "Christian cosmology," it is not a mining of these authorities for facts about nature.

What then is theology of nature if, in fact, there is such a thing? One alternative is that theology of nature supplies no scientific information but does survive as a philosophy or metaphysics of world. This view too is not without its problems. Reflective analyses of world-for-us and ontological analyses of world features have their own sorts of evidences that can be publically argued. Why then should a reflection that originates in redemption necessarily oppose or replace such intuitively grounded or speculatively argued concepts as process, event, relation, motion, or world participation? Even as a theological anthropology is not necessarily a competitor with philosophical anthropology, neither is a theology of world one among many philosophies of world.

The phrase, "the theology of something," does not have the same straightforward and clear meaning as other grammatically similar expressions; for instance, "history of," or "statistics of." It does, of course, suggest an interpretation shaped by a theological perspective, but that does not say very much. Why would the "something," the candidate for interpretation, need to add to the myriad interpretations of world a *theological* interpretation? The question is sharpened if we agree that theological interpretation will not add factual claims to the other inquiries. Here we must attend to the perspective or orientation that fosters and guides theology, the conviction that whatever exists is not only part of the world system but in its very being is shrouded in the mystery that constitutes the very facticity of that system. This mystery is not simply yet unre-

searched and unsolved puzzles that attend the content, behavior, relations, or contexts of things. Thus the building up of knowledge about
these matters does not reduce the mystery of world. The mystery of an
entity is partly that inaccessible concreteness sensed by direct experience
and expressed by poets ("the flower in the crannied wall") and partly the
final horizon, the world itself, which is the matrix of its existence. The
concern of any "theology of" is with the *status* of entities (events, groups,
and soon) as they exist on that ultimate horizon.[3] This is why the interpretive concepts that carry forward a "theology of" do not compete with or
displace the factual claims of observation and analysis. Accordingly,
when a theology of world speaks of world as "real," "significant," or
"good," it is describing the status of world with respect to its fundamental mystery.[4]

THE GENESIS OF WORLD AS CREATION

To think of world or the world order as brought forth by God or gods is
virtually universal among ancient and modern religious faiths. Why is
this the case? The answer may be more evident in archaic and ancient
Near Eastern religions than in the "monotheistic" faiths that sprang from
the religion of Israel. In archaic religions human beings, struggling to
survive the inconstancies of the earth's fecundity, ritualistically and myth-
ically reconnect themselves to the creative powers at work in all things.
Earth itself is a fecundity of powers that must ever be renewed. Creation
myths are accounts of that fecundity.[5] In Hebrew, Jewish, Islamic, and
Christian faiths the ritual renewal of sacred powers recedes in importance. Central to these faiths is the historical event, the traditioned mem-

3. The distinction between the empirically philosophically discerned world and perspectives on the *status* of the world is implied in the classical Catholic theology's claim that God
did not create the world *in* time. This distinction between a timeless God and timeful creation is not without difficulties. But the resistance to thinking of the world as preceded
(and presumably followed) by temporal flow may be at the same time a refusal to see the
"act" of creation as an ordinary empirical event. Thus, instead of describing an externally
observable event, creation is about the world's mysterious dependence on God, hence is
about its status as dependent rather than an empirical origin of the cosmos.

4. To say that creation expresses the (God-dependent) status of world rather than an
empirically described origin is not necessarily to relinquish all content questions to common sense, the sciences, or metaphysics. A perspective while inevitably subjectively structured can at the same time be a distinctive way of being open to disclosures or manifestations. To grasp world as dependent may carry with it "status" discernments about the
world's intrinsic goodness, contingency, reality, or even beauty that may be suppressed in
other perspectives. "Status" discourse is neither ontological nor "subjective" in the ordinary
senses of those terms.

5. For a typology of various creation myths (emergent, world parent, chaos, etc.), see
Charles Long, *Alpha: The Myths of Creation* (New York: Braziller, 1963).

ory, social and individual moral corruption, divine law, and judgement and mercy.[6] Why would such "religions of salvation," centered on social oppression and individual righteousness, think of God as world creator and world as creation? Is this simply a speculative addendum tacked onto the narratives of redemption? In its textual history Israel's legal material and tales of the covenant people preceded its stories of creation. Why did the theme of creation arise at all?

The standard answer to this question is that the logic of salvation, not speculative curiosity, generates the motif of creation. Posited here is a connection between redemptive experience and the world as creation. Theology's task is to uncover this connection. In what follows, I shall draw on the account of redemption in *Good and Evil* to track this connection. According to that account, redemption takes place in agential, interhuman, and sociopolitical spheres. Each of these spheres displays a way of being enmeshed in world.

As biological entities human individuals live from and in the biosphere. Although their basic passions have biological roots, the goods of the biosphere only partially satisfy these desires for survival, organic well-being, being with others, and aesthetic and cognitive pleasures. Idolatrous dynamics arise as human beings try to displace their essentially insecure and anxious situation in the world by attaching themselves in absolutizing ways to various goods at hand, goods of their worldly environment. These dynamics are such that neither the human passions themselves nor the entities that make up the world are evil as such. Redemption takes place when the human being is so "founded" (in God) that its being is shaped by a courage that exists not from false securers but in consent to the tragic insecurity of the world. With courage come new relations to world, relations of consent, existential risk of the self, openness, empathy, and appreciation of the mysteries and beauties of the world. Accordingly, in the sphere of human agents redemption is a way of being in, toward, and even for world.

A different dynamics corrupts the sphere of the interhuman. Alienation, *ressentiment,* and guilt arise as responses to interhuman violation and become relatively permanent and ineradicable structures of relation. Redemption involves a dynamics of reconciliation and communion in which the wounds of violation and guilt are healed not by payments and punishments but by forgiveness. Here, too, something is at work in the dynamics that does not originate simply in the interhuman and whose

6. Anderson, *Creation versus Chaos,* chap. 4.

agapic nature overrides the specific legal, vengeful, or territorial claims of the violators and victims. Metaphors for God in the interpersonal sphere are the Thou, face, forgiveness, and love. In the sphere of the social and political, human evil means violence, oppression, and subjugation by entrenched powers, a situation that calls for emancipation and theonomous societal structures. God is present here as the ideal of justice, unidentifiable with the agendas, traditions, and social organizations of any particular group or society.

Two things get our attention about the way redemption works in these spheres. First, world is present in an intrinsic way in all of these redemptions. The physical cosmos, the realm of living things, and history are presupposed by all three dynamics. The world as a realm of needed and desirable "goods" is presupposed and desired, rendered absolute by idolatry, exploited and used by societal powers. And when redemption effects new freedoms of agents, a new agapic communion of thous in relation, or an emancipated society, the entities, relations, and processes of world are what carry these transformations. In redemption then, world is not excluded but presupposed, and world relations of wonder, empathy, responsibility, nonexploitation, and aesthetic appreciation all come with these redemptions.

Second, the redemptive transformations of these spheres are open-ended with respect to the world. The founding act, the divine presence, never specifies some piece of the world as the locus and limit of human freedom, the interhuman setting, or the societal context. Preeempted is any and all privileging of a worldly territory (earth or heaven, this or that continent, coasts or plains), world stratum (plant life, animals, the micro world), or types of entities and environments as *that* to which wonder, empathy, and responsibility are restricted. The redemptive activity of God (founding) has to do with world as such, any and all possible environments in which human beings live, move, and have their being.

This nonrestriction or nonprivileging has several implications. First, the one who redemptively founds, that is, breaks the power of idolized worldly goods over human beings, can be neither one of the world's entities nor the world totality itself. Because no worldly entity nor the world totality can in fact "found," that is, be the ultimate meaning of things, there would be no redemption at all if the redeeming power were some piece of world. Second, that which opens up and restores human beings to the world and promotes their cooperation with each other and with the world is not and cannot be an alien to that world but rather must be the power or creativity of the world itself. If world means a realm to which God has no relation and exercises no activity, it is surely not possible that God can effect the human sphere in the direction of redemption; that is, agential freedom, cooperation, emancipation. If world is utterly strange, alien, or opposite to God, an utterly autonomous resistance to God's activity, redemption could never mean consent to, appreciation of, or responsibility for world. This, then, is the "logic" of redemption that makes it impossible for the communities of redemption to think of God as a worldless or world-indifferent redeemer. Instead, they conclude that only the one on whom the world order depends, whose creative activity relates to the world as such, could be the founder of meaning, the agapic and merciful face, the criterion of justice. And if God is not worldless or world indifferent, then neither is it possible to think of world or nature as Godless, as utterly unrelated to God. The traditional symbol of this general relation of the world to God is world as creation.[7]

CREATION: UNPACKING A SYMBOL

Creation is surely one of the Christian movement's deep symbols. Having to do with the status of the world, it connects the mystery of the world and the mystery of God. More specifically, it expresses why there is a mystery of the world. We should not be surprised to learn that the mystery that connects God and world (creation) does not lend itself to discursive inquiry. This is because we have no cognitive access to what metaphors of creation express. We do not observe or experience in any direct way either the way the world depends on God or the divine creative activity. A second obstacle is tossed up by the legacy of past interpretation that confuses the matter of the symbol with problems of cosmic origin and gaps in scientific explanation.[8] A third obstacle is the perpetual

---

7. This interpretation of the way creation arises from faith and for theology both resembles and departs from Schleiermacher's view. See *The Christian Faith*, trans. H. R. Mackintosh and J. S. Stewart (Edinburgh: T. & T. Clark, 1928), 142–56. For Schleiermacher the doctrine of creation arises not from the struggle with the puzzle of the world but with the very structure of piety. However, he assigns the doctrine not to the way piety is determinate under the conditions of redemption but to the general piety that redemption presupposes. He thus argues that the structure of utter dependence (piety) in the immediate self-consciousness is inseparable from the human being's sense of world entanglement. Thus, the individual's sense of dependence on God coexists with a sense that the whole world order depends on God. I have departed from this approach because of the privileging of redemption as the way God comes forth as God. Accordingly, the sense of the world as dependent on God comes not with the general structure of piety but with the transition of the human being from the hold of idolatry to freedom by way of being-founded.

8. On the side of the scientists, Fred Hoyle exemplifies this position when he claims that scientific explanation of the universe displaces the religious symbol of creation (*Nature of the Universe* [New York: Harper, 1951]). On the religion side, the confusion is perpetuated

tendency of religious communities, forgetful of the negative and meta-phorical character of all theological expressions, to apply in a direct way some intraworld relation, act, or causality to the mysterious connection of world and God.

Dependence

The most general way to express the meaning of creation is to say that the world depends on God. The world's ultimate status is the status of dependence, sometimes expressed in the metaphor of God as ground. We must acknowledge at the outset that this term names a linguistically unique situation and does not simply repeat any of the many ways worldly entities depend on each other. Thus, we are not to confuse the dependence of the world on God with dependence as an ontological fea-ture of any and all actual things. All things depend on the environmental conditions of their being, on the particular strand of the past from which they came, and on the world system as a whole. But this ontological fea-ture of worldly entities does not directly express the ultimate status of the world as dependent, the mystery of the very facticity of the world. As a term for creation, dependence is of course a metaphor taken from intraworld relations. This metaphor carries with it a second metaphor. To speak of something's dependence is at the same time to assume a differentiation, an independence. That which depends on *A* is not itself *A*. The world's dependence on and independence from God are both part of the symbol, world as creation. These two aspects of the symbol are unavoidable if we acknowledge that God's *redemptive* activity is the basis for the cipher of divine creativity and for affirming world as creation. Redemption as the breaking of the power of idols deabsolutizes world and establishes an irreducible differentiation between that which redeems or founds and that which does not (world). As something that is not God,

by contemporary "creationists" who see the Genesis account of creation as an *alternative* to scientific cosmology. See Roland Frye, *Is God a Creationist?: The Religious Case Against Creation Science* (New York: Charles Scribner's Sons, 1983); and Langdon Gilkey, *Creationism on Trial: Evolution and God at Little Rock* (Minneapolis: Winston Press, 1985). A nonfundamentalist way of confusing creation and cosmic origins is the view that the Big Bang concept some-how confirms the religious doctrine. Ernan McMullin points out that this, like the old phys-icotheology of the eighteenth century, is a "gap" argument ("Natural Science and Belief," in Russell, ed., *Physics*, #5). Ian Barbour also takes the position that "the religious idea of creation is not dependent on particular physical cosmologies, ancient or modern" ("Cre-ation and Cosmology," in Ted Peters, ed., *Cosmos and Creation* [Nashville: Abingdon Press, 1989], 129). Peters likewise points out the problems of combining creation with the Big Bang theory (129).

has no absolute or ultimate status, and has its own reality, world is independent. Existing because of divine creative activity, it is dependent.

But what exactly is affirmed by this language of dependence? The Western religious tradition has employed additional metaphors to specify the meaning of dependence: efficient cause, teleological or final cause, artistic shaping, action, supplying sufficient conditions for, ordering, intervention, and influencing. All of these metaphors are taken from the way intraworldly things influence each other, bring about the new, or effect changes in the environment. Granting that none of the metaphors directly describe the concrete way the world depends on God, is it possible that some of the metaphors are better expressions of the world's dependence on God than others?

Here the theology of God turns to the redemptive coming forth of God as God for norms under which to assess the metaphors of dependence. God's redemptive activity can be such a norm only if it is a special case of God's creative activity at work throughout the world. I argued previously that redemption appresents God as the world's Creativity, active in the total environment in which redemption takes place. If that is the case, there can be no sharp differentiation between human redemptive dependence on God and world's dependence on the divine Creativity. In both cases dependence means receiving from God conditions that promote the independence of what is real (the entity, the human being, the cell) in larger orders of harmony and cooperation. Because the units of reality (entities in their environment) exist eventfully over time, this dependence is limited neither to some primordial moment nor to occasional interventions but is an ongoing, temporal activity.

In agential redemption God is a founding presence that releases agents from structures of idolatry into various world-oriented freedoms. In interhuman redemption God is the infinite Thou who presses alienated relation beyond guilt, resentment, penalty, and vengeance to reconciliation. In sociopolitical redemption God is the justice ideal by which acts of oppression and injustice are measured. If redemption is the way human beings experience God, then the initial clue to how things depend on God is provided by redemptive activity. These redemptions attest a divine action (creativity) that would bring self-destructive, other-violating, society-corrupting human beings into a harmonious being-with-others in which each being is honored in itself.

In the classical Catholic theology of God, the doctrine of creation *ex nihilo* functioned to eliminate concepts of co-creators with God and coeternal materials used in creation, both of which qualify the dependence of the world on God.[9] Postponing these issues until later, I note now an ambiguity in the concept *ex nihilo*. On the one hand it can be a way of asserting that God is the utter and only determiner of world and world is utterly and totally determined by God. Since *ex nihilo* in this sense contradicts the essential independence of the world as attested both in everyday experience and in redemption, and since it presupposes a literalized version of the metaphor of sovereignty, it is not a viable concept. On the other hand insofar as *ex nihilo* is a way of affirming God's activity of establishing the conditions of and drive toward cooperation and harmony, it names an absolute condition of there being a world, without which world never forms.[10] Accordingly, world as a world system and any specific world system such as our cosmic epoch depends in an absolute way on God.

Independence

Because it affirms the world's dependence on God, the symbol of world as creation also *differentiates* God and the world. But what does this metaphor of independence mean as an expression of the symbol, world as creation? In our common sense world participation, our experience of world-for-us, we constantly negotiate with entities that possess a certain independence. These entities resist all of our attempts to reduce them to our wishes and needs. Insofar as they are real at all, they resist our attempts to manage them. In both the human world and the world of nature, we experience the influencings, spontaneities, and irreducible contents of what is other to ourselves. In the spheres of redemption we experience the world's independence as beauty, significance, and vulnerability. Embodied and self-transcending agents, interhuman relations, and institutions with their historical momentums and gathered power all display independence in relation to divine redemptive activities.

What then is this independence we take for granted in everyday life and the transformations of redemption? Three features constitute the independence of ordinary, worldly entities existing in their environments. First, independence is the degree to which an entity is not simply the property of another entity. In ancient philosophy this is one of the mean-

---

9. For an extended account of the basis intentions of the classical doctrine of creation *ex nihilo*, see Gilkey, *Maker*, chap. 3.

10. Grace Jentzen takes this position in her revision of the concept of creation *ex nihilo* (*God's World and God's Body* [Philadephia: Westminster Press, 1984], 137).

ings of the term *substance*.[11] Second, independence is the degree to which the contents of an entity are not identical with, an exact replication of, or reducible to the contents of something else. Insofar as there is such an identity—and we recall at this point that contents are relative to positions in spacetime and to relations—the distinction between that entity and any other collapses. Third, independence names the degree to which an entity is not simply determined by some external causality but rather contributes to its own being. Independence means then being a true subject of properties, differentiability of content, and autonomy of action. All of these features come together in the metaphor of independence to say that the world is not-God. Accordingly, world as creation is not simply a property of God like holiness or love. It is not an exact replication of whatever content constitutes God's being. And, having its own events, processes, spontaneities and self-initiations, it is not simply determined by God.

Dependence and independence are the most general marks of the world's status as created. Accordingly, to reduce the meaning of creation simply to dependence would assign the world's independence to some primordial source other than God's creative activity. But entities can have these properties of independence only if there is a world in the first place, only if they are part of a world system. The world itself can have the character of independence from God only if there is a Creativity that ever brings about the world. Independence is thus neither in isolation from or in opposition to but rather derivative of dependence. At the same time, all the senses in which the world depends on God's creativity concern a differentiated, independent world.

WORLD POLARITIES: IMPLICATIONS OF WORLD AS CREATION

Dependence and independence express a theological perspective on world only at the most formal level. When we reflect further on these themes, we discover certain implications that have in fact found frequent expression in biblical texts and subsequent theological interpretations. The four implied themes may best be understood as two conceptual polarities: (1) mystery and intelligibility (meaning); and (2) goodness and the tragic. It is important not to construe these implied themes and polari-

---

11. "Substance in the truest and primary and most definite sense of the word is that which is neither predicable of a subject nor present in a subject; for instance, the individual man or horse" (Aristotle, *Categories*, chap. 5). See Richard McKeon, *The Basic Works of Aristotle* (New York: Random House, 1941), 7.

ties as straightforward metaphysical descriptions of world totality. Rooted as they are in the way God comes forth in redemption, they first of all express postures toward the world, a kind of hermeneutics of world interpretation that takes place in everyday life. Thus, faith and redemption orient human beings toward the world as mysterious and meaningful, beautiful and tragic. These implications are more "postulates of practical, theological reason" than rationally derived predicates of pure reason. In spite of their postural character, however, they express convictions about the status of the world, not just about the postures themselves. These convictions are "implications" at work in the "logic of redemption." For instance, if the world is the dependent-independent creation of God, it must have the character of mystery, intelligibility, and the like. To some degree these affirmations are confirmed in our actual, everyday experiences of world.

Mystery and Intelligibility

Christian theology's past resistances to modern cosmology, rational theology's attempts to demonstrate God's existence, and styles of certainty in the way theology has been written, have all fostered the suspicion that the "doctrine of creation" is a metaphysical hubris that enters where angels fear to tread. The hubris element originates with the apparent claim that Christian theology, unlike science and philosophy, has cracked the problem posed by the world. There is truth in this charge. Christian theology of world does subject the ultimate status of the world to symbolic interpretation. But the result of this interpretation is not to eliminate but to express and protect the mystery of the world. One negative consequence of world as creation is the abandonment of any and all claims of knowledge of world totality.[12] For Christian theology, human beings have not and cannot accomplish the divinelike cognitive feat of comprehending world in its ultimate origin or actual totality. What we call the universe occupies a single cosmic epoch that originated between twelve and fifteen billion years ago and appears destined to come to an end. This universe is *a* world, not world either in the sense of possible worlds or worlds of succeeding cosmic epochs. Our universe may be *the* world in

---

12. "The God whom man knows is the God who has humbled himself by making place for the world. The rationality of human theology is an embodied rationality. This means that reason is circumscribed by a domain it cannot completely penetrate. . . . The created order is found to be a world of facticity, which is neither completely opaque to man, nor completely transparent to reason" (Michael Wyschogrod, *The Body of Faith: God in the People Israel* [San Francisco: Harper & Row, 1983], 13–14). "The idea of creation cannot be grounded because creation is the idea of the ungrounded" (168).

our perspective. It is not all worlds together or world totality. And there is a theological reason for this agnosticism about knowledge of totality. If world is an dependent-independent work of God (creation), that work will constitute the world's mystery. Mystery is intrinsic to anything and everything whose ground is the mystery of Creativity itself.[13]

Theology is also suspected of cognitive hubris because of what seems to be its denial of world mystery, its claim that world as creation is meaningful, significant, or intelligible. These terms express the conviction, partially confirmed in everyday experience, that there is some correspondence between our attempts to understand, get along in, and aesthetically enjoy the world and the way the world is constituted. If the world were simply a chaotic jumble, all of these attempts would fail. But theological discourse about the world's meaning or intelligibility has to do not only with the immediate environments of everyday life but with the ultimate status of the world. Because world is creation, it has the sort of significance something has that is valued or willed. Because it is creation, the world's facticity is not just the facticity of a sheer accident but of a valuing Creativity. The meaningfulness (significance, intelligibility) of world does not qualify or reduce its mystery. It is the meaningfulness of what is ultimately mysterious.

Goodness and the Tragic

The second polarity juxtaposes the world's goodness (beauty) and its tragic character. In the classical Christian formulation, the world's goodness is an inevitable, derivative effect of its origin in that which is perfectly good. A perfect goodness (God) can bring about what is contingent but not what is evil. I have no quarrel with this basic axiom providing it is clear that the term *evil* is not applied to such properties of world as incompatibility, maladaptibility, and vulnerability to destruction. If "good" means the necessarily successful realization of an entity's distinctive entelechy, then very little about the world is "good." Schleiermacher opposed the "natural heresy" of Manicheanism by a negative definition of the world's goodness. Nothing about the world's createdness as such is an intrinsic obstacle to the fulfillment of God consciousness.[14] I offer a slight revision of this proposal. A world entity is good insofar as its very

13. See Dietrich Bonhoeffer's exposition of Gen. 1:1–2 (*Creation and Fall: A Theological Interpretation of Genesis 1–3* [New York: Macmillan, 1959]). "Man no longer lives in the beginning—he has lost the beginning. Now he finds he is in the middle, knowing neither the end nor the beginning . . ." (10). "Thinking cannot answer its own last 'why,' because an answer would again produce a 'why'" (9).

14. Schleiermacher, *The Christian Faith*, Part One, Section Three (233).

constitution enables it to be receptive to the divine attempt to draw it into harmonious cooperation with others. Thus, even the natural egocentrism of autonomous and independent entities may be good if it is not an utter resistance to cooperation. This fundamental goodness of things is then the presupposition of world as harmonious, creative, beautiful, and diverse.

The other side of the world's goodness is its tragic character. We find the tragic in both scientific and philosophical (ontological) portrayals of world. Here we discover it to be an implication of world as creation. Any world whose entities have the character of independence will have a tragic side. If independence means autonomy, and if world contains a multiplicity of entities, only an absolute external determination can adapt them to each other or to some larger good. Each entity's situation then is inevitably a struggle to fulfill its own entelechy in an environment that contains other entities, processes, and conditions not absolutely ordered to that entity's own aims and needs. Thus, world as creation is a tragic world, a world of entities whose realizations and enjoyments are ever accompanied by frustration, suffering, and demise.

APORIAS AND BOUNDARIES

With each step of this theology of God, I have attempted to mediate the apparent stand-off between anti-theism and classical Christian theism. The motif of creation confronts us once again with this conflict. In some interpretations classical Christian theism propounds world as creation as an alternative to the scientific accounts of world origin and to doctrines of the eternality of world. Hoping to avoid such issues, anti-theism repudiates the language and theme of creation on the grounds that it objectifies God and the meaning of God. Against this repudiation, I argue that world as creation arises necessarily with the way God redemptively comes forth as God. Against the classical view (at least seen as objectivism), I argue that a theology of world as creation is not world description but concerns the ultimate status of world. This means that the theology of God does not aspire to thinking the totality of the world. World as creation is just what frustrates this aspiration. On the other hand, we can only acknowledge that the way religious faiths and theologies often speak about creation sounds very much like totality thinking, either in the sense of objective explanation or in the sense of literalistic, space and time description. Creation discourse translated into totality thinking does perpetuate certain standard confusions. Two of these seem to be ever with us: (1) creation as empirical origin; and (2) creation as either absolute beginning or everlasting process.

To say that God is "maker of heaven and earth" sounds like an explanation. Anything that is "made," (produced, invented, crafted, originated) poses the question of what made it, and that which brings things about is at least in part their explanation. If world is construed as a "made" entity, then God as maker must be its explanation. Thus, the explanatory origin of the world is God. This statement appears to be the logical alternative to another statement. The origin of the world is the Big Bang. This tempts the theologian to locate something unexplained in the scientific theory that devolves to the theological explanation. But the problem of the ontological status of the world and the problem of what presents itself for causal or mathematical explanation arise in quite different orders.[15] The emergence of what we call the cosmos out of a primordial and unstable singular that precedes the Big Bang is surely a problem for nuclear physics. Even if the singular itself remains unexplained, it need not be a gap into which we insert some sort of divine causality. Perhaps cosmological science will discover that the chaotic forces of the singular contain remnants of a former cosmic epoch. The problem still remains a problem of understanding processes, continuities, and causalities in what theology calls world. World, in other words, is not necessarily synonymous with the universe of our present cosmic epoch. If this is so, it is surely the case that world as creation is not a term for the origin of our cosmos, for some divine causality operating in the singular that explains the Big Bang itself.

The second confusion has more the character of an aporia that arises when two ciphers of the divine being are forced to function as objective explanations. The cipher of God's power arises when the religious community connects the facticity of redemption with God. The negative theology element of all ciphers works to prevent that power from being identified with any mundane form of power: force, efficient causality, control. Whatever the power actually is in redemption, it is the power of God and

---

15. For a clear and cogent analysis of these two orders, scientific cosmology and the Big Bang theory of origins, and the status of world as creation, see Howard J. Van Til, "The Scientific Investigation of Cosmic History," in Van Til, ed. *Portraits of Creation: Biblical and Scientific Perspectives on the World's Formation* (Grand Rapids, Mich.: Wm. B. Eerdmans, 1990). In Van Til's view scientific cosmogony does not entail any concept of the status of the universe in relation to God. Nor is it an explanation of the origin of the universe. Thus, the Big Bang theory is about an early portion of the formative history of the universe, not the formative question of the very facticity of the universe. For a similar position, see W. R. Stoeger, "Contemporary Cosmology and its Implications for Science," in the same volume.

not a world process. That means it is in service of God's love, mercy, or creativity. What we cannot do is to take one of the mundane senses of power, such as efficient causality, and argue that God is its perfect exemplification. If mundane power is partial determination, control, or causality, then divine power must be absolute determination and control. With such a move God becomes the power that absolutely determines all outcomes, including the final outcome of world. And with the concept of one final world outcome comes its correlate, the concept of an absolute beginning. It is from this notion of absolutized sovereignty that has prompted some traditional theologies to think of creation as a one-time act that took place a long time ago. Thus, creation *ex nihilo* comes to mean the concept of an absolute beginning of *the* world.

A second objectified cipher has an opposite outcome. The cipher of God's love also arises with the facticity of redemption. The negative theology helps prevent construing this cipher as a piece of contingent divine psychology. Love expresses an eternal disposition of God, God's very being. It is just this eternal disposition that supplies the "motive" for the divine creativity. But if love is creation's eternal dynamism, then Creativity cannot have a limited or finite expression and creation cannot be limited to an act a long time ago. Creation then is not an absolute origin but an eternal activity of God.

If I were forced to resolve this aporia of a finite and an infinite creativity, I would have to choose the second alternative for two reasons. First, the objectified power of the first alternative has a cosmological, even mythological character. Second, the cipher of love is primary to the more derivative metaphor of power in the way God redemptively comes forth as God. Yet, several reasons caution against rushing to resolve the aporia. First, both options require us to think of world as some sort of totality, either as a finite or infinite temporal span. But world totality arises with metaphysical speculation, not world as creation. Second, even at the level of totality thinking, both options are simply inconceivable. We can conceive neither an infinity of universes nor a one-time act of God. Even if we grant the classical notion that time comes into existence with creation, hence there is no "before" of creation, we cannot avoid the mythology that arises when we distinguish between God-without-world (alone) and God-plus-world. The transition between the two takes place in God; hence, time of some sort, a "before" and "after," is brought back into the picture. On the other hand, we cannot conceive any actuality as temporally infinite. Such a notion would require shifts in our way of thinking about time much more radical than the notion of spacetime in twentieth-century physics. Third, both options require us to relate a cipher of God (power or love) to world not just to express the world's dependence-independence but as an enterprise of empirical cosmology. It is not clear to me how one determines the status of world as finitely or infinitely temporal by means of a cipher that expresses the mystery of God. Totalizing thinking, inconceivability, and the cosmological inapplicability of ciphers should prompt theology of creation to remain content with a doctrine of creation that simply sets forth the mysterious dependent and independent relation of world to God.[16]

16. In similar vein, Schleiermacher sees no relation between the speculative issue of the eternality or temporality of the world and piety (*The Christian Faith*, 155).

17
THE EVENT OF JESUS AS CHRIST

Of His earth-visiting feet
None knows the secret, cherished, perilous
The terrible shamefast, frightened, whispered, sweet,
Heart-shattering secret of His way with us.
Alice Meynell, "Christ in the Universe"

Theology of God's third task is construction of a paradigm that interprets the divine activity. This paradigm attempts to connect "the way the world works" according to scientific and ontological analysis of cosmos, nature, and history; the end or aim of divine activity attested in redemption; and the character and content of the divine working (the symbolics of God). In the motif of creation, God's redemptive aims are extended to all that exists. Redemption and creation indicate but give no account of this divine activity. They affirm the facticity and universal scope of the divine working but propose no specific location. This failure to locate the divine activity is a serious lacuna for the inclusive paradigm I shall try to construct. My general account of the "facticity of redemption" has so far omitted that through which redemption historically takes place. And it appears to be the case that we better understand the activity of something when we grasp not only its outcome but that which brought it about, its "through-which." It goes without saying that in the case of God, the divine causal efficacy, influence, or presence is never directly given. Even if we think that Moses' burning bush or the disappearance of leprosy at the hands of Jesus is a direct divine action, what we would have before us is still only the burning bush and a healed body. We are not given the causality itself. Lacking direct access to divine action, we proceed to construct a paradigm from appropriate elements. The one element we have not yet considered is what actually takes place so as to bring about redemption. In other words, God comes forth as God not only in the facticity of redemption (experienced as founding, emancipation, or reconciliation) but in that *through-which* this redemption comes about. This through-which will surely shape the way we understand God's relation to the world.

God comes forth as God in different ways in the epochs, peoples, and regions of human history. In the Christian movement and the redemption it voices, that coming forth takes place in connection with a specific event or set of events in history, namely, the event of Jesus as Christ. To say this is not to restrict God's activity to the Christian movement, thus denying that God redemptively comes forth in any other time, history, or people. The event of Jesus as Christ is itself part of a very long historical trajectory that includes the origin of the nation of Israel and with that the Torah-faith and prophetic-faith of the Jewish people. But for the Christian movement, something decisive happened in connection with the event of Jesus as Christ that created the through-which of redemption as Christians experience it. It is the task of this chapter to say in the briefest way what took place in that event.

Should we think of this account of Jesus as Christ as a "Christology"? Those who permit the specific concepts of two natures, preexisting logos, and anhypostasis to define Christology will want to withhold the term from this interpretation. On the other hand, the analysis is "christological" insofar as that term means the theological attempt to understand the significance of Jesus as Christ.[1] I shall not, however, articulate the significance of the event of Jesus as Christ through the assumptions and methods of the "house of authority." The issue turns on the use or nonuse of historical method toward the materials of the New Testament collection, which materials provide the only access we have to the event and figure of Jesus. When historical method is refused, the texts of the New Testament collection become one-dimensional, collapsed into a single level of descriptive truth. Accordingly, all events about Jesus and all sayings attributed to Jesus recorded in these texts become equally pertinent sources for a Christology. Each title of Jesus is judged to be equally descriptive and true in a harmonized totality of titles. The result is the concept of a preexisting, divine being (the Word) who abandoned the heavenly state to assume flesh. This being then was the very reality (person) of Jesus from birth. Since this divine being was the subject of Jesus, Jesus

---

1. A number of contemporary theologians have offered interpretations of the significance of Jesus in other terms than the two natures. See the collection of essays in John Hick, ed., *The Myth of God Incarnate* (London: SCM, 1977); Monika Helwig, *Jesus as the Compassion of God: New Perspectives on the Tradition of Christianity* (Wilmington, Del.: Michael Glazier, 1983), Introduction; Douglas F. Ottati, *Jesus Christ and Christian Vision* (Philadelphia: Fortress Press, 1989). Ottati would avoid a "metaphysical protrait of two natures in one hypostasis" (chap. 5).

was sinless, was aware of being divine, and knew in advance the necessity of his own death. After the resurrection the enfleshed logos continues in heavenly mode, awaiting to return to earth at the end time.

Once the New Testament collection is acknowledged to be written by human beings who reflect the perspectives and life situations of early Christian communities, "Christology" can no longer proceed from a synthesis of leveled and "true" texts. In a historical perspective the texts of the New Testament reflect different situations, times, and communities. This sets for the interpreter the "archaeological" task of determining what is primitive and what is late, what actually happened to Jesus and what did not, what Jesus actually taught or preached and what the kergymas of the later community attributed to him, and what was the origin and meaning of Jesus' titles. This archaeological work uncovers less a single "Christology" as a variety of ways Jesus was proclaimed and interpreted even in the first generations of the Christian community. A second result is the picture of a community whose initial Easter beginnings prompted it to attribute not only saving significance to Jesus' death but to search for ways of confessing that God was in him. These ways ranged from an early humiliation-exaltation scheme to the Johannine theology of the incarnate Word.

Plural christological traditions of the New Testament do seem to create more problems for the Protestant than the Catholic church. Historically oriented Catholics can at least argue that, however multiple were the New Testament Christologies, an official and true theology arose from a divinely guided development of church teachings (dogma). But history replaces the traditional Protestant appeal to a leveled-out Scripture with multiple interpretations of the significance and figure of Jesus in the canonical texts themselves. Historical methods call for an alternative to both views. Instead of the Catholic notion of truth *a priori* to the developing teachings of the church and the Protestant notion of truth *a priori* to each and every New Testament text, the historically oriented theologian tries to grasp the significance of Jesus as Christ by an account of how the event of Jesus is the "through-which" of redemption. This approach interprets the contemporary facticity of redemption (and the community of redemption) and the historically retrieved event of Jesus as Christ in relation to each other.

The "event of Jesus as Christ" does not mean simply the life of Jesus.[2] What we have in the literature of the New Testament is the record of a

2. I use the expression, Jesus as Christ, and not Jesus as *the* Christ, to avoid a Christian imperialist claim in relation to Judaism. For Christians to claim possession of *the* one and only Messiah implies a negative judgment on Judaism, namely, that *the* Messiah appeared,

community-originating event, the central figure of which was Jesus. There is thus no figure or event of Jesus separated from this larger event of origination, nor do these early texts know any other Jesus than the one proclaimed as Christ.[3] The "as Christ" expresses how the figure and event of Jesus was significant for the new community. The event of Jesus as Christ is then, just that, an event in which a new community, the ecclesia, took historical form.[4]

The origin of the new community in relation to its precipitating figure, Jesus, is an actual happening in history, open to historical investigation. At the same time, the "event of Jesus as Christ" is a theological concept, a perspective on the historical event rooted in an "inner history." This perspective is possible because the new community with its central figure continues to be the through-which of redemption for at least one strand

---

only to be rejected by the Jews. But *the* Messiah of Jewish national hope did not appear. *The* Messiah (for Jews) is the deliverer of the Jewish nation. While the Christian movement, reflecting its Jewish origins, did apply the term *Christos* to Jesus, it was not *the Christos*, but Messiah in a quite different sense. Because the event of Jesus as Christ did fulfill a certain teleological dimension of the faith of Israel, Jesus was dubbed Messiah. This teleological dimension is the potentiality of the faith of Israel to be a universal or Gentile faith. Jesus then is Christ in relation to that possibility, not as *the* deliverer of the Israelite people. In the course of the Christian movement, the term *Christ* tended to lose its titular function and merged with Jesus as a proper name.

3. Wolfhart Pannenberg, while acknowledging the essential connection between Christology and salvation, refuses to make Christology a function of soteriology. For Pannenberg this means the view that Jesus has no significance in himself, only for us, or in his salvific effects. Christology's prior question to his significance beyond himself is "about Jesus himself, the person as he lived on earth." Christology must start from Jesus of Nazareth (*Jesus—God and Man*, trans. L. L. Wilkins and A. Priebe [Philadelphia: Westminster Press, 1968], 48–49). Perhaps Pannenberg's point is that the content of incarnation, Jesus' unity with God and his resurrection, is not reducible to discourse about salvation. But would Pannenberg establish this content apart from the way the initial community responded to and interpreted Jesus? Clearly, the only materials Pannenberg has to work with are texts written within the conviction of Jesus' saving significance. Not even Paul and the Gospel writers had some extrasalvific access to Jesus as "one with God" or as "resurrected." Does Pannenberg? Can he find a way to a nonsoteriological Jesus that then shows Jesus' saving significance? Perhaps the issue turns on the word *significance*. Ordinarily, the significance of something is *for* something else; e.g., the significance of the *magna carta*. What would it mean to claim that the *magna carta* is significant in itself? What then is Jesus' significance "in himself"? In the eyes of God? His own internal interpretation of who he is? I would think we have little or no access to either of these. For similar "event" approaches to Christology, see John Cobb, "The Finality of Christ in a Whiteheadian Perspective," in Dow Kirkpatrick, ed., *The Finality of Christ* (Nashville: Abingdon, 1966). Hans Frei seems to have departed from Pannenberg's notion of "Jesus' significance in himself." He sees Paul and the Gospel writers not focused on Jesus' own faith but his mission and his obedience as the one who was sent (*The Identity of Jesus Christ* [Philadelphia: Fortress Press, 1975], 106).

4. "The various elements [of the Event of Christ] can be identified in different ways; but I should say that this central event must be thought of as including, whatever words may be used in designating them, the personality, life, and teaching of Jesus, the response of loyalty he awakened, his death, his resurrection, the coming of the Spirit, the faith with which the Spirit was received, the creation of the community" (John Knox, *Jesus, Lord, and Christ* [New York: Harper & Row, 1958], 217).

of human history. In this sense the event of Jesus as Christ is an ongoing event. Accordingly, setting forth the event of Jesus as Christ is both a historical and theological endeavor. Historical inquiry gives us a multilayered, developing event and a figure interpreted by various kerygmas of the early community. Theological inquiry attempts to recover that about the total event which makes it the through-which of an ongoing redemption.

THE EVENT OF JESUS AS CHRIST IN ITS RESOLUTION: THE ECCLESIA

A major contention of this book is that God comes forth as God in connection with redemption. Furthermore, insofar as there is a founding that transforms idolatrous passions into freedoms, alienation into reconcilation, and subjugation into emancipation, redemption has a certain facticity. Redemption actually takes place. But how does such redemption happen? It is clear that it does not spontaneously generate in human hearts or societies. At a formal level, we can say that individuals are redemptively transformed in their everyday life settings and societies are changed as they are part of the flow of historical events. That is to say, as a facticity, redemption takes place in and through the historical. More specifically, this means that individuals, relations, and institutions are transformed by the historical mediations of new stories, altered symbolics, new intersubjectivities, changed historical memories, charismatic figures, and new communities and traditions. If this is the case, the facticity of redemption carries with it another facticity, the facticity of that through which redemption is historically mediated. This through-which of historical redemption (at least for the Christian movement) is the new community, the new corporate reality with its intersubjectivity, traditions, narratives, and symbolics. But whence comes the new community? What is its through-which? The answer is the figure and activity of Jesus, the resolution of which is the beginning of the new community. Thus the *resolution* of the event of Jesus as Christ is the birth of the ecclesia. The history of the Christian movement is replete with attempts (theories?) to express the salvific significance of Jesus. The one nontheoretical and historical statement we can make is that a new community did come about in the wake of Jesus' life and death. That will be our entree into the thicket of metaphors and proposals about the significance of the event of Jesus.[5]

5. This method of beginning with the ecclesial community and working back to its central and precipitating figure, Jesus as Christ, was pioneered in various works of John Knox. See the trilogy of works assembled into the volume entitled *Jesus, Lord, and Christ* (New York: Harper & Row, 1958); *The Church and the Reality of Christ* (New York: Harper & Row,

The New Community

The new community that arose as a resolution of the event of Jesus as Christ is a universalized form of the faith of Israel. That is to say, it is a social form of Israelite faith that can exist in connection with any of the ways human beings organize themselves into societies, cultures, or ancestral groups. This is not to say that the ecclesial community is the only "universal" form of faith. Many religious faiths are universal in the sense that they can cross the cultural boundaries in which they initially arose and be taken into different socialities. Although the faith of Israel itself was socially formed by tribal and intertribal (national?) groupings, its way of understanding the sacred had universalistic elements of the one creator God who was active in the life of all peoples. Judaism, itself a form of the faith of Israel, is universal not only in the sense that some of its early forms engaged in proselytizing, but also in its genius for surviving amidst very different and even alien societies. Like other forms of Israelite faith, the ecclesial community was always socially particular, existing over time by taking into itself the language, customs, and social forms of the society of which it was a part. But no such particularities are necessary to ecclesiality. No specific cultural, ethnic, ancestral, or "racial" entity is the condition for there being an ecclesial community. This capacity to exist in the form of the faith of Israel in relation to any and all human societies is ecclesia's most visible and external feature.[6]

What would launch such a community into existence? I have contended that redemption itself has universalizing elements. In the faith of Israel Yahweh is not simply a god but God. Yahweh's activity is not restricted to the covenant people but is as wide as the world itself. As a norm, justice has a certain transcendence over the specific situations of peoples. These motifs of the faith of Israel contain a radical dimension that is given expression in the prophet's word of an absolute demand. Evoking this word are the corruptions, perils, and hopes of the people (and nation) of Israel. But the criterion of justice, the possibility of forgiveness, and the divine pathos are not simply pragmatic calculations that apply to or mirror simply that people. Thus, the faith of Israel exists as a tension between having a national *sine qua non* of hearing the divine word and the *as such* character of that word. The radical element of the pro-

---

1962); *The Humanity and Divinity of Christ: A Study of Pattern in Christology* (Cambridge, Eng.: Cambridge University Press, 1967); and *The Death of Christ: The Cross in New Testament History and Faith* (New York: Abingdon Press, 1958).

6. For a fuller discussion of ecclesia as a distinct kind of community, see my book *Ecclesial Man: A Social Phenomenology of Faith and Reality* (Philadelphia: Fortress Press, 1975), chap. 7.

phetic word is this *as such* dimension, the summons to obey God as such, to hope in and worship as such.[7] What gives the relation to God or the divine summons an *as such* character is its nonrestrictability, its irreducibility to what mediates it (the whole determinate system of language, traditions, and institutions), the irreducibility of the summons to pragmatic self-interested calculations, and the irreducibility or absoluteness of God Godself.

With the event of Jesus as Christ, the prophetic word of divine summons (in grace or demand) breaks with this tense mixture of an ethnic or national *sine qua non* and the *as such* element. That is, the divine word does not absolutely require the existence of any particular ethnicity but can be present to any and all.[8] The early texts of the Christian movement expressed the transethnic and *as such* character of relation to God in a variety of ways: the impending reign of God, the absolute character of faith (as in the parables), the primacy of agape, and the enfleshed logos. If the new community was a universalized form of the faith of Israel, then what launched it was something that lifted the *as such* character of relation to God out of all ethnic and national conditions.

The Relation of the New Community to Judaism

Even as redemption does not take place as a spontaneous generation, a sheer divine intervention over and above historical processes and human responses, neither does the event of Jesus as Christ simply fall onto history from the outside. This event takes place not simply in "history" but in a specific strand of history which John Cobb, using a term from Karl Jaspers, calls Jewish axial existence. The new community arose within this existence but was transplanted outside the specific ethnicity of Judaism. In this transplantation the faith of Israel became also a Gentile faith. What then is the relation between the new community and the communities (various Jewish forms of the faith of Israel) from which it arose? An older theology formulated that relation as a displacement, a new cove-

---

7. Abraham Heschel eloquently communicates this *as such* element of prophetic faith. "To a person endowed with prophetic sight, everyone else appears blind; to a person whose ear perceives God's voice, everyone else appears deaf. No one is just; no knowing is strong enough, no trust complete enough. The prophet hates the approximate, shuns the middle of the road. Man must live on the summit to avoid the abyss. There is nothing to hold to except God" (*The Prophets*, Vol. 1 [New York: Harper & Row, 1962], 16).

8. According to Martin Buber, Deutero-Isaiah was the "originator of a world theology." He proclaimed the rule of God over the nations, thus opposed the claims of other gods to leadership (*The Prophetic Faith* [New York: Macmillan, 1949], 209). Thus Israelite faith itself came to a moment when the God of the people Israel is proclaimed as the God of all peoples. This universalism anticipated the social form of Israelite faith that came about when a Gentile form of that faith arose, namely the ecclesia.

nant displacing an old one. In this interpretation this displacement was part of a divinely orchestrated scheme of salvation history. This displacement motif is part of the background of the long tradition of Christian anti-Semitism, constantly fed by charges that the Jews rejected and killed their own Messiah and by the notion that Christianity as the "new Israel" was the one and only valid form of the faith of Israel. Historically speaking, it is the Christian movement arose initially as a sect of Judaism from which it separated to become a largely Gentile (non-Jewish) faith. Can we formulate this break in some other way than the displacement and discreditation of Judaism, acknowledging in a positive way Judaism's genius and legitimacy?

The task is made more difficult by the fact that the Christian movement is not an entirely different *faith* from the faith of Israel but represents a certain "logic" or tendency in that faith. According to the texts of Israel's faith, the idolatry of individuals and the corruptions of institutions can be exposed and redemption can have its day. The social entity that experienced and narrated these themes was initially a nomadic tribe, then amphictyony of tribes, then a national people. Something happens to faith as it becomes entangled in social forms. The institutions, laws, and traditions necessary to mediate that faith and keep it alive take on the character of a *sine qua non,* an absolute condition that itself must be fiercely defended on behalf of faith itself. An unbreakable correlation develops between faith, redemption, or relation to God and such social forms as the landed nation or the exiled people. At the same time there is something about redemption itself that undermines such a correlation. Individual redemption transforms idolatrous human passions that as such have no designated end but exist toward an open horizon. In redemption that horizon (which idolatry had reduced to the idol) turns out to be the one and only thing that can break the power of the idol, the true horizon of divine being. A similar nonrestriction is at work in the reconciling of alienated relations and in the norm of justice. Thus, while a determinate, historical entity is necessary to the mediation of redemption, the founding, reconciling, and emancipating activity of God cannot be absolutely restricted to its mediating institutions. This is why there developed in the faith of Israel itself the notion that the God of Israel is the creator of all things and thus is at work in the life and doings of other peoples.

Judaism is not simply a replication of the ancient faith of Israel but is a specific, social form of that faith.[9] This is the form that faith took when

---

9. It is important to remember that "Judaism" of the first century covered a variety of movements. The Pharisaic movement and rabbinical Judaism was one of those movements that eventually came to dominance. John Dominic Crossan identifies—but without any in-

the people of Israel developed a way of being faithful under the alien conditions of the diaspora. Judaism, too, exists in a perpetual tension between the institutions necessary for successful existence in the diaspora situation (for instance, halakah, the rabbinate, Talmud) and the incipient universal elements in faith itself. Judaism is a form of the faith of Israel in which a specific, ancestrally organized people has learned to exist in the alien conditions of a dominant culture apart from its own land and nation. The social form of ancestral identity is thus the *sine qua non* of Judaic obedience and worship of God.

I have contended that the new community is the faith of Israel in universal, that is, nonethnic form, and that this gives social form to the *as such* element of prophetic faith. Does such a contention disestablish or discredit Judaism? Does it foster an intrinsic opposition between Judaism and the Christian movement? If the question is simply a comparison of the two as "religions" or corporate modes of faith, I see no basis for arguing the superiority of the one over the other. Judged by certain criteria, Judaism has a "genius" absent in the Christian movement. This genius is the capacity to preserve an authentic faith and life before God while existing in cultural environments hostile to that faith. The successful resistance to cultural determination is at the same time a resistance against the demonic influences and structures of virtually any human society. By way of narrative, Scriptures, traditions, halakah, Talmud, synagogues, rabbis, and the familial structures of an ethnic people, Judaism makes the everyday life of its people constantly subject to matters of faith.

Judged by this criterion, the Christian movement comes off a poor second. Its departure from the ethnic *sine qua non* opens it to enculturation into any society of which it is part.[10] Having no ethnic carrier with a specific halakah, it either develops a timeless institutionality, dogma, and casuistry of its own (for instance, Catholicism) that becomes a new *sine qua non*, which as such departs from the ecclesial form of faith, or it exists in a constant compromise with culture, diluting or corrupting faith and tradition by political, ethical, or aesthetic cultural syntheses.[11] Thus, Juda-

---

tended disvaluation—"inclusive" and "exclusive" tendencies in first-century Judaism. He sees inclusive Judaism continuing in the early Christian movement and exclusive Judaism in rabbinic Judaism (*The Historical Jesus: The Life of a Mediterranean Peasant* [San Francisco: Harper San Francisco, 1991], 418–22).

10. To say that Judaism is an ethnic faith and the faith of the Christian movement does not mean simply that there is a specifically Jewish people but no specifically Christian people. The Christian movement, a Gentile form of the faith of Israel, inevitably embodies itself in particular ethnicities, in which case it takes on an ethnic character. Yet as a "Gentile" faith, it cannot be identified with any one of these ethnicities.

11. "Ecclesial" (as over against ecclesiastical) names the *type* of religious community, at least expressed in an ideal way, in which any and all ethnic, national, or territorial forms

ism is less prone than the Christian movement to open its symbols and community to therapeutic, religious syncretism, obscurantism, scientism, and prevailing political movements. In its formative period (the first four or so centuries), the Christian movement did differentiate itself from its cultural environment by way of an official institutionality, an official doctrine, and certain ethical rigorisms. This solution to the problem of survival and identity created a new institutional *sine qua non* for relation to God that was eventually relativized by movements of protest. Lacking ethnic definition and possessing only a relative means of maintaining identity, the Christian movement is constantly open to cultural assimilation.

The "genius" of the Christian movement is its way of carrying the faith of Israel into any and all societal and cultural frameworks without an ethnic *sine qua non*. Its burden is the constant rotation that goes on between absolutistic ways of preserving identity (biblicism, fundamentalism, and so on) that take on the the status of *sine qua nons* of relation to God and the critique of such in the name of unconditional grace.[12] The Christian movement both needs and relativizes the Torah element of the faith of Israel. I conclude then that Judaism and the Christian movement are not oppositional faiths but two quite legitimate forms of the faith of Israel.[13] Accordingly, there would surely be a great impoverishment if the Judaic form of faith were to disappear or if the faith of Israel were confined to its Judaic form.[14] Unfortunately, mutual caricaturing continues to mark the interrelation of these two faiths. The Christian caricature of Ju-

can serve as its cultural framework. "Anti-ecclesial" is the tendency to make one of these forms definitive and necessary to faith.

12. Paul Tillich expressed this paradox in the phrase Protestant principle and Catholic substance. All actual religious faiths, including Judaism with its prophetic dimension, experience and embody some form of this tension. That is, all actual religious faiths require determinate, institutional forms through which they exist as faiths, which forms tend to displace or suppress the *as such* element of the divine word.

13. In a more general way, Crossan points out the perils of both Judaic and Christian (universalistic) forms of faith: "to be human is to balance particularity and universality, and, although the balance may always tip one way or the other, either extreme is equally inhuman. You can lose your soul at either end of the spectrum, and one can and should ask, with equal legitimacy: did Judaism give too little in failing to convert the Roman Empire? Did Christianity give too much in succeeding?" (*The Historical Jesus*, 422–23).

14. Paul Van Buren makes a strong case for this point, that is, the full legitimacy of both Judaic and Christian (Gentile) forms of the faith of Israel. Thus, "the differences between us arise not because one of us is right and the other wrong, but because they are God's people whereas we are God's elect church" (*Discerning the Way: A Theology of the Jewish Christian Reality* [New York: Seabury, 1980], 197). For Van Buren, both forms of faith attempt to walk in God's Way. But what happened in the event of Christ, the origin of church, was the "bringing of Gentiles into the story" (321). Thus the church, the ecclesia, has a distinctive mission, but that does not include displacing God's people, the Jews. Rather, the ecclesia is called to live alongside the people of Israel.

daism is of a Messiah-rejecting people, the implication being that Judaism should be absorbed into Christianity. In the eyes of some Jews, the Christian movement is an intellectualizing of faith into belief in dogmas, a tritheism, and an idolatry (the worship of a pseudo-Messiah), and an aggressive oppressor of other faiths, the implication being that it is unfortunate that Christianity ever arose.[15]

THE EVENT OF JESUS AS CHRIST: THE PRECIPITATING FIGURE

According to this "archaeology" of the conditions of redemption, the new community that arose as the resolution of the event of Jesus as Christ is the historical through-which of redemption. But if this community is not simply spontaneously generated and if it is not simply the direct effect of a supernatural intervention, then it too has a historical through-which. What then is the through-which of this new, universal form of the faith of Israel? The question can be only partially answered at the level of "external history." That is to say, historians can never arrive at the exact point in the event of Jesus where they demonstrate by historical evidence that the figure, teachings, death, and resurrection of Jesus gave birth to the new community. The historian's sources are not written by people who themselves knew Jesus in person but by people dependent on earlier traditions. The texts record the way the first and succeeding generations of the Christian movement responded to the event of Jesus. One conviction runs through all of these responses, and here we have a third facticity. In addition to the facticity (that is, actuality) of redemption itself and the facticity of the community of redemption, there is the fact that the new community understood Jesus as the through-which of its very existence. This conviction is a perennial feature of ecclesia. It is our task to explore what it can mean.

The Kerygmas: Their Intended Factuality

The kerygmas of the early Christian movement that attest to Jesus as the through-which of the new community are framed by participants in that community. All kerygmas bring together contemporary redemptive experience and historical memory. Insofar as a kerygma attests a through-which of an actual historical resolution that begins the new community,

---

15. Both Judaism and the Christian movement are imperiled in advanced industrial society, the Christian movement as it reshapes itself into therapeutic and other cultural contents, the Jewish movement as its ethnic character becomes more and more diluted by assimilation and by cultural assaults on halakah and other crucial historical bearers of the faith.

one aspect of its content is something actual in history. More specifically, these kerygmas attest that the through-which of redemptive existence is not simply a symbol, but Jesus as a historical reality. As historical, this conviction is open to historical inquiry and thus is ever relative to the evidences of historical method. Since historical method deals in probabilities, it can never *absolutely* confirm or disconfirm the historical conviction of the new community that its through-which is this actual figure. As to the community itself, a certain appresentation appears to be at work in its historical conviction. Even as the actuality of redemption appresents a symbolics of the one and only thing that can found or serve as a norm for justice, so the actuality of the mediation of redemption in the new community appresents not just a historical vacuum or figure X but the *kind* of figure and event necessary to bring forth the new universal form of the faith of Israel. A minimum version of this appresentation and its event is that the figure and its event so embodied an *as such* relation to God that it broke the *sine qua non* of ethnicity (as a condition of redemption) and transformed the faith of Israel into a universal form. This is in fact what we find in the accounts of Jesus in the New Testament record. This appresentation also has a rather minimal confirmation in those historical studies that attempt to get behind the kerygmatic way of expressing Jesus' significance to Jesus' actual sayings, deeds, and fate.

Needless to say the historically retrieved Jesus varies from historian to historian. There does, however, appear to be a kind of minimum agreement among most historians.[16] Jesus was born between 5 and 8 B.C.E. and was executed during the rule of Pilate after 26 C.E. He spoke Aramaic. The length and chronology of his public activity is unknown. He was baptized by John and thus is associated in some way with that movement. He labored as an itinerant teacher and probably healer in the towns of Galilee. He had a special advocacy relation to the poor and the outcast and his teaching attracted followers. His activity and teachings brought him into conflict with Jewish leaders and eventually the local Roman procurator. He was arrested, tried, convicted, and executed by crucifixion in Jerusalem by the Roman government. His way of teaching had the ring of a direct authority. The center of his message was the impending rule of God to which the proper response is repentance. Whether he expected

16. See James P. Mackey, *Jesus the Man and the Myth: A Contemporary Christology* (New York: Paulist Press, 1979); James D. G. Dunn, *The Evidence for Jesus* (Philadelphia: Westminster Press, 1985); Hans Conzelmann, *Jesus* (Philadelphia: Fortress Press, 1973); Martin Dibelius, *Jesus* (Philadelphia: Westminster Press, 1949); William M. Thompson, *The Jesus Debate: A Survey and Synthesis* (New York: Paulist Press, 1985); and Crossan, *The Historical Jesus.*

the eminent end of things and interpreted the coming rule that way is disputed. His teaching addressed Israel, his own people, and took for granted the basic convictions and motifs of the Jewish faith of the time: Scripture, law, Israel, God, creation. He seems to have taught in parables. By way of parables of the rule of God, he pressed behind the superficial piety and detailed halakah to the heart of the matter, the commandment of love. His relation to God was a relation of absolute faith. As to his self-consciousness about his own mission or even significance, most scholars see no way to get to this beyond simply putting together what he did and taught.

We should be wary of identifying this minimal and ever-changing historical reconstruction with the "real" Jesus. The reconstruction is simply what is yielded by certain ways of working with historical evidences. The "real" Jesus may well be closer to the one who evoked the later titles, metaphors, and even legendary stories. Does the historical reconstruction provide any indication, any hint, why Jesus could evoke the titles applied to him? Do we find in this picture any signs of something that would bring about a new, universalized form of the faith of Israel? Keeping in mind that the answer to the question has the character of historical probability, I do sense something about the Jesus of the historical retrieval that would open a religious community to any and all human societies. This is not necessarily to say that Jesus had a self-conscious mission to the Gentile world or that he explicitly thematized a universalized community of faith. Yet something new does faintly glimmer in the historically constructed picture of this figure. He seems to exist before God in an immediate and direct way. The message of the impending rule of God carries with it no detailed national scenario. The stories of his healing and wonder-working (which may not survive as such the historian's suspicious eye) focus not so much on the miracle but on the absolute posture of faith that calls it forth, a faith that itself is not built on conformity to the complex cultic and moral paraphernalias of religion.[17] In the parables relation to God is simply *as such,* a matter of direct trust, without resentment, calculation, or preoccupation with status. God's summons to live in sheer trust, love, or faith is simply an absolute summons, without qualifications, and as such bypasses all the ways religion must institutionalize, qualify, and manage that summons.

I contended previously that there is an *as such* element in any and all redemption. Further, the prophetic vision of justice and the divine de-

---

17. See Günther Bornkamm, *Jesus of Nazareth,* trans. Irene and Frank McClusky (1963; Minneapolis: Fortress Press, 1994), chap. 5, 6.

mand is stated simply *as such*. Insofar as we exist before God *as such*, hear the divine summons to live toward the neighbor in love *as such*, all of the religious tradition's inevitable cultic and casuistic conditions for knowing, obeying, or worshiping God take a back seat. Even in the minimal picture of Jesus that historical method yields, we find no preoccupation with such conditions. In one way Jesus takes for granted the cultic and religious traditions of the time. He uses Scriptures, lives within the halakah, worships according to cultic requirements. But almost none of that has much importance, not only in the way he appears in the later kerygmas but in the picture historians reconstruct. The radicalism of Jesus is this "innocent" life of faith and trust before God. Furthermore, the Jesus of this historical picture so embodied and voiced this radical demand, this *as such* relation to God with its implicit relativization of even his own ethnic religion and its implicit criticism of Roman culture and power, that it brought him into conflict with the religious and political leadership of his day. Suffering is intrinsic to any and all conflict. Jesus' persistent voicing, acting out, and confronting his generation with an *as such* relation to God ended in a suffering unto death. Even in the minimal historical portrait we sense some connection between the radicalized existence and mission of Jesus and his humiliating execution. I conclude then that the tone, events, and message of Jesus, the total event of that figure, is that God summons, loves, and imparts grace simply *as such*, and insofar as it is *as such*, it has no single ethnicity, class, gender, or nation as its absolute *sine qua non*.

The kerygmas of the new community all work from the conviction that an actual historical figure, Jesus, is the occasion of redemption. Historians can probably agree that the new community arose in some way from this figure. Thus, for both the community's kerygma and for historical analysis, Jesus is the center and the through-which of the new community. What then is the relation between the kerygmatic conviction about Jesus and the historically retrieved Jesus? One thing is clear. The actual occurrence and process of redemption in the new community is neither dependent on the historical reconstruction for its facticity nor is it indifferent to the proximate picture that reconstruction yields. The reason redemption (being-founded, reconciled alienation, social emancipation) does not depend in some absolute way on the approximations of the historian is simply that it happens. It does not move from possibilities resident in historical knowledge to its facticity. Idolatry is not redemptively transformed only insofar as the person checks in regularly with the latest scholarship. In other words, redemption does not happen by means of *degrees of historical certitude* about the historically studied Jesus. This factical redemption does appresent a social through-which (the new community) and beyond that the through-which (Jesus as Christ) of that community. This is why the community's memory and tradition is enriched by historical retrievals of the early kergymas and the figure they proclaim. But its existence as a redemptive community does not wax or wane with varying trends of historical scholarship.

The issue here is the *theological* status of the historically retrieved picture of Jesus. This issue has been posed in such phrases as "the historical Jesus and the kerygmatic Christ," or "the Jesus of history and the Christ of the creeds." Essentially ambiguous, these phrases should not, without further analysis, be permitted to determine the question. On the one hand, these oppositions can refer to the difference between the *historically* retrieved figure of Jesus in his actual deeds and life and the *historically* retrieved proclaimed Jesus of the post-Easter Christian community. This historical differentiation as such poses no theological problem. On the other hand, the oppositional phrase can refer to Jesus as historically retrieved (including the retrieval of the early kerygmatic pictures) and Jesus as the through-which of the new community of faith. Here it is clear that while faith and the proclaiming community have always related to Jesus as their historical through-which, that relation has never been merely derived from or brought into existence by historical research. This is the point Rudolf Bultmann kept pressing. But to acknowledge the nonderivation of faith from historical research does not mean that faith or the new community is indifferent to that research or can as easily as not entertain Jesus as a mythical figure.

This interpretation of the theological significance of the historically retrieved figure of Jesus departs from both "conservative" and "liberal" approaches. Insofar as theological conservatives make redemption dependent on a belief-ful and even cognitive relation to what was formulated in the New Testament or at Nicea, it is required to bestow on these texts whatever inerrancy they need to be the objects of belief-ful certitude. In this view, a historical approach to these ancient literatures is vastly restricted if not even repudiated. Theological liberalism of a certain kind posits a similar dependence of faith on the historically retrieved figure of Jesus that corrects the "Christ of dogma." Here the emphasis is on the prekerygmatic figure, uncorrupted by "dogmatic" developments. But this "real" predogmatic Jesus is historically abstracted from the only Jesus the record gives us, the through-which of the new community. Further, one of the liberal approaches abstracts Jesus from the redemptive community in its notion that redemption somehow takes place through some sort of direct, imitative relation to the "real" Jesus.

The Kerygma: Jesus as Christ

The historical reconstruction of a Jesus behind the various layers of early kerygma is inevitably thin, abstracting Jesus from the response he evoked and from judgments of his significance. At best it shows glimmers, traces of a figure who evoked both resistance and discipleship. In the literature of the New Testament Jesus is proclaimed as the through-which of the new community and thus of the redemption it mediates. Is there such a thing as *the* kerygma and thus a Jesus of *the* kerygma? Here the historian faces a problem as complex as the reconstruction of the historical figure. The New Testament is a collection of texts written at different times and places mostly in the last half of the first century c.e. The attempt to reconstruct pre-Easter responses to Jesus or even the post-Easter Palestinian Jesus movement yields very little, perhaps a kerygma of Jesus as the prophet of God, or the humiliated Jesus whom God exalted. With the expansion of the Jesus movement among non-Jews in Asia Minor comes a variety of ways of understanding Jesus' saving significance.[18] This significance is expressed through various titles and through fundamental metaphors present in Jewish and even Hellenistic faiths. Jesus is dubbed *Kurios* or lord, Son of man, Son of God, and Christ. His saving significance is expressed in metaphors that would make sense of the humiliating defeat that ended his life (sacrifice, ransom, the suffering Servant) and metaphors that attempt to express how God is connected to him (by adoption, as a self-emptying heavenly being, as preexisting logos, or Wisdom). All of these expressions have kerygmatic intent. They would express the way in which the whole drama of Jesus has continuing, saving significance.

Two observations are important to make at this point. There is little if any conceptual-theoretical material in these titles and metaphors. The New Testament texts do not conceptually spell out what it means to say Jesus is a sacrifice or a ransom, or what it means to say the logos "became" (*egéneto*) "flesh" (*sarx*). The metaphors and titles then are fertile ground for later attempts to give a coherent conceptual account of Jesus' saving significance. What in fact happened is that later theologians attempted to construct out of a selected metaphor, for instance, propitia-

---

18. Attempts to identify the kerygmas of the New Testament or the stages of christological thinking are legion. Some distinguish very early ways of confessing Jesus (as eschatological prophet, as humilated-exalted) from later themes of preexistence and incarnation. See Edward Schillebeeckx, *Jesus: An Experiment in Christology*, trans. H. Hoskins (New York: Crossroad, 1981), Part 3, chaps. 1 and 2; John Knox, *Humanity and Divinity*, chap. 1; James D. G. Dunn, *Christology in the Making: A New Testament Inquiry into the Origins of the Doctrine of the Incarnation* (Philadelphia: Westminster Press, 1980); and Willi Marxsen, *The Beginning of Christology: A Study in Its Problems*, trans. Paul Achtemeier (Philadelphia: Fortress Press, 1969).

tion, a theory of Jesus' saving significance. The result was a way of interpreting the significance of Jesus as something suprahistorical, for instance, a transaction between the Son and God the Father. This legacy of "theories" built on the titles and metaphors is more a burden that strains credulity and sets up unnecessary barriers to response to the event of Jesus as Christ than something that assists that response.

Second, there seems to be no single kerygma which serves as the "essence" of the variety of interpretations to be found in the New Testament. What we have instead is a variety of ways (kerygmas) of understanding Jesus' continuing, saving significance. These various ways of understanding Jesus' saving significance do share something in common. Most generally, they all assume that Jesus is an actual historical and human figure. They are also united in what we might call general convictions about this human being, Jesus. In one way or another the various titles, metaphors, saga-like stories (for instance, the birth narratives), and apocalyptic scenarios give expression to three fundamental Christological convictions. First, the event and figure of Jesus is the through-which of the new universal community, the ecclesia, and thus of the new age. Proclaiming Jesus' resurrection was one way this conviction was set forth.[19] Second, Jesus is the through-which or agent of redemption by way of suffering, humiliation, and death. Third, this whole event and figure is a drama of the work of God. Or, in other words, "God was in Christ." Coming together in the event of Jesus as Christ and determining the meaning of "Christ" are the *universalization* of the faith of Israel through a *suffering* agent *of God*; or, motifs of resurrection, suffering, and divinity. Three succinct declamations express these motifs: "God raised him from the dead"; "Christ died for our sins"; and "God was in Christ."

An underlying conviction of the New Testament kerygmas is that the very existence of the new community is a sign that the figure and event of Jesus is not simply futile, one more victory of the awful powers of human evil, one more confirmation of cynicism and despair. On the contrary, and again from the kerygmatic perspective, the event of Jesus issued in a victory over evil powers that made what he was and did available to the future, a victory powerful enough to give rise to the new community. The way the kerygmas expressed this conviction was to say that "God raised him from the dead."[20] The apocalyptic notion of a gen-

---

19. John Knox, *The Church and the Reality of Christ*, chap. 3.
20. According to Gerd Lüdemann, this fairly frequent formulaic expression is older than the writings in which it occurs (1 Thessalonians, 2 Corinthians, Galatians, Romans) and is as early as Paul's earliest writings (*The Resurrection of Jesus: History, Experience, Theology* [Minneapolis: Fortress Press, 1994], 24).

eral resurrection of the dead at the end time is thus applied to the figure of Jesus.

While the resurrection of Jesus is a theme in virtually all the primitive kerygmas, there is no agreement on its exact meaning as an event. It clearly did not mean the belief that Jesus was resuscitated back to ordinary life. But what the Gospel tradition and also Paul have to work with is not the event itself but traditions that record appearances of Jesus. Historical method can make little headway in determining at this point "what really happened."[21] It cannot reconstruct the event in the same way it would reconstruct the execution of Jesus. Nor can theological method penetrate behind the various kerygmas to discover "what really happened." It can, however, ask about the significance or import of this proclaimed event. Here we find three themes voiced in the New Testament literatures, all of which have been picked up in one way or another by contemporary theologies. First (and this may be the earliest kerygmatic formulation), Jesus' resurrection is significant as that which vindicates Jesus' life and mission and rescues it from mere defeat. Jesus was humiliated but then exalted. Apart from the resurrection, Jesus is one more martyred prophet. This version of the significance of the resurrection has content only when accompanied by some notion of what Jesus' mission actually was. If we think that the significance of Jesus' life was his embodiment of a radical *as such* relation to God that universalizes the availability of redemption, then *what* is vindicated is just that.

Second, the resurrection as a transformation of Jesus' mode of existence is the presupposition of the rise of the new community. This can mean either that the resurrection is a way of expressing the rise of the new community (compare Bultmann) or the presupposed but rather undesignated event through which the new community came into existence (compare Pannenberg). The primary way the New Testament authors express this meaning of the resurrection is through the apocalyptic language of a new age, a new aeon, the beginning of the end time, or the ecclesia as the new Israel.

The third way of voicing the significance of the resurrection of Jesus is to relate it to the problem of individual mortality and salvation. Here the

---

21. According to Lüdemann, what the historian *can* get to and reconstruct behind the phrase, "God raised him from the dead," are the visions of Jesus (that is, appearances) experienced by Peter and other followers. Thus, he distinguishes the traditions of vision experiences and the tradition of empty tomb (*The Resurrection of Jesus*, 171, 174). Pannenberg likewise makes this distinction but finds historical reasons (the proclamation of Jesus' resurrection in Jerusalem) for saying the tomb was in fact empty. Further, the fact that the two independent traditions merge and complement each other makes Jesus' resurrection "historically very probable" (*Jesus, God, and Man*, 101, 105). I suspect we could search far and wide and not find a secular historian who would concur in this judgment.

resurrection of Jesus is a transformation that gives grounds for hope in the face of death. Jesus' resurrection is then the "first fruits" of a more general phenomenon. All three of these motifs are expressions of hope, the conviction that the most terrible sufferings and defeats are subject to reversal. Resurrection then becomes the symbol for the dimension of hope that structures genuine faith.

The second conviction present in the various New Testament kerygmas is that Jesus' humiliation, suffering, and death are themselves redemptive.[22] Like the other two deep convictions, the picture of the suffering, dying Jesus became a fundamental part of the new community, memorialized in its liturgies and arts, a structural aspect of its pieties, and ever reinterpreted by theologians. The kerygmatic conviction that Jesus died "for us" is what prompted the Gospel tradition to record Jesus' death in such detail. And while virtually all of the New Testament authors share this conviction, there is no single theological or conceptual agreement as to what the "for us" means. Instead of a theoretical articulation, the earliest Christian authors set forth the "for us" in a variety of metaphors: the Suffering Servant of Isaiah 53, ritual sacrifice, ransom, and propitiation. We can guess why the event of Jesus' suffering and death evoked the conviction that it had salvific meaning. Such a conviction would not have arisen simply from the grief and disappointment of Jesus' followers. Grief and anger may rise from a sense that an injustice had been done, but that can easily as not end in a fatalistic acquiescence that experiences again how threatening innocency succumbs to self-protective powers. Only if there is a sense that this drama of suffering was reversed in the resurrection would we have a motive for thinking the suffering itself has a meaning. If the total event of mission, suffering, death, and resurrection is the through-which of the new redemptive community, then the suffering aspect of the event takes on the character of "for us."

The third conviction present in various New Testament representations of the significance of the figure of Jesus is that "God was in Christ."[23] Here too there is a certain deep consensus expressed in a variety of formulations. This theme is explicitly or implicitly at work in some of the

---

22. For an attempt to discover the origin of the concept that the death of Jesus could be itself a saving event, see Sam K. Williams, *Jesus' Death as Saving Event: The Background and Origin of a Concept* (Missoula, Mont.: Scholars Press, 1975), 24.

23. John Knox proposes a three-stage development of this conviction: an early adoptionist phase ("God has made Jesus, whom you call crucified, both Lord and Christ," Acts 2:36); a kenotic phase (Philippians 2) that voices the preexistent Christ emptying himself to become human being, then to be exalted; and a final docetic phase where the eternal Lord takes on a human appearance (*Humanity and Divinity of Christ*, chap. 1).

titles of Jesus. To say he is God's annointed (Christ) is to voice the conviction that he is sent by God, that God is at work in his life and mission. To speak of him as emptying himself and taking on the form of a servant only to be exalted connects him with a divine preexistence, and to say that he is the Word that became flesh and lived among us is to say that his very existence embodies that which is divine. Again, these expressions are not precise conceptual formulations of the meaning of "God was in Christ." Two thousand years of conciliar, doctrinal, and even philosophical interpretations will attempt that.

To summarize, in the kerygmas of the early Christian movement, themes of resurrection, suffering and death, and divine presence come together to interpret the significance of the event and figure of Jesus. Together the three themes specify the meaning of the claim that he is "Christ." As has often been pointed out, to say that Jesus is Christ in this sense departs from the messianic tradition of Judaism. There, messiah is the deliverer of the oppressed and exiled people of Israel. Ethnicity and nationality remain the framework for this expectation. The new community connects messianic promise to the universalizable aspect of the faith of Israel and thus defines messiah as the one through whom the faith of Israel is made universally available. Jesus as Christ is the one whose suffering and exaltation are the through-which of a redemption now available in the new (universal) community, and this through-which is a work, a presence, of God. These convictions were expressed in a variety of metaphors, in the quasi cosmology of Jewish apocalyptic, and even in the language of myth, that is, in notions that resemble ordinary cosmological speculations. Our next task is to reinterpret theologically the three convictions that express the "event of Jesus as Christ."

18

THE FIGURE OF JESUS: UNIVERSALITY, PATHOS, AND EMPATHY

> No hurt I did not feel, no death
> That was not mine; mine each last breath
> That, crying, met an answering cry
> From the Compassion that was I.
> All suffering mine, and mine its rod
> Mine, pity like the pity of God.
> *Edna St. Vincent Millay, "Renascence"*

> And then it seemed that One who did create
> Compassion, who alone invented pity,
> Walked, as though called, in at that north-east gate,
> Out from the muttering city,

> Threaded the little crowd, trod the brown grass,
> Bent o'er the speaker close, saw the tear rise,
> And saw Himself, as one looks in a glass,
> In those impassioned eyes.
> *Alice Meynell, "In Sleep"*

The previous chapter mixed historical and theological perspectives to describe the "event of Jesus as Christ" as attested in the kerygmas of the first sixty or so years of the Christian movement. These kerygmas or interpretations of the significance of Jesus share the convictions that Jesus' resurrection, suffering, and "divinity" altogether are the through-which of the new community and the redemption it experiences. The new community (*ecclesia*) then is the resolution or outcome of the precipitating event of Jesus. If the event of Jesus as Christ is to be in any way a guide to how we understand the divine activity, we must move from description to theological reinterpretation. This reinterpretation will not try to show how the event of Jesus as Christ itself displays the divine activity. First, it displays no such thing. Second, the problem of the divine activity calls for a paradigm that requires more elements than simply the event of Jesus. The task rather is to discover how the event of Jesus as Christ is the through-which of the new community and thus of redemption.

I must acknowledge that such a reinterpretation inevitably has a speculative dimension. This is for two reasons. First, it cannot settle its claims about the significance of Jesus as Christ by way of direct intuitive grounding. The historical character of that event intervenes in any such method. Second, it cannot simply repeat the content of canonical or conciliar texts in a way that assumes those texts necessarily contain or express truth. Christological reinterpretation, in other words, is neither the compilation of exegeted texts nor the consultation of experience. It works rather in synthetic fashion attempting to identify the way in which certain contents and symbolisms of the ancient historical event and figure are correlated with the conditions of redemption in the new community. And this surely is a kind of speculation.

Several constraints or negative criteria attend this task. Because of the historical character of the New Testament, I cannot simply assume that the Pauline, Johannine, or other such interpretations of Jesus are so unquestioningly and finally true that they are the necessary beginning points of Christology. These texts illumine the novel character of the event but are not authoritative objects of belief. Nor can I directly appropriate the cosmological elements of the New Testament that make the event of Jesus the central event of the cosmos and thus of innumerable galaxies or apocalyptic end time schemes that presuppose some sort of geocentrism. Nor is it possible to make sense of the event and figure of Jesus by treating the motifs of the kerygmas as if each one pertained to some separate dynamics of salvation; for instance, Jesus' death, or resurrection, or his "divinity." From this method have come theories of the atonement and docetic speculations about Jesus' divinity that obscure rather than disclose the event's significance. Also closed to us is any procedure than smacks of a tritheistic trinity, according to which one of the "persons" of God's being acted in an independent way and underwent something excluded to the other "persons." The notion of Jesus as *a* preexistent divine being both mythologizes divine being and dehumanizes Jesus. It may be a way of justifying the cultic worship of Jesus, but it obscures what actually happened in the event of Jesus as Christ.

THE UNIVERSALIZATION OF THE FAITH OF ISRAEL

I have argued that the outcome of the event of Jesus as Christ is the new community in which the faith of Israel became transethnically available. This universalization is both a historical fact and a deep conviction of the early kerygmas. Through this universalization the redemptive (ap)-presence of God becomes available across cultural boundaries. I also argued that what precipitated this universalization was the *as such* or absolute character of piety, faith, or relation to God, embodied in Jesus' acts, and voiced in his message. This theme is present in the various kerygmas and a trace of it shows even in historical reconstructions of the figure of Jesus.

The problem of the interrelation between the necessary cultural carriers and paraphernalias of religion and the relativizing *as such* dimension of faith or redemption is not confined to communities rooted in the faith of Israel. There is an inevitable tension between the absolute claims of faith and the absolute claims of its historical mediations whose traditions, institutions, and social systems tend to become *sine qua nons* or absolute conditions of relation to God. Mediating institutions thus preside over the delivery of tradition, monitor organizations, and set punishments in order to make the divine demand concrete and to protect it against what would dilute it. For the same reason and in spite of its universal form, the ecclesial community must embody itself in social structures in order to survive over time. Thus, as a historical particularity, the church privileged the male gender and European culture, appropriating that culture's cosmologies and institutional forms. Tragically, the ecclesial community constantly corrupts the event of Jesus as Christ in order to render it culturally specific, functional, and enduring. This is precisely the point of the exchange between the Grand Inquisitor and the compassionate Jesus who, having returned to a town in medieval Russia, listens silently to the Inquisitor's reasons for having to reject him. "Thou wast warned." he says to Him. "Thou hast had no lack of admonitions and warnings, but Thou didst not listen to those warnings; Thou didst reject the only way by which men might be made happy. But, fortunately, departing Thou didst hand on the work to us. Thou hast established by Thy Word, Thou has given to us the right to bind and to unbind, and now, of course Thou canst not think of taking it away." And again, "And if it is a mystery, we too have a right to preach a mystery, and to teach them that it's not the free judgment of their hearts, not love that matters, but a mystery which they must follow blindly, even against their conscience. So we have done. We have corrected Thy work and founded it upon miracle, mystery, and authority."[1] The outcome of the event of Jesus as Christ and the meaning

---

1. Fyodor Dostoyevski, *The Brothers Karamazov*, The Modern Library (New York: Random House, n.d.), 261, 266.

of the figure and work of Jesus is, to be sure, redemption, not so much in the sense of an utterly new set of teachings that depart from the faith of Israel or its Judaic form but in the sense of an absolute demand and compassion of God toward which the one proper response is simply trust, the faithful expectation of God's coming reign.

The figure of Jesus as reported in the kergymas and as it glimmers in historical reconstructions is of one who intimately and almost naively relates to God in such a way that the paraphernalias of religious traditions, while not repudiated, are ignored, sometimes exposed in their self-absolutization, certainly relativized in relation to God's demand, love, and ever-coming rule. Once the Christian movement began to try to make sense of this event and figure by way of suprahistorical, cosmic schemes of divine forensics and conflicts with demonic powers, it interpreted Jesus' "innocent" piety negatively as sinlessness (either because the hypostasis or actual being of Jesus was the logos or because the need for a superfluity of merit required an innocent victim) and positively as an actual ontological fulfillment (in order to be the Exemplum of divine-human nature). Both views arise as requirements of totalistic theories of Jesus.[2] When we concern ourselves with the historically reconstructed Jesus and even the Jesus whose precipitating work is the new community, we find this "innocence" of Jesus to be that peculiar quality of relation to God simply *as such*.[3]

The *as such* element in the reconstructed life and teaching of Jesus and in the kerygmatic portraits opened the possibility of a universal form of the faith of Israel. The way the new community testified to this new thing

2. In the light of the typology George Rupp proposes to replace the standard triad of view of the work of Christ (cf. Gustav Aulèn), my view follows the "processive" rather than the "transactional" type. See George Rupp, *Christologies and Cultures: Toward a Typology of Religious World Views* (The Hague: Mouton, 1974). The transactional theories assume the possibility of a transhistorical determination of human destiny, thus Christ's work takes place "independently of its historic mediation" (7). The focus of the processive type (e.g., Hegel, John Cobb) is on the way Christ and the event of Christ affect actual historical processes.

3. John Dominic Crossan expresses what I am calling the *as such* element as follows: "He was neither broker nor mediator but, somewhat paradoxically, the announcer that neither should exist between humanity and divinity or between humanity and itself. Miracle and parable, healing and eating were calculated to force individuals into unmediated physical and spiritual contact with God and unmediated physical and spiritual contact with each other. He announced, in other words, the brokerless Kingdom of God" (*The Historical Jesus: The Life of a Mediterranean Peasant* [San Francisco: Harper San Francisco, 1991]). Compare this to Monika K. Hellwig's account of Jesus' message of the Kingdom of God: Jesus "lived as though God reigned and none else had power." He responded to God and lived in the world as if the "compassionate providence of God" were the only thing to be considered (*Jesus the Compassion of God: New Perspectives on the Tradition of Christianity* [Wilmington, Del.: Michael Glazier, 1983], chap. 5).

was to speak of an event that turned the despairing and defeated follow-ers of Jesus into the nucleus of the new community, namely the resurrec-tion of Jesus, followed by the coming of the Spirit. Whatever the event of resurrection is in itself, it is present in the memory of the church as the catalyst of the new community.

THE PATHOS OF THE AS-SUCH

It is a historical fact that Jesus' career ended in a humiliating death. Simply in itself and abstracted out of the event of Jesus as Christ, that death has no salvific efficiency. It is simply one more horrible defeat of someone who threatened the self-interests of local powers. On the other hand, suffering is part of the warp and woof of the event of Jesus as Christ. But does this say very much? Is not suffering intrinsic to human life as such? In addition to sharing the vulnerabilities of all living things, human beings in their self-transcending and interrelational lives experi-ence intense pains of grief, humiliation, and anxiety. Furthermore, tragic sufferings are enormously intensified by the workings of human evil: by the fears, self-deceptions, and malices of idolatry, the pathetic acts of in-terhuman violation, and the dehumanizing horrors worked by oppressive institutions. As a human being Jesus surely suffered both the ordinary events of illness, injury, and anxiety, and the consequences of living under the shadow of social oppression. He knew well the situation of the poor and marginalized.

But there is a much more specific reason why suffering and even death are intrinsic to the event of Jesus. A pathos tracks the figure of Jesus, reflecting the fact that his public activity necessarily evoked resistance, rejection, and persecution. The pathos of Jesus is not simply the tragic pathos of the human condition but the pathos that necessarily comes with relating to God *as such*, that is, in such trust and faith that the mediating paraphernalia of religion and the social conditions of grace are pressed into the background or are revealed in their demonic potentialities. And it is clear from the way the new community remembered and attested to Jesus that the God Jesus prayed to was not simply an ultimate, all-determining power. Indeed, relation to that sort of deity would also in-volve suffering, namely the violation any creature would undergo in be-ing subjected to sheer external determination. The God of Jesus' trust is one whose own pathos springs from a compassionate relation to her-his children. Throughout the various kerygmas, the figure of Jesus and the God of Jesus are expressed in the language of compassion, forgiveness, and agape. And where there is compassion there is suffering. For this reason pathos is the tone of the life and message of any and all prophets.[4] Pathos is the major tone of the prophet's response to the condition of a specific people. In prophetism the *as such* element may take the form of a transcendent norm of justice whose setting is the situation of a national people. The pathos of Jesus is likewise a response to the particular sufferings of his own people. But his *as such* or absolute relation to God gives it another dimension. He responds to his people's sufferings not simply because they are his people, living in the circle of the inherited cultural legacy, but simply because they suffer. For to relate to God and the divine empathy *as such* is to relate to something that has no boundaries, no restrictions. An intensified pathos comes with such boundless empathy and sensibility to any and all who suffer, not only those who suffer the horrors of social oppression but those who are themselves caught up in the oppressive system.

R. L. Vanstone has persuasively shown that this ever enlarging openness toward the other is intrinsic to love itself. For Vanstone, genuine love is a laborious act of unsparing self-giving that holds nothing back. As such it is oriented simply (as such?) to the other's capacity to receive it and ever seeks to enlarge that capacity. Thus, genuine love cannot have some self-limiting qualification built into it that in advance restricts itself to some aspect of the other or to some specifically designated other. The reason is that once love is concerned with enlarging the other's capacity to receive love, it must promote all conditions that pertain to that, including the others of that other. Thus the telos or entelechy of genuine love is all others. And since genuine love desires a true other that retains its true alterity, it is always an act of risk that courts the possibility of non-response, resistance, or failure at every turn.[5] This is just what we find in the kerygmatic accounts of the figure of Jesus, a self-giving love simply *as such* that risks failure, antipathy, and hatred.

Suffering is intrinsic to the figure of Jesus for a second reason. Jesus' empathetic love was not a private and interior phenomenon. Born in his *as such* relation to God and having the character of compassion or empathy, its location was not simply interiority but public activity.[6] The Jesus of the recorded memory is a Jesus who confronted his own people and their leaders with his *as such* message of God's summons and impending rule. His own *as such* relation to God was lived out in public activities of

4. See Abraham Heschel, *The Prophets*, Vol. 2 (New York: Harper & Row, 1962), chaps. 1–3.
5. William H. Vanstone, *The Risk of Love* (New York: Oxford University Press, 1978), chap. 3.
6. For a phenomenology of compassion that uncovers compassion's necessarily public, active, and involved dimension, see Wendy L. Farley, *Tragic Vision and Divine Compassion: A Contemporary Theodicy* (Louisville: Westminster/John Knox Press, 1990), 75.

controversy, teaching, and social relations with "sinners."[7] According to the narratives, this public life of Jesus evoked a resistance so determined that it would be satisfied with nothing less than a humiliating execution. From one point of view Jesus' death is a drama of high irony. Pictured here is an apparently harmless, politically naive, itinerant teacher who evoked an antipathy powerful enough to end his life.[8] This extreme resistance shows us how radically threatening to public life is an *as such* relation to God, a relation that shows a certain indifference to the societal and institutional paraphernalia of religion and challenges their status as absolute conditions of grace and human well-being. This determined and threatened resistance is not directed against a program of specific religious or political reform but against someone whose acts and teachings challenged the absolute necessity of any specific religious and political institutionality.

Here we have a second pathos connected with the figure of Jesus, the pathos that his public way of living his *as such* relation to God brought down upon him, the pathos of both risking and experiencing resistance, rejection, and persecution unto death. Rather than being accidental to the figure and event of Jesus, suffering is intrinsic as the pathos element of an *as such* relation to God and as the pathos element of the public life of that relation. Pathos and death ever shadowed his being and mission. And what his being and mission procured for us was the resolution of the event, the new community of universal redemption. This universalization of the faith of Israel, this cross-cultural mode of divine presence that carried with it its own new forms of risk and corruption, had a price, namely the existential and public pathos and even death of Jesus. In this sense it is not surprising to find the Christian movement saying that "Christ died for our sins."

THE EMPATHIC UNION

The third deep conviction of the kergymas of the early Christian movement was that "God was in Christ." From the post-Easter perspective of

---

7. Portrayed here is not some "inner life" of Jesus but the picture of Jesus that historical method is able to retrieve as it reconstructs his teachings and actions. We cannot, of course, describe Jesus' actual relation to God. We can, as historical method permits, discern or reconstruct Jesus' piety on the basis of the way he talked about (absolute) faith, the *as such* demands of the Kingdom, and his compassionate acts toward those around him.

8. It is tempting to exaggerate the motif of Jesus as self-conscious revolutionary. That he came into conflict with both the Roman and Jewish establishment seems to be a fact. Crossan illumines this fact in his very detailed description of peasant turmoil in first-century Palestine. For Crossan the two key elements are free healing and common eating, thus a

the new community, this claim is that the relativizing of all ethnic *sine qua nons* of grace and the universalizing of the faith of Israel is brought forth by God. Even as the rise of Yahweh worship with Abraham, the founding of a people of the Torah on a land, and the new institutionality of the diaspora could all be said to be workings of God, so can that claim be made for the rise of a universalized form of Abraham's faith. And insofar as the new community experienced or remembered Jesus as the through-which of this event, it will confess that Jesus too is a working of God, that God is "in" him.

This deep conviction that "God was in Christ" evokes the theological task of reinterpreting the messianic symbolism in such a way as not to tax credulity by literalism and outmoded cosmology. This is to say, the Christian movement should not make the ability to simply repeat ancient modes of thinking a condition for grasping the significance of the figure of Jesus. Three ancient ways of understanding how God is "in" Christ especially deserve a critical and suspicious eye. The first claims for Jesus' death (or resurrection, or incarnation) some suprahistorical meaning. For instance, Jesus' death is the once-for-all (in the space and time of the cosmos) condition for divine grace, or Jesus' death-resurrection is an event that overthrows heavenly, cosmic powers. Forgiveness and even the confrontation with the "powers of this world" surely are a dimension of the event of Jesus as Christ but they are not abstractable from the aim and resolution of that event in the new community.

A second interpretation assumes that the lack of vision, understanding, or knowledge of God is *the* primary human problem and thus makes "revelation" the primary aim and outcome of the event. *The* point of Christology, in that case, is a *revealing* of the divine-human unity, the divine love, or even the divine union with perishing. Again, disclosure surely is a dimension of the event of Jesus as Christ, not so much as an end in itself as something that attends the redemption that takes place in the new, universalized form of the faith of Israel. Revelation is not an independent and abstractable aim of the event but is a feature of what comes with the new community.

A third way of interpreting God's presence "in" Jesus is the anthropological turn of certain liberal Protestant Christologies. Here *the* point of the event and figure of Jesus is the accomplishment of a definitive instance of divine-human relation; thus Jesus as the realization of God-

kind of "religious and economic egalitarianism that negated alike and at once the hierarchical and patronal normalcies of Jewish religion and Roman power" (*The Historical Jesus*, 422).

consciousness (F. O. E. Schleiermacher), the absolute synthesis of flesh and Spirit (G. W. F. Hegel), the "symbol" of new being and Godmanhood (Paul Tillich), or the new structure of human existence in which the human subjective aim and the divinely originated initial aim coincide (John Cobb). With the exception of Tillich who, content with the symbol, makes no empirical claim, these anthropologies seem to make the empirical claim that Jesus actually was a perfected or complete instance of the divine-human relation. Given their rejection of authority theology, it is not clear how these authors know this about Jesus. They seem to posit a miraculous instance of perfection in the midst of history, something Schleiermacher especially would resist. This problem aside, these anthropological Christologies seem to assume that this perfect instance of divine-human unity functions as a timeless Exemplum for subsequent history, a concept that turns the point of the event away from its resolution in the new universal community to a definitive instance to be remembered or an ideal to be emulated.

The following interpretation of the way God is "in" Jesus posits at the outside two positive principles. First, that which God is "in" is an individual who, without qualification, is fully human. This principle excludes from the outset any and all interpretations that require the divine presence (logos, wisdom, person) to displace some aspect of Jesus' humanity and this includes the docetic if not mythical notion that God (logos) Godself is the individual person of Jesus which then takes on human features. Second, whatever way God is "in" Jesus is not an exception to the way God can be "in" or present to other human beings. While this is not to deny all senses of Jesus' uniqueness or "finality," it does eliminate ontological versions of such. Uniqueness and finality arise with Jesus as the through-which of the event of the new community.

Let us begin by restating the early community's fundamental conviction; namely, that God is active in Jesus as the through-which of the rise of the new community and thus of redemption. In this event and figure of Jesus we have to do with God. Accordingly, adoption, incarnation, kenosis, and Jesus' death as a sacrifice are all specific ways of saying how the event has to do with God. Another way of saying it is that the *as such* character of Jesus' relation to God brings forth a new *as such* or universalized form of the faith of Israel. God then is "in" Jesus in whatever sense is necessary to bring forth the new, universalized form of the faith of Israel.

When we press this phrase, "whatever sense is necessary," we are on the threshold of a mystery, in fact *the* mystery of how God in fact moves the world, works to transform history, and founds the individual in its passionate life. And even if we find grounds for speaking of God as love, creativity, or even as suffering, this language does not give us any direct picture of the concrete way human beings are open to or united with God. Nor does the repetition or exegesis of any particular biblical verse relay to our understanding the concrete interrelation of Jesus and God. For instance, *ho logos sarx egeneto*, (the word became flesh) or *unus . . . assumptione humanitatis in Deum* (one . . . by the assumption of humanness into God), do not say just what the *egeneto* or the *assumptio* precisely mean.[9] I shall reinterpret this language of union by way of the anthropological materials set forth in *Good and Evil*, certain traces that we find in the historical depiction of the figure of Jesus, the interpretations of the early kerygmas, and an exploration of the interhuman relation of empathy.

As fully and actually human, Jesus embodies the general agential structures of human existence. This means that he too is constituted by bodily passions, experiences the tragic ambiguities of existence, and participates in the deep social structures of a specific culture already infected by corporate evil. Any account of Jesus that withholds such things from Jesus is surely docetic. We can presume that the trace or tone or piety in Jesus' life is a being-founded in God that releases him toward various human freedoms. But his public activity makes it clear that whatever this releasement is, it carries him into public life on behalf of the marginalized of his day. Thus, in Jesus, relation to God and empathetic concern come to the same thing. In Jesus the various spheres of redemptive existence seem to be present: a certain freedom from the hold of idolatry, intense interhuman relations, and a sense of injustice on behalf of many whom he met. All together show an empathetic existence carried into public life.

At the same time and according to the various kerygmas, Jesus' piety and public activities take place in connection with his relation to God. What determines this sensibility, this way of being open to God? We can only conclude that something about Jesus' relation to God orients Jesus empathetically and as such to any and all he meets. And what is that but the divine empathy? In Jesus then being-founded means a sensibility to the divine empathy that opens him empathetically to those around him, an empathy that calls forth severe negation of the conditions that stifle,

9. "The Athanasian Creed," #35. See Philip Schaff, *Creeds of Christendom*, Vol. 2 (New York: Harper Brothers, 1882), 69.

impoverish, and oppress. Jesus thus appears to be one with the divine empathy. What does it mean to say this?

Located in the sphere of the interhuman, empathy is not just a subjective, interior phenomenon. Rather, empathy, concerned suffering participation in the life of a genuine other, is a kind of activity and even efficacy, not in the sense of an external force, but something that evokes response. The other can respond to empathy by contemptuously construing it as a weakness or by exploiting it for self-interest. Or the suffering that empathy embodies can evoke in the other a responding empathy, a sensibility to suffering empathy. Here we have in the sphere of the interhuman a union or merger of empathies.

But another dimension comes with sensibility to divine, suffering empathy. As infinite the divine empathy has no restrictions. No territorial privilege, legacy of class and tradition, gender, or status qualify its *as such* character. It would ever work to enlarge the capacity to receive it and promote the conditions pertaining to that capacity. Thus the divine empathy coincides with creativity itself. To be sensible to, embody, and act out God's suffering empathy is to have a posture that also is simply *as such*. This unrestricted empathy spreads throughout one's being and orients one toward any and all need. I am saying then that Jesus has a sensibility to a divine empathy that has no qualifiers, no restrictions, and is simply *as such*. And this *as such* empathy becomes the tone and public activity of Jesus' life. Here being-founded means not simply the liberation from the demons of personal suffering or desire but existing in suffering empathy toward whatever looms ahead. This deep way in which the divine and human can come together may be as close to the union between the divine and the human that human language permits.

How does this interpretation of "God was in Christ" compare to the orthodox incarnationalist tradition of Nicea and Chalcedon? If by incarnation we mean that *a* being (the logos) was from the beginning the being of Jesus and thus adapted itself (by kenosis) to the features of human nature, then the concept of empathic union is a departure from that tradition. On the other hand, empathic union retains most of the features of the Nicean-Chalcedonian Christologies. According to the orthodox Christology, that which is in Christ (the logos) is divine fully and without diminution. In the empathic union, it is God, not a demi-god, not *a* god, that is with and in Jesus. According to the orthodox (Johannine) Christology, it is the logos that is "in" Christ. I take that to mean that what is "in" Christ is the immanent, world-moving aspect of God, God as relation. This immanent aspect can be called word, wisdom, reason (compare

Neoplatonic Christianity), even spirit. I have termed this immanent, world-moving aspect, the divine empathy, and prefer it to the more philosophical language of logos. But to think of this world-relating aspect as *a* divine being, one among three divine beings, moves toward tritheism and departs from the orthodox tradition itself. Further, the negations of Chalcedon quite properly apply to the empathic union. The divine (empathy) and human (empathy) are together "inconfusedly, unchangeably, indivisibly, inseparably."[10] In one important respect the notion of an empathic union departs from the classical Christology. In the classical view, the divine may "assume flesh" or "take our nature" but this in no way means that God Godself can thereby suffer. But the empathetic union is just that, a union that arises with a human sensibility to the divine empathetic suffering.[11]

SUMMARY AND CONCLUSION

The aim of these chapters on the event of Jesus as Christ has been to uncover how this event is the through-which of redemption. I return now to that question. I have argued that the event and figure of the suffering Jesus is the through-which of the new community that universalizes the faith of Israel. That is the "point" of Christology.[12] With this new community, at least in its ideal sense, comes a new intersubjectivity in which the "any and all" of the stranger is implicitly present, and a new universalizing symbolism whose parameters and focus is not any one form of nationality or culture; thus, sacrament, word, faith, spirit, love. At the center of this symbolism and the cultic acts that repeat it is the picture of the messianic pathos, the suffering messiah. I have argued that it is here in suffering empathy that God and Jesus are united.

How then does this universalized community and symbolism relate to the three spheres of redemption—to reconciliation, agential freedom, and emancipation? As to the sphere of reconciliation, the alienation of relation transforms the vulnerable face of the other into an accusing face. The

10. "The Creed of Chalcedon," Schaff, *Creeds* 2:62.
11. I owe much of this interpretation of Jesus' relation to God as an empathic union to Monika Hellwig. She too attempts to get beyond mythological construals of Nicea and Chalcedon to the essential paradox and mystery of God's relation to Jesus. See *Jesus the Compassion of God*, chap. 8. In similar vein, Paul Fiddes argues (like Vanstone) that if suffering is intrinsic to love, and if God is suffering love, then Jesus' suffering is somehow connected with the divine suffering. See *The Creative Suffering of God* (Oxford: Oxford University Press, 1989), chap. 5.
12. Schubert Ogden, *The Point of Christology: New Perspectives on the Tradition* (Wilmington, Del.: Michael Glazier, 1983), chap. 1.

customs and laws of any specific ethnicity tend to serve as the framework for that accusation. If a specific casuistry mediates the accusations of the interhuman, then reconciliation is possible only as the ethnic framework specifies it in advance. Here social structures do not eliminate the interhuman but they do dominate and manage it. Reconciliation then is defined by the natural intimacy and social loyalty of the specific group. But a universalized form of redemption alters the *status* of the cultural management of reconciliation in a community by relativizing the culture itself, especially in its role of mediating the divine command. In the new community the reconciling act is opened across cultural boundaries to any and all alienations, thus relativizing the power of the socially entrenched and casuistic accusing face.

As we have seen, justice is never reducible to ethnic, national, or cultural considerations. When its mediation is restricted to nations and their traditions, however, its intrinsic *as such* character becomes subject to or managed by the self-interest and power orientations of the social entity. Hence, justice can become identified with the legal tradition or with the well-being of the particular society. In the universalized form of the faith of Israel, justice is thematized in its *as such* character. The nation itself is thus subjected to this irreducible norm, and the norm opens that nation toward responsibility to larger social environments.

In the sphere of the individual, redemption means a being-founded that transforms idolatrous passions into passionate freedoms. But such founding is always mediated through community symbolisms and narratives. In this mediation, the individual's responsibilities and even freedoms are rendered in relatively precise form by institutional regulation. This precision of cultic act and moral responsibility is inevitable to any and all religious communities. In the new community the status of precisely defined obligations and violations is relativized in such a way that beliefs, casuistry, and cultic requirements have an open face. They express not simply the needs of the specific religion to manage its own social processes but something in principle, something as such, something that even places the system of mediations in the background.

To describe the effect of universalized mediation on redemption is not to argue the superiority of the new community to nonuniversalized faiths. The history of the Christian movement shows all too well how new demonic possibilities can arise with the universalization of the faith of Israel. For the very need to *be* a religion, that is, to develop social forms (doctrines, morals, organizational structures) enabling it to exist at all, tends to define and tame the universalization. When this happens, universalization becomes a not-so-masked form of religious imperialism, a new universal conformity to whatever the new community has developed. Such universalization is surely a corruption of the new community, whose universal character means negatively the relativization but not eschewal of any and all institutional mediations and positively the attestation and embodiment of the *as such* character of relation to God.

19

DIVINE EMPATHY: PRELIMINARY CONSIDERATIONS

For I feel it, I feel it—infinite love is suffering too—yea, in the fulness of knowledge it suffers, it yearns, it mourns; and that is a blind self-seeking which waits to be freed from the sorrow wherewith the whole creation groaneth and travaileth. Surely it is not true blessedness to be free from sorrow, while there is sorrow and sin in the world: sorrow is then a part of love, and love does not seek to throw it off.

George Eliot, Adam Bede

How should I know but roses might lead lives as glad as mine?
Elizabeth Barrett Browning, "The Deserted Garden"

Paradigms of divine activity must inevitably consult a variety of sources. In chapters 11 through 18 I assembled sources pertinent to such a paradigm. We face now the task of weaving these sources into an interpretation of the divine activity. I must concede at the outset that any account of the divine activity contains speculative elements. This is not to say that the claim itself (God is active in and toward the world) is simply a speculation. The facticity of redemption and the redemptive coming forth of God presuppose and indicate a divine activity. And although ciphers of redemption and creativity do concern the divine activity, they do not as such discuss how the world is in fact disposed by God. Nor do we find specific accounts of God's activity in the biblical narrative. Present in those texts are narratives of God's doings (for instance, the creation narrative, a vision narrative, the defeat of an army, a specific wonder-working) and also of divine promises to judge, forgive, or restore. But the exegesis of these narratives and metaphors does not yield any specific meaning of God's activity. One reason for this is that such texts contain little or no materials about what the world itself is.

The symbolics of God leaves us then with the task of articulating how it is that God is active in the world. The facticity of redemption and its symbolics makes this task possible; paradigmatic speculation carries it out. Speculative extrapolation is unavoidable because we are never outside the relation of God and world in such a way as to comprehend each term and with that the relation between the terms. Nor are we ever privy to the divine activity itself. In this situation of grasping the *facticity* of the activity (through redemption) but without direct apprehension of it, all we can do is to construct a paradigm that incorporates the relevant materials. This paradigm will attempt to bring together the divine aim as it is manifested in redemption and the ciphers of God, the locus of the divine activity (as in the event of Jesus as the Christ), the general creative relation of God and the world, and the way the world is manifested in the sciences and in an ontology of the world. It should not be necessary to say that the result of this construction is not *the* but *a* paradigm of the divine activity. This is so not only because theological interpretation varies with its historical time and place but because the interpretation of the world is not simply a static given. Instead of an official Christian cosmology, what we have are ever-changing scientific and philosophical accounts of cosmos, nature, and history.

The possibility of a paradigm of the divine activity is rooted in the fact that God's redemptive coming forth as God and its ciphers point to an actual redemptive-creative activity of God. But what obliges interpreters of Christian faith to go ahead with such a construction? What makes this third task of the theology of God something other than an exercise in curiosity? Generally speaking, theology would interpret the divine activity for the same reason it pursues its other themes. It would bring (as far as possible) the convictions of faith into modes of understanding, hoping to thereby assist whatever (teaching, proclaiming, piety) would profit from such understanding. But there is a specific reason that makes thinking the divine activity if not necessary at least important. Paradigms for understanding the divine activity have been part of the Christian movement virtually from the beginning. Some of these paradigms have exercised a powerful influence on segments of Christendom. They range from literalistic and cosmological ways of relating God as *a* being to *the* world to sophisticated philosophical accounts of how God affects the world's basic constituents (*res verae*). In these paradigms we find patriarchal elements, monarchical metaphors, and traces of ancient cosmologies. One reason that theodicy questions are so severe for members of the Christian movement goes back to a paradigm that relates God to the world as an overriding and all-determinative causality. This legacy of past paradigms surely calls for continuing inspection and critique. But to engage in paradigm critique in a theological and not just formal way carries with it implications for alternative ways of thinking the divine activity. Accordingly, if we do not settle for a passive acceptance of these paradigms but examine them in a critical way, we have already begun the trek toward an alternate paradigm. While paradigm construction is more than simply stating a metaphor, any proposed paradigm may in fact carry with it a dominant metaphor; for instance, final causality, the mind-body relation, or the dialogical interrelations of thous. The paradigm I shall propose contains just such a metaphor, namely the influential power (efficacy) of human empathy.

SOME GUIDING PRINCIPLES

Paradigm construction inevitably takes place under certain constraints, principles that eliminate certain assumptions and procedures and privileges others. Because paradigm constructors will be aware of only a fraction of these exclusions and commitments, all paradigms are subject to deconstructive efforts to uncover the hidden and fluid text beneath the text. On the other hand, many exclusions and commitments are deliberately adopted in the course of paradigm construction. Consider then the following three negative constraints. The most general constraint at work here is an oft-stated theme of the theology of God. *Paradigm constructions are not based in a direct access to God's active relation to the world.* Insofar as redemption is actually experienced, we can subject it to a more or less direct inspection. Insofar as certain world processes and features are manifest, our account of them is subject to both empirical and intuitive control. What eludes us is the actual way in which the divine activity disposes world processes such that they are "created," "governed," "influenced," and the like.[1] An implication of this negation is that any and all proposals to discover the divine activity as some yet unknown aspect of world processes (puzzles of the particle world, evolution, and so forth)

1. See Owen Thomas, ed., *God's Activity in the World: The Contemporary Problem* (Chico, Calif.: Scholars Press, 1983). Many of the contributors to this volume are united on this point. Even G. Ernest Wright ("God Who Acts") insists that such language is historical testimony, not philosophical analysis (19). Schubert Ogden draws on Rudolf Bultmann and Charles Hartshorne to argue that language about the divine activity is existential and analogical. Langdon Gilkey expresses in a very sharp way how the rise of Western sciences has made problematic the older discourse about divine deeds (31). And Frank Dilley ("Does the 'God Who Acts' Really Act?") eliminates virtually all of the standard ways of justifying language about divine activity.

are misled. We cannot insert God as the missing link of an empirical explanation.

A second negative constraint excludes *panpsychist accounts of the ultimate constituents of world process.* To think that something like life and responsiveness characterizes the world "all the way down" is for me both aesthetically and metaphysically attractive. Yet, it is clearly the case that at the macro level of composite entities, there is a differentiation between living and nonliving things. To posit something like life for the ultimate constituents of the world is a step I am unable to take. Even if panpsychism were established, we would still have to acknowledge that much of the cosmos is comprised of complex entities (crystals, metals, asteroids) which do not experience or behave like living entities.

A third constraint is theological in character. When we examine instances of the divine activity in the Hebrew Scriptures or the New Testament, *what we are not given is a direct, unopposable, and determining causality.* Some instances ("miracles"?) appear to be totally due to a divine cause (a burning bush, the drowning of the Egyptians, the collapsing of the Jericho walls), but these events almost never have to do with the actual redemptive transformation of human agents or communities. At the same time, the through-which of redemption, the event of Jesus as the Christ, is clearly not an external and overriding casuality unrelated to human response. This event took place amidst historical contingencies and evoked undetermined responses of anger, resistance, and betrayal. In this event God's redemptive activity concurs with the independence and responsiveness of worldly entities.

Three guiding principles express positive convictions. The first is the principle of positivity. Stated in negative form, this principle is *a rejection of universals distributed into isolated strata.*[2] If the world is not simply a hierarchy of stratified universals from the most general to the most specific (for instance, universals of the essence of living things, of the human, of the female gender, of a particular ethnicity, of a particular locale, and so forth) but rather is comprised of processing entities, events, relations, and ecosystems, what we can expect is that every specific instance that embodies a generic feature changes that feature by its embodiment. If this is the case, we cannot assume that the features described in the sciences or in ontologies of world are changeless universals. This is not to say there are no abstractable generalities. There are people who are Burmese

---

2. See my book *Ecclesial Man: A Social Phenomenology of Faith and Reality* (Philadelphia: Fortress Press, 1975), 57–65.

and not Irish and who are females and not males. Rather, it affirms that the abstractable generalities undergo modification in their actual embodiments. And if that is the case, a *theology* of world cannot assume that world is synonymous with the aggregate of general features proposed by the sciences or ontology.[3]

A second conviction concerns the status of metaphysics and is based on the outcome of chapter 11. *Anti-theist critiques of metaphysics chasten and qualify but do not eliminate metaphysics.* One of the several meanings of metaphysics that has continuing validity and importance is the formulation of generic features of what we experience as our world: world-for-us, world constituents, root metaphors. When we utterly repudiate this undertaking, we end up reducing the world either to subjective experience or to the "objective" descriptions of the sciences. Rather than excluding the abstracting analyses of levels and constituents of being, the principle of positivity says that all actual things modify by their very concreteness the general features they share with other things.

The third conviction has a theological character. *The activity of God in redemption is an exemplification rather than a unique instance of God's activity in the world.* Negatively expressed, this means that God does not dispose the world, relate to entities and events, in some utterly different way from what human beings experience in redemption. Accordingly, divine creativity is something like a redemptive process. This conviction has a procedural implication. Because we can express the divine activity in a much more concrete way as redemption appresents it, we proceed by allowing redemption to determine the aim and content of the divine activity. We then extrapolate how that activity works in any and all created entities. But as we leave redemption and the human sphere, our discourse becomes more abstract, more general, and less intuitively grounded. If this principle is defensible, then we would expect something like a natural egocentrism and a natural self-securing at work in all living entities. Further, we would expect them all to exist interdependently with others in their environment, and presume that their struggle for survival and their self-fulfillment to be a part of their relations to others.

RETRIEVING ELEMENTS FROM THE SOURCES

Paradigms of the divine activity do not spontaneously generate themselves but are constructed from sources that bespeak both the divine aims

---

3. Although Edmund Husserl thought and wrote in the philosophical style of essentialist philosophy, his complex idea of intentionality was actually a displacement of essentialism. That is, the meanings and references of concrete human acts are constantly reforming as motives, perspectives, valuings, and agendas change. Thus, that which any concrete act of

and how the world works. Sciences and philosophies tell us something of how the world works; theologies of redemption, creation, and divine symbolics express something of the aim and content of God's activity. Sciences, philosophies, and theologies of world are what we have to work with when we construct a paradigm of God's activity.

Themes Descriptive of How the World Proceeds

What sort of world is it that is disposed by the divine activity? To accept this question as valid is to refuse to derive what the world is from religious sources alone (Scripture, dogma, encyclicals, popular piety), an act that suppresses all scientific and philosophical accounts of the world. And if "world" means cosmos, nature (life), and history, it is appropriate to consult whatever studies those spheres. Four general themes descriptive of how the world works are present in sciences and philosophies of the world: entities, openness, tragedy, and cooperation.

The first general feature of world working is the unit of that working, the *entity*. Here we cannot avoid a mix of common sense orientation, ontology of world, and speculation. According to both common sense and physical and biological sciences, that in which the world persists through time are entities of one sort of another: individual human beings, animals, plants, cells, molecules, atoms. This entitized way of looking at the world may not go "all the way down." At the bottom of the world of quantum physics, there may not be entities but "energies" or something else we can talk about only metaphorically and mathematically. Some philosophers (Gottfried Leibniz, A. N. Whitehead) see reality as constituted by an ultimate entity or *res vera*. I shall neither adopt nor reject such a proposal. It does seem to be the case that the world of both human experience and the sciences is made up of entities that behave in a certain way. Thus it is the entity that exists in and constitutes the open, flexible, and tragic world and at the same time is the unit of direction and cooperation.

Some notion of entities seems necessary if we are to understand how it is that God disposes the world. In what follows I shall sketch a theory of entities that applies most closely to human entities, which is applicable in a more distant way to all forms of life, and which we can only speculatively apply to nonliving types of entities. We would expect, however, the

---

meaning grasps or experiences is quite unique, however much one might extract from it a generalized content. Husserl's student, Martin Heidegger, saw the implications of the uniqueness of concrete acts and expressed them in such notions as that which is manifest, "that which unconceals itself," the *being* of entities, and openness as the proper stance toward being.

features of entities to vary in intensity and complexity over this range of distribution.

First, all entities are composites. Accordingly, they have parts that exist in some unitary relation to each other. Given the processive character of the world, these internal relations are more a dynamic system than an unchanging structure. Each entity, then, is an ecosystem in miniature. To the degree that entities are complex systems of internal relations, that is to say, syntheses, they are the result of some sort of unifying process, a harmonization of things in relation to each other, and, as dynamic syntheses, entities obtain some degree of fit between their structure and activity. In other words, they have some degree of beauty.

Second, no entity has an utterly passive relation to the forces, energies, or other entities that bear upon it. To be an entity at all is to respond to the environment, which responses originate in the entity itself. I shall call this the entity as self-initiating. To use language ordinarily restricted to human beings, to be an entity is to have a natural egocentrism, autonomy, or self-determination. Entities, therefore, are not reducible to things or thingness.

Third, entities always exist in environments and therefore in relation to and interdependent with other entities. This means that all entities have very specific "social" and environmental conditions of their existence. To be an entity then involves some kind of activity in an environment that supports the conditions needed by that entity to exist. Because of the self-orientation or autonomy of the entity, this activity will have the character of struggling with the obstacles and perils of the environment; that is, to overcome as far as possible the maladaptive aspects of the entity's situation. Thus, the entity is launched into competitive and even antagonistic relations to other entities in its environment.

Fourth, as dynamic, self-initiating, and responsive, no entity has its being all at once in the mode of fulfillment. Rather, to be an entity is to exist in the mode of eros (need, desire, struggle). It is because of this eros quality that the entity is oriented to what is other than itself; to other entities or to the conditions of its environment. Eros can orient the entity to an other whose beauty attracts the entity or to that which enhances the well-being of the entity along with its others. This is why entities can be attracted toward cooperation. The eros aspect of entities will surely vary with the entity's complexity. At one level eros will prompt the entity to pragmatic or self-fulfilling relations to other entities. At a second level the beauty of other entities will evoke an aesthetic enjoyment that in some sense draws the entity beyond issues of survival or self-fulfillment. At still another level, the other will engage the empathy of the entity, evoking a kind of "fellow feeling" or even a sense of obligation.

Finally, entities experience their own situation as problematic. If it is the case that entities are in some sense perceptive of what goes on around them, are constituted by eros, and are able to respond to other entities as beautiful or threatening, it would seem that they sense to some degree the perils and possibilities of their situation. Thus, entities experience something like anxiety, suffering, and even alienation as they battle other entities in their struggle for life and well-being. Needless to say, these "anthropomorphic" features of entities become intensified at the macro level of animal life and further intensified as animal life becomes neurologically complex. If it is the case that entities are preoccupied and structured by these problematics, then something like the human experience of being released from the hold of anxiety and self-oriented idolatry may pertain to all entities. Needless to say, what this would mean would have to befit the level of the entity in question.

Second, *openness* is a term for the world's temporal proceeding into novelty. To deny the world's openness is to interpret causality through the root metaphor of the machine. In this metaphor actual things are explainable without remainder by external forces. Challenging this notion are evidences of openness in the indeterminacy of the particle world, the random character of the operations in microbiology, and the unpredictable complexities and ambiguities of history. World openness is manifest in a variety of levels. It is the assymmetry and cumulative character of temporal passage. That is, no passage of time ever merely repeats a previous instance but builds on and adds to it.[4] It is the spontaneous (reactive, responsive, creative) character of living entities, each of which has an interior aspect. It is the flexibility of the environment of things in relation to each other without which spontaneous action would be impossible. Flexibility provides the space for the entity's specific development, for ever-changing relations between entities, and for the possibility of the entity's capacity to alter or introduce changes in its environment.

Third, because the world is open (a flexible realm of spontaneous action and indeterminacy), it is also *tragic*. For those who would restrict the genre of the tragic to the realm of history and the human, this language is unnecessarily anthropomorphic and metaphorical. Yet if the tragic refers to the root of suffering or ill-being in something *structural*, then some-

---

4. For extensive analyses of both time and the temporal character of things, see Robert Neville, *Recovering the Measure: Interpretation and Nature* (Albany: SUNY Press, 1989), chaps. 9 and 10.

thing like the tragic characterizes the world as we know it. Injury, disease, and demise all attend the profligacy of reproduction and superfluous populations of the young of most living species. All living things are structured by a split between what they strive for and what actually happens. Struggle is their very mode of being. Structurally necessary to life itself is the maladjustment that holds between the flexible conditions needed for individuals and even species to exist together in an environment and what would promote the good of each individual. Cosmos, nature, and history are not designed to promote what each and every participant needs or desires. The very movement of the world in these three spheres leaves behind it a detritus of individuals, species, and whole ecosystems.

Fourth, "world" as we know it is not simply a term for chaos, suffering, or randomness. Open and tragic, it also requires a kind of *cooperation.* That is to say, it is comprised of entities and environments that have obtained a sufficient unity or synthesis of aspects as to endure over a period of time. Simply to come into existence requires a movement in which aspects come together into a unity. Even the existence of an atom requires the overcoming of the repulsions and mutual annihilations that take place in the subparticle world.[5] Another level of synthesis takes place when macromolecules appear on the scene and with living cells. Living things are made up of complex, dynamic, interdependent subsystems: neurological, reproductive, skeletal, muscular, metabolic. And as life develops, synthesis takes the form of cooperation. Bisexual reproduction is a kind of cooperation. Within species individuals cooperate when they protect the conditions of reproduction, defend the young, or attend to the good of the pride, flock, or pod. In some instances forms of interspecies cooperation develop. At the human level cooperation takes on complex institutional forms and finds expression in moral sanctions and legal formulas.

When we put these themes together, we have a world made up of synthesized, spontaneously acting but vulnerable entities that exist in sys-

5. According to James Trefil, particles—electrons, for instance—originate prior to .01 of the Big Bang. From .001 to .01 is the particle era. But all particles have anti-particles—positrons, for instance—and a mutual annihilation occurs on contact. With falling temperatures, conditions arose favorable to nonannihilating contacts and making possible nuclei. But there, too, violent collisions prevented the nuclei from forming atoms until conditions changed again. At every step of the Big Bang, an overcoming of collisions, repulsions, and mutual annihilation made possible new compounds. The end of the story is the actual compounds of atoms, molecules, elements, crystals, etc., that constitute the universe. See *The Moment of Creation: Big Bang Physics from Before the First Millisecond to the Present Universe* (New York: Charles Scribner's Sons, 1983), chap. 2.

tems which themselves are ever threatened but that exhibit tendencies in certain directions; that is, toward further syntheses, and toward the urge to unite with or cooperate with other entities and even types of entities.

Themes Descriptive of the Divine Aim

The rich contents of redemption, the event of Jesus as Christ, and the symbolics of God all point to a single metaphor for God's activity, the metaphor of divine empathy. This metaphor more or less coincides with such terms as *chesed,* agape, sympathy, and compassion. If redemption means a founding that imparts courage to anxious and idolatrous agents, a reconciling love imparted to human relations, and an emancipating norm of justice for oppressed groups, that which redeems is a kind of compassion, an acting on behalf of needy others. And if the meaning of the event of Jesus as Christ is that the divine empathy and the empathy of Jesus are so united that Jesus embraces the suffering necessary to embody a universalizing as-such relation, then the empathy of God is also a pathos, a "fellow-feeling" that suffers because its creativity inevitably moves the world in the direction of complex and intensified experiencings and therefore in the direction of intensified suffering.

To use the term *empathy* in this way does pass over some finely tuned distinctions at work in philosophical texts. These texts distinguish empathy, sympathy (fellow-feeling), compassion, and love. For Edith Stein empathy is a transcendentally based capacity to perceive the other in its experiencing (*Erleben*).[6] For instance, we empathetically perceive that another is grieving or in pain. Sympathy or fellow-feeling (*Miteinanderfühlen*) is not just a perception of but a participation in the life of the other.[7] Compassion is a participation in the *suffering* or misery of the other and as such is itself an activity. Love is an unqualified suffering self-impartation of one's being to or for the sake of the other. Love, then, is the strongest way an entity can feelingly respond to the vulnerable other and empathy (in Stein's sense) is the weakest.[8] These fine distinctions tend to collapse when we apply them to the divine activity. The reason is that all four terms express relations or responses at work in the sphere of the interhuman. As metaphors for the divine activity, they tend to merge. We

6. Edith Stein, *On the Problem of Empathy,* trans. W. Stein (The Hague: Nijhoff, 1964).

7. Max Scheler, *The Nature of Sympathy,* trans. P. Heath (London: Routledge and Kegan Paul, 1954), Part 1, and pp. 13–14.

8. For the distinction between love and fellow-feeling, see Scheler, *Nature of Sympathy,* 141–44. For a full phenomenology of love that locates it in the sphere of intersubjectivity, see Robert Johann, *The Meaning of Love: An Essay Toward a Metaphysics of Intersubjectivity* (Mahwah, N.J.: Paulist Press, 1954).

cannot imagine a divine empathy that is without sympathy, or a divine impartation of love without compassion. The divine activity has all four of these features: participative suffering, self-impartation, perception of our experiencing, and compassion. Divine empathy here will be an inclusive term for this collection of metaphors.

The divine empathy carries with it a subtheme that has a counterpart in the way the world works. Empathy not only feels with another but would ease the other's suffering and promote the other's well-being. Empathy cannot then arbitrarily restrict its reach or scope. It cannot say, thus far and no farther. Empathy, therefore, is always and simply *as such*. It cannot desire a good for one aspect of the other and not another aspect. Nor can it limit its intent simply to the other as a being isolated from the conditions of its being and from its others in an ecosystem. Empathy thus is ever an operation of enlargement, a universalization. This universalization is the very meaning of the event of Jesus as Christ. If we regard the contents of redemption and the contents of that event as indications of the divine aim, we must conclude that as empathic the divine activity ever works to enlarge or universalize the goods of what is local and specific. As an efficacious empathy, God works to bring about the syntheses I am calling entities by promoting attractions between what is self-isolating and competitive.[9] As efficacious empathy, God works to bring about cooperative relations between entities, thus relations in which the entities themselves can flourish and in which more complex levels of things can ensue. God as empathy is thus the ground of the cooperative, directional aspect of world processes. This is one of the things we mean when we say that God is "maker of heaven and earth."

DIVINE ACTIVITY MINUS "CHRISTIAN COSMOLOGY"

Understanding the divine activity in a coherent way is never merely a logical derivation or a formal problem. It changes with the paradigm shifts, the root metaphors, and the prevailing cognitive commitments of historical times and places. The rise of modernity itself—not to mention postmodernity—has had a radical effect on our capacity to interpret the divine activity in a coherent way. The classical Catholic theology of God, especially as it comes to fruition in the High Middle Ages, interpreted

9. For the efficacious character of love, see Theresa Low Ching's comprehensive interpretation of the theology of Juan Luis Segundo, *Efficacious Love: Its Meaning and Function in the Theology of Juan Luis Segundo* (Lanham, Md.: University Press of America, 1989).

God's activity in a world largely of its own making. Accordingly, it is somewhat misleading to say that this theology separated and granted autonomy to philosophy and cosmology. The reaction of the church to Johannes Kepler, Giordano Bruno, and Galileo indicates the presence of a powerful and official "Christian cosmology." That to which or in which God was active was a hierarchically stratified cosmos ranging from heavenly angelic beings to layers of ecclesiastical and secular powers, all serving to mediate the divine causality. Hierarchical in structure, this cosmos was at the same time a developing drama of angelic fall and subsequent dominion, human fall and restoration in the incarnate one, and an eschatological fulfillment in the double destiny of heaven and hell. Insofar as this cosmology remains intact, there is a certain self-evidence to the claim that God is the source and director of this theater.

The story of the demise of this medieval world picture and drama under the impact of Renaissance and Enlightenment sciences is a familiar one. The geocentric, hierarchical cosmos with its teleological drama is replaced by world explanations that require no ontotheological appeal. Secondary causes, mathematically formulated laws, gravity, evolution, multiple galaxies, and sun systems displaced the immediate and mediate divine operations. In some interpretations this displacement meant the "death of God," at least of the God whose meaning was bound up with Christian cosmology. The demise of Christian cosmology left the theology of God with a new and severe problem: How can one even imagine a divine activity in a cosmos or nature whose processes are quite explainable on their own terms? Responding to this problem were three new forms of "natural theology" that I shall call the Newtonian, the Leibnizian, and the Bergsonian.

The Newtonian type closely examines the "godless" world system in order to discover some lacuna in the scientific or cosmological accounts. Isaac Newton himself proposed that space is an attribute and sensorium of God and that God continues to exercise the twofold function of keeping the stars from collapsing into a single meld "maintaining the stability of the solar system in the face of perturbations of planetary motions by other planets."[10] Proposals of this sort continue today in those who would posit God as some sort of "field of force." One problem with the Newtonian type is that its insertion of God into the gap of scientific puzzles sets

10. See Dudley Shuere, "Isaac Newton," in Paul Edwards, ed., *The Encyclopedia of Philosophy*, Vol. 5 (New York: Macmillan, 1967), 490.

up the situation of withdrawing or inserting the divine activity as those puzzles are solved. A second problem is that the divine activity must be the same sort of operation that scientific explanation requires.

The Leibnizian type of response takes a step back from scientific and cosmological explanation to the philosophical problem of *res verae*, the ultimate constituents of reality. Interpreting these constituents as monads, Leibniz could describe the divine activity as the condition of their harmonious being together.[11] Alfred North Whitehead's philosophy of actual entities is the most detailed and most enduring proposal of this type. For Whitehead the *res verae* are temporal occasions (not unlike the occasions of human experience), each coming to a resolution by way of its subjective aim apprehending relevant future possibilities. God's function is to contain (somewhat like Plato's Receptacle) and constantly reenvision these possibilities so they will be available and relevant to the entity. Since this gradation is not just for the sake of each entity but for the ordering of all of them together, it is the very condition of a processing, ordered, and beautiful world.

Even if we accept Whitehead's metaphysical apparatus of actual entities and the grading function of the Primordial Nature of God, we still face the question why any entity would be drawn toward possibilities that have to do with goods other than its own. What would motivate the entity to break out of the circle of its own eros? Although for Whitehead feeling (affective experience) is primordial to knowing, this focus on *possibilities* (eternal objects) smacks of an intellectualized interpretation of what attracts entities to act. By way of the notion of the Consequent Nature of God, process thinkers have voiced the theme of God's suffering. But that which moves the world is not so much the suffering, Consequent Nature, as the Primordial Nature whose re-presentation of possibilities to each new entity sounds more like a very large computer than a sympathetic Thou. In this form of Leibnizian natural theology, God suffers but the suffering has no efficacy.

The Bergsonian type of natural theology would locate the divine activity neither in a leftover scientific puzzle nor in *res verae* but in some sort of force or energy (*nisus*) that ever pushes the world system toward novelty.[12] In this interpretation God is that which accounts for the fact that things do evolve and they do so in a certain direction. The strength of the

---

11. See Gottfried Wilhelm von Leibniz, *Monadology and Other Essays*, trans. Paul and Anne Martin Schrecker, Library of Liberal Arts (New York: Bobbs-Merril, 1965), 162–63.

12. See Samuel Alexander, *Space, Time, and Deity*, Vol. 2 (New York: Dover Publications, 1966), 346–47; Lloyd Morgan, *Emergent Evolution* (New York: Henry Holt, 1927), 34, 36, 301.

nisus approach is that it does not depend on a speculative construction of the ultimate units of world process and it does take into consideration the directional aspect of process. Its weakness, at least for a theology of God, is its symbolic thinness, its distance from any sense of God as Thou, and its inability to relate the divine activity to entities and their situations.

I have reviewed in an outrageously simplistic typology a few main types of the natural theology that would reformulate the divine activity in the wake of the displacement of Christian cosmology by Copernicus, Newton, Charles Darwin, and Albert Einstein. Here we must note a response that repudiates both Christian cosmology and natural theology. This is the response of anti-theism that sees natural theology as an idol. Theologies of this sort would work as far as possible within the discourse of Scripture and the religious community, posit a sharp contrast between philosophical and theological thinking, and by reason of the divine Thou would eschew the task of formulating the divine activity. In the first two parts of this book I attempted to mediate anti-theism and the classical Catholic theology of God. Can these two approaches be mediated in the third task of the theology of God, the thinking of the divine activity?[13] At first sight there appears to be an utter opposition between the God who redemptively comes forth as God in and through the event of Jesus as Christ and the God of the proposals of natural theology. At the same time, we recall that the God who redemptively comes forth as God is at the same time the Creativity of things. Even as the theology of God works to understand what God's redemptive activity is and how that activity generates a symbolics of God, it also faces the task of understanding what it means to say that God's creative (redemptive) activity disposes the world as such. Can we think God as redemptive Thou and God as world-disposer together? Can we relate God to the host of problems that arise with the way the world works and retain the God who redemptively comes forth as God? Can we interpret the divine activity as itself creative, as that which ever brings about what we call the world? These are the questions of our final chapter.

---

13. Robert Johann's *The Meaning of Love* is another example of an attempt to mediate Thomas Aquinas and contemporary continental philosophy (Gabriel Marcel, Lavelle, Maurice Nédoncelle). He would get beyond both the Thomist objectification and the phenomenological psychologization of love (Introduction).

20

THE EFFICACY OF THE DIVINE EMPATHY

My will and my desire were turned by love,
The love that moves the sun and other stars.

So I looked back as she directed me,
And saw a hundred little spheres whose rays
Gave beauty to each other mutually.

Dante, Paradise

The world that stands so firm on its foundation,
With all its many harmonies diverse,
The elements with all their contentation,
Yet held in bonds that nothing can disperse
Phoebus that doth the earth in light immerse
The moon that hath the lordship of the night—
All these depend on Love and on his might.

Chaucer, Troilus and Cressida

The God who redemptively comes forth as God is the Creativity that
disposes the world. Christian theology has employed many metaphors
to bespeak this Creativity. God is that on which all things *depend.* God's
creation is *continuous.* God *providentially* governs the world. God is the
ground and *power* of being, the basis of the creative advance. What are
these metaphors actually talking about? I shall assume that such terms
as "being," "world," or "creation" refer to the total process in which
entities and their ecosystems come about. If that is the case, the question about God's creativity is the question of the base or ground of this
ongoing process.

At each step of this theology of God, I have confronted the face-off
between metaphysical and antimetaphysical (anti-theism) approaches
to God. When we take up the question of the divine activity, this face-
off continues to concern us. Alfred North Whitehead's metaphysics
offers the most detailed version of how God specifically disposes

world process, namely as an ever-adjusting envisioning of relevant possibilities for processing occasions and as that which gathers up and retains all past happenings. On the anti-theist side, Emmanuel Levinas (under his rather idiosyncratic usage of metaphysics) restricts his speaking of God to that eternal "face" which is a trace of the face of the finite other whose vulnerability summons persons to responsibility. Can the metaphysical problem of Whitehead, God's way of disposing finite entities in a certain direction, and the anti-theist posture of Levinas be brought together? Certain elements in the theology of God summon us to this rapprochement. The God who redemptively comes forth as God, the God of the event of Jesus as Christ, is surely a Thou, a "face" of empathetic suffering. At the same time, this God cannot be either a piece of the world or a world-indifferent entity. The empathetic, suffering God of redemption is also the Creativity that disposes the world. I shall attempt to bring these two things together in three steps: an imaginative construction of the conditions necessary for a world process in which entities come about, a theory of the divine empathetic creative activity, and an application of this theory to certain perennial issues that arise when we consider God's relation to the world.

ENTITIES IN THE MAKING

Contemporary natural sciences provide us with certain general facts about the world. First, world process contains various kinds of directions including entropy, the development of environments of greater complexity, and the teleonomic growth of particular individuals over their life span. Second, entities (atoms, molecules, cells, plants) come about by way of processes of syntheses, the unification of diverse aspects. Various kinds of unification bring forth entities and with them the world. Third, something is at work that opens entities to other entities and to their environments. At the level of life and possibly even other levels, we find not just competition but cooperation that fosters conditions of mutual enhancement and continuing syntheses. Syntheses, cooperation, enlargement of perspective are all involved in the generation of entities and their environments and with this generation come situations that never existed before. Finally, even if it is the case that entities are constituted by relations and exist in an ecosystem, the primary unit that receives, struggles, responds, or exists is the entity rather than the relation, event, or system.

How is it that syntheses and cooperation exist at all? Living entities with some degree of self-determination and responsiveness will serve as the privileged example for the following analysis. If an entity is a synthesis or composite and if it displays in its actions some degree of fit between form and function, it possesses a kind of beauty that can be satisfying to whatever experiences it. And if an entity is both needy and self-determining, it will persist over time in the mode of eros, desiring the conditions and environments appropriate to its need. Accordingly, an entity's relation to other entities is not neutral or indifferent but is alert both to the possible threat and the attractiveness or beauty of the other. Further, if entities are responsive and erotic, struggling for existence and well-being, they will be structured in some sense by self-orientation, and insofar as they struggle in their situation, their affective tone will include awareness of their imperiled situation. Accordingly, the human experience of the self-destructive effects of autonomy, anxiety, and idolatry is present in some form in all living entities. For synthesis and cooperation to take place, the entity must be drawn out of its self-preoccupation into the world of the other. If syntheses and their ecosystems are to come about at all, the entities cannot be simply "windowless monads" (Gottfried Leibniz), existing solipsistically in relation to each other. One way to account for a nonsolipsistic interdependence of entities is to hypothesize a preestablished harmony (Leibniz). I shall pursue the other alternative, hypothesizing something that works in an ongoing way to draw entities out of their isolation or autonomy toward each other. To say that cooperation is preestablished in relation to a particular set of entities at a point in time is to appeal to the fact that entities and their ecosystems have come about. But what prompts or evokes this gregariousness of entities from which comes the world.

One reason for the gregariousness, the eros to cooperation, of entities, is the mutual attraction of beauty and eros. Insofar as beauty is unreducible to mere use and has an in-itself quality, to desire or appreciate the beautiful other is a kind of self-transcending. At the same time, the entity's orientation to the other's beauty occurs within the dynamics of self-fulfillment. Distinguishable from this erotic relation is the empathetic entering into the other's being and the sympathetic "fellow feeling" with the other's suffering. Beyond such sympathetic orientation to the single other is the sympathetic apprehension of the other with its others, an apprehension of others-together-in-peril. Here we have different senses or degrees in which the entity can be drawn out of its natural solipsism, its struggling self-preoccupation, and even out of its aesthetic or eros relation to the other. This drawing out is the condition of the entity's willingness to labor for an environment of mutual enhancement. For it is just such an environment that entities need and that cooperation would bring about. In Whitehead's correction of the Leibnizian solipsism, the focus is on the objective problem of making available to the entity concrete *possi-bilities* that have to do with mutual enhancement. I have no inclination to repudiate the entity's need to envision relevant possibilities for itself. But if entities are first of all composites of passion or desire, and oriented to their own survival, we cannot avoid the Levinasian problem of motiva-tion, the problem of transforming the solipsistic orientation of the entity into participation in the life of the other and in the situation of others-together-in-peril. Accordingly, the entity needs not only available options (graded eternal objects) but an orientation of empathy that pushes it to-ward synthesis and cooperation.

EFFICACIOUS EMPATHY

The thesis of this chapter is that the divine empathy is what disposes world process in directions of synthesis, cooperation, and novelty. This thesis connects the content of the divine aim displayed in redemption and the kind of world we know. If we extrapolate the facticity of redemp-tion to the whole processing world, we conclude that the *aim* of Creativity is something like redemption, the promotion of the reality, freedom, and cooperative interrelation of entities. If we look at this aim from within the event of Jesus as Christ, we conclude that this redemption ever seeks an enlargement, a universal reach that embraces all things together. Further-more, this activity of universalization originates from the divine empathy, which is itself a suffering. These conclusions form the basis of a way of understanding the divine activity. The world proceeds by means of something that attracts (motivates) autonomous entities into cooperation and mutual enhancement. In addition to whatever role God plays as a condition of finite temporality, as ground of relevant possibility, God as Thou (or face) is what motivates entities in the direction of an ever-enlarg-ing cooperation and thus new syntheses. Since entities come about in the first place as the result of syntheses, God is the ground of both the coming about of entities and their subsequent complexification, enlargement, and unitings. In this interpretation the divine empathy is not simply what motivates the divine activity but is itself what is efficacious.

Since God's actual concrete activity is, like God's own being, not given directly to either intuitive experience or discourse, we can never con-cretely envision or fully specify the actual work of the divine empathy. We can exclude one interpretation of the divine empathy as efficacious. If the world as creation has an independent as well as dependent aspect, and if the sciences and ontology of the world are right in their account of self-initiating entities, random processes, and the tragic, then empathetic action cannot mean a direct and irresistable causal determination. If re-demption is the divine Creativity at work in the sphere of the human and if redemption works by enjoining human response, then Creativity (redemption writ large) will likewise engage the responses of entities. But how is it that empathy, something we usually think of as something subjective or psychological, disposes world process?

Recall that as a metaphor for the divine activity, empathy has connota-tions of sympathy, compassion, and love. Does human empathy in this strong sense have an efficacious or influential character? It seems clear that love, compassion, and sympathy as well as their counterparts of ha-tred, contempt, and indifference are not simply hidden internal postures. To experience another's sympathetic participation in one's grief or anoth-er's contemptuous dismissal is to be affected in one's being. And when these modes of relation endure over a long time, as when a parent rou-tinely treats a child with contempt (or sympathy), they will evoke re-sponses and shape character. Participative fellow-feeling can ease, com-fort, and encourage self-esteem. Furthermore, empathy toward another can evoke a response of empathy and bring forth a mutual empathetic relation. And since true empathy desires the other to remain itself and to retain its integrity, it refuses to control and manage. Accordingly, empathy assists rather than suppresses the other's self-initiation and freedom.

Granting that human empathy can be efficacious, is there any way of conceiving the efficacy of divine empathy? On the basis of this theory of entities, I can say generally that God functions to draw self-oriented enti-ties out of the circle of fear and solipsism into union and cooperation with others. If entities (and therefore a world) are to form at all, they must be attracted out of their self-orientation not just toward the beauty of the other but to an empathetic concern for the larger environment of others, to others-together-in-peril. Only in this more comprehensive tran-scending is the entity attracted to acts of mutual enhancement. Here we find something at work throughout world process analogous to the re-demption of anxious, idolatrous human agents. In the redemption of hu-man individuals, elemental passions driven by anxiety and structured by idolatrous self-securing are transformed into freedoms only if the human being is "founded" and given meaning by the "one and only" thing able so to do. In the larger world of (living) entities, there is a similar struggle for life and well-being in modes of anxiety and self-concern. Their "re-demption" takes place as they are moved toward union with other enti-ties as the "one and only" thing that is concerned for the mutual enhance-ment of all entities together appeals to and enlarges their empathy.

What does God do to engage or illicit an entity's enlarging empathy? The question is unanswerable not only at the level of world creativity but for the redemptive founding and transformation of human agents. But some specification may be possible. Two quite different but not necessarily exclusive ways of understanding divine empathetic efficacy present themselves, the one more anti-theistic, the other more "metaphysical." Both would specify how the divine empathy draws entities toward cooperation and mutual enhancement by evoking their empathy. According to the anti-theist interpretation, God as Thou makes its own empathetic suffering available to entities. As entities grasp the vulnerable beauty of others in their environment, they are at the same time grasping and experiencing the mystery at work in that beauty, a suffering Thou whose empathy bestows on others a pathos that draws entities out of themselves. Here we would have the dialogical philosophy of I-Thou and "face" (Martin Buber, Emmanuel Levinas) applied to a theory of how God disposes the world. In this interpretation the pathos of the other simply cannot of itself penetrate the entity's self-orientation until or unless it is connected to the Pathos in which everything takes place. Apart from this connection the entity grasps its others only in modes of use, competition, or self-fulfillment.

According to the "metaphysical" interpretation, the divine empathy presents itself in mediated form, presenting to self-oriented entities a vision of others-together-in-peril. Here God is the "one and only" thing able to empathetically envision the total pathos of world process. Only in the light of such a vision will entities be drawn together into cooperation. To make the same point from the side of the entity, entities can be drawn toward larger systems of mutual enhancement only if the larger pathos of things is presented to them along with their specific perceptions. In other words, God makes available to the entity the corporate plight of things. Here God is not merely the receptacle of possibilities but the receptacle of the larger pathos of things. This spectacle of a larger pathos can be neither an unchanging structure nor simply preestablished because the vulnerability of entities, their actual pathos, changes from moment to moment.[1]

---

1. Prominent throughout this essay has been the theme of the tragic character of world process and with that the pathos that attends God's efficacious empathy. David Ford of Cambridge University (in conversation) observed that the high role of the tragic in my book *Good and Evil* omits an important dimension of redemption, namely joy. A similar criticism could be made of my interpretation of the divine Creativity. Does God simply "suffer" the world into existence? Is there no divine enjoyment? I venture a two-step reply. First, I do accent the divine pathos to correct theologies of God that place God triumphantly and experientially beyond suffering. In those theologies God is the inevitably successful and free determiner of whatever is. But even Chaucer was revolted by such a picture: "Love will

A few clarifications are in order. The first concerns the previously discussed matter of creation *ex nihilo*. It would seem from this account of divine creativity that divine empathy must *presuppose* the existence of entities in order to be creative. Have we not said that entities are the primary units of process and that God functions to attract them into union and cooperation? Here we recall, first of all, that the outcome of this attraction is a new synthesis or entity.

Second, this creating by uniting goes "all the way down." A kind of unity had to take place prior to the Big Bang for there to even be nuclei and atoms. But when we confront the situation in which primordial entities themselves are brought about, a curtain drops before us. Something confronts us that no analogies of world, world process, or divine activity can reach. If God's creativity is the condition of the coming about of entities, we can never bestow on entities the metaphysical status of utter independence. Our principle must then be, Where there are entities, the creativity of God is their condition. In this sense creation is *ex nihilo*.

Second, is the notion of divine empathetic efficacy necessarily parochial? Is it, in other words, necessarily restricted to the spheres of history and life, thus having no conceivable application in the particle or subparticle world or the macro world of suns and galaxies? Has our privileged example of living entities as the units of divine creativity excluded creativity from the nonliving? Panpsychism offers an obvious solution to this question. Although my theory of entities borders on panpsychism, I have not pressed it to the level of *res verae* for the following reasons. Even if it were the case at some micro level that process advanced by way of units of feeling, it is still the case that history and life are comprised of such complex things as cells, plants, and human beings. If the divine empathy cannot attract things of this sort, it helps little to say that God moves the world along by influencing microunits of feeling. If that were the only way God disposed the world, we would have to posit some deterministic relation between the microunits and the composites of the everyday world. Yet the view I am offering comes close to panpsychism. The difference is that "below" the sphere of life or nature, we simply have no way of understanding the divine activity.

not be constrained by mastery, when mastery comes the God of love anon stretching his wings and farewell: he is gone" (*Canterbury Tales*, trans. N. Coghill [Baltimore: Penguin Books, 1951], 55). And I am convinced that if world process moves by substitution and decay, and if God is in any way at work in that movement, pathos must somehow be involved. But this formulation does suppress the divine enjoyment. The other side of the world's tragic conflict and decay is that things do appear. The world does come about. Beautiful entities, movements, and structures arise. And surely, if God is not a sheer indifference, there is something like a divine enjoyment that marks the tone of Creativity, possibly even the dominant tone.

Yet two things prompt me to think that the divine activity in the particle world resembles the empathetic efficacy at work in nature and history. First, even in the particle world, entities come about by way of synthesis. There seems to be, even at the level of the coming to be of atoms themselves, a drift toward unity. Second, there are good reasons to think that the way the divine activity occurs in the lives of human beings (redemption) and in nature (as the attraction to cooperation) is in continuity with that activity throughout the world. It surely is the case that the divine activity accommodates itself, to use a term from Calvin, to the levels and types of entities. Accordingly, we would not expect an identical function throughout the world. Thus, for instance, human beings experience the divine empathetic efficacy as grace, forgiveness, reconciling love, and normative justice—terms inapplicable to other spheres of the world.

Third, this interpretation of the divine activity emphasizes synthesis, cooperation, and "drift to order." God appears then to promote structure (logos) rather than novelty. Is something other than God (for instance, the self-initiations of entities) the source of novelty? It should be clear that the very fact of process bespeaks novelty. The coming about of an entity is itself a novelty. Thus, the synthesis or unity that constitutes an entity, for instance, a single human being, is not only an organization of aspects and a continuity over time, but is something new. In addition, the divine empathy works to attract the entity beyond itself as a fixed and self-valued content into the world of others and others-together-in-peril. This effort to enlarge the entity's orientation results in ever more complex entities and environments, entities (for instance, human beings) that themselves perform unimaginably subtle and complex acts of creativity that ensue in language, aesthetics, institutions, and moralities. Novelty thus is intrinsic to world process and takes on new dimensions in life, history, and human *Existenz*.

Fourth, does not the privileging of the entity (which at the human level means the agent) perpetuate the abstraction of individualism? Here I must acknowledge that an important element has been left out of the analysis. I recall at this point that redemption itself is not reducible to the transformation of individuals. Prior to human agency and even making it possible is the interhuman, the sphere of relation, and organizing both into continuities over time are the institutions of historical life. All three spheres undergo corruption and all three are open to redemption. Nor is the event of Jesus as Christ reducible to the experience and teaching of Jesus as if the "point" of Christology were the communication of something about Jesus pertinent only to future generations of individuals. The outcome of the event of Jesus as Christ was the new, universalizing community, which became the historical through-which of redemption for subsequent generations. We have here the two dimensions of the divine activity. In the one the divine empathy is united with the sensibility of a human individual (Jesus) who thus voices and lives out such a radical critique that it opens the faith of Israel to a universal enlargement.

But a second dimension is present in this event that goes far beyond the entity's (Jesus') response. This is the forming of a community that embodied (to a certain extent) the critique and response of Jesus. To say that a community is the through-which of redemption means that the existence, faith, and teaching of Jesus became institutionally embodied. And with that come various social sedimentations: a characteristic inter-subjectivity, traditions and traditionings, scriptures, forms of organization, rites, basic symbols, and legacies of interpretation. And it was in the form of an enduring community that the response of Jesus (the divine empathetic activity in relation to *an* individual) was mediated. And only with a social embodiment of the divine activity does it take the form of a *norm* for human corporate life. But as both history and our experience testify, this historical embodiment (the ecclesia) contained from the very beginning compromises and corruptions of the as-such or radical faith of Jesus, corruptions that prompt some types of Christian piety to attempt to avoid or abandon the ecclesia in order to have Jesus alone.

We have here two dimensions of the divine activity; one that appeals to and transforms the entity in relation to its environment, the other that socially embodies and mediates that entity's vision. And this sets up the ongoing dialectic that constitutes historical passage. Individuals in their social settings drawn by the divine empathy transcend and criticize their setting. This criticism and insight becomes communally and even institutionally embodied, which embodiment itself is corrupted, and new individuals respond to that corruption. And neither the individual critical response nor the social sedimentation can be omitted in any account of the divine activity that works both to draw individuals into criticism, self-transcending cooperation, and, through cooperation, to sediment the new into forms of duration. Thus, the divine activity fosters both destabilizing and enduring patterns of mutual enhancement. This dialectic of historical passage is not an exception but an exemplification of the way God is active throughout the world. That is to say, entities not only respond to God's enlarging attraction into the life of others, they press their environments to take on structures and legacies of influence to be passed on to future others. This entity-environment dialectic goes on in the sphere of nature, and beyond that in all the levels and spheres of the world.

Fifth, is this interpretation of the divine activity a kind of sentimentalism that suppresses the prophetic theme of divine judgment? Is it possible to say that an empathetic God judges? Any account of divine judgment in the framework I have offered will have to disconnect it from what I have called the tragic structure of world process. Contingency, chaos, maladjustment, and suffering are not signs of divine judgment but rather are attendants of world process as such. Even as the need for redemption arises insofar as an entity refuses the summons of the divine empathy toward others-together-in-peril, so judgment arises when that summons is refused. But the signs of this judgment are not the inescapable vulnerabilities of life: disease, injury, and the like. Rather they arise as the outcome of the entity's insistence to remain in the circle of its autonomy, thus the set of corruptions that weave their way into the very being of the entity, alienate its relations, and undermine its corporate life. Judgments as negative consequences do visit imperialistic nations, racist societies, and controlling and sadistic human beings. They take the form of meaningless lives, empty relations, the absence of aesthetics, oppressive social structures, and the dynamics of malice. And these things can and do intensify and exploit the tragic side of life by promoting starvation, murder, and disease. Even as the entity's refusal of the divine empathy issues in judgment, so the divine empathy persists in the face of that refusal. In human redemption this persistence is experienced as grace and forgiveness.

Finally, is this notion of divine efficacious empathy a "natural theology"? Would it be possible to begin, not with the way God redemptively comes forth as God and the attending symbolics, but with a metaphysics of world process that would show the necessity of divine empathetic efficacy? As a *theology* of God, this essay makes no such attempt. In the inevitable mode of a speculative construction, I have rather tried to formulate a way of understanding the divine activity that relates how the world works and the indications of redemption. I must acknowledge, however, that the closer one comes to specifying the divine activity in relation to how the world works, the more one has identified something about world process not totally accountable by a science or philosophy of the world. Hence, there may be an incipient natural theology here in a minimal if not maximal sense. Minimally, a natural theology of world tries to show how the world or world process is open to the divine activity. This proposal does go this far. Maximally, natural theology would try to show that something about world process can be what it is only because of the divine activity. This I have not attempted to do. I would not say such an endeavor is impossible or unimportant, but I do not see it as part of a *theology* of God.

SOME REINTERPRETATIONS

I would conclude what has now become a very long exploration with an attempt to relate this interpretation of the divine activity to theodicy, eschatology, and liberation theology.

Theodicy

Does the notion of divine empathetic efficacy constitute a theodicy? We recall at this point the ambiguity of the idea of theodicy. This idea wavers between a logical conundrum and a religious and existential pathos of courage. As a conundrum, theodicy means the task of showing how the absolute power and unqualified goodness of God can be consistent with the reality of evil. As a religious and existential pathos of courage, theodicy is the human being's capacity to remain open to the divine efficacy in the face of radical suffering. The book of Job offers a theodicy not as a logical solution to the conundrum but as a pathos of courage. The proposal of these pages makes no attempt to solve the theodicy conundrum. This is because I do not interpret divine power as a literal, unqualified, and inclusive determination of created being. The dynamics of redemption and the event of Jesus as Christ depict the activity of God as taking place in connection with unpredictable human responses and adamant resistance. Thus, foreordination, predestination, or omnipotence cannot mean determinative or causal ways God relates to the world. Such an interpretation is speculative in a way that corrupts and undermines a theological approach that would subject itself to the way God redemptively comes forth as God. That is, such notions (foreordination and so forth) do not arise from the indications of redemption, nor do they concern themselves with the way the cosmos, nature, and history actually display themselves. This is not to say that the metaphor of power is utterly inapplicable to God. To say that God is empathetically efficacious is to say that God (through empathy) is an ongoing empowering of entities in their environment. There is no special pleading here. In human interrelations empathy (sympathy, love) also is a kind of empowerment.

I have set forth a number of ways in which the very being of the world has a tragic character. Demise, competitive struggle, randomness, maladjustment, and suffering are intrinsic to world process. Why these things add up to a *tragic* situation is that all these things are necessary if entities are to arise in the first place, have self-initiating powers, and experience the world in modes of enjoyment and self-fulfillment. How is the divine activity related to this tragic dimension of world process? The traditional theistic position is that God "permits" such things. This notion is sometimes elaborated in the following way: God is truly and really omnipotent but freely chooses not to be omnipotent—that is, withholds its own capacity to determine everything according to its will—when it chooses to create.[2] I find this to be a very odd notion. If omnipotence is a genuine attribute, it will not come and go like human character changes. If it is not a genuine attribute but a term for the way God relates to whatever is not God, then what does it mean to say God has it but gives it up when the not-God, a world, appears? If omnipotence is thus a world-relation term, then God abandons that relation (omnipotence) the instant relation is called for, that is, the coming about of world. But the most serious problem with the position is its assumption that power means all-determination, its derivation of that cipher not from redemption but from something else, and its refusal to let the negative theology serve as a qualifier in the "omni" part of the concept.

In place of the discourse of omnipotence and its stepchild, the idea of divine permission, I would propose that in a very real sense God Godself is implicated in the tragic character of world process. If the divine empathy is that which would attract entities out of their circle of autonomy to participate empathetically in the situation of others-together-in-peril, if God works to enlarge the perspective of entities so that they will cooperate and unite, and if this urging is the condition of "higher" or at least more complex levels of the world, then the direction of the divine activity is toward a situation where suffering is more and not less intense. As entities form, unite, and become transformed into more complex entities in more complex ecosystems, the tragic character of the world is enormously intensified. At the same time, the entity's capacity of self-initiation, complexity of perception, grand passions, and aesthetic sensibility

---

2. This seems to be the position of Keith Ward who rejects the traditional notion of God's self-sufficiency and acknowledges that God limits God's self by the very act of creation. Thus both God's will and knowledge are limited by creatures able to oppose God. Even though love is the reason God brings others into being, creation is not necessary to God. This seems to make the divine creativity and self-giving love contingent on there being a world, hence, they characterize God only *after* creation. If this is so, it would seem that the world exists not *because* of love but as the result of a sheer act of will. I find it difficult, in other words, to put together Ward's notion that love is what prompts creation and his view that only with creation does love come about. The old view of God's self-sufficiency seems here to be retained (*Rational Theology and the Creativity of God* [New York: St. Martin's Press, 1974], chap. 4 and pp. 85–86.)

all increase in intensity. Here we have the deepest meaning of the divine pathos. God does not simply *risk* suffering but actually must promote it in order to have entities that themselves can empathetically exist. This is not to say that God wills or promotes "evil" unless we identify evil with suffering or the tragic character of the world. In this analysis, evil as it might apply to living entities does not mean their suffering but their resistance to the divine empathy, their insistence on remaining within the "safe" circle of their autonomy, their merely competitive and conflictual relations with others. The divine efficacious empathy is without exception opposed to evil in this sense. To act out of this opposition means to set entities on the path of larger harmonies and complexities, and therefore more intense experiences of frustration and suffering. Thus, God wills and promotes suffering in the same way that parents do when they will and guide their children toward maturity and thus toward greater and more intense experiences of maladjustment, disappointment, grief, and suffering. Few parents would wish their children to die in childhood or be lobotomized in order to avoid the suffering that comes with the increased sensitivity of maturity.

I must confess that I have been repelled by the way popular piety sometimes responds to death or a catastrophic event by saying "it was the will of God." Yet there is something about piety that properly refuses to think that misery and suffering are utterly outside God's concern or activity. Such piety senses what I have tried to articulate, that God by fostering union and cooperation tragically draws the world toward greater intensities of suffering.[3] This notion of God as suffering love goes one step beyond the view that God suffers simply because God experiences a nonideal world. The divine pathos is convoluted not simply because God empathetically senses the world's suffering but because God's very creativity presses unities and syntheses that carry with them more intense forms of suffering. Similarly, when creatures are empathetically drawn by the divine pathos toward unity with others, they open themselves to more intense experiences of suffering, even as they are capable of greater joys

3. Friedrich Schleiermacher has no concept of divine suffering, but he does articulate piety's sense that everything, including evil, depends on God: "It is to be maintained that all evil, in the full meaning of that word, is just as much wholly dependent on God as that which is in opposition to it, i.e., good" (*The Christian Faith*, trans. H. R. Mackintosh and J. S. Stewart [Edinburgh: T. & T. Clark, 1928], 185). The basis of this statement is the proposition that expresses the concept of divine preservation. "The religious self-consciousness by means of which we place all that affects or influences us in absolute dependence on God, coincides entirely with the view that all such things are conditioned and determined by the interdependence of nature" (170).

and fulfillments. The paradox of divine suffering is thus repeated in each creature.[4]

Even as God promotes suffering, so God is the source of chaos and randomness. This is inevitably the case if God's creativity effects the bringing about of self-initiating entities. If the world proceeds by way of such entities, it cannot be predictable. The unrolling of time cannot be a mere conformation or replication of the past. For self-initiation brings about the unpredictable new. If nonbeing means the randomness that comes with self-initiating entities, then God is the author of nonbeing. Nonbeing has, however, a second meaning. The fact that what comes about is contingent, in peril to competitors, and dependent on its environment depends in one sense on God's creativity. Its created status makes it contingent and therefore subject to demise. But God does not make entities subject to peril in any direct way. The condition of their ephemerality is that their power to be is always a struggle conducted in the face of nonbeing. Nonbeing in this sense does not come forth from God but is the coeternal condition of creativity itself.[5] Since nonbeing is a "non," it is not a coeternal *something* in competition with God. Such an interpretation unnecessarily mythologizes nonbeing.

Eschatology

In a literalistic and even cosmological sense, eschatology means convictions or theological formulations that concern the final outcome of the world and-or the final destiny of individual human beings. In its decosmologized sense it means convictions or theological formulations that concern the reality of human hope, the fate in store for apparently undefeatable corporate evil, and the futurity dimension of redemption. In reviewing these concerns, I find it impossible to formulate eschatological hope in ways that entail cosmological assertions; for instance, assertions that presuppose an anthropocentric or geocentric universe. In my judgment theologies of this sort verge on science fiction. But the concerns of decosmologized eschatology are all resident in the notion of divine

---

4. For a closely argued case for God as "suffering love" and a criticism of the Augustinian and Plotinian view of God as *apatheia*, see Nicolas Wolterstorff, "Suffering Love," in Thomas V. Morris, ed., *Philosophy and the Christian Faith* (South Bend: University of Notre Dame Press, 1975), 196–237. In similar fashion, Geddes MacGregor argues that infinite creativity and love must be infinitely sacrificial (*He Who Lets Be: A Theology of Love* [New York: Seabury Press, 1975], 15).

5. For the nothingness (*das Nichtige*) that is not part of the "light and shadow" of creation, see Karl Barth, *Church Dogmatics*, Vol. III, 3., #50. See also Nicolas Berdyaev, *The Destiny of Man*, trans. N. Duddington (New York: Harper & Row, 1960), 29. Jacob Boehme's notion of the *Ungrund* is clearly the background of Berdyaev's concept of the *me-on* or nothing.

empathetic efficacy. The self-initiations of entities and the chaos element in world process (nonbeing) undermine eschatology as certain knowledge of what *will* happen in the future. At the same time, the facticity of redemption and the event of Jesus as Christ bespeak an ever-active God, a God whose empathetic relation to the world never ceases. In redemptive transformation, individuals are released from anxious and idolatrous attachments into an open future. Futurity, then, is a structural aspect of agential redemption. It is also structurally present in societal emancipation. When the divine empathy works corporately to create community, it takes the form of norms (justice) that function to expose societal corruption and to lead the society toward a new future. Thus, to trust in, believe in, or worship God means to relate to an efficacy that will be at work in every imaginable future.

Liberation

This theology of God has said little about the specific struggles of embattled and victimized minorities, women, or poor people. These struggles are, needless to say, the concrete context of theology and therefore the theology of God. The management of designated groups (ethnic, gendered, racial) by those in power is virtually a structural feature of human history. This situation of subjugated victims is where theology begins as it attests to the possibility and facticity of redemptive transformation. This book has connected itself to these struggles only in an indirect way. It has not advocated the cause of any specific oppressed group. That is to say, it has not offered specific political, contextual, historical, and psychological accounts of the situation of the poor, the dynamics of oppression, the subterranean oppressive structures of the society, or strategies of change. It rather takes up metaphors, beliefs, and issues that arise when theologians would ground their liberating discourse in the event of Jesus as Christ or in the empowerment of God. Questions of the meaning of God, how God comes forth as God, and what God actually does in and toward the world do not disappear, neither are they resolved, in the theological genres of advocacy and social criticism. They continue in the background of these genres as presupposed but often unestablished symbolics and paradigms. Some of these genres in fact unwittingly promote discourses that are easily co-opted by victimizing powers when they adopt an easy pragmatism that implies "God" is not to be trusted or worshiped but rather deployed. Here God is not so much a reality as a deployed symbol. With the deployment of God comes a dilution, a taming of the transcendent and radical criticism that justice requires. In this book I have offered an account of that subterranean world of images and discourses to which liberation theologies are inevitably connected. The God who liberates or who is the source of liberation is just the God who redemptively comes forth as God, who is the redemptive Creativity at work not simply in one selected community but in the world, and whose creativity has the character of a persistent empathic drawing of entities and societies out of their parochial corruptions to ever larger spheres of coresponsibility and cooperation.

INDEX